KANT'S
CRITIQUE OF JUDGEMENT

IMMANUEL KANT

THE CRITIQUE OF JUDGEMENT

Translated with Analytical Indexes

by

JAMES CREED MEREDITH

LITT. D. (T.C.D.)

OXFORD

AT THE CLARENDON PRESS

Oxford University Press, Ely House, London W. 1

GLASGOW NEW YORK TORONTO MELBOURNE WELLINGTON
CAPE TOWN IBADAN NAIROBI DAR ES SALAAM LUSAKA ADDIS ABABA
DELHI BOMBAY CALCUTTA MADRAS KARACHI LAHORE DACCA
KUALA LUMPUR SINGAPORE HONG KONG TOKYO

ISBN 0 19 824138 0

$c \cdot |$

Printed lithographically in Great Britain at the
University Press, Oxford, from sheets of the first
editions of *The Critique of Aesthetic Judgement* and
of *The Critique of Teleological Judgement* (1928)
1952
Reprinted 1957, 1961, 1964, 1969, 1973

PUBLISHER'S NOTE

THIS volume contains the late Judge J. C. Meredith's translations of Kant's *Critique of Aesthetic Judgement* and *Critique of Teleological Judgement* together with an Analytical Index to each. The introductions and notes that accompanied the translations in the original two volumes have now been dropped in order to make the translations available in a single volume.

CONTENTS

CRITIQUE OF JUDGEMENT

BY

IMMANUEL KANT

PART I
CRITIQUE OF AESTHETIC JUDGEMENT

PREFACE

TO THE FIRST EDITION, 1790

THE faculty of knowledge from *a priori* principles may be called *pure reason*, and the general investigation into its possibility and bounds the Critique of pure reason. This is permissible although 'pure reason', as was the case with the same use of terms in our first work, is only intended to denote reason in its theoretical employment, and although there is no desire to bring under review its faculty as practical reason and its special principles as such. That Critique is, then, an investigation addressed simply to our faculty of knowing things *a priori*. Hence it makes our *cognitive faculties* its sole concern, to the exclusion of the feeling of pleasure or displeasure and the faculty of desire; and among the cognitive faculties it confines its attention to *understanding* and its *a priori* principles, to the exclusion of *judgement* and *reason*, (faculties that also belong to theoretical cognition,) because it turns out in the sequel that there is no cognitive faculty other than understanding capable of affording constitutive *a priori* principles of knowledge. Accordingly the Critique which sifts these faculties one and all, so as to try the possible claims of each of the other faculties to a share in the clear possession of knowledge from roots of its own, retains nothing but what *understanding* prescribes *a priori* as a law for nature as the complex of phenomena—the form of these being similarly furnished *a priori*. All other pure concepts it relegates to the rank of ideas, which for our faculty of theoretical cognition are transcendent: though they are not without their use nor redundant, but discharge certain functions as regulative principles.

For these concepts serve partly to restrain the officious pretensions of understanding, which, presuming on its ability to supply *a priori* the conditions of the possibility of all things

168 which it is capable of knowing, behaves as if it had thus determined these bounds as those of the possibility of all things 5 generally, and partly also to lead understanding, in its study of nature, according to a principle of completeness, unattainable as this remains for it, and so to promote the ultimate aim of all knowledge.

Properly, therefore, it was *understanding*—which, so far as 10 it contains constitutive *a priori* cognitive principles, has its special realm, and one, moreover, in our *faculty of knowledge*— that the Critique, called in a general way that of Pure Reason, was intended to establish in secure but particular possession against all other competitors. In the same way *reason*, which 15 contains constitutive *a priori* principles solely in respect of the *faculty of desire*, gets its holding assigned to it by the Critique of Practical Reason.

But now comes *judgement*, which in the order of our cognitive faculties forms a middle term between understanding 20 and reason. Has *it* also got independent *a priori* principles? If so, are they constitutive, or are they merely regulative, thus indicating no special realm? And do they give a rule *a priori* to the feeling of pleasure and displeasure, as the middle term between the faculties of cognition and desire, just as under- 25 standing prescribes laws *a priori* for the former and reason for the latter? This is the topic to which the present Critique is devoted.

A Critique of pure reason, i.e. of our faculty of judging on *a priori* principles, would be incomplete if the critical ex- 30 amination of judgement, which is a faculty of knowledge, and, as such, lays claim to independent principles, were not dealt with separately. Still, however, its principles cannot, in a system of pure philosophy, form a separate constituent part intermediate between the theoretical and practical divisions, but may when 35

needful be annexed to one or other as occasion requires. For
if such a system is some day worked out under the general
name of Metaphysic—and its full and complete execution is
both possible and of the utmost importance for the employ-
5 ment of reason in all departments of its activity—the critical
examination of the ground for this edifice must have been previously carried down to the very depths of the foundations of
the faculty of principles independent of experience, lest in some
quarter it might give way, and, sinking, inevitably bring with it
10 the ruin of all.

We may readily gather, however, from the nature of the 169
faculty of judgement (whose correct employment is so necessary and universally requisite that it is just this faculty that is
intended when we speak of sound understanding) that the
15 discovery of a peculiar principle belonging to it—and some
such it must contain in itself *a priori*, for otherwise it would
not be a cognitive faculty the distinctive character of which is
obvious to the most commonplace criticism—must be a task
involving considerable difficulties. For this principle is one
20 which must not be derived from *a priori* concepts, seeing that
these are the property of understanding, and judgement is only
directed to their application. It has, therefore, itself to furnish
a concept, and one from which, properly, we get no cognition of
a thing, but which it can itself employ as a rule only—but not as
25 an objective rule to which it can adapt its judgement, because,
for that, another faculty of judgement would again be required to
enable us to decide whether the case was one for the application
of the rule or not.

It is chiefly in those estimates that are called aesthetic, and
30 which relate to the beautiful and sublime, whether of nature or
of art, that one meets with the above difficulty about a principle (be it subjective or objective). And yet the critical search
for a principle of judgement in their case is the most important
item in a Critique of this faculty. For, although they do not
35 of themselves contribute a whit to the knowledge of things,

they still belong wholly to the faculty of knowledge, and evidence an immediate bearing of this faculty upon the feeling of pleasure or displeasure according to some *a priori* principle, and do so without confusing this principle with what is capable of being a determining ground of the faculty of desire, for the latter 5 has its principles *a priori* in concepts of reason.—Logical estimates of nature, however, stand on a different footing. They deal with cases in which experience presents a conformity to law in things, which the understanding's general concept of the sensible is no longer adequate to render intelligible or explic- 10 able, and in which judgement may have recourse to itself for a principle of the reference of the natural thing to the unknowable supersensible and, indeed, must employ some such principle, though with a regard only to itself and the knowledge of nature. For in these cases the application of such an *a priori* 15 principle for the *cognition* of what is in the world is both possible and necessary, and withal opens out prospects which are profitable for practical reason. But here there is no immediate reference to the feeling of pleasure or displeasure. But this is precisely the riddle in the principle of judgement that 20 170 necessitates a separate division for this faculty in the Critique, —for there was nothing to prevent the formation of logical estimates according to concepts (from which no immediate conclusion can ever be drawn to the feeling of pleasure or displeasure) having been treated, with a critical statement of its 25 limitations, in an appendage to the theoretical part of philosophy.

The present investigation of taste, as a faculty of aesthetic judgement, not being undertaken with a view to the formation or culture of taste, (which will pursue its course in the future, as in the past, independently of such inquiries,) but 30 being merely directed to its transcendental aspects, I feel assured of its indulgent criticism in respect of any shortcomings on that score. But in all that is relevant to the transcendental aspect it must be prepared to stand the test of the most rigorous examination. Yet even here I venture to 35 hope that the difficulty of unravelling a problem so involved in its nature may serve as an excuse for a certain amount of hardly avoidable obscurity in its solution, provided that the accuracy of our statement of the principle is proved with all 5 requisite clearness. I admit that the mode of deriving the phenomena of judgement from that principle has not all the lucidity that is rightly demanded elsewhere, where the subject is cognition by concepts, and that I believe I have in fact attained in the second part of this work.

10 With this, then, I bring my entire critical undertaking to a close. I shall hasten to the doctrinal part, in order, as far as possible, to snatch from my advancing years what time may yet be favourable to the task. It is obvious that no separate division of Doctrine is reserved for the faculty of judgement, seeing that 15 with judgement Critique takes the place of Theory ; but, following the division of philosophy into theoretical and practical, and of pure philosophy in the same way, the whole ground will be covered by the Metaphysics of Nature and of Morals.

INTRODUCTION

I

Division of Philosophy

PHILOSOPHY may be said to contain the principles of the rational cognition that concepts afford us of things (not merely, as with Logic, the principles of the form of thought in general irrespective of the Objects), and, thus interpreted, the course, usually adopted, of dividing it into *theoretical* and *practical* is perfectly sound. But this makes imperative a specific distinction on the part of the concepts by which the principles of this rational cognition get their Object assigned to them, for if the concepts are not distinct they fail to justify a division, which always presupposes that the principles belonging to the rational cognition of the several parts of the science in question are themselves mutually exclusive.

Now there are but two kinds of concepts, and these yield a corresponding number of distinct principles of the possibility of their objects. The concepts referred to are those *of nature* and that *of freedom*. By the first of these a *theoretical* cognition from *a priori* principles becomes possible. In respect of such cognition, however, the second, by its very concept, imports no more than a negative principle (that of simple antithesis), while for the determination of the will, on the other hand, it establishes fundamental principles which enlarge the scope of its activity, and which on that account are called *practical*. Hence the division of philosophy falls properly into two parts, quite distinct in their principles—a theoretical, as *Philosophy of Nature*, and a practical, as *Philosophy of Morals* (for this is what the practical legislation of reason by the concept of

freedom is called).　Hitherto, however, in the application of
these expressions to the division of the different principles, and
with them to the division of philosophy, a gross misuse of the
terms has prevailed ; for what is practical according to concepts
5 of nature has been taken as identical with what is practical
according to the concept of freedom, with the result that a 172
division has been made under these heads of theoretical and
practical, by which, in effect, there has been no division at all
(seeing that both parts might have similar principles).

10　The will—for this is what is said—is the faculty of desire
and, as such, is just one of the many natural causes in the
world, the one, namely, which acts by concepts ; and whatever
is represented as possible (or necessary) through the efficacy of
will is called practically possible (or necessary) : the intention
15 being to distinguish its possibility (or necessity) from the
physical possibility or necessity of an effect the causality of
whose cause is not determined to its production by concepts
(but rather, as with lifeless matter, by mechanism, and, as with
the lower animals, by instinct).—Now, the question in re-
20 spect of the practical faculty : whether, that is to say, the
concept, by which the causality of the will gets its rule, is a
concept of nature or of freedom, is here left quite open.

The latter distinction, however, is essential.　For, let the
concept determining the causality be a concept of nature, and
25 then the principles are *technically-practical* ; but, let it be a
concept of freedom, and they are *morally-practical.*　Now,
in the division of a rational science the difference between
objects that require different principles for their cognition is the
difference on which everything turns.　Hence technically-
30 practical principles belong to theoretical philosophy (natural
science), whereas those morally-practical alone form the second
part, that is, practical philosophy (ethical science).

All technically-practical rules (i.e. those of art and skill
generally, or even of prudence, as a skill in exercising an
35 influence over men and their wills) must, so far as their

B

principles rest upon concepts, be reckoned only as corollaries
to theoretical philosophy. For they only touch the possibility
of things according to concepts of nature, and this embraces,
not alone the means discoverable in nature for the purpose, but
even the will itself (as a faculty of desire, and consequently a 5
natural faculty), so far as it is determinable on these rules by
natural motives. Still these practical rules are not called laws
(like physical laws), but only precepts. This is due to the
fact that the will does not stand simply under the natural
concept, but also under the concept of freedom. In the latter 10
connexion its principles are called laws, and these principles,
with the addition of what follows from them, alone constitute
the second or practical part of philosophy.

The solution of the problems of pure geometry is not allo-
173 cated to a special part of that science, nor does the art of land- 15
surveying merit the name of practical, in contradistinction to
pure, as a second part of the general science of geometry, and
with equally little, or perhaps less, right can the mechanical or
chemical art of experiment or of observation be ranked as
a practical part of the science of nature, or, in fine, domestic, 20
agricultural, or political economy, the art of social intercourse,
the principles of dietetics, or even general instruction as to
the attainment of happiness, or as much as the control of
the inclinations or the restraining of the affections with a
view thereto, be denominated practical philosophy—not to 25
mention forming these latter into a second part of philosophy
in general. For, between them all, the above contain nothing
more than rules of skill, which are thus only technically
practical—the skill being directed to producing an effect which
is possible according to natural concepts of causes and effects. 30
As these concepts belong to theoretical philosophy they are
subject to those precepts as mere corollaries of theoretical
philosophy (i. e. as corollaries of natural science), and so
cannot claim any place in any special philosophy called
practical. On the other hand the morally practical precepts, 35

which are founded entirely on the concept of freedom, to the complete exclusion of grounds taken from nature for the determination of the will, form quite a special kind of precepts. These, too, like the rules obeyed by nature, are, without qualification, called laws,—though they do not, like the latter, rest on sensible conditions, but upon a supersensible principle,—and they must needs have a separate part of philosophy allotted to them as their own, corresponding to the theoretical part, and termed practical philosophy.

Hence it is evident that a complex of practical precepts furnished by philosophy does not form a special part of philosophy, co-ordinate with the theoretical, by reason of its precepts being practical—for that they might be, notwithstanding that their principles were derived wholly from the theoretical knowledge of nature (as technically-practical rules). But an adequate reason only exists where their principle, being in no way borrowed from the concept of nature, which is always sensibly conditioned, rests consequently on the supersensible, which the concept of freedom alone makes cognizable by means of its formal laws, and where, therefore, they are morally-practical, i.e. not merely precepts and rules in this or that interest, but laws independent of all antecedent reference to ends or aims.

II

THE REALM OF PHILOSOPHY IN GENERAL

THE employment of our faculty of cognition from principles, and with it philosophy, is coextensive with the applicability of *a priori* concepts.

Now a division of the complex of all the objects to which those concepts are referred for the purpose, where possible, of compassing their knowledge, may be made according to the varied competence or incompetence of our faculty in that connexion.

Concepts, so far as they are referred to objects apart from the question of whether knowledge of them is possible or not, have their field, which is determined simply by the relation 5 in which their Object stands to our faculty of cognition in general.—The part of this field in which knowledge is possible for us, is a territory (*territorium*) for these concepts and the requisite cognitive faculty. The part of the territory over which they exercise legislative authority is the realm (*ditio*) of 10 these concepts, and their appropriate cognitive faculty. Empirical concepts have, therefore, their territory, doubtless, in nature as the complex of all sensible objects, but they have no realm (only a dwelling-place, *domicilium*), for, although they are formed according to law, they are not themselves legis- 15 lative, but the rules founded on them are empirical, and consequently contingent.

Our entire faculty of cognition has two realms, that of natural concepts and that of the concept of freedom, for through both it prescribes laws *a priori*. In accordance with 20 this distinction, then, philosophy is divisible into theoretical and practical. But the territory upon which its realm is established, and over which it *exercises* its legislative authority, is still always confined to the complex of the objects of all possible experience, taken as no more than mere phenomena, for 25 otherwise legislation by the understanding in respect of them is unthinkable.

The function of prescribing laws by means of concepts of nature is discharged by understanding, and is theoretical. That of prescribing laws by means of the concept of freedom 30 is discharged by reason and is merely practical. It is only in the practical sphere that reason can prescribe laws; in respect of theoretical knowledge (of nature) it can only (as by the 175 understanding advised in the law) deduce from given laws their logical consequences, which still always remain restricted 35 to nature. But we cannot reverse this and say that where rules are practical reason is then and there *legislative*, since the rules might be technically practical.

Understanding and reason, therefore, have two distinct
5 jurisdictions over one and the same territory of experience. But neither can interfere with the other. For the concept of freedom just as little disturbs the legislation of nature, as the concept of nature influences legislation through the concept of freedom.—That it is possible for us at least to think without
10 contradiction of both these jurisdictions, and their appropriate faculties, as coexisting in the same Subject, was shown by the Critique of Pure Reason, since it disposed of the objections on the other side by detecting their dialectical illusion.

Still, how does it happen that these two different realms do
15 not form *one* realm, seeing that, while they do not limit each other in their legislation, they continually do so in their effects in the sensible world? The explanation lies in the fact that the concept of nature represents its objects in intuition doubtless, yet not as things-in-themselves, but as mere phenomena,
20 whereas the concept of freedom represents in its Object what is no doubt a thing-in-itself, but it does not make it intuitable, and further that neither the one nor the other is capable, therefore, of furnishing a theoretical cognition of its Object (or even of the thinking Subject) as a thing-in-itself, or, as this would be,
25 of the supersensible—the idea of which has certainly to be introduced as the basis of the possibility of all those objects of experience, although it cannot itself ever be elevated or extended into a cognition.

Our entire cognitive faculty is, therefore, presented with an
30 unbounded, but, also, inaccessible field—the field of the supersensible—in which we seek in vain for a territory, and on which, therefore, we can have no realm for theoretical cognition, be it for concepts of understanding or of reason. This field we must indeed occupy with ideas in the interest as well
35 of the theoretical as the practical employment of reason, but in

connexion with the laws arising from the concept of freedom we cannot procure for these ideas any but practical reality, which, accordingly, fails to advance our theoretical cognition one step towards the supersensible.

Albeit, then, between the realm of the natural concept, as the 5
176. sensible, and the realm of the concept of freedom, as the supersensible, there is a great gulf fixed, so that it is not possible to pass from the former to the latter (by means of the theoretical employment of reason), just as if they were so many separate worlds, the first of which is powerless to exercise influence on 10 the second : still the latter is *meant* to influence the former— that is to say, the concept of freedom is meant to actualize in the sensible world the end proposed by its laws ; and nature must consequently also be capable of being regarded in such a way that in the conformity to law of its form it at least 15 harmonizes with the possibility of the ends to be effectuated in it according to the laws of freedom.—There must, therefore, be a ground of the *unity* of the surpersensible that lies at the basis of nature, with what the concept of freedom contains in a practical way, and although the concept of this ground neither theoreti- 20 cally nor practically attains to a knowledge of it, and so has no peculiar realm of its own, still it renders possible the transition from the mode of thought according to the principles of the one to that according to the principles of the other.

III 25

THE CRITIQUE OF JUDGEMENT AS A MEANS OF CONNECTING THE TWO PARTS OF PHILOSOPHY IN A WHOLE

THE Critique which deals with what our cognitive faculties are capable of yielding *a priori* has properly speaking no realm in respect of Objects ; for it is not a doctrine, its sole business 30 being to investigate whether, having regard to the general bearings of our faculties, a doctrine is possible by their means,

and if so, how. Its field extends to all their pretensions, with a view to confining them within their legitimate bounds. But what is shut out of the division of Philosophy may still be admitted as a principal part into the general Critique of our
5 faculty of pure cognition, in the event, namely, of its containing principles which are not in themselves available either for theoretical or practical employment.

Concepts of nature contain the ground of all theoretical cognition *a priori* and rest, as we saw, upon the legislative
10 authority of understanding.—The concept of freedom contains the ground of all sensuously unconditioned practical precepts *a priori*, and rests upon that of reason. Both faculties, therefore, besides their application in point of logical form to principles of whatever origin, have, in addition, their own peculiar
15 jurisdiction in the matter of their content, and so, there being 177 no further (*a priori*) jurisdiction above them, the division of Philosophy into theoretical and practical is justified.

But there is still further in the family of our higher cognitive faculties a middle term between understanding and reason.
20 This is *judgement,* of which we may reasonably presume by analogy that it may likewise contain, if not a special authority to prescribe laws, still a principle peculiar to itself upon which laws are sought, although one merely subjective *a priori.* This principle, even if it has no field of objects appropriate to it as
25 its realm, may still have some territory or other with a certain character, for which just this very principle alone may be valid.

But in addition to the above considerations there is yet (to judge by analogy) a further ground, upon which judgement may
30 be brought into line with another arrangement of our powers of representation, and one that appears to be of even greater importance than that of its kinship with the family of cognitive faculties. For all faculties of the soul, or capacities, are re-ducible to three, which do not admit of any further derivation
35 from a common ground : the *faculty of knowledge*, the *feeling*

178 *of pleasure or displeasure*, and the *faculty of desire*.[1] For the

[1] Where one has reason to suppose that a relation subsists between concepts, that are used as empirical principles, and the faculty of pure cognition *a priori*, it is worth while attempting, in consideration of this connexion, to give them a transcendental definition—a definition, that is, 5 by pure categories, so far as these by themselves adequately indicate the distinction of the concept in question from others. This course follows that of the mathematician, who leaves the empirical data of his problem indeterminate, and only brings their relation in pure synthesis under the concepts of pure arithmetic, and thus generalizes his solution. 10 —I have been taken to task for adopting a similar procedure (*Critique of Practical Reason*, Preface, p. 16) and fault has been found with my definition of the faculty of desire, as *a faculty which by means of its representations is the cause of the actuality of the objects of those representations*: for mere *wishes* would still be desires, and yet in their case every 15 one is ready to abandon all claim to being able by means of them alone to call their Object into existence.—But this proves no more than the presence of desires in man by which he is in contradiction with himself. For in such a case he seeks the production of the Object by means of his representation alone, without any hope of its being effectual, since he is 20 conscious that his mechanical powers (if I may so call those which are not psychological), which would have to be determined by that representation, are either unequal to the task of realizing the Object (by the intervention of means, therefore) or else are addressed to what is quite impossible. as, for example, to undo the past (*O mihi praeteritos*, &c.) or, 25 to be able to annihilate the interval that, with intolerable delay, divides us from the wished-for moment.—Now, conscious as we are in such fantastic desires of the inefficiency of our representations, (or even of their futility,) as *causes* of their objects, there is still involved in every *wish* a reference of the same as cause, and therefore the representation 30 of its *causality*, and this is especially discernible where the wish, as *longing*, is an affection. For such affections, since they dilate the heart and render it inert and thus exhaust its powers, show that a strain is kept on being exerted and re-exerted on these powers by the representations, but that the mind is allowed continually to relapse and get languid 35 upon recognition of the impossibility before it. Even prayers for the aversion of great, and, so far as we can see, inevitable evils, and many superstitious means for attaining ends impossible of attainment by natural means, prove the causal reference of representations to their Objects— a causality which not even the consciousness of inefficiency for pro- 40 ducing the effect can deter from straining towards it.—But why our nature should be furnished with a propensity to consciously vain desires is a teleological problem of anthropology. It would seem that were we

faculty of cognition understanding alone is legislative, if (as must be the case where it is considered on its own account free of confusion with the faculty of desire) this faculty, as that of *theoretical cognition*, is referred to nature, in respect of which
5 alone (as phenomenon) it is possible for us to prescribe laws by means of *a priori* concepts of nature, which are properly pure concepts of understanding.—For the faculty of desire, as a higher faculty operating under the concept of freedom, only reason (in which alone this concept has a place) prescribes
10 laws *a priori*.—Now between the faculties of knowledge and desire stands the feeling of pleasure, just as judgement is intermediate between understanding and reason.   Hence we may, provisionally at least, assume that judgement likewise contains an *a priori* principle of its own, and that, since
15 pleasure or displeasure is necessarily combined with the faculty of desire (be it antecedent to its principle, as with the lower desires, or, as with the higher, only supervening upon its 179 determination by the moral law), it will effect a transition from the faculty of pure knowledge, i. e. from the realm of concepts
20 of nature, to that of the concept of freedom, just as in its logical employment it makes possible the transition from understanding to reason.

Hence, despite the fact of Philosophy being only divisible into two principal parts, the theoretical and the practical, and
25 despite the fact of all that we may have to say of the special principles of judgement having to be assigned to its theoretical part, i. e. to rational cognition according to concepts of nature : still the Critique of pure reason, which must settle this whole question before the above system is taken in hand, so as to
30 substantiate its possibility, consists of three parts : the Critique

not to be determined to the exertion of our power before we had assured ourselves of the efficiency of our faculty for producing an Object, our power would remain to a large extent unused.   For as a rule we only first learn to know our powers by making trial of them.   This deceit of
35 vain desires is therefore only the result of a beneficent disposition in our nature.

of pure understanding, of pure judgement, and of pure reason, which faculties are called pure on the ground of their being legislative *a priori*.

IV

JUDGEMENT AS A FACULTY BY WHICH LAWS ARE PRESCRIBED *A PRIORI*

JUDGEMENT in general is the faculty of thinking the particular as contained under the universal. If the universal (the rule, principle, or law,) is given, then the judgement which subsumes the particular under it *is determinant*. This is so even where such a judgement is transcendental and, as such, provides the conditions *a priori* in conformity with which alone subsumption under that universal can be effected. If, however, only the particular is given and the universal has to be found for it, then the judgement is simply *reflective*.

The determinant judgement determines under universal transcendental laws furnished by understanding and is subsumptive only ; the law is marked out for it *a priori*, and it has no need to devise a law for its own guidance to enable it to subordinate the particular in nature to the universal.—But there are such manifold forms of nature, so many modifications, as it were, of the universal transcendental concepts of nature, left undetermined by the laws furnished by pure understanding *a priori* as above mentioned, and for the reason that these laws only touch the general possibility of a nature, (as an object of sense,) that there must needs also be laws in this behalf. These laws, being empirical, may be contingent as far as the light of *our* understanding goes, but still, if they are to be called laws, (as the concept of a nature requires,) they must be regarded as necessary on a principle, unknown though it be to us, of the unity of the manifold.—The reflective judgement which is compelled to ascend from the particular in nature to the universal, stands, therefore, in need of a principle. This principle it cannot borrow from experience, because what it has to do is to establish just the unity of all empirical principles under higher, though likewise empirical, principles, and thence the possibility of the systematic subordination of higher and 5 lower. Such a transcendental principle, therefore, the reflective judgement can only give as a law from and to itself. It cannot derive it from any other quarter (as it would then be a determinant judgement). Nor can it prescribe it to nature, for reflection on the laws of nature adjusts itself to nature, and 10 not nature to the conditions according to which we strive to obtain a concept of it,—a concept that is quite contingent in respect of these conditions.

Now the principle sought can only be this : as universal laws of nature have their ground in our understanding, which 15 prescribes them to nature (though only according to the universal concept of it as nature), particular empirical laws must be regarded, in respect of that which is left undetermined in them by these universal laws, according to a unity such as they would have if an understanding (though it be not ours) 20 had supplied them for the benefit of our cognitive faculties, so as to render possible a system of experience according to particular natural laws. This is not to be taken as implying that such an understanding must be actually assumed, (for it is only the reflective judgement which avails itself of this idea as 25 a principle for the purpose of reflection and not for determining anything) ; but this faculty rather gives by this means a law to itself alone and not to nature.

Now the concept of an Object, so far as it contains at the same time the ground of the actuality of this Object, is called 30 its *end*, and the agreement of a thing with that constitution of things which is only possible according to ends, is called the *finality* of its form. Accordingly the principle of judgement, in respect of the form of the things of nature under empirical laws generally, is the *finality of nature* in its multiplicity. In other 35 words, by this concept nature is represented as if an under- 181

standing contained the ground of the unity of the manifold of
its empirical laws.

The finality of nature is, therefore, a particular *a priori*
concept, which has its origin solely in the reflective judgement.
For we cannot ascribe to the products of nature anything like 5
a reference of nature in them to ends, but we can only make
use of this concept to reflect upon them in respect of the nexus
of phenomena in nature—a nexus given according to empirical
laws. Furthermore, this concept is entirely different from
practical finality (in human art or even morals), though it is 10
doubtless thought after this analogy.

V

THE PRINCIPLE OF THE FORMAL FINALITY OF NATURE IS A TRANSCENDENTAL PRINCIPLE OF JUDGEMENT.

A TRANSCENDENTAL principle is one through which we 15
represent *a priori* the universal condition under which alone
things can become Objects of our cognition generally. A principle, on the other hand, is called metaphysical, where it
represents *a priori* the condition under which alone Objects
whose concept has to be given empirically, may become further 20
determined *a priori*. Thus the principle of the cognition of
bodies as substances, and as changeable substances, is transcendental where the statement is that their change must have
a cause : but it is metaphysical where it asserts that their
change must have an *external* cause. For in the first case 25
bodies need only be thought through ontological predicates
(pure concepts of understanding), e. g. as substance, to enable
the proposition to be cognized *a priori* ; whereas, in the second
case, the empirical concept of a body (as a movable thing in
space) must be introduced to support the proposition, although, 30
once this is done, it may be seen quite *a priori* that the
latter predicate (movement only by means of an external cause)

applies to body.—In this way, as I shall show presently, the
principle of the finality of nature (in the multiplicity of its
empirical laws) is a transcendental principle. For the concept
of Objects, regarded as standing under this principle, is only
5 the pure concept of objects of possible empirical cognition
generally, and involves nothing empirical. On the other hand 182
the principle of practical finality, implied in the idea of the
determination of a free *will*, would be a metaphysical principle,
because the concept of a faculty of desire, as will, has to be
10 given empirically, i.e. is not included among transcendental
predicates. But both these principles are, none the less, not
empirical, but *a priori* principles ; because no further experience
is required for the synthesis of the predicate with the empirical
concept of the subject of their judgements, but it may be
15 apprehended quite *a priori.*

That the concept of a finality of nature belongs to transcendental principles is abundantly evident from the maxims of
judgement upon which we rely *a priori* in the investigation of
nature, and which yet have to do with no more than the
20 possibility of experience, and consequently of the knowledge
of nature,—but of nature not merely in a general way, but as
determined by a manifold of particular laws.—These maxims
crop up frequently enough in the course of this science, though
only in a scattered way. They are aphorisms of metaphysical
25 wisdom, making their appearance in a number of rules the
necessity of which cannot be demonstrated from concepts.
' Nature takes the shortest way (*lex parsimoniae*) ; yet it makes
no leap, either in the sequence of its changes, or in the juxtaposi-
tion of specifically different forms (*lex continui in natura*) ; its
30 vast variety in empirical laws is, for all that, unity under a few
principles (*principia praeter necessitatem non sunt multiplicanda*)' ;
and so forth.

If we propose to assign the origin of these elementary rules,
and attempt to do so on psychological lines, we go straight in
35 the teeth of their sense. For they tell us, not what happens,

i.e. according to what rule our powers of judgement actually discharge their functions, and how we judge, but how we ought to judge ; and we cannot get this logical objective necessity where the principles are merely empirical. Hence the finality of nature for our cognitive faculties and their employment, which 5 manifestly radiates from them, is a transcendental principle of judgements, and so needs also a transcendental Deduction, by means of which the ground for this mode of judging must be traced to the *a priori* sources of knowledge.

Now, looking at the grounds of the possibility of an experience, 10 183 the first thing, of course, that meets us is something necessary— namely, the universal laws apart from which nature in general (as an object of sense) cannot be thought. These rest on the categories, applied to the formal conditions of all intuition possible for us, so far as it is also given *a priori*. Under these 15 laws judgement is determinant ; for it has nothing else to do than to subsume under given laws. For instance, understand- ing says : all change has its cause (universal law of nature) ; transcendental judgement has nothing further to do than to furnish *a priori* the condition of subsumption under the concept 20 of understanding placed before it : this we get in the succession of the determinations of one and the same thing. Now for nature in general, as an object of possible experience, that law is cognized as absolutely necessary.—But besides this formal time-condition, the objects of empirical cognition are deter- 25 mined, or, so far as we can judge *a priori*, are determinable, in divers ways, so that specifically differentiated natures, over and above what they have in common as things of nature in general, are further capable of being causes in an infinite variety of ways ; and each of these modes must, on the concept of 30 a cause in general, have its rule, which is a law, and, conse- quently, imports necessity : although owing to the constitution and limitations of our faculties of cognition we may entirely fail to see this necessity. Accordingly, in respect of nature's merely empirical laws, we must think in nature a possibility of 35

an endless multiplicity of empirical laws, which yet are contingent so far as our insight goes, i.e. cannot be cognized *a priori*. In respect of these we estimate the unity of nature according to empirical laws, and the possibility of the unity of experience,
5 as a system according to empirical laws, to be contingent. But, now, such a unity is one which must be necessarily presupposed and assumed, as otherwise we should not have a thoroughgoing connexion of empirical cognition in a whole of experience. For the universal laws of nature, while provid-
10 ing, certainly, for such a connexion among things generically, as things of nature in general, do not do so for them specifically as such particular things of nature. Hence judgement is compelled, for its own guidance, to adopt it as an *a priori* principle, that what is for human insight contingent in the
15 particular (empirical) laws of nature contains nevertheless unity of law in the synthesis of its manifold in an intrinsically possible experience—unfathomable, though still thinkable, as such unity 184 may, no doubt, be for us. Consequently, as the unity of law in a synthesis, which is cognized by us in obedience to
20 a necessary aim (a need of understanding), though recognized at the same time as contingent, is represented as a finality of Objects (here of nature), so judgement, which, in respect of things under possible (yet to be discovered) empirical laws, is merely reflective, must regard nature in respect of the latter
25 according to a *principle of finality* for our cognitive faculty, which then finds expression in the above maxims of judgement. Now this transcendental concept of a finality of nature is neither a concept of nature nor of freedom, since it attributes nothing at all to the Object, i.e. to nature, but only represents
30 the unique mode in which we must proceed in our reflection upon the objects of nature with a view to getting a thoroughly interconnected whole of experience, and so is a subjective principle, i.e. maxim, of judgement. For this reason, too, just as if it were a lucky chance that favoured us, we are rejoiced (properly speaking relieved of a want) where we meet with such

systematic unity under merely empirical laws : although we must necessarily assume the presence of such a unity, apart from any ability on our part to apprehend or prove its existence.

In order to convince ourselves of the correctness of this 5 Deduction of the concept before us, and the necessity of assuming it as a transcendental principle of cognition, let us just bethink ourselves of the magnitude of the task. We have to form a connected experience from given perceptions of a nature containing a maybe endless multiplicity of empirical 10 laws, and this problem has its seat *a priori* in our understanding. This understanding is no doubt *a priori* in possession of universal laws of nature, apart from which nature would be incapable of being an object of experience at all. But over and above this it needs a certain order of nature in its par- 15 ticular rules which are only capable of being brought to its knowledge empirically, and which, so far as it is concerned, are contingent. These rules, without which we would have no means of advance from the universal analogy of a possible experience in general to a particular, must be regarded by 20 understanding as laws, i. e. as necessary—for otherwise they would not form an order of nature—though it be unable to cognize or ever get an insight into their necessity. Albeit, 185 then, it can determine nothing *a priori* in respect of these (Objects), it must, in pursuit of such empirical so-called laws, 25 lay at the basis of all reflection upon them an *a priori* principle, to the effect, namely, that a cognizable order of nature is possible according to them. A principle of this kind is expressed in the following propositions. There is in nature a subordination of genera and species comprehensible by us : 30 Each of these genera again approximates to the others on a common principle, so that a transition may be possible from one to the other, and thereby to a higher genus : While it seems at the outset unavoidable for our understanding to assume for the specific variety of natural operations a like number of 35

various kinds of causality, yet these may all be reduced to a small number of principles, the quest for which is our business ; and so forth. This adaptation of nature to our cognitive faculties is presupposed *a priori* by judgement on behalf of its
5 reflection upon it according to empirical laws. But understanding all the while recognizes it objectively as contingent, and it is merely judgement that attributes it to nature as transcendental finality, i.e. a finality in respect of the Subject's faculty of cognition. For, were it not for this presupposition, we should
10 have no order of nature in accordance with empirical laws, and, consequently, no guiding-thread for an experience that has to be brought to bear upon these in all their variety, or for an investigation of them.

For it is quite conceivable that, despite all the uniformity of
15 the things of nature according to universal laws, without which we would not have the form of general empirical knowledge at all, the specific variety of the empirical laws of nature, with their effects, might still be so great as to make it impossible for our understanding to discover in nature an intelligible
20 order, to divide its products into genera and species so as to avail ourselves of the principles of explanation and comprehension of one for explaining and interpreting another, and out of material coming to hand in such confusion (properly speaking only infinitely multiform and ill-adapted to our power
25 of apprehension) to make a consistent context of experience.

Thus judgement, also, is equipped with an *a priori* principle for the possibility of nature, but only in a subjective respect. By means of this it prescribes a law, not to nature (as autonomy), but to itself (as heautonomy), to guide its reflection upon 186
30 nature. This law may be called *the law of the specification of nature* in respect of its empirical laws. It is not one cognized *a priori* in nature, but judgement adopts it in the interests of a natural order, cognizable by our understanding, in the division which it makes of nature's universal laws when it
35 seeks to subordinate to them a variety of particular laws. So

C

when it is said that nature specifies its universal laws on a
principle of finality for our cognitive faculties, i. e. of suitability
for the human understanding and its necessary function of
finding the universal for the particular presented to it by
perception, and again for varieties (which are, of course, common 5
for each species) connexion in the unity of principle, we do not
thereby either prescribe a law to nature, or learn one from it
by observation—although the principle in question may be
confirmed by this means.   For it is not a principle of the determinant but merely of the reflective judgement.   All that is 10
intended is that, no matter what is the order and disposition of
nature in respect of its universal laws, we must investigate its
empirical laws throughout on that principle and the maxims
founded thereon, because only so far as that principle applies
can we make any headway in the employment of our under- 15
standing in experience, or gain knowledge.

VI

THE ASSOCIATION OF THE FEELING OF PLEASURE WITH THE CONCEPT OF THE FINALITY OF NATURE

THE conceived harmony of nature in the manifold of its 20
particular laws with our need of finding universality of
principles for it must, so far as our insight goes, be deemed
contingent, but withal indispensable for the requirements of
our understanding, and, consequently, a finality by which
nature is in accord with our aim, but only so far as this is 25
directed to knowledge.—The universal laws of understanding,
which are equally laws of nature, are, although arising from
spontaneity, just as necessary for nature as the laws of motion
applicable to matter.   Their origin does not presuppose any
regard to our cognitive faculties, seeing that it is only by their 30
means that we first come by any conception of the meaning of
187 a knowledge of things (of nature), and they of necessity apply

to nature as Object of our cognition in general. But it is contingent, so far as we can see, that the order of nature in its particular laws, with their wealth of at least possible variety and heterogeneity transcending all our powers of compre-
5 hension, should still in actual fact be commensurate with these powers. To find out this order is an undertaking on the part of our understanding, which pursues it with a regard to a necessary end of its own, that, namely, of introducing into nature unity of principle. This end must, then, be attributed
10 to nature by judgement, since no law can be here prescribed to it by understanding.

The attainment of every aim is coupled with a feeling of pleasure. Now where such attainment has for its condition a representation *a priori*—as here a principle for the reflective
15 judgement in general—the feeling of pleasure also is determined by a ground which is *a priori* and valid for all men: and that, too, merely by virtue of the reference of the Object to our faculty of cognition. As the concept of finality here takes no cognizance whatever of the faculty of desire, it differs
20 entirely from all practical finality of nature.

As a matter of fact, we do not, and cannot, find in ourselves the slightest effect on the feeling of pleasure from the coincidence of perceptions with the laws in accordance with the universal concepts of nature (the Categories), since in their
25 case understanding necessarily follows the bent of its own nature without ulterior aim. But, while this is so, the discovery, on the other hand, that two or more empirical heterogeneous laws of nature are allied under one principle that embraces them both, is the ground of a very appreciable
30 pleasure, often even of admiration, and such, too, as does not wear off even though we are already familiar enough with its object. It is true that we no longer notice any decided pleasure in the comprehensibility of nature, or in the unity of its divisions into genera and species, without which the empirical concepts, that
35 afford us our knowledge of nature in its particular laws, would

not be possible. Still it is certain that the pleasure appeared in due course, and only by reason of the most ordinary experience being impossible without it, has it become gradually fused with simple cognition, and no longer arrests particular attention.—Something, then, that makes us attentive in our 5 estimate of nature to its finality for our understanding—an endeavour to bring, where possible, its heterogeneous laws under higher, though still always empirical, laws—is required, 188 in order that, on meeting with success, pleasure may be felt in this their accord with our cognitive faculty, which accord 10 is regarded by us as purely contingent. As against this a representation of nature would be altogether displeasing to us, were we to be forewarned by it that, on the least investigation carried beyond the commonest experience, we should come in contact with such a heterogeneity of its 15 laws as would make the union of its particular laws under universal empirical laws impossible for our understanding. For this would conflict with the principle of the subjectively final specification of nature in its genera, and with our own reflective judgement in respect thereof. 20

Yet this presupposition of judgement is so indeterminate on the question of the extent of the prevalence of that ideal finality of nature for our cognitive faculties, that if we are told that a more searching or enlarged knowledge of nature, derived from observation, must eventually bring us into contact with 25 a multiplicity of laws that no human understanding could reduce to a principle, we can reconcile ourselves to the thought. But still we listen more gladly to others who hold out to us the hope that the more intimately we come to know the secrets of nature, or the better we are able to compare it with 30 external members as yet unknown to us, the more simple shall we find it in its principles, and the further our experience advances the more harmonious shall we find it in the apparent heterogeneity of its empirical laws. For our judgement makes it imperative upon us to proceed on the principle of the con- 35

formity of nature to our faculty of cognition, so far as that
principle extends, without deciding—for the rule is not given
to us by a determinant judgement—whether bounds are anywhere set to it or not. For while in respect of the rational
5 employment of our cognitive faculty bounds may be definitely
determined, in the empirical field no such determination of
bounds is possible.

VII

THE AESTHETIC REPRESENTATION OF THE FINALITY OF
10 NATURE

THAT which is purely subjective in the representation of an
Object, i. e. what constitutes its reference to the Subject, not to
the object, is its aesthetic quality. On the other hand, that
which in such a representation serves, or is available, for the
15 determination of the object (for the purpose of knowledge), is 189
its logical validity. In the cognition of an object of sense
both sides are presented conjointly. In the sense-represen-
tation of external things the Quality of space in which we intuite
them is the merely subjective side of my representation of them
20 (by which what the things are in themselves as Objects is left
quite open), and it is on account of that reference that the
object in being intuited in space is also thought merely as
a phenomemon. But despite its purely subjective Quality,
space is still a constituent of the knowledge of things as phe-
25 nomena. *Sensation* (here external) also agrees in expressing
a merely subjective side of our representations of external
things, but one which is properly their matter (through which
we are given something with real existence), just as space is
the mere *a priori* form of the possibility of their intuition ; and
30 so sensation is, none the less, also employed in the cognition
of external Objects.

But that subjective side of a representation *which is incapable
of becoming an element of cognition,* is the *pleasure* or *displeasure*
connected with it ; for through it I cognize nothing in the

object of the representation, although it may easily be the result of the operation of some cognition or other. Now the finality of a thing, so far as represented in our perception of it, is in no way a quality of the object itself (for a quality of this kind is not one that can be perceived), although it may be in- 5 ferred from a cognition of things. In the finality, therefore, which is prior to the cognition of an Object, and which, even apart from any desire to make use of the representation of it for the purpose of a cognition, is yet immediately connected with it, we have the subjective quality belonging to it that is 10 incapable of becoming a constituent of knowledge. Hence we only apply the term 'final' to the object on account of its representation being immediately coupled with the feeling of pleasure : and this representation itself is an aesthetic represen- tation of the finality.—The only question is whether such 15 a representation of finality exists at all.

If pleasure is connected with the mere apprehension (*appre- hensio*) of the form of an object of intuition, apart from any reference it may have to a concept for the purpose of a definite cognition, this does not make the representation referable to 20 the Object, but solely to the Subject. In such a case the pleasure can express nothing but the conformity of the Object to the cognitive faculties brought into play in the reflective 190 judgement, and so far as they are in play, and hence merely a subjective formal finality of the Object. For that apprehen- 25 sion of forms in the imagination can never take place without the reflective judgement, even when it has no intention of so doing, comparing them at least with its faculty of referring intuitions to concepts. If, now, in this comparison, imagina- tion (as the faculty of intuitions *a priori*) is undesignedly 30 brought into accord with understanding, (as the faculty of con- cepts,) by means of a given representation, and a feeling of pleasure is thereby aroused, then the object must be regarded as final for the reflective judgement. A judgement of this kind is an aesthetic judgement upon the finality of the Object, which 35

does not depend upon any present concept of the object, and does not provide one. When the form of an object (as opposed to the matter of its representation, as sensation) is, in the mere act of reflecting upon it, without regard to any concept to be
5 obtained from it, estimated as the ground of a pleasure in the representation of such an Object, then this pleasure is also judged to be combined necessarily with the representation of it, and so not merely for the Subject apprehending this form, but for all in general who pass judgement. The object is then
10 called beautiful ; and the faculty of judging by means of such a pleasure (and so also with universal validity) is called taste. For since the ground of the pleasure is made to reside merely in the form of the object for reflection generally, consequently not in any sensation of the object, and without any reference,
15 either, to any concept that might have something or other in view, it is with the conformity to law in the empirical employ-ment of judgement generally (unity of imagination and under-standing) in the Subject, and with this alone, that the repre-sentation of the Object in reflection, the conditions of which
20 are universally valid *a priori*, accords. And, as this accordance of the object with the faculties of the Subject is contingent, it gives rise to a representation of a finality on the part of the object in respect of the cognitive faculties of the Subject.

Here, now, is a pleasure which—as is the case with all
25 pleasure or displeasure that is not brought about through the agency of the concept of freedom (i. e. through the antecedent determination of the higher faculty of desire by means of pure reason)—no concepts could ever enable us to regard as necessarily connected with the representation of an object.
30 It must always be only through reflective perception that it is 191 cognized as conjoined with this representation. As with all empirical judgements, it is, consequently, unable to announce objective necessity or lay claim to *a priori* validity. But, then, the judgement of taste in fact only lays claim, like every
35 other empirical judgement, to be valid for every one, and,

despite its inner contingency this is always possible. The only point that is strange or out of the way about it, is that it is not an empirical concept, but a feeling of pleasure (and so not a concept at all), that is yet exacted from every one by the judge- 5 ment of taste, just as if it were a predicate united to the cognition of the Object, and that is meant to be conjoined with its representation.

A singular empirical judgement, as, for example, the judgement of one who perceives a movable drop of water in a rock-crystal, rightly looks to every one finding the fact as 10 stated, since the judgement has been formed according to the universal conditions of the determinant judgement under the laws of a possible experience generally. In the same way one who feels pleasure in simple reflection on the form of an object, without having any concept in mind, rightly lays claim to the 15 agreement of every one, although this judgement is empirical and a singular judgement. For the ground of this pleasure is found in the universal, though subjective, condition of reflective judgements, namely the final harmony of an object (be it a product of nature or of art) with the mutual relation of 20 the faculties of cognition, (imagination and understanding,) which are requisite for every empirical cognition. The pleasure in judgements of taste is, therefore, dependent doubtless on an empirical representation, and cannot be united *a priori* to any concept (one cannot determine *a priori* what object 25 will be in accordance with taste or not—one must find out the object that is so) ; but then it is only made the determining ground of this judgement by virtue of our consciousness of its resting simply upon reflection and the universal, though only subjective, conditions of the harmony of that 30 reflection with the knowledge of objects generally, for which the form of the Object is final.

This is why judgements of taste are subjected to a Critique in respect of their possibility. For their possibility presupposes an *a priori* principle, although that principle is neither a cognitive 35 principle for understanding nor a practical principle for the 192 will, and is thus in no way determinant *a priori*.

Susceptibility to pleasure arising from reflection on the forms of things (whether of nature or of art) betokens, however, not 5 only a finality on the part of Objects in their relation to the reflective judgement in the Subject, in accordance with the concept of nature, but also, conversely, a finality on the part of the Subject, answering to the concept of freedom, in respect of the form, or even formlessness, of objects. The result is that 10 the aesthetic judgement refers not merely, as a judgement of taste, to the beautiful, but also, as springing from a higher intellectual feeling, to the *sublime*. Hence the above-mentioned Critique of Aesthetic Judgement must be divided on these lines into two main parts.

15

VIII

THE LOGICAL REPRESENTATION OF THE FINALITY OF NATURE

THERE are two ways in which finality may be represented in an object given in experience. It may be made to turn on 20 what is purely subjective. In this case the object is considered in respect of its form as present in *apprehension* (*apprehensio*) prior to any concept ; and the harmony of this form with the cognitive faculties, promoting the combination of the intuition with concepts for cognition generally, is represented as a finality 25 of the form of the object. Or, on the other hand, the representation of finality may be made to turn on what is objective, in which case it is represented as the harmony of the form of the object with the possibility of the thing itself according to an antecedent concept of it containing the ground of this form. We have 30 seen that the representation of the former kind of finality rests on the pleasure immediately felt in mere reflection on the form of the object. But that of the latter kind of finality, as it refers the form of the Object, not to the Subject's cognitive faculties engaged in its apprehension, but to a definite cognition of the object under a given concept, has nothing to do with a feeling of pleasure in things, but only with understanding and its estimate of them.   Where the concept of an object is given, 5 the function of judgement, in its employment of that concept for cognition, consists in *presentation* (*exhibitio*), i. e. in placing beside the concept an intuition corresponding to it.   Here it may be that our own imagination is the agent employed, as in

193 the case of art, where we realize a preconceived concept of an 10 object which we set before ourselves as an end.   Or the agent may be nature in its technic, (as in the case of organic bodies,) when we read into it our own concept of an end to assist our estimate of its product.   In this case what is represented is not a mere *finality* of nature in the form of the thing, but 15 this very product as a *natural end.*—Although our concept that nature, in its empirical laws, is subjectively final in its forms is in no way a concept of the Object, but only a principle of judgement for providing itself with concepts in the vast multiplicity of nature, so that it may be able to take its 20 bearings, yet, on the analogy of an end, as it were a regard to our cognitive faculties is here attributed to nature.   *Natural beauty* may, therefore, be looked on as the *presentation* of the concept of formal, i. e. merely subjective, finality and *natural ends* as the presentation of the concept of a real, i. e. objective, finality. 25 The former of these we estimate by taste (aesthetically by means of the feeling of pleasure), the latter by understanding and reason (logically according to concepts).

On these considerations is based the division of the Critique of Judgement into that of the *aesthetic* and the *teleological* 30 judgement.   By the first is meant the faculty of estimating formal finality (otherwise called subjective) by the feeling of pleasure or displeasure, by the second the faculty of estimating the real finality (objective) of nature by understanding and reason.   35

In a Critique of Judgement the part dealing with aesthetic judgement is essentially relevant, as it alone contains a principle introduced by judgement completely *a priori* as the basis of its reflection upon nature. This is the principle of nature's formal
5 finality for our cognitive faculties in its particular (empirical) laws—a principle without which understanding could not feel itself at home in nature : whereas no reason is assignable *a priori*, nor is so much as the possibility of one apparent from the concept of nature as an object of experience, whether in its universal or
10 in its particular aspects, why there should be objective ends of nature, i. e. things only possible as natural ends. But it is only judgement that, without being itself possessed *a priori* of a principle in that behalf, in actually occurring cases (of certain products) contains the rule for making use of the concept of
15 ends in the interest of reason, after that the above transcen- 194 dental principle has already prepared understanding to apply to nature the concept of an end (at least in respect of its form).

But the transcendental principle by which a finality of nature, in its subjective reference to our cognitive faculties, is
20 represented in the form of a thing as a principle of its estimation, leaves quite undetermined the question of where and in what cases we have to make our estimate of the object as a product according to a principle of finality, instead of simply according to universal laws of nature. It resigns to the
25 *aesthetic* judgement the task of deciding the conformity of this product (in its form) to our cognitive faculties as a question of taste (a matter which the aesthetic judgement decides, not by any harmony with concepts, but by feeling). On the other hand judgement as teleologically employed
30 assigns the determinate conditions under which something (e.g. an organized body) is to be estimated after the idea of an end of nature. But it can adduce no principle from the concept of nature, as an object of experience, to give it its authority to ascribe *a priori* to nature a reference to ends, or
35 even only indeterminately to assume them from actual ex-

perience in the case of such products. The reason of this is that in order to be able merely empirically to cognize objective finality in a certain object, many particular experiences must be collected and reviewed under the unity of their principle.— Aesthetic judgement is, therefore, a special faculty of estima- 5 ting according to a rule, but not according to concepts. The teleological is not a special faculty, but only general reflective judgement proceeding, as it always does in theoretical cognition, according to concepts, but in respect of certain objects of nature, following special principles—those, namely, of a 10 judgement that is merely reflective and does not determine Objects. Hence, as regards its application, it belongs to the theoretical part of philosophy, and on account of its special principles, which are not determinant, as principles belonging to doctrine have to be, it must also form a special part of the 15 Critique. On the other hand the aesthetic judgement contributes nothing to the cognition of its objects. Hence it must *only* be allocated to the Critique of the judging Subject and of its faculties of knowledge so far as these are capable of possessing *a priori* principles, be their use (theoretical or 20 practical) otherwise what it may—a Critique which is the propaedeutic of all philosophy.

195

IX

JOINDER OF THE LEGISLATIONS OF UNDERSTANDING
AND REASON BY MEANS OF JUDGEMENT 25

UNDERSTANDING prescribes laws *a priori* for nature as an Object of sense, so that we may have a theoretical knowledge of it in a possible experience. Reason prescribes laws *a priori* for freedom and its peculiar causality as the supersensible in the Subject, so that we may have a purely practical know- 30 ledge. The realm of the concept of nature under the one legislation, and that of the concept of freedom under the other, are completely cut off from all reciprocal influence, that they might severally (each according to its own principles) exert upon the other, by the broad gulf that divides the super- 35

sensible from phenomena. The concept of freedom determines nothing in respect of the theoretical cognition of nature; and the concept of nature likewise nothing in respect of the practical laws of freedom. To that extent, then, it is not
5 possible to throw a bridge from the one realm to the other.—Yet although the determining grounds of causality according to the concept of freedom (and the practical rule that this contains) have no place in nature, and the sensible cannot determine the supersensible in the Subject; still the converse
10 is possible (not, it is true, in respect of the knowledge of nature, but of the consequences arising from the supersensible and bearing on the sensible). So much indeed is implied in the concept of a causality by freedom, the *operation* of which, in conformity with the formal laws of freedom, is to take effect
15 in the world. The word *cause*, however, in its application to the supersensible only signifies the *ground* that determines the causality of things of nature to an effect in conformity with their appropriate natural laws, but at the same time also in unison with the formal principle of the laws of reason—a
20 ground which, while its possibility is impenetrable, may still be completely cleared of the charge of contradiction that it is alleged to involve.[1] The effect in accordance with

---

[1] One of the various supposed contradictions in this complete distinction of the causality of nature from that through freedom, is expressed
25 in the objection that when I speak of *hindrances* opposed by nature to causality according to laws of freedom (moral laws) or of *assistance* lent to it by nature, I am all the time admitting an *influence* of the former upon the latter. But the misinterpretation is easily avoided, if attention is only paid to the meaning of the statement. The resistance or further-
30 ance is not between nature and freedom, but between the former as phenomenon and *the effects* of the latter as phenomena in the world of sense. Even the causality of freedom (of pure and practical reason) is the causality of a natural cause subordinated to freedom (a causality of the Subject regarded as man, and consequently as a phenomenon), and
35 one, the ground of whose determination is contained in the intelligible, that is thought under freedom, in a manner that is not further or otherwise explicable (just as in the case of that intelligible that forms the supersensible substrate of nature).

196 the concept of freedom is the final end which (or the manifestation of which in the sensible world) is to exist, and this
presupposes the condition of the possibility of that end in nature
(i.e. in the nature of the Subject as a being of the sensible
world, namely, as man). It is so presupposed *a priori*, and with- 5
out regard to the practical, by judgement. This faculty, with its
concept of a *finality* of nature, provides us with the mediating
concept between concepts of nature and the concept of freedom
—a concept that makes possible the transition from the pure
theoretical [legislation of understanding] to the pure practical 10
[legislation of reason] and from conformity to law in accordance
with the former to final ends according to the latter. For through
that concept we cognize the possibility of the final end that can
only be actualized in nature and in harmony with its laws.

Understanding, by the possibility of its supplying *a priori* 15
laws for nature, furnishes a proof of the fact that nature is
cognized by us only as phenomenon, and in so doing points to
its having a supersensible substrate ; but this substrate it leaves
quite *undetermined*. Judgement by the *a priori* principle of its
estimation of nature according to its possible particular laws 20
provides this supersensible substrate (within as well as without
us) with *determinability through the intellectual faculty*. But
reason gives *determination* to the same *a priori* by its practical
law. Thus judgement makes possible the transition from the
realm of the concept of nature to that of the concept of freedom. 25

In respect of the faculties of the soul generally, regarded
as higher faculties, i.e. as faculties containing an autonomy,
understanding is the one that contains the *constitutive a priori*
principles for the *faculty of cognition* (the theoretical knowledge
of nature). The *feeling of pleasure and displeasure* is provided 30
for by the judgement in its independence from concepts and
from sensations that refer to the determination of the faculty
197 of desire and would thus be capable of being immediately
practical. For the *faculty of desire* there is reason, which is
practical without mediation of any pleasure of whatsoever 35

origin, and which determines for it, as a higher faculty, the final end that is attended at the same time with pure intellectual delight in the Object.—Judgement's concept of a finality of nature falls, besides, under the head of natural concepts, but 5 only as a regulative principle of the cognitive faculties—although the aesthetic judgement on certain objects (of nature or of art) which occasions that concept, is a constitutive principle in respect of the feeling of pleasure or displeasure. The spontaneity in the play of the cognitive faculties whose harmonious accord con- 10 tains the ground of this pleasure, makes the concept in question, in its consequences, a suitable mediating link connecting the realm of the concept of nature with that of the concept of freedom, as this accord at the same time promotes the sensibility of the mind for moral feeling. The following table may facilitate 15 the review of all the above faculties in their systematic unity.[1]

List of Mental Faculties	*Cognitive Faculties*
Cognitive faculties	Understanding
Feeling of pleasure and displeasure	Judgement
Faculty of desire	Reason

20 *A priori Principles*	*Application*
Conformity to law	Nature
Finality	Art
Final End	Freedom

---

[1] It has been thought somewhat suspicious that my divisions in pure 25 philosophy should almost always come out threefold. But it is due to the nature of the case. If a division is to be *a priori* it must be either analytic, according to the law of contradiction—and then it is always twofold (quodlibet ens est aut A aut non A)—or else it is *synthetic*. If it is to be derived in the latter case from *a priori* concepts (not, as in 30 mathematics, from the *a priori* intuition corresponding to the concept,) then, to meet the requirements of synthetic unity in general, namely (1) a condition, (2) a conditioned, (3) the concept arising from the union of the conditioned with its condition, the division must of necessity be trichotomous.

THE CRITIQUE OF JUDGEMENT

PART I

CRITIQUE OF AESTHETIC JUDGEMENT

FIRST SECTION

ANALYTIC OF AESTHETIC JUDGEMENT

FIRST BOOK

ANALYTIC OF THE BEAUTIFUL

FIRST MOMENT

OF THE JUDGEMENT OF TASTE[1] : MOMENT OF QUALITY

§ 1

The judgement of taste is aesthetic.

IF we wish to discern whether anything is beautiful or not, we do not refer the representation of it to the Object by means of understanding with a view to cognition, but by means of the imagination (acting perhaps in conjunction with understanding) we refer the representation to the Subject and its feeling of pleasure or displeasure. The judgement of taste, therefore, is not a cognitive judgement, and so not logical, but is aesthetic—which means that it is one whose determining ground *cannot be*

[1] The definition of taste here relied upon is that it is the faculty of estimating the beautiful. But the discovery of what is required for calling an object beautiful must be reserved for the analysis of judgements of taste. In my search for the moments to which attention is paid by this judgement in its reflection, I have followed the guidance of the logical functions of judging (for a judgement of taste always involves a reference to understanding). I have brought the moment of quality first under review, because this is what the aesthetic judgement on the beautiful looks to in the first instance.

D

other than subjective. Every reference of representations is
capable of being objective, even that of sensations (in which
case it signifies the real in an empirical representation).   The
204 one exception to this is the feeling of pleasure or displeasure.
This denotes nothing in the object, but is a feeling which the 5
Subject has of itself and of the manner in which it is affected
by the representation.

To apprehend a regular and appropriate building with one's
cognitive faculties, be the mode of representation clear or
confused, is quite a different thing from being conscious of 10
this representation with an accompanying sensation of delight.
Here the representation is referred wholly to the Subject,
and what is more to its feeling of life—under the name of
the feeling of pleasure or displeasure—and this forms the basis
of a quite separate faculty of discriminating and estimating, that 15
contributes nothing to knowledge.   All it does is to compare
the given representation in the Subject with the entire faculty
of representations of which the mind is conscious in the feeling
of its state.   Given representations in a judgement may be
empirical, and so aesthetic ; but the judgement which is pro- 20
nounced by their means is logical, provided it refers them to
the Object.   Conversely, be the given representations even
rational, but referred in a judgement solely to the Subject (to
its feeling), they are always to that extent aesthetic.

§ 2   25

*The delight which determines the judgement of
taste is independent of all interest.*

THE delight which we connect with the representation of the
real existence of an object is called interest.   Such a delight,
therefore, always involves a reference to the faculty of desire, 30
either as its determining ground, or else as necessarily implicated
with its determining ground.   Now, where the question is

whether something is beautiful, we do not want to know, whether we, or any one else, are, or even could be, concerned in the real existence of the thing, but rather what estimate we form of it on mere contemplation (intuition or reflection). If 5 any one asks me whether I consider that the palace I see before me is beautiful, I may, perhaps, reply that I do not care for things of that sort that are merely made to be gaped at. Or I may reply in the same strain as that Iroquois *sachem* who said that nothing in Paris pleased him better than the eating-houses. 10 I may even go a step further and inveigh with the vigour of 205 a *Rousseau* against the vanity of the great who spend the sweat of the people on such superfluous things. Or, in fine, I may quite easily persuade myself that if I found myself on an uninhabited island, without hope of ever again coming among men, 15 and could conjure such a palace into existence by a mere wish, I should still not trouble to do so, so long as I had a hut there that was comfortable enough for me. All this may be admitted and approved ; only it is not the point now at issue. All one wants to know is whether the mere representation of the object 20 is to my liking, no matter how indifferent I may be to the real existence of the object of this representation. It is quite plain that in order to say that the object *is beautiful*, and to show that I have taste, everything turns on the meaning which I can give to this representation, and not on any factor which 25 makes me dependent on the real existence of the object. Every one must allow that a judgement on the beautiful which is tinged with the slightest interest, is very partial and not a pure judgement of taste. One must not be in the least prepossessed in favour of the real existence of the thing, but must 30 preserve complete indifference in this respect, in order to play the part of judge in matters of taste.

This proposition, which is of the utmost importance, cannot be better explained than by contrasting the pure disinterested [1]

---

[1] A judgement upon an object of our delight may be wholly *disinterested* 35 but withal very *interesting*, i.e. it relies on no interest, but it produces

delight which appears in the judgement of taste with that allied
to an interest—especially if we can also assure ourselves that
there are no other kinds of interest beyond those presently to
be mentioned.

§ 3   5

Delight IN THE AGREEABLE *is coupled with interest.*

That is AGREEABLE *which the senses find pleasing in sensation.*
This at once affords a convenient opportunity for condemning
and directing particular attention to a prevalent confusion of
the double meaning of which the word ' sensation ' is capable. 10
All delight (as is said or thought) is itself sensation (of a
206 pleasure). Consequently everything that pleases, and for the
very reason that it pleases, is agreeable—and according to its
different degrees, or its relations to other agreeable sensations,
is attractive, charming, delicious, enjoyable, &c. But if this is 15
conceded, then impressions of sense, which determine inclination,
or principles of reason, which determine the will, or mere contemplated forms of intuition, which determine judgement, are
all on a par in everything relevant to their effect upon the
feeling of pleasure, for this would be agreeableness in the 20
sensation of one's state ; and since, in the last resort, all the
elaborate work of our faculties must issue in and unite in the
practical as its goal, we could credit our faculties with no other
appreciation of things and the worth of things, than that consisting in the gratification which they promise. How this is 25
attained is in the end immaterial ; and, as the choice of the
means is here the only thing that can make a difference, men
might indeed blame one another for folly or imprudence, but
never for baseness or wickedness ; for they are all, each accord-

one. Of this kind are all pure moral judgements. But, of themselves, 30
judgements of taste do not even set up any interest whatsoever. Only
in society is it *interesting* to have taste—a point which will be explained
in the sequel.

ing to his own way of looking at things, pursuing one goal, which for each is the gratification in question.

When a modification of the feeling of pleasure or displeasure is termed sensation, this expression is given quite a different
5 meaning to that which it bears when I call the representation of a thing (through sense as a receptivity pertaining to the faculty of knowledge) sensation. For in the latter case the representation is referred to the Object, but in the former it is referred solely to the Subject and is not available for any cognition, not
10 even for that by which the Subject *cognizes* itself.

Now in the above definition the word sensation is used to denote an objective representation of sense ; and, to avoid continually running the risk of misinterpretation, we shall call that which must always remain purely subjective, and is absolutely
15 incapable of forming a representation of an object, by the familiar name of feeling. The green colour of the meadows belongs to *objective* sensation, as the perception of an object of sense ; but its agreeableness to *subjective* sensation, by which no object is represented : i.e. to feeling, through which the
20 object is regarded as an Object of delight (which involves no cognition of the object).

Now, that a judgement on an object by which its agreeable- 207 ness is affirmed, expresses an interest in it, is evident from the fact that through sensation it provokes a desire for similar objects,
25 consequently the delight presupposes, not the simple judgement about it, but the bearing its real existence has upon my state so far as affected by such an Object. Hence we do not merely say of the agreeable that it *pleases*, but that it *gratifies*. I do not accord it a simple approval, but inclination is aroused by
30 it, and where agreeableness is of the liveliest type a judgement on the character of the Object is so entirely out of place, that those who are always intent only on enjoyment (for that is the word used to denote intensity of gratification) would fain dispense with all judgement.

§ 4

Delight IN THE GOOD *is coupled with interest.*

THAT is *good* which by means of reason commends itself by
its mere concept. We call that *good for something* (useful)
which only pleases as a means ; but that which pleases on its
own account we call *good in itself.* In both cases the concept
of an end is implied, and consequently the relation of reason
to (at least possible) willing, and thus a delight in the *existence*
of an Object or action, i. e. some interest or other.

To deem something good, I must always know what sort of
a thing the object is intended to be, i. e. I must have a concept
of it. That is not necessary to enable me to see beauty in
a thing. Flowers, free patterns, lines aimlessly intertwining—
technically termed foliage,—have no signification, depend upon
no definite concept, and yet please. Delight in the beautiful
must depend upon the reflection on an object precursory to
some (not definitely determined) concept. It is thus also
differentiated from the agreeable, which rests entirely upon
sensation.

In many cases, no doubt, the agreeable and the good seem
convertible terms. Thus it is commonly said that all (especially lasting) gratification is of itself good ; which is almost
equivalent to saying that to be permanently agreeable and to
be good are identical. But it is readily apparent that this is
merely a vicious confusion of words, for the concepts appro-
208 priate to these expressions are far from interchangeable. The
agreeable, which, as such, represents the object solely in
relation to sense, must in the first instance be brought under
principles of reason through the concept of an end, to be, as an
object of will, called good. But that the reference to delight is
wholly different where what gratifies is at the same time called
good, is evident from the fact that with the good the question

always is whether it is mediately or immediately good, i.e. useful
or good in itself; whereas with the agreeable this point can
never arise, since the word always means what pleases immediately—and it is just the same with what I call beautiful.

5   Even in everyday parlance a distinction is drawn between
the agreeable and the good. We do not scruple to say of
a dish that stimulates the palate with spices and other condi-
ments that it is agreeable—owning all the while that it is not
good : because, while it immediately *satisfies* the senses, it is
10 mediately displeasing, i.e. in the eye of reason that looks
ahead to the consequences. Even in our estimate of health
this same distinction may be traced. To all that possess it, it
is immediately agreeable—at least negatively, i.e. as remoteness
of all bodily pains. But, if we are to say that it is good, we
15 must further apply to reason to direct it to ends, that is, we
must regard it as a state that puts us in a congenial mood
for all we have to do. Finally, in respect of happiness every
one believes that the greatest aggregate of the pleasures
of life, taking duration as well as number into account, merits
20 the name of a true, nay even of the highest, good. But reason
sets its face against this too. Agreeableness is enjoyment.
But if this is all that we are bent on, it would be foolish to be
scrupulous about the means that procure it for us—whether it
be obtained passively by the bounty of nature or actively and
25 by the work of our own hands. But that there is any intrinsic
worth in the real existence of a man who merely lives for
enjoyment, however busy he may be in this respect, even when
in so doing he serves others—all equally with himself intent
only on enjoyment—as an excellent means to that one end,
30 and does so, moreover, because through sympathy he shares
all their gratifications,—this is a view to which reason will
never let itself be brought round. Only by what a man does
heedless of enjoyment, in complete freedom and independently
of what he can procure passively from the hand of nature, does
35 he give to his existence, as the real existence of a person, an 209

absolute worth. Happiness, with all its plethora of pleasures, is far from being an unconditioned good.[1]

But, despite all this difference between the agreeable and the good, they both agree in being invariably coupled with an interest in their object. This is true, not alone of the agree- 5 able, § 3, and of the mediately good, i. e. the useful, which pleases as a means to some pleasure, but also of that which is good absolutely and from every point of view, namely the moral good which carries with it the highest interest. For the good is the Object of will, i. e. of a rationally determined faculty of 10 desire). But to will something, and to take a delight in its existence, i. e. to take an interest in it, are identical.

§ 5

Comparison of the three specifically different kinds of delight.

BOTH the Agreeable and the Good involve a reference to 15 the faculty of desire, and are thus attended, the former with a delight pathologically conditioned (by stimuli), the latter with a pure practical delight. Such delight is determined not merely by the representation of the object, but also by the represented bond of connexion between the Subject 20 and the real existence of the object. It is not merely the object, but also its real existence, that pleases. On the other hand the judgement of taste is simply *contemplative*, i. e. it is a judgement which is indifferent as to the existence of an object, and only decides how its character 25 stands with the feeling of pleasure and displeasure. But not even is this contemplation itself directed to concepts ; for the

---

[1] An obligation to enjoyment is a patent absurdity. And the same, then, must also be said of a supposed obligation to actions that have merely enjoyment for their aim, no matter how spiritually this enjoy- 30 ment may be refined in thought (or embellished), and even if it be a mystical, so-called heavenly, enjoyment.

judgement of taste is not a cognitive judgement (neither a theoretical one nor a practical), and hence, also, is not *grounded* on concepts, nor yet *intentionally directed* to them.

The agreeable, the beautiful, and the good thus denote
5 three different relations of representations to the feeling of pleasure and displeasure, as a feeling in respect of which we 210 distinguish different objects or modes of representation. Also, the corresponding expressions which indicate our satisfaction in them are different. The *agreeable* is what GRATIFIES a man;
10 the *beautiful* what simply PLEASES him; the *good* what is ESTEEMED (*approved*), i.e. that on which he sets an objective worth. Agreeableness is a significant factor even with irrational animals; beauty has purport and significance only for human beings, i.e. for beings at once animal and rational (but not
15 merely for them as rational—intelligent beings—but only for them as at once animal and rational); whereas the good is good for every rational being in general;—a proposition which can only receive its complete justification and explanation in the sequel. Of all these three kinds of delight, that of taste in
20 the beautiful may be said to be the one and only disinterested and *free* delight; for, with it, no interest, whether sense or reason, extorts approval. And so we may say that delight, in the three cases mentioned, is related to *inclination*, to *favour*, or to *respect*. For FAVOUR is the only free liking. An
25 object of inclination, and one which a law of reason imposes upon our desire, leaves us no freedom to turn anything into an object of pleasure. All interest presupposes a want, or calls one forth; and, being a ground determining approval, deprives the judgement on the object of its freedom.

30 So far as the interest of inclination in the case of the agreeable goes, every one says : Hunger is the best sauce; and people with a healthy appetite relish everything, so long as it is something they can eat. Such delight, consequently, gives no indication of taste having anything to say to the choice.
35 Only when men have got all they want can we tell who among

the crowd has taste or not. Similarly there may be correct habits (conduct) without virtue, politeness without good-will, propriety without honour, &c. For where the moral law dictates, there is, objectively, no room left for free choice as to what one has to do ; and to show taste in the way one carries 5 out these dictates, or in estimating the way others do so, is a totally different matter from displaying the moral frame of one's mind. For the latter involves a command and produces a need of something, whereas moral taste only plays with the objects of delight without devoting itself sincerely to any. 10

211 DEFINITION OF THE BEAUTIFUL DERIVED FROM THE
FIRST MOMENT

Taste is the faculty of estimating an object or a mode of representation by means of a delight or aversion *apart from any interest.* The object of such a delight is called *beautiful.* 15

SECOND MOMENT

OF THE JUDGEMENT OF TASTE : MOMENT OF QUANTITY

§ 6

*The beautiful is that which, apart from concepts, is represented
as the Object of a* UNIVERSAL *delight.* 20

THIS definition of the beautiful is deducible from the foregoing definition of it as an object of delight apart from any interest. For where any one is conscious that his delight in an object is with him independent of interest, it is inevitable that he should look on the object as one containing a ground 25 of delight for all men. For, since the delight is not based on any inclination of the Subject (or on any other deliberate interest), but the Subject feels himself completely *free* in respect of the

liking which he accords to the object, he can find as reason for
his delight no personal conditions to which his own subjective
self might alone be party. Hence he must regard it as resting on
what he may also presuppose in every other person ; and there-
5 fore he must believe that he has reason for demanding a similar
delight from every one. Accordingly he will speak of the beautiful as if beauty were a quality of the object and the judgement
logical (forming a cognition of the Object by concepts of it) ;
although it is only aesthetic, and contains merely a reference
10 of the representation of the object to the Subject ;—because
it still bears this resemblance to the logical judgement, that it
may be presupposed to be valid for all men. But this universality cannot spring from concepts. For from concepts there is
no transition to the feeling of pleasure or displeasure (save in
15 the case of pure practical laws, which, however, carry an
interest with them ; and such an interest does not attach
to the pure judgement of taste). The result is that the judge- 212
ment of taste, with its attendant consciousness of detachment
from all interest, must involve a claim to validity for all
20 men, and must do so apart from universality attached to
Objects, i.e. there must be coupled with it a claim to subjective
universality.

§ 7

Comparison of the beautiful with the agreeable and the good
25 *by means of the above characteristic.*

As regards the *agreeable* every one concedes that his judgement, which he bases on a private feeling, and in which he
declares that an object pleases him, is restricted merely to
himself personally. Thus he does not take it amiss if, when
30 he says that Canary-wine is agreeable, another corrects the
expression and reminds him that he ought to say : It is agreeable *to me*. This applies not only to the taste of the tongue,
the palate, and the throat, but to what may with any one be
agreeable to eye or ear. A violet colour is to one soft and

lovely : to another dull and faded.   One man likes the tone
of wind instruments, another prefers that of string instruments.
To quarrel over such points with the idea of condemning
another's judgement as incorrect when it differs from our own,
as if the opposition between the two judgements were logical, 5
would be folly.   With the agreeable, therefore, the axiom holds
good : *Every one has his own taste* (that of sense).

The beautiful stands on quite a different footing.   It would,
on the contrary, be ridiculous if any one who plumed
himself on his taste were to think of justifying himself by 10
saying : This object (the building we see, the dress that
person has on, the concert we hear, the poem submitted to our
criticism) is beautiful *for me*.   For if it merely pleases *him*, he
must not call it *beautiful*.   Many things may for him possess
charm and agreeableness—no one cares about that ; but when 15
he puts a thing on a pedestal and calls it beautiful, he demands
the same delight from others.   He judges not merely for himself, but for all men, and then speaks of beauty as if it were
a property of things.   Thus he says the *thing* is beautiful ; and
it is not as if he counted on others agreeing in his judgement 20
213 of liking owing to his having found them in such agreement on a number of occasions, but he *demands* this agreement
of them.   He blames them if they judge differently, and denies
them taste, which he still requires of them as something they
ought to have ; and to this extent it is not open to men to say : 25
Every one has his own taste.   This would be equivalent to
saying that there is no such thing at all as taste, i.e. no aesthetic
judgement capable of making a rightful claim upon the assent
of all men.

Yet even in the case of the agreeable we find that the 30
estimates men form do betray a prevalent agreement among
them, which leads to our crediting some with taste and denying
it to others, and that, too, not as an organic sense but as
a critical faculty in respect of the agreeable generally.   So of

one who knows how to entertain his guests with pleasures (of
enjoyment through all the senses) in such a way that one and
all are pleased, we say that he has taste. But the universality
here is only understood in a comparative sense ; and the rules
5 that apply are, like all empirical rules, *general* only, not
universal,—the latter being what the judgement of taste upon
the beautiful deals or claims to deal in. It is a judgement in
respect of sociability so far as resting on empirical rules. In
respect of the good it is true that judgements also rightly assert
10 a claim to validity for every one ; but the good is only represented as an Object of universal delight *by means of a concept*,
which is the case neither with the agreeable nor the beautiful.

§ 8

In a judgement of taste the universality of delight is only
15 *represented as subjective.*

THIS particular form of the universality of an aesthetic
judgement, which is to be met with in a judgement of taste, is
a significant feature, not for the logician certainly, but for the
transcendental philosopher. It calls for no small effort on his
20 part to discover its origin, but in return it brings to light
a property of our cognitive faculty which, without this analysis,
would have remained unknown.

First, one must get firmly into one's mind that by the
judgement of taste (upon the beautiful) the delight in an 21
25 object is imputed to *every one*, yet without being founded on
a concept (for then it would be the good), and that this claim
to universality is such an essential factor of a judgement by
which we describe anything as *beautiful*, that were it not for its
being present to the mind it would never enter into any one's
30 head to use this expression, but everything that pleased without
a concept would be ranked as agreeable. For in respect of the
agreeable every one is allowed to have his own opinion, and
no one insists upon others agreeing with his judgement of

taste, which is what is invariably done in the judgement of taste about beauty. The first of these I may call the taste of sense, the second, the taste of reflection : the first laying down judgements merely private, the second, on the other hand, judgements ostensibly of general validity (public), but 5 both alike being aesthetic (not practical) judgements about an object merely in respect of the bearings of its representation on the feeling of pleasure or displeasure. Now it does seem strange that while with the taste of sense it is not alone experience that shows that its judgement (of pleasure or displeasure 10 in something) is not universally valid, but every one willingly refrains from imputing this agreement to others (despite the frequent actual prevalence of a considerable consensus of general opinion even in these judgements), the taste of reflection, which, as experience teaches, has often enough to 15 put up with a rude dismissal of its claims to universal validity of its judgement (upon the beautiful), can (as it actually does) find it possible for all that, to formulate judgements capable of demanding this agreement in its universality. Such agreement it does in fact require from every one for each of its judgements 20 of taste,—the persons who pass these judgements not quarrelling over the possibility of such a claim, but only failing in particular cases to come to terms as to the correct application of this faculty.

First of all we have here to note that a universality which 25 does not rest upon concepts of the Object (even though these are only empirical) is in no way logical, but aesthetic, i. e. does not involve any objective quantity of the judgement, but only one that is subjective. For this universality I use the expression *general validity*, which denotes the validity of the reference of 30 a representation, not to the cognitive faculties, but to the feeling of pleasure or displeasure for every Subject. (The same expression, however, may also be employed for the logical 215 quantity of the judgement, provided we add *objective* universal validity, to distinguish it from the merely subjective validity which is always aesthetic.)

Now a judgement that has *objective universal validity* has always got the subjective also, i. e. if the judgement is valid for everything which is contained under a given concept, it is valid also for all who represent an object by means of this concept. But from a *subjective universal validity*, i. e. the aesthetic, that does not rest on any concept, no conclusion can be drawn to the logical ; because judgements of that kind have no bearing upon the Object. But for this very reason the aesthetic universality attributed to a judgement must also be of a special kind, seeing that it does not join the predicate of beauty to the concept of the *Object* taken in its entire logical sphere, and yet does extend this predicate over the whole sphere of *judging Subjects*.

In their logical quantity all judgements of taste are *singular* judgements. For, since I must present the object immediately to my feeling of pleasure or displeasure, and that, too, without the aid of concepts, such judgements cannot have the quantity of judgements with objective general validity. Yet by taking the singular representation of the Object of the judgement of taste, and by comparison converting it into a concept according to the conditions determining that judgement, we can arrive at a logically universal judgement. For instance, by a judgement of taste I describe the rose at which I am looking as beautiful. The judgement, on the other hand, resulting from the comparison of a number of singular representations : Roses in general are beautiful, is no longer pronounced as a purely aesthetic judgement, but as a logical judgement founded on one that is aesthetic. Now the judgement, 'The rose is agreeable' (to smell) is also, no doubt, an aesthetic and singular judgement, but then it is not one of taste but of sense. For it has this point of difference from a judgement of taste, that the latter imports an *aesthetic quantity* of universality, i. e. of validity for every one which is not to be met with

in a judgement upon the agreeable. It is only judgements
upon the good which, while also determining the delight in an
object, possess logical and not mere aesthetic universality; for
it is as involving a cognition of the Object that they are valid
of it, and on that account valid for every one.   5

In forming an estimate of Objects merely from concepts, all
representation of beauty goes by the board. There can,
therefore, be no rule according to which any one is to be com-
216 pelled to recognize anything as beautiful. Whether a dress, a
house, or a flower is beautiful is a matter upon which one declines 10
to allow one's judgement to be swayed by any reasons or principles. We want to get a look at the Object with our own
eyes, just as if our delight depended on sensation. And yet,
if upon so doing, we call the object beautiful, we believe
ourselves to be speaking with a universal voice, and lay claim 15
to the concurrence of every one, whereas no private sensation
would be decisive except for the observer alone and *his* liking.

Here, now, we may perceive that nothing is postulated in
the judgement of taste but such a *universal voice* in respect of
delight that is not mediated by concepts; consequently, only 20
the *possibility* of an aesthetic judgement capable of being at
the same time deemed valid for every one. The judgement of
taste itself does not *postulate* the agreement of every one (for
it is only competent for a logically universal judgement to do
this, in that it is able to bring forward reasons); it only *imputes* 25
this agreement to every one, as an instance of the rule in respect
of which it looks for confirmation, not from concepts, but from
the concurrence of others. The universal voice is, therefore,
only an idea—resting upon grounds the investigation of which
is here postponed. It may be a matter of uncertainty whether 30
a person who thinks he is laying down a judgement of taste
is, in fact, judging in conformity with that idea; but that
this idea is what is contemplated in his judgement, and that,
consequently, it is meant to be a judgement of taste, is pro-

claimed by his use of the expression 'beauty'. For himself he can be certain on the point from his mere consciousness of the separation of everything belonging to the agreeable and the good from the delight remaining to him ; and this is all for
5 which he promises himself the agreement of every one—a claim which, under these conditions, he would also be warranted in making, were it not that he frequently sinned against them, and thus passed an erroneous judgement of taste.

§ 9

10 *Investigation of the question of the relative priority in a judgement of taste of the feeling of pleasure and the estimating of the object.*

THE solution of this problem is the key to the Critique of taste, and so is worthy of all attention.
15 Were the pleasure in a given object to be the antecedent, and were the universal communicability of this pleasure to be 217 all that the judgement of taste is meant to allow to the representation of the object, such a sequence would be self-contradictory. For a pleasure of that kind would be nothing
20 but the feeling of mere agreeableness to the senses, and so, from its very nature, would possess no more than private validity, seeing that it would be immediately dependent on the representation through which the object *is given*.

Hence it is the universal capacity for being communicated
25 incident to the mental state in the given representation which, as the subjective condition of the judgement of taste, must be fundamental, with the pleasure in the object as its consequent. Nothing, however, is capable of being universally communicated but cognition and representation so far as appurtenant to
30 cognition. For it is only as thus appurtenant that the representation is objective, and it is this alone that gives it a universal point of reference with which the power of representation of every one is obliged to harmonize. If, then,

E

the determining ground of the judgement as to this universal communicability of the representation is to be merely subjective, that is to say, is to be conceived independently of any concept of the object, it can be nothing else than the mental state that presents itself in the mutual relation of the powers of 5 representation so far as they refer a given representation *to cognition in general.*

The cognitive powers brought into play by this representation are here engaged in a free play, since no definite concept restricts them to a particular rule of cognition.   Hence the 10 mental state in this representation must be one of a feeling of the free play of the powers of representation in a given representation for a cognition in general.   Now a representation, whereby an object is given, involves, in order that it may become a source of cognition at all, *imagination* for bringing together 15 the manifold of intuition, and *understanding* for the unity of the concept uniting the representations.   This state of *free play* of the cognitive faculties attending a representation by which an object is given must admit of universal communication: because cognition, as a definition of the Object with which 20 given representations (in any Subject whatever) are to accord, is the one and only representation which is valid for every one.

As the subjective universal communicability of the mode of representation in a judgement of taste is to subsist apart from the presupposition of any definite concept, it can be 25
218 nothing else than the mental state present in the free play of imagination and understanding (so far as these are in mutual accord, as is requisite for *cognition in general*): for we are conscious that this subjective relation suitable for a cognition in general must be just as valid for every one, and consequently 30 as universally communicable, as is any determinate cognition, which always rests upon that relation as its subjective condition.

Now this purely subjective (aesthetic) estimating of the object, or of the representation through which it is given, is

antecedent to the pleasure in it, and is the basis of this pleasure in the harmony of the cognitive faculties. Again, the above-described universality of the subjective conditions of estimating objects forms the sole foundation of this universal
5 subjective validity of the delight which we connect with the representation of the object that we call beautiful.

That an ability to communicate one's mental state, even though it be only in respect of our cognitive faculties, is attended with a pleasure, is a fact which might easily be
10 demonstrated from the natural propensity of mankind to social life, i.e. empirically and psychologically. But what we have here in view calls for something more than this. In a judgement of taste the pleasure felt by us is exacted from every one else as necessary, just as if, when we call something beautiful,
15 beauty was to be regarded as a quality of the object forming part of its inherent determination according to concepts ; although beauty is for itself, apart from any reference to the feeling of the Subject, nothing. But the discussion of this question must be reserved until we have answered the further one of whether,
20 and how, aesthetic judgements are possible *a priori*.

At present we are exercised with the lesser question of the way in which we become conscious, in a judgement of taste, of a reciprocal subjective common accord of the powers of cognition. Is it aesthetically by sensation and our mere
25 internal sense ? Or is it intellectually by consciousness of our intentional activity in bringing these powers into play ?

Now if the given representation occasioning the judgement of taste were a concept which united understanding and imagination in the estimate of the object so as to give a
30 cognition of the Object, the consciousness of this relation would be intellectual (as in the objective schematism of judgement dealt with in the Critique). But, then, in that case the judgement would not be laid down with respect to pleasure and displeasure, and so would not be a judgement of taste. 219
35 But, now, the judgement of taste determines the Object,

independently of concepts, in respect of delight and of the predicate of beauty.   There is, therefore, no other way for the subjective unity of the relation in question to make itself known than by sensation.   The quickening of both faculties (imagina-tion and understanding) to an indefinite, but yet, thanks to 5 the given representation, harmonious activity, such as belongs to cognition generally, is the sensation whose universal com-municability is postulated by the judgement of taste.   An objective relation can, of course, only be thought, yet in so far as, in respect of its conditions, it is subjective, it may be felt in 10 its effect upon the mind, and, in the case of a relation (like that of the powers of representation to a faculty of cognition generally) which does not rest on any concept, no other consciousness of it is possible beyond that through sensation of its effect upon the mind—an effect consisting in the more 15 facile play of both mental powers (imagination and understand-ing) as quickened by their mutual accord.   A representation which is singular and independent of comparison with other representations, and, being such, yet accords with the conditions of the universality that is the general concern of understanding, 20 is one that brings the cognitive faculties into that proportionate accord which we require for all cognition and which we therefore deem valid for every one who is so constituted as to judge by means of understanding and sense conjointly (i.e. for every man).   25

DEFINITION OF THE BEAUTIFUL DRAWN FROM THE SECOND MOMENT

The *beautiful* is that which, apart from a concept, pleases universally.

THIRD MOMENT

§ 10

5 *Finality in general.*

LET us define the meaning of 'an end' in transcendental terms (i. e. without presupposing anything empirical, such as the feeling of pleasure). An end is the object of a concept so 220 far as this concept is regarded as the cause of the object (the 10 real ground of its possibility) ; and the causality of a *concept* in respect of its *Object* is finality (*forma finalis*). Where, then, not the cognition of an object merely, but the object itself (its form or real existence) as an effect, is thought to be possible only through a concept of it, there we imagine an end. The 15 representation of the effect is here the determining ground of its cause and takes the lead of it. The consciousness of the causality of a representation in respect of the state of the Subject as one tending *to preserve a continuance* of that state, may here be said to denote in a general way what is called pleasure ; 20 whereas displeasure is that representation which contains the ground for converting the state of the representations into their opposite (for hindering or removing them).

The faculty of desire, so far as determinable only through concepts, i. e. so as to act in conformity with the representation 25 of an end, would be the will. But an Object, or state of mind, or even an action may, although its possibility does not necessarily presuppose the representation of an end, be called final simply on account of its possibility being only explicable and intelligible for us by virtue of an assumption on our part of 30 a fundamental causality according to ends, i. e. a will that would have so ordained it according to a certain represented rule. Finality, therefore, may exist apart from an end, in so far as we do not locate the causes of this form in a will, but yet are able to render the explanation of its possibility intelligible to ourselves only by deriving it from a will. Now we are not always obliged to look with the eye of reason into what we observe (i.e. to consider it in its possibility). So we may at least observe a finality of form, and trace it in objects—though by reflection only—without resting it on an end (as the material of the *nexus finalis*).

221   § 11   10

The sole foundation of the judgement of taste is the FORM OF FINALITY *of an object (or mode of representing it).*

WHENEVER an end is regarded as a source of delight it always imports an interest as determining ground of the judgement on the object of pleasure. Hence the judgement of taste cannot rest on any subjective end as its ground. But neither can any representation of an objective end, i.e. of the possibility of the object itself on principles of final connexion, determine the judgement of taste, and, consequently, neither can any concept of the good. For the judgement of taste is an aesthetic and not a cognitive judgement, and so does not deal with any *concept* of the nature or of the internal or external possibility, by this or that cause, of the object, but simply with the relative bearing of the representative powers so far as determined by a representation.   25

Now this relation, present when an object is characterized as beautiful, is coupled with the feeling of pleasure. This pleasure is by the judgment of taste pronounced valid for every one ; hence an agreeableness attending the representation is just as incapable of containing the determining ground of the judgement as the representation of the perfection of the object or the concept of the good. We are thus left with the subjective

finality in the representation of an object, exclusive of any
end (objective or subjective)—consequently the bare form of
finality in the representation whereby an object is *given* to us,
so far as we are conscious of it—as that which is alone capable
5 of constituting the delight which, apart from any concept, we
estimate as universally communicable, and so of forming the
determining ground of the judgment of taste.

§ 12

The judgement of taste rests upon a priori *grounds.*

10 To determine *a priori* the connexion of the feeling of
pleasure or displeasure as an effect, with some representation
or other (sensation or concept) as its cause, is utterly impossible ; for that would be a causal relation which, (with objects of experience,) is always one that can only be cognized 222
15 *a posteriori* and with the help of experience. True, in the
Critique of Practical Reason we did actually derive *a priori*
from universal moral concepts the feeling of respect (as a particular and peculiar modification of this feeling which does not
strictly answer either to the pleasure or displeasure which we
20 receive from empirical objects). But there we were further
able to cross the border of experience and call in aid a causality
resting on a supersensible attribute of the Subject, namely that
of freedom. But even there it was not this *feeling* exactly
that we deduced from the idea of the moral as cause, but from
25 this was derived simply the determination of the will. But the
mental state present in the determination of the will by any
means is at once in itself a feeling of pleasure and identical
with it, and so does not issue from it as an effect. Such an
effect must only be assumed where the concept of the moral
30 as a good precedes the determination of the will by the law ;
for in that case it would be futile to derive the pleasure combined with the concept from this concept as a mere cognition.

Now the pleasure in aesthetic judgements stands on a similar footing : only that here it is merely contemplative and does not bring about an interest in the Object; whereas in the moral judgement it is practical. The consciousness of mere formal finality in the play of the cognitive faculties of the Subject attending a representation whereby an object is given, is 5 the pleasure itself, because it involves a determining ground of the Subject's activity in respect of the quickening of its cognitive powers, and thus an internal causality (which is final) in respect of cognition generally, but without being limited to a definite cognition, and consequently a mere form of the sub- 10 jective finality of a representation in an aesthetic judgement. This pleasure is also in no way practical, neither resembling that from the pathological ground of agreeableness nor that from the intellectual ground of the represented good. But still it involves an inherent causality, that, namely, of *preserving* 15 *a continuance* of the state of the representation itself and the active engagement of the cognitive powers without ulterior aim. We *dwell* on the contemplation of the beautiful because this contemplation strengthens and reproduces itself. The case is analogous (but analogous only) to the way we linger on 20 a charm in the representation of an object which keeps arresting the attention, the mind all the while remaining passive.

223

§ 13

The pure judgement of taste is independent of charm and emotion. 25

EVERY interest vitiates the judgement of taste and robs it of its impartiality. This is especially so where instead of, like the interest of reason, making finality take the lead of the feeling of pleasure, it grounds it upon this feeling—which is what always happen in aesthetic judgements upon anything so 30 far as it gratifies or pains. Hence judgements so influenced can either lay no claim at all to a universally valid delight, or else must abate their claim in proportion as sensations of the kind in question enter into the determining grounds of taste. Taste that requires an added element of *charm* and *emotion* for its delight, not to speak of adopting this as the measure of its 5 approval, has not yet emerged from barbarism.

And yet charms are frequently not alone ranked with beauty (which ought properly to be a question merely of the form) as supplementary to the aesthetic universal delight, but they have been accredited as intrinsic beauties, and con- 10 sequently the matter of delight passed off for the form. This is a misconception which, like many others that have still an underlying element of truth, may be removed by a careful definition of these concepts.

A judgement of taste which is uninfluenced by charm or 15 emotion, (though these may be associated with the delight in the beautiful,) and whose determining ground, therefore, is simply finality of form, is *a pure judgement of taste*.

§ 14

Exemplification.

20 AESTHETIC, just like theoretical (logical) judgements, are divisible into empirical and pure. The first are those by which agreeableness or disagreeableness, the second those by which beauty, is predicated of an object or its mode of representation. The former are judgements of sense (material 25 aesthetic judgements), the latter (as formal) alone judgements of taste proper.

A judgement of taste, therefore, is only pure so far as its 224 determining ground is tainted with no merely empirical delight. But such a taint is always present where charm or 30 emotion have a share in the judgement by which something is to be described as beautiful.

Here now there is a recrudescence of a number of specious

pleas that go the length of putting forward the case that charm is not merely a necessary ingredient of beauty, but is even of itself sufficient to merit the name of beautiful. A mere colour, such as the green of a plot of grass, or a mere tone (as distinguished from sound or noise), like that of a violin, is 5 described by most people as in itself beautiful, notwithstanding the fact that both seem to depend merely on the matter of the representations—in other words, simply on sensation, which only entitles them to be called agreeable. But it will at the same time be observed that sensations of colour as well as of 10 tone are only entitled to be immediately regarded as beautiful where, in either case, they are *pure*. This is a determination which at once goes to their form, and it is the only one which these representations possess that admits with certainty of being universally communicated. For it is not to be 15 assumed that even the quality of the sensations agrees in all Subjects, and we can hardly take it for granted that the agreeableness of a colour, or of the tone of a musical instrument, which we judge to be preferable to that of another, is given a like preference in the estimate of every one. 20

Assuming with *Euler* that colours are isochronous vibrations (*pulsus*) of the aether, as tones are of the air set in vibration by sound, and, what is most important, that the mind not alone perceives by sense their effect in stimulating the organs, but also, by reflection, the regular play of the impressions, (and 25 consequently the form in which different representations are united,)—which I, still, in no way doubt—then colour and tone would not be mere sensations. They would be nothing short of formal determinations of the unity of a manifold of sensations, and in that case could even be ranked as intrinsic 30 beauties.

But the purity of a simple mode of sensation means that its uniformity is not disturbed or broken by any foreign sensation. It belongs merely to the form; for abstraction may there be made from the quality of the mode of such sensation (what colour or tone, if any, it represents). For this reason all simple colours are regarded as beautiful so far as pure. Composite colours have not this advantage, because, 225 not being simple, there is no standard for estimating whether they should be called pure or impure.

But as for the beauty ascribed to the object on account of its form, and the supposition that it is capable of being enhanced by charm, this is a common error and one very prejudicial to genuine, uncorrupted, sincere taste. Nevertheless charms may be added to beauty to lend to the mind, beyond a bare delight, an adventitious interest in the representation of the object, and thus to advocate taste and its cultivation. This applies especially where taste is as yet crude and untrained. But they are positively subversive of the judgement of taste, if allowed to obtrude themselves as grounds of estimating beauty. For so far are they from contributing to beauty, that it is only where taste is still weak and untrained, that, like aliens, they are admitted as a favour, and only on terms that they do not violate that beautiful form.

In painting, sculpture, and in fact in all the formative arts, in architecture and horticulture, so far as fine arts, the *design* is what is essential. Here it is not what gratifies in sensation but merely what pleases by its form, that is the fundamental prerequisite for taste. The colours which give brilliancy to the sketch are part of the charm. They may no doubt, in their own way, enliven the object for sensation, but make it really worth looking at and beautiful they cannot. Indeed, more often than not the requirements of the beautiful form restrict them to a very narrow compass, and, even where charm is admitted, it is only this form that gives them a place of honour.

All form of objects of sense (both of external and also, mediately, of internal sense) is either *figure* or *play*. In the latter case it is either play of figures (in space: mimic and dance), or mere play of sensations (in time). The *charm* of colours, or of the agreeable tones of instruments, may be added: but the *design* in the former and the *composition* in the latter constitute the proper object of the pure judgement of taste. To 5 say that the purity alike of colours and of tones, or their variety and contrast, seem to contribute to beauty, is by no means to imply that, because in themselves agreeable, they therefore yield an addition to the delight in the form and one on a par with it. The real meaning rather is that they make 10 this form more clearly, definitely, and completely intuitable, and besides stimulate the representation by their charm, as they excite and sustain the attention directed to the object itself.

Even what is called *ornamentation* (*parerga*), i.e. what is 15 only an adjunct, and not an intrinsic constituent in the complete representation of the object, in augmenting the delight of taste does so only by means of its form. Thus it is with the frames of pictures or the drapery on statues, or the colonnades of palaces. But if the ornamentation does not itself enter into 20 the composition of the beautiful form—if it is introduced like a gold frame merely to win approval for the picture by means of its charm—it is then called *finery* and takes away from the genuine beauty.

Emotion—a sensation where an agreeable feeling is pro- 25 duced merely by means of a momentary check followed by a more powerful outpouring of the vital force—is quite foreign to beauty. Sublimity (with which the feeling of emotion is connected) requires, however, a different standard of estimation from that relied upon by taste. A pure judgement of 30 taste has, then, for its determining ground neither charm nor emotion, in a word, no sensation as matter of the aesthetic judgement.

§ 15

The judgement of taste is entirely independent of the concept of perfection.

Objective finality can only be cognized by means of a reference of the manifold to a definite end, and hence only through a concept. This alone makes it clear that the beautiful, which is estimated on the ground of a mere formal finality, i.e. a finality apart from an end, is wholly independent of the representation of the good. For the latter presupposes an objective finality, i.e. the reference of the object to a definite end.

Objective finality is either external, i.e. the *utility*, or internal, i.e. the *perfection*, of the object. That the delight in an object on account of which we call it beautiful is incapable of resting on the representation of its utility, is abundantly evident from the two preceding articles; for in that case, it would not be an immediate delight in the object, which latter is the essential condition of the judgement upon beauty. But in an objective, internal finality, i.e. perfection, we have what is more akin to the predicate of beauty, and so this has been held even by philosophers of reputation to be convertible with beauty, though subject to the qualification : *where it is thought in a confused way.* In a Critique of taste it is of the utmost importance to decide whether beauty is really reducible to the concept of perfection.

For estimating objective finality we always require the concept of an end, and, where such finality has to be, not an external one (utility), but an internal one, the concept of an internal end containing the ground of the internal possibility of the object. Now an end is in general that, the *concept* of which may be regarded as the ground of the possibility of the object itself. So in order to represent an objective finality in a thing we must first have a concept of *what sort of a thing it is to be.* The agreement of the manifold in a thing with this

227

concept (which supplies the rule of its synthesis) is the *qualitative perfection* of the thing.   *Quantitative* perfection is entirely
distinct from this.   It consists in the completeness of anything
after its kind, and is a mere concept of quantity (of totality).
In its case the question of *what the thing is to be* is regarded 5
as definitely disposed of, and we only ask whether it
is possessed of *all* the requisites that go to make it such.
What is formal in the representation of a thing, i. e. the agreement of its manifold with a unity (i. e. irrespective of what it is
to be) does not, of itself, afford us any cognition whatsoever of 10
objective finality.   For since abstraction is made from this
unity as *end* (what the thing is to be) nothing is left but the
subjective finality of the representations in the mind of the
Subject intuiting.   This gives a certain finality of the representative state of the Subject, in which the Subject feels itself quite 15
at home in its effort to grasp a given form in the imagination,
but no perfection of any Object, the latter not being here
thought through any concept.   For instance, if in a forest
I light upon a plot of grass, round which trees stand in a circle,
and if I do not then form any representation of an end, as that 20
it is meant to be used, say, for country dances, then not the least
228 hint of a concept of perfection is given by the mere form.   To
suppose a formal *objective* finality that is yet devoid of an end,
i. e. the mere form of a *perfection* (apart from any matter or
concept of that to which the agreement relates, even though 25
there was the mere general idea of a conformity to law) is
a veritable contradiction.

Now the judgement of taste is an aesthetic judgement,
i. e. one resting on subjective grounds.   No concept can be its
determining ground, and hence not one of a definite end. 30
Beauty, therefore, as a formal subjective finality, involves no
thought whatsoever of a perfection of the object, as a would-
be formal finality which yet, for all that, is objective : and
the distinction between the concepts of the beautiful and the

good, which represents both as differing only in their logical
form, the first being merely a confused, the second a clearly
defined, concept of perfection, while otherwise alike in content
and origin, all goes for nothing : for then there would be no
5 *specific* difference between them, but the judgement of taste
would be just as much a cognitive judgement as one by which
something is described as good—just as the man in the street,
when he says that deceit is wrong, bases his judgement on confused, but the philosopher on clear grounds, while both appeal
10 in reality to identical principles of reason.   But I have already
stated that an aesthetic judgement is quite unique, and affords
absolutely no, (not even a confused,) knowledge of the Object.
It is only through a logical judgement that we get knowledge.
The aesthetic judgement, on the other hand, refers the repre-
15 sentation, by which an Object is given, solely to the Subject,
and brings to our notice no quality of the object, but only the
final form in the determination of the powers of representation engaged upon it.   The judgement is called aesthetic for
the very reason that its determining ground cannot be a con-
20 cept, but is rather the feeling (of the internal sense) of the
concert in the play of the mental powers as a thing only
capable of being felt.   If, on the other hand, confused concepts, and the objective judgement based on them, are going
to be called aesthetic, we shall find ourselves with an under-
25 standing judging by sense, or a sense representing its objects
by concepts—a mere choice of contradictions.   The faculty
of concepts, be they confused or be they clear, is understanding ; and although understanding has (as in all judgements) its
rôle in the judgement of taste, as an aesthetic judgement,
30 its rôle there is not that of a faculty for cognizing an object, 229
but of a faculty for determining that judgement and its
representation (without a concept) according to its relation
to the Subject and its internal feeling, and for doing so in so far
as that judgement is possible according to a universal rule.

§ 16

A judgement of taste by which an object is described as beautiful
under the condition of a definite concept is not pure.

THERE are two kinds of beauty : free beauty (*pulchritudo*
vaga), or beauty which is merely dependent (*pulchritudo* 5
adhaerens). The first presupposes no concept of what the
object should be ; the second does presuppose such a concept
and, with it, an answering perfection of the object. Those of
the first kind are said to be (self-subsisting) beauties of this
thing or that thing ; the other kind of beauty, being attached 10
to a concept (conditioned beauty), is ascribed to Objects which
come under the concept of a particular end.

Flowers are free beauties of nature. Hardly any one but
a botanist knows the true nature of a flower, and even he,
while recognizing in the flower the reproductive organ of the 15
plant, pays no attention to this natural end when using his taste
to judge of its beauty. Hence no perfection of any kind—no
internal finality, as something to which the arrangement of the
manifold is related—underlies this judgement. Many birds
(the parrot, the humming-bird, the bird of paradise), and 20
a number of crustacea, are self-subsisting beauties which are
not appurtenant to any object defined with respect to its end,
but please freely and on their own account. So designs *à la*
grecque, foliage for framework or on wall-papers, &c., have no
intrinsic meaning ; they represent nothing—no Object under 25
a definite concept—and are free beauties. We may also rank
in the same class what in music are called fantasias (without
a theme), and, indeed, all music that is not set to words.

In the estimate of a free beauty (according to mere form) we
have the pure judgement of taste. No concept is here pre- 30
supposed of any end for which the manifold should serve
230 the given Object, and which the latter, therefore, should
represent—an incumbrance which would only restrict the

freedom of the imagination that, as it were, is at play in the contemplation of the outward form.

But the beauty of man (including under this head that of a man, woman, or child), the beauty of a horse, or of a building 5 (such as a church, palace, arsenal, or summer-house), presupposes a concept of the end that defines what the thing has to be, and consequently a concept of its perfection ; and is therefore merely appendant beauty. Now, just as it is a clog on the purity of the judgement of taste to have the agreeable 10 (of sensation) joined with beauty to which properly only the form is relevant, so to combine the good with beauty, (the good, namely, of the manifold to the thing itself according to its end,) mars its purity.

Much might be added to a building that would immediately 15 please the eye, were it not intended for a church. A figure might be beautified with all manner of flourishes and light but regular lines, as is done by the New Zealanders with their tattooing, were we dealing with anything but the figure of a human being. And here is one whose rugged features 20 might be softened and given a more pleasing aspect, only he has got to be a man, or is, perhaps, a warrior that has to have a warlike appearance.

Now the delight in the manifold of a thing, in reference to the internal end that determines its possibility, is a delight based 25 on a concept, whereas delight in the beautiful is such as does not presuppose any concept, but is immediately coupled with the representation through which the object is given (not through which it is thought). If, now, the judgement of taste in respect of the latter delight is made dependent upon the 30 end involved in the former delight as a judgement of reason, and is thus placed under a restriction, then it is no longer a free and pure judgement of taste.

Taste, it is true, stands to gain by this combination of intellectual delight with the aesthetic. For it becomes fixed, 35 and, while not universal, it enables rules to be prescribed for it in respect of certain definite final Objects. But these rules are then not rules of taste, but merely rules for establishing a union of taste with reason, i.e. of the beautiful with the good—rules by which the former becomes available as an intentional instrument in respect of the latter, for the purpose 5 of bringing that temper of the mind which is self-sustaining 231 and of subjective universal validity to the support and maintenance of that mode of thought which, while possessing objective universal validity, can only be preserved by a resolute effort. But, strictly speaking, perfection neither gains by 10 beauty, nor beauty by perfection. The truth is rather this, when we compare the representation through which an object is given to us with the Object (in respect of what it is meant to be) by means of a concept, we cannot help reviewing it also in respect of the sensation in the Subject. Hence there results 15 a gain to the *entire faculty* of our representative power when harmony prevails between both states of mind.

In respect of an object with a definite internal end, a judgement of taste would only be pure where the person judging either has no concept of this end, or else makes abstraction 20 from it in his judgement. But in cases like this, although such a person should lay down a correct judgement of taste, since he would be estimating the object as a free beauty, he would still be found fault with by another who saw nothing in its beauty but a dependent quality (i.e. who looked to the end 25 of the object) and would be accused by him of false taste, though both would, in their own way, be judging correctly : the one according to what he had present to his senses, the other according to what was present in his thoughts. This distinction enables us to settle many disputes about beauty on the part of 30 critics ; for we may show them how one side is dealing with free beauty, and the other with that which is dependent : the former passing a pure judgement of taste, the latter one that is applied intentionally.

§ 17

The Ideal of beauty.

THERE can be no objective rule of taste by which what is beautiful may be defined by means of concepts. For every
5 judgement from that source is aesthetic, i.e. its determining ground is the feeling of the Subject, and not any concept of an Object. It is only throwing away labour to look for a principle of taste that affords a universal criterion of the beautiful by definite concepts; because what is sought is a thing im-
10 possible and inherently contradictory. But in the universal communicability of the sensation (of delight or aversion)—a communicability, too, that exists apart from any concept— in the accord, so far as possible, of all ages and nations **232** as to this feeling in the representation of certain objects, we
15 have the empirical criterion, weak indeed and scarce sufficient to raise a presumption, of the derivation of a taste, thus confirmed by examples, from grounds deep-seated and shared alike by all men, underlying their agreement in estimating the forms under which objects are given to them.
20 For this reason some products of taste are looked on as *exemplary*—not meaning thereby that by imitating others taste may be acquired. For taste must be an original faculty; whereas one who imitates a model, while showing skill commensurate with his success, only displays taste as himself a
25 critic of this model.[1] Hence it follows that the highest model, the archetype of taste, is a mere idea, which each person must beget in his own consciousness, and according to which he

---

[1] Models of taste with respect to the arts of speech must be composed in a dead and learned language; the first, to prevent their having to
30 suffer the changes that inevitably overtake living ones, making dignified expressions become degraded, common ones antiquated, and ones newly coined after a short currency obsolete; the second to ensure its having a grammar that is not subject to the caprices of fashion, but has fixed rules of its own.

must form his estimate of everything that is an Object of taste,
or that is an example of critical taste, and even of universal
taste itself.   Properly speaking, an *idea* signifies a concept of
reason, and an *ideal* the representation of an individual existence
as adequate to an idea.   Hence this archetype of taste—which 5
rests, indeed, upon reason's indeterminate idea of a maximum, but is not, however, capable of being represented by
means of concepts, but only in an individual presentation—
may more appropriately be called the ideal of the beautiful.
While not having this ideal in our possession, we still strive to 10
beget it within us.   But it is bound to be merely an ideal of
the imagination, seeing that it rests, not upon concepts, but
upon the presentation—the faculty of presentation being the
imagination.—Now, how do we arrive at such an ideal of
beauty?   Is it *a priori* or empirically?   Further, what species 15
of the beautiful admits of an ideal?

First of all, we do well to observe that the beauty for which
an ideal has to be sought cannot be a beauty that is *free and
at large*, but must be one *fixed* by a concept of objective finality.
Hence it cannot belong to the Object of an altogether pure 20
judgement of taste, but must attach to one that is partly intellectual.   In other words, where an ideal is to have place
among the grounds upon which any estimate is formed, then
beneath grounds of that kind there must lie some idea of
reason according to determinate concepts, by which the end 25
underlying the internal possibility of the object is determined *a priori*.   An ideal of beautiful flowers, of a beautiful
suite of furniture, or of a beautiful view, is unthinkable.   But,
it may also be impossible to represent an ideal of a beauty
dependent on definite ends, e.g. a beautiful residence, a beau- 30
tiful tree, a beautiful garden, &c., presumably because their
ends are not sufficiently defined and fixed by their concept,
with the result that their finality is nearly as free as with beauty
that is quite *at large*.   Only what has in itself the end of its

233

real existence—only *man* that is able himself to determine his ends by reason, or, where he has to derive them from external perception, can still compare them with essential and universal ends, and then further pronounce aesthetically upon their accord 5 with such ends, only he, among all objects in the world, admits, therefore, of an ideal of *beauty*, just as humanity in his person, as intelligence, alone admits of the ideal of *perfection*.

Two factors are here involved. *First*, there is the aesthetic *normal idea*, which is an individual intuition (of the imagina-10 tion). This represents the norm by which we judge of a man as a member of a particular animal species. *Secondly*, there is the *rational idea*. This deals with the ends of humanity so far as capable of sensuous representation, and converts them into a principle for estimating his outward form, through which these 15 ends are revealed in their phenomenal effect. The normal idea must draw from experience the constituents which it requires for the form of an animal of a particular kind. But the greatest finality in the construction of this form—that which would serve as a universal norm for forming an estimate of 20 each individual of the species in question—the image that, as it were, forms an intentional basis underlying the technic of nature, to which no separate individual, but only the race as a whole, is adequate, has its seat merely in the idea of the judging Subject. Yet it is, with all its proportions, an aesthetic 25 idea, and, as such, capable of being fully presented *in concreto* in a model image. Now, how is this effected? In order to render the process to some extent intelligible (for who can wrest nature's whole secret from her?), let us attempt a psychological explanation.

30 It is of note that the imagination, in a manner quite incom- 234 prehensible to us, is able on occasion, even after a long lapse of time, not alone to recall the signs for concepts, but also to reproduce the image and shape of an object out of a countless number of others of a different, or even of the very same, kind. 35 And, further, if the mind is engaged upon comparisons, we

may well suppose that it can in actual fact, though the process
is unconscious, superimpose as it were one image upon another,
and from the coincidence of a number of the same kind
arrive at a mean contour which serves as a common standard for all.   Say, for instance, a person has seen a thousand 5
full-grown men.   Now if he wishes to judge normal size
determined upon a comparative estimate, then imagination (to
my mind) allows a great number of these images (perhaps the
whole thousand) to fall one upon the other, and, if I may be
allowed to extend to the case the analogy of optical presenta- 10
tion, in the space where they come most together, and within
the contour where the place is illuminated by the greatest con-
centration of colour, one gets a perception of the *average size*,
which alike in height and breadth is equally removed from the
extreme limits of the greatest and smallest statures ; and this 15
is the stature of a beautiful man.   (The same result could be
obtained in a mechanical way, by taking the measures of all
the thousand, and adding together their heights, and their
breadths (and thicknesses), and dividing the sum in each case by
a thousand.)   But the power of imagination does all this by 20
means of a dynamical effect upon the organ of internal sense,
arising from the frequent apprehension of such forms.   If,
again, for our average man we seek on similar lines for the
average head, and for this the average nose, and so on, then we
get the figure that underlies the normal idea of a beautiful man 25
in the country where the comparison is instituted.   For this
reason a negro must necessarily (under these empirical conditions) have a different normal idea of the beauty of forms
from what a white man has, and the Chinaman one different
from the European.   And the process would be just the same 30
with the *model* of a beautiful horse or dog (of a particular
breed).—This *normal idea* is not derived from proportions
taken from experience *as definite rules* : rather is it according
to this idea that rules for forming estimates first become pos-

sible. It is an intermediate between all singular intuitions of individuals, with their manifold variations—a floating image for the whole genus, which nature has set as an archetype underlying those of her products that belong to the same species, but 235 5 which in no single case she seems to have completely attained. But the normal idea is far from giving the complete *archetype* of *beauty* in the genus. It only gives the form that constitutes the indispensable condition of all beauty, and, consequently, only *correctness* in the presentation of the genus. It is, as the 10 famous *Doryphorus* of *Polycletus* was called, the *rule* (and *Myron's* Cow might be similarly employed for its kind). It cannot, for that very reason, contain anything specifically characteristic ; for otherwise it would not be the *normal idea* for the genus. Further, it is not by beauty that its presenta- 15 tion pleases, but merely because it does not contradict any of the conditions under which alone a thing belonging to this genus can be beautiful. The presentation is merely academically correct.[1]

But the *ideal* of the beautiful is still something different 20 from its *normal idea*. For reasons already stated it is only to be sought in the *human figure*. Here the ideal consists in the expression of the *moral*, apart from which the object would not please at once universally and positively (not merely negatively

[1] It will be found that a perfectly regular face—one that a painter 25 might fix his eye on for a model—ordinarily conveys nothing. This is because it is devoid of anything characteristic, and so the idea of the race is expressed in it rather than the specific qualities of a person. The exaggeration of what is characteristic in this way, i. e. exaggeration violating the normal idea (the finality of the race), is called *caricature*. 30 Also experience shows that these quite regular faces indicate as a rule internally only a mediocre type of man ; presumably—if one may assume that nature in its external form expresses the proportions of the internal —because, where none of the mental qualities exceed the proportion requisite to constitute a man free from faults, nothing can be expected 35 in the way of what is called *genius,* in which nature seems to make a departure from its wonted relations of the mental powers in favour of some special one.

in a presentation academically correct).   The visible expression
of moral ideas that govern men inwardly can, of course, only
be drawn from experience ; but their combination with all that
our reason connects with the morally good in the idea of the
highest finality—benevolence, purity, strength, or equanimity, 5
&c.—may be made, as it were, visible in bodily manifestation
(as effect of what is internal), and this embodiment involves
a union of pure ideas of reason and great imaginative power,
in one who would even form an estimate of it, not to speak
of being the author of its presentation.   The correctness of 10
236 such an ideal of beauty is evidenced by its not permitting
any sensuous charm to mingle with the delight in its Object,
in which it still allows us to take a great interest.   This fact in
turn shows that an estimate formed according to such a standard
can never be purely aesthetic, and that one formed according 15
to an ideal of beauty cannot be a simple judgement of taste.

DEFINITION OF THE BEAUTIFUL DERIVED FROM THIS THIRD MOMENT

Beauty is the form of *finality* in an object, so far as perceived in it *apart from the representation of an end*.[1]   20

---

[1] As telling against this explanation, the instance may be adduced, that
there are things in which we see a form suggesting adaptation to an
end, without any end being cognized in them—as, for example, the stone
implements frequently obtained from sepulchral tumuli and supplied
with a hole, as if for [inserting] a handle ; and although these by their 25
shape manifestly indicate a finality, the end of which is unknown, they
are not on that account described as beautiful.   But the very fact of their
being regarded as art-products involves an immediate recognition that
their shape is attributed to some purpose or other and to a definite end.
For this reason there is no immediate delight whatever in their con- 30
templation.   A flower, on the other hand, such as a tulip, is regarded
as beautiful, because we meet with a certain finality in its perception,
which, in our estimate of it, is not referred to any end whatever.

FOURTH MOMENT

§ 18

5   *Nature of the modality in a judgement of taste.*

I MAY assert in the case of every representation that the
synthesis of a pleasure with the representation (as a cognition)
is at least *possible.* Of what I call *agreeable* I assert that it
actually causes pleasure in me. But what we have in mind in
10 the case of the *beautiful* is a *necessary* reference on its part to
delight. However, this necessity is of a special kind. It is not
a theoretical objective necessity—such as would let us cognize
a priori that every one *will feel* this delight in the object that 237
is called beautiful by me. Nor yet is it a practical necessity,
15 in which case, thanks to concepts of a pure rational will in
which free agents are supplied with a rule, this delight is the
necessary consequence of an objective law, and simply means
that one ought absolutely (without ulterior object) to act in
a certain way. Rather, being such a necessity as is thought
20 in an aesthetic judgement, it can only be termed *exemplary.*
In other words it is a necessity of the assent of *all* to a judgement regarded as exemplifying a universal rule incapable of
formulation. Since an aesthetic judgement is not an objective
or cognitive judgement, this necessity is not derivable from
25 definite concepts, and so is not apodictic. Much less is it
inferable from universality of experience (of a thorough-going
agreement of judgements about the beauty of a certain object).
For, apart from the fact that experience would hardly furnish
evidences sufficiently numerous for this purpose, empirical
30 judgements do not afford any foundation for a concept of the
necessity of these judgements.

§ 19

The subjective necessity attributed to a judgement of taste is conditioned.

THE judgement of taste exacts agreement from every one ; and a person who describes something as beautiful insists that every one *ought* to give the object in question his approval and follow suit in describing it as beautiful. The *ought* in aesthetic judgements, therefore, despite an accordance with all the requisite data for passing judgement, is still only pronounced conditionally. We are suitors for agreement from every one else, because we are fortified with a ground common to all. Further, we would be able to count on this agreement, provided we were always assured of the correct subsumption of the case under that ground as the rule of approval.

§ 20

The condition of the necessity advanced by a judgement of taste is the idea of a common sense.

WERE judgements of taste (like cognitive judgements) in possession of a definite objective principle, then one who in his judgement followed such a principle would claim unconditioned necessity for it. Again, were they devoid of any principle, as are those of the mere taste of sense, then no thought of any necessity on their part would enter one's head. Therefore they must have a subjective principle, and one which determines what pleases or displeases, by means of feeling only and not through concepts, but yet with universal validity. Such a principle, however, could only be regarded as a *common sense*. This differs essentially from common understanding, which is also sometimes called common sense (*sensus communis*): for the judgement of the latter is not one by feeling, but always one by concepts, though usually only in the shape of obscurely represented principles.

The judgement of taste, therefore, depends on our pre-supposing the existence of a common sense. (But this is not to be taken to mean some external sense, but the effect arising from the free play of our powers of cognition.) Only under the presupposition, I repeat, of such a common sense, are we able to lay down a judgement of taste.

§ 21

Have we reason for presupposing a common sense?

COGNITIONS and judgements must, together with their atten-dant conviction, admit of being universally communicated ; for otherwise a correspondence with the Object would not be due to them. They would be a conglomerate constituting a mere subjective play of the powers of representation, just as scepticism would have it. But if cognitions are to admit of communication, then our mental state, i.e. the way the cog-nitive powers are attuned for cognition generally, and, in fact, the relative proportion suitable for a representation (by which an object is given to us) from which cognition is to result, must also admit of being universally communicated, as, without this, which is the subjective condition of the act of knowing, know-ledge, as an effect, would not arise. And this is always what actually happens where a given object, through the intervention of sense, sets the imagination at work in arranging the manifold, and the imagination, in turn, the understanding in giving to this arrangement the unity of concepts. But this disposition of the cognitive powers has a relative proportion differing with the diversity of the Objects that are given. However, there must be one in which this internal ratio suitable for quickening (one faculty by the other) is best adapted for both mental powers in respect of cognition (of given objects) generally ; and this 239 disposition can only be determined through feeling (and not by concepts). Since, now, this disposition itself must admit of being universally communicated, and hence also the feeling of it (in the case of a given representation), while again, the universal communicability of a feeling presupposes a common sense : it follows that our assumption of it is well founded. 5 And here, too, we do not have to take our stand on psychological observations, but we assume a common sense as the necessary condition of the universal communicability of our knowledge, which is presupposed in every logic and every principle of knowledge that is not one of scepticism.   10

§ 22

The necessity of the universal assent that is thought in a judgement of taste, is a subjective necessity which, under the presupposition of a common sense, is represented as objective.

In all judgements by which we describe anything as beautiful 15 we tolerate no one else being of a different opinion, and in taking up this position we do not rest our judgement upon concepts, but only on our feeling. Accordingly we introduce this fundamental feeling not as a private feeling, but as a public sense. Now, for this purpose, experience cannot 20 be made the ground of this common sense, for the latter is invoked to justify judgements containing an 'ought'. The assertion is not that every one *will* fall in with our judgement, but rather that every one *ought* to agree with it. Here I put forward my judgement of taste as an example of the judge- 25 ment of common sense, and attribute to it on that account *exemplary* validity. Hence common sense is a mere ideal norm. With this as presupposition, a judgement that acccords with it, as well as the delight in an Object expressed in that judgement, is rightly converted into a rule for every one. For 30 the principle, while it is only subjective, being yet assumed as subjectively universal (a necessary idea for every one), could, in what concerns the consensus of different judging Subjects, demand universal assent like an objective principle, provided we were assured of our subsumption under it being correct.

This indeterminate norm of a common sense is, as a matter of fact, presupposed by us ; as is shown by our presuming to lay down judgements of taste. But does such a common sense in fact exist as a constitutive principle of the possibility of experience, or is it formed for us as a regulative principle by a still higher principle of reason, that for higher ends first seeks to beget in us a common sense? Is taste, in other words, a natural and original faculty, or is it only the idea of one that is artificial and to be acquired by us, so that a judgement of taste, with its demand for universal assent, is but a requirement of reason for generating such a con*sensus*, and does the ' ought ', i.e. the objective necessity of the coincidence of the feeling of all with the particular feeling of each, only betoken the possibility of arriving at some sort of unanimity in these matters, and the judgement of taste only adduce an example of the application of this principle? These are questions which as yet we are neither willing nor in a position to investigate. For the present we have only to resolve the faculty of taste into its elements, and to unite these ultimately in the idea of a common sense.

DEFINITION OF THE BEAUTIFUL DRAWN FROM THE
FOURTH MOMENT

The beautiful is that which, apart from a concept, is cognized as object of a *necessary* delight.

GENERAL REMARK ON THE FIRST SECTION OF THE ANALYTIC

The result to be extracted from the foregoing analysis is in effect this : that everything runs up into the concept of taste as a critical faculty by which an object is estimated in reference to the *free conformity to law* of the imagination. If, now, imagination must in the judgement of taste be regarded in its freedom, then, to begin with, it is not taken as reproductive, as in its subjection to the laws of association, but as productive and exerting an activity of its own (as originator of arbitrary 5 forms of possible intuitions). And although in the apprehension of a given object of sense it is tied down to a definite form of this Object and, to that extent, does not enjoy free play, (as it does in poetry,) still it is easy to conceive that the object may supply ready-made to the imagination just such a form of the 10 arrangement of the manifold, as the imagination, if it were left to itself, would freely project in harmony with the general *conformity to law of the understanding.* But that the *imagination* should be both *free* and *of itself conformable to law*, i.e. carry autonomy with it, is a contradiction. The understanding alone 15 gives the law. Where, however, the imagination is compelled to follow a course laid down by a definite law, then what the form of the product is to be is determined by concepts ; but, in that case, as already shown, the delight is not delight in the beautiful, but in the good, (in perfection, though it be no more 20 than formal perfection), and the judgement is not one due to taste. Hence it is only a conformity to law without a law, and a subjective harmonizing of the imagination and the understanding without an objective one—which latter would mean that the representation was referred to a definite concept of the 25 object—that can consist with the free conformity to law of the understanding (which has also been called finality apart from an end) and with the specific character of a judgement of taste.

Now geometrically regular figures, a circle, a square, a cube, 30 and the like, are commonly brought forward by critics of taste as the most simple and unquestionable examples of beauty. And yet the very reason why they are called regular, is because the only way of representing them is by looking on them as mere

presentations of a determinate concept by which the figure has
its rule (according to which alone it is possible) prescribed for
it. One or other of these two views must, therefore, be wrong :
either the verdict of the critics that attributes beauty to such
5 figures, or else our own, which makes finality apart from any
concept necessary for beauty.

One would scarce think it necessary for a man to have taste
to take more delight in a circle than in a scrawled outline, in
an equilateral and equiangular quadrilateral than in one that
10 is all lob-sided, and, as it were, deformed. The requirements
of common understanding ensure such a preference without the
least demand upon taste. Where some purpose is perceived, as,
for instance, that of forming an estimate of the area of a plot of
land, or rendering intelligible the relation of divided parts to
15 one another and to the whole, then regular figures, and those
of the simplest kind, are needed ; and the delight does not
rest immediately upon the way the figure strikes the eye, but
upon its serviceability for all manner of possible purposes. A 242
room with the walls making oblique angles, a plot laid out in a
20 garden in a similar way, even any violation of symmetry, as
well in the figure of animals (e.g. being one-eyed) as in that of
buildings, or of flower-beds, is displeasing because of its
perversity of form, not alone in a practical way in respect of
some definite use to which the thing may be put, but for
25 an estimate that looks to all manner of possible purposes.
With the judgement of taste the case is different. For, when
it is pure, it combines delight or aversion immediately with the
bare *contemplation* of the object irrespective of its use or of
any end.

30 The regularity that conduces to the concept of an object is,
in fact, the indispensable condition (*conditio sine qua non*) of
grasping the object as a single representation and giving to the
manifold its determinate form. This determination is an end
in respect of knowledge ; and in this connexion it is invariably
35 coupled with delight (such as attends the accomplishment of

any, even problematical, purpose). Here, however, we have merely the value set upon the solution that satisfies the problem, and not a free and indeterminately final entertainment of the mental powers with what is called beautiful. In the latter case understanding is at the service of imagination, in the former this relation is reversed.

With a thing that owes its possibility to a purpose, a building, or even an animal, its regularity, which consists in symmetry, must express the unity of the intuition accompanying the concept of its end, and belongs with it to cognition. But where all that is intended is the maintenance of a free play of the powers of representation (subject, however, to the condition that there is to be nothing for understanding to take exception to), in ornamental gardens, in the decoration of rooms, in all kinds of furniture that shows good taste, &c., regularity in the shape of constraint is to be avoided as far as possible. Thus English taste in gardens, and fantastic taste in furniture, push the freedom of imagination to the verge of what is grotesque— the idea being that in this divorce from all constraint of rules the precise instance is being afforded where taste can exhibit its perfection in projects of the imagination to the fullest extent.

All stiff regularity (such as borders on mathematical regularity) is inherently repugnant to taste, in that the contemplation of it affords us no lasting entertainment. Indeed, where it has neither cognition nor some definite practical end expressly in view, we get heartily tired of it. On the other hand, anything that gives the imagination scope for unstudied and final play is always fresh to us. We do not grow to hate the very sight of it. *Marsden* in his description of Sumatra observes that the free beauties of nature so surround the beholder on all sides that they cease to have much attraction for him. On the other hand he found a pepper garden full of charm, on coming across it in mid-forest with its rows of parallel stakes on which the plant twines itself. From all this he infers that wild, and

in its appearance quite irregular beauty, is only pleasing as
a change to one whose eyes have become surfeited with regular
beauty.   But he need only have made the experiment of
passing one day in his pepper garden to realize that once the
5 regularity has enabled the understanding to put itself in accord
with the order that is its constant requirement, instead of the
object diverting him any longer, it imposes an irksome constraint upon the imagination : whereas nature subject to no
constraint of artificial rules, and lavish, as it there is, in its
10 luxuriant variety can supply constant food for his taste.—Even
a bird's song, which we can reduce to no musical rule, seems
to have more freedom in it, and thus to be richer for taste,
than the human voice singing in accordance with all the rules
that the art of music prescribes ; for we grow tired much
15 sooner of frequent and lengthy repetitions of the latter.   Yet
here most likely our sympathy with the mirth of a dear little
creature is confused with the beauty of its song, for if exactly
imitated by man (as has been sometimes done with the notes
of the nightingale) it would strike our ear as wholly destitute
20 of taste.

Further, beautiful objects have to be distinguished from
beautiful views of objects (where the distance often prevents a
clear perception).   In the latter case taste appears to fasten,
not so much on what the imagination *grasps* in this field, as on
25 the incentive it receives to indulge in poetic fiction, i. e. in the
peculiar fancies with which the mind entertains itself as it is
being continually stirred by the variety that strikes the eye.   It
is just as when we watch the changing shapes of the fire or of
a rippling brook: neither of which are things of beauty, but 244
30 they convey a charm to the imagination, because they sustain
its free play.

SECOND BOOK

ANALYTIC OF THE SUBLIME

§ 23

*Transition from the faculty of estimating the beautiful to that
of estimating the sublime.*   5

THE beautiful and the sublime agree on the point of pleasing
on their own account.   Further they agree in not presupposing
either a judgement of sense or one logically determinant, but
one of reflection.   Hence it follows that the delight does not
depend upon a sensation, as with the agreeable, nor upon 10
a definite concept, as does the delight in the good, although
it has, for all that, an indeterminate reference to concepts.
Consequently the delight is connected with the mere presentation or faculty of presentation, and is thus taken to express the
accord, in a given intuition, of the faculty of presentation, or 15
the imagination, with the *faculty of concepts* that belongs to
understanding or reason, in the sense of the former assisting
the latter.   Hence both kinds of judgements are *singular*, and
yet such as profess to be universally valid in respect of every
Subject, despite the fact that their claims are directed merely 20
to the feeling of pleasure and not to any knowledge of the
object.

There are, however, also important and striking differences
between the two.   The beautiful in nature is a question of the
form of the object, and this consists in limitation, whereas the 25
sublime is to be found in an object even devoid of form, so
far as it immediately involves, or else by its presence provokes,
a representation of *limitlessness*, yet with a super-added thought
of its totality.   Accordingly the beautiful seems to be regarded
as a presentation of an indeterminate concept of understanding, 30

the sublime as a presentation of an indeterminate concept of reason. Hence the delight is in the former case coupled with the representation of *Quality*, but in this case with that of *Quantity*. Moreover, the former delight is very different from the latter in kind. For the beautiful is directly attended with a feeling of the furtherance of life, and is thus compatible with charms and a playful imagination. On the other hand, the 245 feeling of the sublime is a pleasure that only arises indirectly, being brought about by the feeling of a momentary check to the vital forces followed at once by a discharge all the more powerful, and so it is an emotion that seems to be no sport, but dead earnest in the affairs of the imagination. Hence charms are repugnant to it ; and, since the mind is not simply attracted by the object, but is also alternately repelled thereby, the delight in the sublime does not so much involve positive pleasure as admiration or respect, i.e. merits the name of a negative pleasure.

But the most important and vital distinction between the sublime and the beautiful is certainly this : that if, as is allowable, we here confine our attention in the first instance to the sublime in Objects of nature, (that of art being always restricted by the conditions of an agreement with nature,) we observe that whereas natural beauty (such as is self-subsisting) conveys a finality in its form making the object appear, as it were, preadapted to our power of judgement, so that it thus forms of itself an object of our delight, that which, without our indulging in any refinements of thought, but, simply in our apprehension of it, excites the feeling of the sublime, may appear, indeed, in point of form to contravene the ends of our power of judgement, to be ill-adapted to our faculty of presentation, and to be, as it were, an outrage on the imagination, and yet it is judged all the more sublime on that account.

From this it may be seen at once that we express ourselves on the whole inaccurately if we term any *Object of nature* sublime, although we may with perfect propriety call many such

objects beautiful.   For how can that which is apprehended as
inherently contra-final be noted with an expression of approval?
All that we can say is that the object lends itself to the presentation of a sublimity discoverable in the mind.   For the
sublime, in the strict sense of the word, cannot be contained 5
in any sensuous form, but rather concerns ideas of reason,
which, although no adequate presentation of them is possible,
may be excited and called into the mind by that very inadequacy itself which does admit of sensuous presentation.   Thus
the broad ocean agitated by storms cannot be called sublime. 10
Its aspect is horrible, and one must have stored one's mind in
246 advance with a rich stock of ideas, if such an intuition is to raise
it to the pitch of a feeling which is itself sublime—sublime
because the mind has been incited to abandon sensibility, and
employ itself upon ideas involving higher finality.   15

Self-subsisting natural beauty reveals to us a technic of
nature which shows it in the light of a system ordered in
accordance with laws the principle of which is not to be found
within the range of our entire faculty of understanding.   This
principle is that of a finality relative to the employment of judge- 20
ment in respect of phenomena which have thus to be assigned,
not merely to nature regarded as aimless mechanism, but also
to nature regarded after the analogy of art.   Hence it gives
a veritable extension, not, of course, to our knowledge of
Objects of nature, but to our conception of nature itself— 25
nature as mere mechanism being enlarged to the conception
of nature as art—an extension inviting profound inquiries as
to the possibility of such a form.   But in what we are wont to
call sublime in nature there is such an absence of anything
leading to particular objective principles and corresponding 30
forms of nature, that it is rather in its chaos, or in its wildest
and most irregular disorder and desolation, provided it gives
signs of magnitude and power, that nature chiefly excites the
ideas of the sublime.   Hence we see that the concept of the

sublime in nature is far less important and rich in consequences
than that of its beauty.   It gives on the whole no indication of
anything final in nature itself, but only in the possible *employment* of our intuitions of it in inducing a feeling in our own
5 selves of a finality quite independent of nature.   For the
beautiful in nature we must seek a ground external to ourselves,
but for the sublime one merely in ourselves and the attitude
of mind that introduces sublimity into the representation of
nature.   This is a very needful preliminary remark.   It
10 entirely separates the ideas of the sublime from that of
a finality of *nature*, and makes the theory of the sublime
a mere appendage to the aesthetic estimate of the finality
of nature, because it does not give a representation of any
particular form in nature, but involves no more than the
15 development of a final employment by the imagination of
its own representation.

§ 24   247

Subdivision of an investigation of the feeling of the sublime.

IN the division of the moments of an aesthetic estimate of
20 objects in respect of the feeling of the sublime, the course of
the Analytic will be able to follow the same principle as in the
analysis of judgements of taste.   For, the judgement being one
of the aesthetic reflective judgement, the delight in the sublime,
just like that in the beautiful, must in its *Quantity* be shown
25 to be universally valid, in its *Quality* independent of interest,
in its *Relation* subjective finality, and the latter, in its *Modality*,
necessary.   Hence the method here will not depart from the
lines followed in the preceding section : unless something is
made of the point that there, where the aesthetic Judgement
30 bore on the form of the Object, we began with the investigation
of its Quality, whereas here, considering the formlessness that
may belong to what we call Sublime, we begin with that of its
Quantity, as first moment of the aesthetic judgement on the

sublime—a divergence of method the reason for which is evident from § 23.

But the analysis of the sublime obliges a division not required by that of the beautiful, namely one into the *mathematically* and the *dynamically* sublime.   5

For the feeling of the sublime involves as its characteristic feature a mental *movement* combined with the estimate of the object, whereas taste in respect of the beautiful presupposes that the mind is in *restful* contemplation, and preserves it in this state.   But this movement has to be estimated as subjec- 10 tively final (since the sublime pleases).   Hence it is referred through the imagination either to the *faculty of cognition* or to that of *desire*; but to whichever faculty the reference is made the finality of the given representation is estimated only in respect of these faculties (apart from end or interest).   Accordingly the 15 first is attributed to the Object as a *mathematical*, the second as a *dynamical*, affection of the imagination.   Hence we get the above double mode of representing an Object as sublime.

248   A.   THE MATHEMATICALLY SUBLIME

§ 25   20

Definition of the term ' sublime '.

Sublime is the name given to what is *absolutely great*.   But to be great and to be a magnitude are entirely different concepts (*magnitudo* and *quantitas*).   In the same way to *assert without qualification* (*simpliciter*) that something is great, is quite a dif- 25 ferent thing from saying that it is *absolutely great* (*absolute, non comparative magnum*).   The latter is *what is beyond all comparison great*.—What, then, is the meaning of the assertion that anything is great, or small, or of medium size ?   What is indicated is not a pure concept of understanding, still less an 30 intuition of sense ; and just as little is it a concept of reason,

for it does not import any principle of cognition. It must, therefore, be a concept of judgement, or have its source in one, and must introduce as basis of the judgement a subjective finality of the representation with reference to the power of
5 judgement.   Given a multiplicity of the homogeneous together constituting one thing, and we may at once cognize from the thing itself that it is a *magnitude* (*quantum*).   No comparison with other things is required.   But to determine *how great* it is always requires something else, which itself has magnitude,
10 for its measure.   Now, since in the estimate of magnitude we have to take into account not merely the multiplicity (number of units) but also the magnitude of the unit (the measure), and since the magnitude of this unit in turn always requires something else as its measure and as the standard of its
15 comparison, and so on, we see that the computation of the magnitude of phenomena is, in all cases, utterly incapable of affording us any absolute concept of a magnitude, and can, instead, only afford one that is always based on comparison.

If, now, I assert without qualification that anything is great,
20 it would seem that I have nothing in the way of a comparison present to my mind, or at least nothing involving an objective measure, for no attempt is thus made to determine how great the object is.   But, despite the standard of comparison being merely subjective, the claim of the judgement is none the less
25 one to universal agreement ; the judgements : 'That man is beautiful' and 'He is tall' do not purport to speak only for the judging Subject, but, like theoretical judgements, they demand the assent of every one.

Now in a judgement that without qualification describes 249
30 anything as great, it is not merely meant that the object has a magnitude, but greatness is ascribed to it pre-eminently among many other objects of a like kind, yet without the extent of this pre-eminence being determined.   Hence a standard is certainly laid at the basis of the judgement, which standard is

presupposed to be one that can be taken as the same for every
one, but which is available only for an aesthetic estimate of
the greatness, and not for one that is logical (mathematically
determined), for the standard is a merely subjective one underlying the reflective judgement upon the greatness. Furthermore, 5
this standard may be empirical, as, let us say, the average size
of the men known to us, of animals of a certain kind, of trees,
of houses, of mountains, and so forth.   Or it may be a standard
given *a priori*, which by reason of the imperfections of the
judging Subject is restricted to subjective conditions of presen- 10
tation *in concreto* : as, in the practical sphere, the greatness of
a particular virtue, or of public liberty and justice in a country ;
or, in the theoretical sphere, the greatness of the accuracy or
inaccuracy of an experiment or measurement, &c.

Here, now, it is of note that, although we have no interest 15
whatever in the Object, i. e. its real existence may be a matter
of no concern to us, still its mere greatness, regarded even as
devoid of form, is able to convey a universally communicable
delight and so involve the consciousness of a subjective finality
in the employment of our cognitive faculties, but not, be it 20
remembered, a delight in the Object, for the latter may be
formless, but, in contradistinction to what is the case with the
beautiful, where the reflective judgement finds itself set to
a key that is final in respect of cognition generally, a delight in
an extension affecting the imagination itself.   25

If (subject as above) we say of an object, without qualification, that it is great, this is not a mathematically determinant,
but a mere reflective judgement upon its representation, which
is subjectively final for a particular employment of our cognitive
faculties in the estimation of magnitude, and we then always 30
couple with the representation a kind of respect, just as we do
a kind of contempt with what we call absolutely small.   Moreover, the estimate of things as great or small extends to
everything, even to all their qualities.   Thus we call even

their beauty great or small. The reason of this is to be found 250
in the fact that we have only got to present a thing in intuition,
as the precept of judgement directs, (consequently to represent it
aesthetically,) for it to be in its entirety a phenomenon, and
5 hence a quantum.

If, however, we call anything not alone great, but, without
qualification, absolutely, and in every respect (beyond all comparison) great, that is to say, sublime, we soon perceive that
for this it is not permissible to seek an appropriate standard
10 outside itself, but merely in itself. It is a greatness comparable
to itself alone. Hence it comes that the sublime is not to be
looked for in the things of nature, but only in our own ideas.
But it must be left to the Deduction to show in which of them
it resides.

15 The above definition may also be expressed in this way :
that is sublime in comparison with which all else is small. Here
we readily see that nothing can be given in nature, no matter
how great we may judge it to be, which, regarded in some other
relation, may not be degraded to the level of the infinitely
20 little, and nothing so small which in comparison with some
still smaller standard may not for our imagination be enlarged
to the greatness of a world. Telescopes have put within our
reach an abundance of material to go upon in making the first
observation, and microscopes the same in making the second.
25 Nothing, therefore, which can be an object of the senses is to
be termed sublime when treated on this footing. But precisely
because there is a striving in our imagination towards progress
ad infinitum, while reason demands absolute totality, as a real
idea, that same inability on the part of our faculty for the
30 estimation of the magnitude of things of the world of sense to
attain to this idea, is the awakening of a feeling of a supersensible
faculty within us ; and it is the use to which judgement naturally
puts particular objects on behalf of this latter feeling, and not
the object of sense, that is absolutely great, and every other

contrasted employment small. Consequently it is the disposition of soul evoked by a particular representation engaging the attention of the reflective judgement, and not the Object, that is to be called sublime.

The foregoing formulae defining the sublime may, therefore, be supplemented by yet another : *The sublime is that, the mere capacity of thinking which evidences a faculty of mind transcending every standard of sense.*

251

§ 26

The estimation of the magnitude of natural things requisite for the idea of the sublime.

THE estimation of magnitude by means of concepts of number (or their signs in algebra) is mathematical, but that in mere intuition (by the eye) is aesthetic. Now we can only get definite concepts of *how great* anything is by having recourse to numbers (or, at any rate, by getting approximate measurements by means of numerical series progressing *ad infinitum*), the unit being the measure ; and to this extent all logical estimation of magnitude is mathematical. But, as the magnitude of the measure has to be assumed as a known quantity, if, to form an estimate of this, we must again have recourse to numbers involving another standard for their unit, and consequently must again proceed mathematically, we can never arrive at a first or fundamental measure, and so cannot get any definite concept of a given magnitude. The estimation of the magnitude of the fundamental measure must, therefore, consist merely in the immediate grasp which we can get of it in intuition, and the use to which our imagination can put this in presenting the numerical concepts : i. e. all estimation of the magnitude of objects of nature is in the last resort aesthetic (i. e. subjectively and not objectively determined).

Now for the mathematical estimation of magnitude there is,

of course, no greatest possible (for the power of numbers extends to infinity), but for the aesthetic estimation there certainly is, and of it I say that where it is considered an absolute measure beyond which no greater is possible subjectively (i. e. for the 5 judging Subject), it then conveys the idea of the sublime, and calls forth that emotion which no mathematical estimation of magnitudes by numbers can evoke (unless in so far as the fundamental aesthetic measure is kept vividly present to the imagination) : because the latter presents only the relative 10 magnitude due to comparison with others of a like kind, whereas the former presents magnitude absolutely, so far as the mind can grasp it in an intuition.

To take in a quantum intuitively in the imagination so as to be able to use it as a measure, or unit for estimating magnitude 15 by numbers, involves two operations of this faculty : *apprehension* (*apprehensio*) and *comprehension* (*comprehensio aesthetica*). Apprehension presents no difficulty : for this process can be carried on *ad infinitum*; but with the advance of apprehension 252 comprehension becomes more difficult at every step and soon 20 attains its maximum, and this is the aesthetically greatest fundamental measure for the estimation of magnitude. For if the apprehension has reached a point beyond which the representations of sensuous intuition in the case of the parts first apprehended begin to disappear from the imagination as 25 this advances to the apprehension of yet others, as much, then, is lost at one end as is gained at the other, and for comprehension we get a maximum which the imagination cannot exceed.

This explains Savary's observations in his account of Egypt, that in order to get the full emotional effect of the size of 30 the Pyramids we must avoid coming too near just as much as remaining too far away. For in the latter case the representation of the apprehended parts (the tiers of stones) is but obscure, and produces no effect upon the aesthetic judgement of the Subject. In the former, however, it takes the eye some time to complete the apprehension from the base to the summit; but in this interval the first tiers always in part disappear before the imagination has taken in the last, and so the comprehension is never complete.—The same explanation may also sufficiently account for the bewilderment, or sort of perplexity, which, as is said, seizes the visitor on first entering St. Peter's in Rome.   For here a feeling comes home to him of the inadequacy of his imagination for presenting the idea of a whole within which that imagination attains its maximum, and, in its fruitless efforts to extend this limit, recoils upon itself, but in so doing succumbs to an emotional delight.

At present I am not disposed to deal with the ground of this delight, connected, as it is, with a representation in which we would least of all look for it—a representation, namely, that lets us see its own inadequacy, and consequently its subjective want of finality for our judgement in the estimation of magnitude—but confine myself to the remark that if the aesthetic judgement is to be *pure (unmixed with any teleological judgement* which, as such, belongs to reason), and if we are to give a suitable example of it for the Critique of *aesthetic* judgement, we must not point to the sublime in works of art, e.g. buildings, statues and the like, where a human end determines the form as well as the magnitude, nor yet in things of nature, *that in their very concept import a definite end*, e.g. animals of a recognized natural order, but in rude nature merely as involving magnitude (and only in this so far as it does not convey any charm or any emotion arising from actual danger).   For in a representation of this kind nature contains nothing monstrous (nor what is either magnificent or horrible)—the magnitude apprehended may be increased to any extent provided imagination is able to grasp it all in one whole.   An object is *monstrous* where by its size it defeats the end that forms its concept.   The *colossal* is the mere presentation of a concept which is almost too great for presentation, i.e. borders on the relatively monstrous; for

the end to be attained by the presentation of a concept is made harder to realize by the intuition of the object being almost too great for our faculty of apprehension.—A pure judgement upon the sublime must, however, have no end belonging to the
5 Object as its determining ground, if it is to be aesthetic and not to be tainted with any judgement of understanding or reason.

Since whatever is to be a source of pleasure, apart from interest, to the merely reflective judgement must involve in its
10 representation subjective, and, as such, universally valid finality —though here, however, no finality of the *form* of the object underlies our estimate of it (as it does in the case of the beautiful)—the question arises, What is this subjective finality, and what enables it to be prescribed as a norm so as to yield
15 a ground for universally valid delight in the mere estimation of magnitude, and that, too, in a case where it is pushed to the point at which our faculty of imagination breaks down in presenting the concept of a magnitude, and proves unequal to its task?

In the successive aggregation of units requisite for the
20 representation of magnitudes the imagination of itself advances *ad infinitum* without let or hindrance—understanding, however, conducting it by means of concepts of number for which the former must supply the schema.   This procedure belongs to the logical estimation of magnitude, and, as such, is doubt-
25 less something objectively final according to the concept of an end (as all measurement is), but it is not anything which for the aesthetic judgement is final or pleasing.   Further, in this intentional finality there is nothing compelling us to tax the 254 utmost powers of the imagination, and drive it as far as ever it
30 can reach in its presentations, so as to enlarge the size of the measure, and thus make the single intuition holding the many in one (the *comprehension*) as great as possible.   For in the estimation of magnitude by the understanding (arithmetic) we

get just as far, whether the comprehension of the units is pushed to the number 10 (as in the decimal scale) or only to 4 (as in the quaternary); the further production of magnitude being carried out by the successive aggregation of units, or, if the quantum is given in intuition, by apprehension, merely pro- 5 gressively (not comprehensively), according to an adopted principle of progression.   In this mathematical estimation of magnitude understanding is as well served and as satisfied whether imagination selects for the unit a magnitude which one can take in at a glance, e. g. a foot, or a perch, or else a 10 German mile, or even the earth's diameter, the apprehension of which is indeed possible, but not its comprehension in an intuition of the imagination (i. e. it is not possible by means of a *comprehensio aesthetica,* though quite so by means of a *comprehensio logica* in a numerical concept).   In each case 15 the logical estimation of magnitude advances *ad infinitum* with nothing to stop it.

The mind, however, hearkens now to the voice of reason, which for all given magnitudes—even for those which can never be completely apprehended, though (in sensuous repre- 20 sentation) estimated as completely given—requires totality, and consequently comprehension in *one* intuition, and which calls for a *presentation* answering to all the above members of a progressively increasing numerical series, and does not exempt even the infinite (space and time past) from this requirement, 25 but rather renders it inevitable for us to regard this infinite (in the judgement of common reason) as *completely given* (i. e. given in its totality).

But the infinite is absolutely (not merely comparatively) great. In comparison with this all else (in the way of magnitudes of the 30 same order) is small.   But the point of capital importance is that the mere ability even to think it as *a whole* indicates a faculty of mind transcending every standard of sense.   For the latter would entail a comprehension yielding as unit a standard

bearing to the infinite a definite ratio expressible in numbers, which is impossible. Still the *mere ability even to think* the given infinite without contradiction, is something that requires the presence in the human mind of a faculty that is itself supersen- 255
5 sible. For it is only through this faculty and its idea of a nou-
menon, which latter, while not itself admitting of any intuition,
is yet introduced as substrate underlying the intuition of the
world as mere phenomenon, that the infinite of the world of sense,
in the pure intellectual estimation of magnitude, is *completely*
10 comprehended *under* a concept, although in the mathematical
estimation *by means of numerical concepts* it can never be completely thought. Even a faculty enabling the infinite of supersensible intuition to be regarded as given (in its intelligible substrate), transcends every standard of sensibility, and is great
15 beyond all comparison even with the faculty of mathematical
estimation : not, of course, from a theoretical point of view that
looks to the interests of our faculty of knowledge, but as a
broadening of the mind that from another (the practical) point
of view feels itself empowered to pass beyond the narrow
20 confines of sensibility.

Nature, therefore, is sublime in such of its phenomena as in
their intuition convey the idea of their infinity. But this can
only occur through the inadequacy of even the greatest effort
of our imagination in the estimation of the magnitude of an
25 object. But, now, in the case of the mathematical estimation of
magnitude imagination is quite competent to supply a measure
equal to the requirements of any object. For the numerical
concepts of the understanding can by progressive synthesis
make any measure adequate to any given magnitude. Hence
30 it must be the *aesthetic* estimation of magnitude in which we
get at once a feeling of the effort towards a comprehension that
exceeds the faculty of imagination for mentally grasping the
progressive apprehension in a whole of intuition, and, with it,
a perception of the inadequacy of this faculty, which has no

bounds to its progress, for taking in and using for the estimation of magnitude a fundamental measure that understanding could turn to account without the least trouble.   Now the proper unchangeable fundamental measure of nature is its absolute whole, which, with it, regarded as a phenomenon, means 5 infinity comprehended.   But, since this fundamental measure is a self-contradictory concept, (owing to the impossibility of the absolute totality of an endless progression,) it follows that where the size of a natural Object is such that the imagination spends its whole faculty of comprehension upon it in vain, it must 10 carry our concept of nature to a supersensible substrate (underlying both nature and our faculty of thought) which is great beyond every standard of sense.   Thus, instead of the 256 object, it is rather the cast of the mind in appreciating it that we have to estimate as *sublime*.   15

Therefore, just as the aesthetic judgement in its estimate of the beautiful refers the imagination in its free play to the *understanding*, to bring out its agreement with the *concepts* of the latter in general (apart from their determination) : so in its estimate of a thing as sublime it refers that faculty to *reason* to 20 bring out its subjective accord with *ideas* of reason (indeterminately indicated), i.e. to induce a temper of mind conformable to that which the influence of definite (practical) ideas would produce upon feeling, and in common accord with it.

This makes it evident that true sublimity must be sought 25 only in the mind of the judging Subject, and not in the Object of nature that occasions this attitude by the estimate formed of it.   Who would apply the term 'sublime' even to shapeless mountain masses towering one above the other in wild disorder, with their pyramids of ice, or to the dark tempestuous ocean, 30 or such like things ?   But in the contemplation of them, without any regard to their form, the mind abandons itself to the imagination and to a reason placed, though quite apart from any definite end, in conjunction therewith, and merely broadening

its view, and it feels itself elevated in its own estimate of itself
on finding all the might of imagination still unequal to its ideas.

We get examples of the mathematically sublime of nature in
mere intuition in all those instances where our imagination is
afforded, not so much a greater numerical concept as a large
unit as measure (for shortening the numerical series). A tree
judged by the height of man gives, at all events, a standard for
a mountain ; and, supposing this is, say, a mile high, it can
serve as unit for the number expressing the earth's diameter, so
as to make it intuitable ; similarly the earth's diameter for the
known planetary system ; this again for the system of the Milky
Way ; and the immeasurable host of such systems, which go by
the name of nebulae, and most likely in turn themselves form
such a system, holds out no prospect of a limit. Now in the
aesthetic estimate of such an immeasurable whole, the sublime
does not lie so much in the greatness of the number, as in the
fact that in our onward advance we always arrive at proportionately greater units. The systematic division of the cosmos
conduces to this result. For it represents all that is great in 257
nature as in turn becoming little ; or, to be more exact, it
represents our imagination in all its boundlessness, and with it
nature, as sinking into insignificance before the ideas of reason,
once their adequate presentation is attempted.

§ 27

Quality of the delight in our estimate of the sublime.

THE feeling of our incapacity to attain to an idea *that is a law
for us*, is RESPECT. Now the idea of the comprehension of any
phenomenon whatever, that may be given us, in a whole of
intuition, is an idea imposed upon us by a law of reason, which
recognizes no definite, universally valid and unchangeable
measure except the absolute whole. But our imagination, even
when taxing itself to the uttermost on the score of this required

comprehension of a given object in a whole of intuition, (and so with a view to the presentation of the idea of reason,) betrays its limits and its inadequacy, but still, at the same time, its proper vocation of making itself adequate to the same as a law.   Therefore the feeling of the sublime in nature is respect 5 for our own vocation, which we attribute to an Object of nature by a certain subreption (substitution of a respect for the Object in place of one for the idea of humanity in our own self—the Subject) ; and this feeling renders, as it were, intuitable the supremacy of our cognitive faculties on the rational side over 10 the greatest faculty of sensibility.

The feeling of the sublime is, therefore, at once a feeling of displeasure, arising from the inadequacy of imagination in the aesthetic estimation of magnitude to attain to its estimation by reason, and a simultaneously awakened pleasure, arising from 15 this very judgement of the inadequacy of the greatest faculty of sense being in accord with ideas of reason, so far as the effort to attain to these is for us a law.   It is, in other words, for us a law (of reason), which goes to make us what we are, that we should esteem as small in comparison with ideas of 20 reason everything which for us is great in nature as an object of sense ; and that which makes us alive to the feeling of this 258 supersensible side of our being harmonizes with that law.   Now the greatest effort of the imagination in the presentation of the unit for the estimation of magnitude involves in itself a reference 25 to something *absolutely great*, consequently a reference also to the law of reason that this alone is to be adopted as the supreme measure of what is great.   Therefore the inner perception of the inadequacy of every standard of sense to serve for the rational estimation of magnitude is a coming into accord with reason's 30 laws, and a displeasure that makes us alive to the feeling of the supersensible side of our being, according to which it is final, and consequently a pleasure, to find every standard of sensibility falling short of the ideas of reason.

The mind feels itself *set in motion* in the representation of the
sublime in nature ; whereas in the aesthetic judgement upon
what is beautiful therein it is in *restful* contemplation. This
movement, especially in its inception, may be compared with
5 a vibration, i. e. with a rapidly alternating repulsion and attraction
produced by one and the same Object. The point of excess
for the imagination (towards which it is driven in the apprehension of the intuition) is like an abyss in which it fears to
lose itself ; yet again for the rational idea of the supersensible
10 it is not excessive, but conformable to law, and directed to
drawing out such an effort on the part of the imagination : and
so in turn as much a source of attraction as it was repellent to
mere sensibility. But the judgement itself all the while stead-
fastly preserves its aesthetic character, because it represents,
15 without being grounded on any definite concept of the Object,
merely the subjective play of the mental powers (imagination
and reason) as harmonious by virtue of their very contrast.
For just as in the estimate of the beautiful imagination and
understanding by their concert generate subjective finality of
20 the mental faculties, so imagination and *reason* do so here by
their conflict—that is to say they induce a feeling of our possessing a pure and self-sufficient reason, or a faculty for the estimation of magnitude, whose pre-eminence can only be made
intuitively evident by the inadequacy of that faculty which in
25 the presentation of magnitudes (of objects of sense) is itself
unbounded.

Measurement of a space (as apprehension) is at the same
time a description of it, and so an objective movement in the
imagination and a progression. On the other hand the com-
30 prehension of the manifold in the unity, not of thought, but of
intuition, and consequently the comprehension of the succes-
sively apprehended parts at one glance, is a retrogression that
removes the time-condition in the progression of the imagina- 259
tion, and renders *co-existence* intuitable. Therefore, since the

time-series is a condition of the internal sense and of an
intuition, it is a subjective movement of the imagination by
which it does violence to the internal sense—a violence which
must be proportionately more striking the greater the quantum
which the imagination comprehends in one intuition.   The 5
effort, therefore, to receive in a single intuition a measure for
magnitudes which it takes an appreciable time to apprehend,
is a mode of representation which, subjectively considered,
is contra-final, but, objectively, is requisite for the estimation
of magnitude, and is consequently final.   Here the very same 10
violence that is wrought on the Subject through the imagination
is estimated as final *for the whole province* of the mind.

The *quality* of the feeling of the sublime consists in its
being, in respect of the faculty of forming aesthetic estimates,
a feeling of displeasure at an object, which yet, at the same 15
time, is represented as being final—a representation which
derives its possibility from the fact that the Subject's very
incapacity betrays the consciousness of an unlimited faculty of
the same Subject, and that the mind can only form an aesthetic
estimate of the latter faculty by means of that incapacity.   20

In the case of the logical estimation of magnitude the impossibility of ever arriving at absolute totality by the progressive
measurement of things of the sensible world in time and space
was cognized as an objective impossibility, i.e. one of *thinking*
the infinite as given, and not as simply subjective, i.e. an in- 25
capacity for *grasping* it ; for nothing turns there on the amount
of the comprehension in one intuition, as measure, but everything depends on a numerical concept.   But in an aesthetic
estimation of magnitude the numerical concept must drop
out of count or undergo a change.   The only thing that is final 30
for such estimation is the comprehension on the part of imagination in respect of the unit of measure (the concept of a law of
the successive production of the concept of magnitude being
consequently avoided).—If, now, a magnitude begins to tax the

utmost stretch of our faculty of comprehension in an intuition, and still numerical magnitudes—in respect of which we are conscious of the boundlessness of our faculty—call upon the imagination for aesthetic comprehension in a greater unit, 5 the mind then gets a feeling of being aesthetically confined within bounds. Nevertheless, with a view to the extension of imagination necessary for adequacy with what is unbounded in our faculty of reason, namely the idea of the absolute whole, 260 the attendant displeasure, and, consequently, the want of 10 finality in our faculty of imagination, is still represented as final for ideas of reason and their animation. But in this very way the aesthetic judgement itself is subjectively final for reason as source of ideas, i.e. of such an intellectual comprehension as makes all aesthetic comprehension small, and the 15 object is received as sublime with a pleasure that is only possible through the mediation of a displeasure.

B. THE DYNAMICALLY SUBLIME IN NATURE

§ 28

Nature as Might.

20   *Might* is a power which is superior to great hindrances. It is termed *dominion* if it is also superior to the resistance of that which itself possesses might. Nature considered in an aesthetic judgement as might that has no dominion over us, is *dynamically sublime.*

25   If we are to estimate nature as dynamically sublime, it must be represented as a source of fear (though the converse, that every object that is a source of fear is, in our aesthetic judgement, sublime, does not hold). For in forming an aesthetic estimate (no concept being present) the superiority to hin-30 drances can only be estimated according to the greatness of the resistance. Now that which we strive to resist is an evil,

and, if we do not find our powers commensurate to the task, an object of fear. Hence the aesthetic judgement can only deem nature a might, and so dynamically sublime, in so far as it is looked upon as an object of fear.

But we may look upon an object as *fearful*, and yet not be 5 afraid *of* it, if, that is, our estimate takes the form of our simply *picturing to ourselves* the case of our wishing to offer some resistance to it, and recognizing that all such resistance would be quite futile. So the righteous man fears God without being afraid of Him, because he regards the case of his wishing to 10 resist God and His commandments as one which need cause *him* no anxiety. But in every such case, regarded by him as not intrinsically impossible, he cognizes Him as One to be feared.

One who is in a state of fear can no more play the part of 15 a judge of the sublime of nature than one captivated by inclination and appetite can of the beautiful. He flees from the sight of an object filling him with dread; and it is impossible to take delight in terror that is seriously entertained. Hence the agreeableness arising from the cessation of an 20 uneasiness is *a state of joy*. But this, depending upon deliverance from a danger, is a rejoicing accompanied with a resolve never again to put oneself in the way of the danger: in fact we do not like bringing back to mind how we felt on that occasion—not to speak of going in search of an opportunity for 25 experiencing it again.

Bold, overhanging, and, as it were, threatening rocks, thunderclouds piled up the vault of heaven, borne along with flashes and peals, volcanoes in all their violence of destruction, hurricanes leaving desolation in their track, the boundless 30 ocean rising with rebellious force, the high waterfall of some mighty river, and the like, make our power of resistance of trifling moment in comparison with their might. But, provided our own position is secure, their aspect is all the more attractive for its fearfulness ; and we readily call these objects sublime, because they raise the forces of the soul above the height of vulgar commonplace, and discover within us a power of resistance of quite another kind, which gives us courage to be able to measure ourselves against the seeming omnipotence of nature.

In the immeasurableness of nature and the incompetence of our faculty for adopting a standard proportionate to the aesthetic estimation of the magnitude of its *realm,* we found our own limitation.   But with this we also found in our rational faculty another non-sensuous standard, one which has that infinity itself under it as unit, and in comparison with which everything in nature is small, and so found in our minds a pre-eminence over nature even in its immeasurability.   Now in just the same way the irresistibility of the might of nature forces upon us the recognition of our physical helplessness as beings of nature, but at the same time reveals a faculty of estimating ourselves as independent of nature, and discovers a pre-eminence above nature that is the foundation of a self-preservation of quite another kind from that which may be assailed and brought into danger by external nature.   This saves humanity in our own person from humiliation, even though as mortal men we have to submit to external violence. In this way external nature is not estimated in our aesthetic judgement as sublime so far as exciting fear, but rather because it challenges our power (one not of nature) to regard as small those things of which we are wont to be solicitous (worldly goods, health, and life), and hence to regard its might (to which in these matters we are no doubt subject) as exercising over us and our personality no such rude dominion that we should bow down before it, once the question becomes one of our highest principles and of our asserting or forsaking them.   Therefore nature is here called sublime merely because it raises the imagination to a presentation of those cases in which the mind can make itself sensible of the appropriate sublimity of the sphere of its own being, even above nature.

This estimation of ourselves loses nothing by the fact that we must see ourselves safe in order to feel this soul-stirring delight—a fact from which it might be plausibly argued that, as there is no seriousness in the danger, so there is just as little seriousness in the sublimity of our faculty of soul. For here the delight only concerns the *province* of our faculty disclosed in such a case, so far as this faculty has its root in our nature; notwithstanding that its development and exercise is left to ourselves and remains an obligation. Here indeed there is truth—no matter how conscious a man, when he stretches his reflection so far abroad, may be of his actual present helplessness.

This principle has, doubtless, the appearance of being too far-fetched and subtle, and so of lying beyond the reach of an aesthetic judgement. But observation of men proves the reverse, and that it may be the foundation of the commonest judgements, although one is not always conscious of its presence. For what is it that, even to the savage, is the object of the greatest admiration? It is a man who is undaunted, who knows no fear, and who, therefore, does not give way to danger, but sets manfully to work with full deliberation. Even where civilization has reached a high pitch there remains this special reverence for the soldier; only that there is then further required of him that he should also exhibit all the virtues of peace—gentleness, sympathy and even becoming thought for his own person; and for the reason that in this we recognize that his mind is above the threats of danger. And so, comparing the statesman and the general, men may argue as they please as to the pre-eminent respect which is due to either above the other; but the verdict of the aesthetic judgement is for the latter. War itself, provided it is conducted with order and a sacred respect for the rights of civilians, has something sublime about it, and gives nations that carry it on in such a manner a stamp of mind only the more sublime the more numerous the dangers to which they are exposed, and which they are able to meet with fortitude. On the other hand, 5 a prolonged peace favours the predominance of a mere commercial spirit, and with it a debasing self-interest, cowardice, and effeminacy, and tends to degrade the character of the nation.

So far as sublimity is predicated of might, this solution of 10 the concept of it appears at variance with the fact that we are wont to represent God in the tempest, the storm, the earthquake, and the like, as presenting Himself in His wrath, but at the same time also in His sublimity, and yet here it would be alike folly and presumption to imagine a pre-eminence of our minds 15 over the operations and, as it appears, even over the direction of such might. Here, instead of a feeling of the sublimity of our own nature, submission, prostration, and a feeling of utter helplessness seem more to constitute the attitude of mind befitting the manifestation of such an object, and to be that also 20 more customarily associated with the idea of it on the occasion of a natural phenomenon of this kind. In religion, as a rule, prostration, adoration with bowed head, coupled with contrite, timorous posture and voice, seems to be the only becoming demeanour in presence of the Godhead, and accordingly most 25 nations have assumed and still observe it. Yet this cast of mind is far from being intrinsically and necessarily involved in the idea of the *sublimity* of a religion and of its object. The man that is actually in a state of fear, finding in himself good reason to be so, because he is conscious of offending with his 30 evil disposition against a might directed by a will at once irresistible and just, is far from being in the frame of mind for admiring divine greatness, for which a temper of calm reflection and a quite free judgement are required. Only when he becomes conscious of having a disposition that is upright and acceptable to God, do those operations of might serve to stir within him the idea of the sublimity of this Being, so far as he recognizes the existence in himself of a sublimity of disposition consonant with His will, and is thus raised above the dread of such operations of nature, in which he no longer sees God 5 pouring forth the vials of the wrath. Even humility, taking the form of an uncompromising judgement upon his short-comings, which, with the consciousness of good intentions, might readily be glossed over on the ground of the frailty of human nature, is a sublime temper of the mind voluntarily to 10 undergo the pain of remorse as a means of more and more effectually eradicating its cause. In this way religion is intrinsically distinguished from superstition, which latter rears in the mind, not reverence for the sublime, but dread and apprehension of the all-powerful Being to whose will terror- 15 stricken man sees himself subjected, yet without according Him due honour. From this nothing can arise but grace-begging and vain adulation, instead of a religion consisting in a good life.

Sublimity, therefore, does not reside in any of the things of 20 nature, but only in our own mind, in so far as we may become conscious of our superiority over nature within, and thus also over nature without us (as exerting influence upon us). Every-thing that provokes this feeling in us, including the *might* of nature which challenges our strength, is then, though im- 25 properly, called sublime, and it is only under presupposition of this idea within us, and in relation to it, that we are capable of attaining to the idea of the sublimity of that Being which inspires deep respect in us, not by the mere display of its might in nature, but more by the faculty which is planted in us of 30 estimating that might without fear, and of regarding our estate as exalted above it.

§ 29

Modality of the judgement on the sublime in nature.

BEAUTIFUL nature contains countless things as to which we
at once take every one as in their judgement concurring with
our own, and as to which we may further expect this concurrence
without facts finding us far astray.   But in respect of our judgement upon the sublime in nature we cannot so easily vouch
for ready acceptance by others.   For a far higher degree of
culture, not merely of the aesthetic judgement, but also of
the faculties of cognition which lie at its basis, seems to be
requisite to enable us to lay down a judgement upon this
high distinction of natural objects.

The proper mental mood for a feeling of the sublime pos- 265
tulates the mind's susceptibility for ideas, since it is precisely in
the failure of nature to attain to these—and consequently only
under presupposition of this susceptibility and of the straining
of the imagination to use nature as a schema for ideas—that
there is something forbidding to sensibility, but which, for all
that, has an attraction for us, arising from the fact of its being
a dominion which reason exercises over sensibility with a view
to extending it to the requirements of its own realm (the
practical) and letting it look out beyond itself into the infinite,
which for it is an abyss.   In fact, without the development
of moral ideas, that which, thanks to preparatory culture, we
call sublime, merely strikes the untutored man as terrifying.
He will see in the evidences which the ravages of nature
give of her dominion, and in the vast scale of her might,
compared with which his own is diminished to insignificance,
only the misery, peril, and distress that would compass the
man who was thrown to its mercy.   So the simple-minded,
and, for the most part, intelligent, Savoyard peasant, (as Herr
von Sassure relates,) unhesitatingly called all lovers of snow-

mountains fools. And who can tell whether he would have been so wide of the mark, if that student of nature had taken the risk of the dangers to which he exposed himself merely, as most travellers do, for a fad, or so as some day to be able to give a thrilling account of his adventures? But the mind of 5 Sassure was bent on the instruction of mankind, and soul-stirring sensations that excellent man indeed had, and the reader of his travels got them thrown into the bargain.

But the fact that culture is requisite for the judgement upon the sublime in nature (more than for that upon the beautiful) 10 does not involve its being an original product of culture and something introduced in a more or less conventional way into society. Rather is it in human nature that its foundations are laid, and, in fact, in that which, at once with common understanding, we may expect every one to possess and may require 15 of him, namely, a native capacity for the feeling for (practical) ideas, i. e. for moral feeling.

This, now, is the foundation of the necessity of that agreement between other men's judgements upon the sublime and our own, which we make our own imply. For just as we taunt a man 20 who is quite inappreciative when forming an estimate of an object of nature in which we see beauty, with want *of taste*, so we say of a man who remains unaffected in the presence of what we consider sublime, that he has no *feeling*. But we demand both taste and feeling of every man, and, granted 25
266 some degree of culture, we give him credit for both. Still, we do so with this difference : that, in the case of the former, since judgement there refers the imagination merely to the understanding, as the faculty of concepts, we make the requirement as a matter of course, whereas in the case of the latter, 30 since here the judgement refers the imagination to reason, as a faculty of ideas, we do so only under a subjective presupposition, (which, however, we believe we are warranted in making,) namely, that of the moral feeling in man. And, on this

assumption, we attribute necessity to the latter aesthetic judgement also.

In this modality of aesthetic judgements, namely their assumed necessity, lies what is for the Critique of Judgement a moment of capital importance.   For this is exactly what makes an *a priori* principle apparent in their case, and lifts them out of the sphere of empirical psychology, in which otherwise they would remain buried amid the feelings of gratification and pain (only with the senseless epithet of *finer* feeling), so as to place them, and, thanks to them, to place the faculty of judgement itself, in the class of judgements of which the basis of an *a priori* principle is the distinguishing feature, and, thus distinguished, to introduce them into transcendental philosophy.

GENERAL REMARK UPON THE EXPOSITION OF AESTHETIC REFLECTIVE JUDGEMENTS

In relation to the feeling of pleasure an object is to be counted either as *agreeable*, or *beautiful*, or *sublime*, or *good* (absolutely), (*iucundum, pulchrum, sublime, honestum*).

As the motive of desires the *agreeable* is invariably of one and the same kind, no matter what its source or how specifically different the representation (of sense and sensation objectively considered).   Hence in estimating its influence upon the mind the multitude of its charms (simultaneous or successive) is alone relevant, and so only, as it were, the mass of the agreeable sensation, and it is only by its *Quantity*, therefore, that this can be made intelligible.   Further it in no way conduces to our culture, but belongs only to mere enjoyment.—The *beautiful*, on the other hand, requires the representation of a certain *Quality* of the Object, that permits also of being understood and reduced to concepts, (although in the aesthetic judgement it is not so reduced,) and it cultivates, as it instructs us to attend to finality in the feeling of pleasure.—The *sublime* consists merely in the *relation* exhibited by the estimate of the serviceability of the sensible in the representation of nature for a possible supersensible employment.—The *absolutely good*, estimated subjectively according to the feeling it inspires, (the Object of the moral feeling,) as the determinability of the powers of the Subject by means of the representation of an *absolutely necessitating* law, is principally distinguished by the *modality* of a necessity resting upon concepts *a priori*, and involving not a mere *claim*, but a *command* upon every one to assent, and belongs intrinsically not to the aesthetic, but to the pure intellectual judgement. Further, it is not ascribed to nature but to freedom, and that in a determinant and not a merely reflective judgement. But the *determinability of the Subject* by means of this idea, and, what is more, that of a Subject which can be sensible, in the way of a *modification of its state*, to *hindrances* on the part of sensibility, while, at the same time, it can by surmounting them feel superiority over them—a determinability, in other words, as moral feeling—is still so allied to aesthetic judgement and its *formal conditions* as to be capable of being pressed into the service of the aesthetic representation of the conformity to law of action from duty, i.e. of the representation of this as sublime, or even as beautiful, without forfeiting its purity—an impossible result were one to make it naturally bound up with the feeling of the agreeable.

The net result to be extracted from the exposition so far given of both kinds of aesthetic judgements may be summed up in the following brief definitions:

The *beautiful* is what pleases in the mere estimate formed of it (consequently not by intervention of any feeling of sense in accordance with a concept of the understanding). From this it follows at once that it must please apart from all interest.

The *sublime* is what pleases immediately by reason of its opposition to the interest of sense.

Both, as definitions of aesthetic universally valid estimates, have reference to subjective grounds. In the one case the reference is to grounds of sensibility, in so far as these are final on behalf of the contemplative understanding, in the 5 other case in so far as, in their *opposition* to sensibility, they are, on the contrary, final in reference to the ends of practical reason. Both, however, as united in the same Subject, are final in reference to the moral feeling. The beautiful prepares us to love something, even nature, apart from any 10 interest: the sublime to esteem something highly even in opposition to our (sensible) interest.

The sublime may be described in this way: It is an object 268 (of nature) the *representation of which determines the mind to regard the elevation of nature beyond our reach as equivalent to* 15 *a presentation of ideas.*

In a literal sense and according to their logical import, ideas cannot be presented. But if we enlarge our empirical faculty of representation (mathematical or dynamical) with a view to the intuition of nature, reason inevitably steps forward, as the 20 faculty concerned with the independence of the absolute totality, and calls forth the effort of the mind, unavailing though it be, to make the representation of sense adequate to this totality. This effort, and the feeling of the unattainability of the idea by means of imagination, is itself a presentation of the subjective 25 finality of our mind in the employment of the imagination in the interests of the mind's supersensible province, and compels us subjectively to *think* nature itself in its totality as a presentation of something supersensible, without our being able to effectuate this presentation *objectively.*

30 For we readily see that nature in space and time falls entirely short of the unconditioned, consequently also of the absolutely great, which still the commonest reason demands. And by this we are also reminded that we have only to do with nature as phenomenon, and that this itself must be regarded as the

mere presentation of a nature-in-itself (which exists in the idea of reason). But this idea of the supersensible, which no doubt we cannot further determine—so that we cannot *cognize* nature as its presentation, but only *think* it as such—is awakened in us by an object the aesthetic estimating of which strains the 5 imagination to its utmost, whether in respect of its extension (mathematical), or of its might over the mind (dynamical). For it is founded upon the feeling of a sphere of the mind which altogether exceeds the realm of nature (i.e. upon the moral feeling), with regard to which the representation of the 10 object is estimated as subjectively final.

As a matter of fact, a feeling for the sublime in nature is hardly thinkable unless in association with an attitude of mind resembling the moral. And though, like that feeling, the immediate pleasure in the beautiful in nature presupposes 15 and cultivates a certain *liberality* of thought, i.e. makes our delight independent of any mere enjoyment of sense, still it represents freedom rather as in *play* than as exercising a law-ordained *function*, which is the genuine characteristic of human morality, where reason has to impose its dominion 20 upon sensibility. There is, however, this qualification, that in the aesthetic judgement upon the sublime this dominion is represented as exercised through the imagination itself as an instrument of reason.

Thus, too, delight in the sublime in nature is only *negative* 25 (whereas that in the beautiful is *positive*): that is to say it is a feeling of imagination by its own act depriving itself of its freedom by receiving a final determination in accordance with a law other than that of its empirical employment. In this way it gains an extension and a might greater than that which 30 it sacrifices. But the ground of this is concealed from it, and in its place it *feels* the sacrifice or deprivation, as well as its cause, to which it is subjected. The *astonishment* amounting almost to terror, the awe and thrill of devout feeling, that takes hold of one when gazing upon the prospect of mountains ascending to heaven, deep ravines and torrents raging there, deep-shadowed solitudes that invite to brooding melancholy, and the like—all this, when we are assured of our own safety, is 5 not actual fear. Rather is it an attempt to gain access to it through imagination, for the purpose of feeling the might of this faculty in combining the movement of the mind thereby aroused with its serenity, and of thus being superior to internal and, therefore, to external, nature, so far as the latter can have 10 any bearing upon our feeling of well-being. For the imagination, in accordance with laws of association, makes our state of contentment dependent upon physical conditions. But acting in accordance with principles of the schematism of judgement, (consequently so far as it is subordinated to freedom,) it is at 15 the same time an instrument of reason and its ideas. But in this capacity it is a might enabling us to assert our independence as against the influences of nature, to degrade what is great in respect of the latter to the level of what is little, and thus to locate the absolutely great only in the proper estate of 20 the Subject. This reflection of aesthetic judgement by which it raises itself to the point of adequacy with reason, though without any determinate concept of reason, is still a representation of the object as subjectively final, by virtue even of the objective inadequacy of the imagination in its greatest extension for meet- 25 ing the demands of reason (as the faculty of ideas).

Here we have to attend generally to what has been already adverted to, that in the Transcendental Aesthetic of judgement there must be no question of anything but pure aesthetic 270 judgements. Consequently examples are not to be selected 30 from such beautiful or sublime objects as presuppose the concept of an end. For then the finality would be either teleological, or based upon mere sensations of an object (gratification or pain) and so, in the first case, not aesthetic, and, in the second, not merely formal. So, if we call the sight of the

starry heaven *sublime*, we must not found our estimate of it
upon any concepts of worlds inhabited by rational beings, with
the bright spots, which we see filling the space above us, as
their suns moving in orbits prescribed for them with the wisest
regard to ends.   But we must take it, just as it strikes the eye, 5
as a broad and all-embracing canopy : and it is merely under
such a representation that we may posit the sublimity which
the pure aesthetic judgement attributes to this object.   Similarly,
as to the prospect of the ocean, we are not to regard it as we,
with our minds stored with knowledge on a variety of matters, 10
(which, however, is not contained in the immediate intuition,)
are wont to represent it in *thought*, as, let us say, a spacious
realm of aquatic creatures, or as the mighty reservoirs from
which are drawn the vapours that fill the air with clouds of
moisture for the good of the land, or yet as an element which no 15
doubt divides continent from continent, but at the same time
affords the means of the greatest commercial intercourse between them—for in this way we get nothing beyond teleological
judgements.   Instead of this we must be able to see sublimity
in the ocean, regarding it, as the poets do, according to what 20
the impression upon the eye reveals, as, let us say, in its calm,
a clear mirror of water bounded only by the heavens, or, be it
disturbed, as threatening to overwhelm and engulf everything.
The same is to be said of the sublime and beautiful in the
human form.   Here, for determining grounds of the judgement, 25
we must not have recourse to concepts of ends *subserved* by
all its limbs and members, or allow their accordance with these
ends to *influence* our aesthetic judgement, (in such case no
longer pure,) although it is certainly also a necessary condition
of aesthetic delight that they should not conflict with these 30
ends.   Aesthetic finality is the conformity to law of judgement
in its *freedom*.   The delight in the object depends upon the
reference which we seek to give to the imagination, subject to
the proviso that it is to entertain the mind in a free activity.

If, on the other hand, something else,—be it sensation or concept of the understanding—determines the judgement, it is then 271 conformable to law, no doubt, but not an act of *free* judgement.

Hence to speak of intellectual beauty or sublimity is to use 5 expressions which, in the *first* place, are not quite correct. For these are aesthetic modes of representation which would be entirely foreign to us were we merely pure intelligences (or if we even put ourselves in thought in the position of such). *Secondly*, although both, as objects of an intellectual 10 (moral) delight, are compatible with aesthetic delight to the extent of not *resting* upon any interest, still, on the other hand, there is a difficulty in the way of their alliance with such delight, since their function is to *produce* an interest, and, on the assumption that the presentation has to accord with 15 delight in the aesthetic estimate, this interest could only be effected by means of an interest of sense combined with it in the presentation. But in this way the intellectual finality would be violated and rendered impure.

The object of a pure and unconditioned intellectual delight 20 is the moral law in the might which it exerts in us over all *antecedent* motives of the mind. Now, since it is only through sacrifices that this might makes itself known to us aesthetically, (and this involves a deprivation of something— though in the interests of inner freedom—whilst in turn 25 it reveals in us an unfathomable depth of this supersensible faculty, the consequences of which extend beyond reach of the eye of sense,) it follows that the delight, looked at from the aesthetic side (in reference to sensibility) is negative, i.e. opposed to this interest, but from the intellectual side, positive 30 and bound up with an interest. Hence it follows that the intellectual and intrinsically final (moral) good, estimated aesthetically, instead of being represented as beautiful, must rather be represented as sublime, with the result that it arouses more a feeling of respect (which disdains charm) than of love or of the heart being drawn towards it—for human nature does not of its own proper motion accord with the good, but only by virtue of the dominion which reason exercises over sensibility. Conversely, that, too, which we call sublime in external nature, or even internal nature (e. g. certain affections) is only 5 represented as a might of the mind enabling it to overcome this or that hindrance of sensibility by means of moral principles, and it is from this that it derives its interest.

I must dwell a while on the latter point. The idea of the 272 good to which affection is superadded is *enthusiasm*. This 10 state of mind appears to be sublime : so much so that there is a common saying that nothing great can be achieved without it. But now every affection[1] is blind either as to the choice of its end, or, supposing this has been furnished by reason, in the way it is effected—for it is that mental 15 movement whereby the exercise of free deliberation upon fundamental principles, with a view to determining oneself accordingly, is rendered impossible. On this account it cannot merit any delight on the part of reason. Yet, from an aesthetic point of view, enthusiasm is sublime, because it is an 20 effort of one's powers called forth by ideas which give to the mind an impetus of far stronger and more enduring efficacy than the stimulus afforded by sensible representations. But (as seems strange) even *freedom from affection* (*apatheia, phlegma in significatu bono*) in a mind that strenuously follows its un- 25 swerving principles is sublime, and that, too, in a manner

---

[1] There is a specific distinction between *affections* and *passions*. Affections are related merely to feeling ; passions belong to the faculty of desire, and are inclinations that hinder or render impossible all determinability of the elective will by principles. Affections are impetuous 30 and irresponsible : passions are abiding and deliberate. Thus resentment, in the form of anger, is an affection : but in the form of hatred (vindictiveness) it is a passion. Under no circumstances can the latter be called sublime ; for, while the freedom of the mind is, no doubt, *impeded* in the case of affection, in passion it is abrogated. 35

vastly superior, because it has at the same time the delight of pure reason on its side. Such a stamp of mind is alone called noble. This expression, however, comes in time to be applied to things—such as buildings, a garment, literary style,
5 the carriage of one's person, and the like—provided they do not so much excite *astonishment* (the affection attending the representation of novelty exceeding expectation) as *admiration* (an astonishment which does not cease when the novelty wears off)—and this obtains where ideas undesignedly and artlessly
10 accord in their presentation with aesthetic delight.

Every affection of the STRENUOUS TYPE (such, that is, as excites the consciousness of our power of overcoming every resistance *(animus strenuus)*) is *aesthetically sublime*, e. g. anger, even desperation (the *rage of forlorn hope* but not *faint-hearted*
15 despair). On the other hand, affection of the LANGUID TYPE (which converts the very effort of resistance into an object of displeasure *(animus languidus)*) has nothing *noble* about it, 273 though it may take its rank as possessing beauty of the sensuous order. Hence the *emotions* capable of attaining the
20 strength of an affection are very diverse. We have *spirited*, and we have *tender* emotions. When the strength of the latter reaches that of an affection they can be turned to no account. The propensity to indulge in them is *sentimentality*. A sympathetic grief that refuses to be consoled, or one that has to
25 do with imaginary misfortune to which we deliberately give way so far as to allow our fancy to delude us into thinking it actual fact, indicates and goes to make a tender, but at the same time weak, soul, which shows a beautiful side, and may no doubt be called fanciful, but never enthusiastic. Romances,
30 maudlin dramas, shallow homilies, which trifle with so-called (though falsely so) noble sentiments, but in fact make the heart enervated, insensitive to the stern precepts of duty, and incapable of respect for the worth of humanity in our own person and the rights of men (which is something quite other

than their happiness), and in general incapable of all firm principles; even a religious discourse which recommends a cringing and abject grace-begging and favour-seeking, abandoning all reliance on our own ability to resist the evil within us, in place of the vigorous resolution to try to get the better of our inclinations by means of those powers which, miserable sinners though we be, are still left to us; that false humility by which self-abasement, whining hypocritical repentance and a merely passive frame of mind are set down as the method by which alone we can become acceptable to the Supreme Being—these have neither lot nor fellowship with what may be reckoned to belong to beauty, not to speak of sublimity, of mental temperament.

But even impetuous movements of the mind—be they allied under the name of edification with ideas of religion, or, as pertaining merely to culture, with ideas involving a social interest—no matter what tension of the imagination they may produce, can in no way lay claim to the honour of a *sublime* presentation, if they do not leave behind them a temper of mind which, though it be only indirectly, has an influence upon the consciousness of the mind's strength and resoluteness in respect of that which carries with it pure intellectual finality (the supersensible). For, in the absence of this, all these emotions belong only to *motion*, which we welcome in the interests of good health. The agreeable lassitude that follows upon being stirred up in that way by the play of the affections, is a fruition of the state of well-being arising from the restoration of the equilibrium of the various vital forces within us. This, in the last resort, comes to no more than what the Eastern voluptuaries find so soothing when they get their bodies massaged, and all their muscles and joints softly pressed and bent; only that in the first case the principle that occasions the movement is chiefly internal, whereas here it is entirely external. Thus, many a man believes himself edified by a sermon

in which there is no establishment of anything (no system of good maxims); or thinks himself improved by a tragedy, when he is merely glad at having got well rid of the feeling of being bored. Thus the sublime must in every case have
5 reference to our *way of thinking*, i.e. to maxims directed to giving the intellectual side of our nature and the ideas of reason supremacy over sensibility.

We have no reason to fear that the feeling of the sublime will suffer from an abstract mode of presentation like this,
10 which is altogether negative as to what is sensuous. For though the imagination, no doubt, finds nothing beyond the sensible world to which it can lay hold, still this thrusting aside of the sensible barriers gives it a feeling of being unbounded; and that removal is thus a presentation of the infinite. As such it
15 can never be anything more than a negative presentation—but still it expands the soul. Perhaps there is no more sublime passage in the Jewish Law than the commandment: Thou shalt not make unto thee any graven image, or any likeness of any thing that is in heaven or on earth, or under the earth, &c.
20 This commandment can alone explain the enthusiasm which the Jewish people, in their moral period, felt for their religion when comparing themselves with others, or the pride inspired by Mohammedanism. The very same holds good of our representation of the moral law and of our native capacity for
25 morality. The fear that, if we divest this representation of everything that can commend it to the senses, it will thereupon be attended only with a cold and lifeless approbation and not with any moving force or emotion, is wholly unwarranted. The very reverse is the truth. For when nothing any longer meets
30 the eye of sense, and the unmistakable and ineffaceable idea of morality is left in possession of the field, there would be need rather of tempering the ardour of an unbounded imagination to prevent it rising to enthusiasm, than of seeking to lend these ideas the aid of images and childish devices for fear of their

275 being wanting in potency. For this reason governments have gladly let religion be fully equipped with these accessories, seeking in this way to relieve their subjects of the exertion, but to deprive them, at the same time, of the ability, required for expanding their spiritual powers beyond the limits arbitrarily 5 laid down for them, and which facilitate their being treated as though they were merely passive.

This pure, elevating, merely negative presentation of morality involves, on the other hand, no fear of *fanaticism*, which is a *delusion* that would *will some* VISION *beyond all the bounds of* 10 *sensibility*; i.e. would dream according to principles (rational raving). The safeguard is the purely negative character of the presentation. For *the inscrutability of the idea of freedom* precludes all positive presentation. The moral law, however, is a sufficient and original source of determination within us : so it 15 does not for a moment permit us to cast about for a ground of determination external to itself. If enthusiasm is comparable to *delirium*, fanaticism may be compared to *mania*. Of these the latter is least of all compatible with the sublime, for it is *profoundly* ridiculous. In enthusiasm, as an affection, the 20 imagination is unbridled ; in fanaticism, as a deep-seated, brooding passion, it is anomalous. The first is a transitory accident to which the healthiest understanding is liable to become at times the victim ; the second is an undermining disease.

Simplicity (artless finality) is, as it were, the style adopted by 25 nature in the sublime. It is also that of morality. The latter is a second (supersensible) nature, whose laws alone we know, without being able to attain to an intuition of the supersensible faculty within us—that which contains the ground of this legislation. 30

One further remark. The delight in the sublime, no less than in the beautiful, by reason of its universal *communicability* not alone is plainly distinguished from other aesthetic judgements, but also from this same property acquires an interest in

society (in which it admits of such communication). Yet, despite this, we have to note the fact that *isolation from all society* is looked upon as something sublime, provided it rests upon ideas which disregard all sensible interest. To be self-
5 sufficing, and so not to stand in need of society, yet without being unsociable, i.e. without shunning it, is something approaching the sublime—a remark applicable to all superiority to wants. On the other hand, to shun our fellow men from *misanthropy*, because of enmity towards them, or from *anthro-* 276
10 *pophobia*, because we imagine the hand of every man is against us, is partly odious, partly contemptible. There is, however, a misanthropy, (most improperly so called,) the tendency towards which is to be found with advancing years in many right-minded men, that, as far as *good will* goes, is, no doubt,
15 philanthropic enough, but as the result of long and sad experience, is widely removed from *delight* in mankind. We see evidences of this in the propensity to recluseness, in the fanciful desire for a retired country seat, or else (with the young) in the dream of the happiness of being able to spend
20 one's life with a little family on an island unknown to the rest of the world—material of which novelists or writers of Robinsonades know how to make such good use. Falsehood, ingratitude, injustice, the puerility of the ends which we ourselves look upon as great and momentous, and to compass which man
25 inflicts upon his brother man all imaginable evils—these all so contradict the idea of what men might be if they only would, and are so at variance with our active wish to see them better, that, to avoid hating where we cannot love, it seems but a slight sacrifice to forego all the joys of fellowship with our kind.
30 This sadness, which is not directed to the evils which fate brings down upon others, (a sadness which springs from sympathy,) but to those which they inflict upon themselves, (one which is based on antipathy in questions of principle,) is sublime because it is founded on ideas, whereas that springing

from sympathy can only be accounted beautiful.—*Sassure*, who was no less ingenious than profound, in the description of his Alpine travels remarks of *Bonhomme*, one of the Savoy mountains, 'There reigns there a certain *insipid sadness.*' He recognized, therefore, that, besides this, there is an *interesting* sadness, such as is inspired by the sight of some desolate place into which men might fain withdraw themselves so as to hear no more of the world without, and be no longer versed in its affairs, a place, however, which must yet not be so altogether inhospitable as only to afford a most miserable retreat for a human being.—I only make this observation as a reminder that even melancholy, (but not dispirited sadness,) may take its place among the *vigorous* affections, provided it has its root in moral ideas. If, however, it is grounded upon sympathy, and, as such, is lovable, it belongs only to the *languid* affections. And this serves to call attention to the mental temperament which in the first case alone is *sublime.*

---

277   The transcendental exposition of aesthetic judgements now brought to a close may be compared with the physiological, as worked out by Burke and many acute men among us, so that we may see where a merely empirical exposition of the sublime and beautiful would bring us.   Burke,[1] who deserves to be called the foremost author in this method of treatment, deduces, on these lines, 'that the feeling of the sublime is grounded on the impulse towards self-preservation and on *fear*, i.e. on a pain, which, since it does not go the length of disordering the bodily parts, calls forth movements which, as they clear the vessels, whether fine or gross, of a dangerous and troublesome encumbrance, are capable of producing delight ;

[1] See p. 223 of the German translation of his work : *Philosophical In-vestigations as to the Origin of our Conceptions of the Beautiful and Sublime.* Riga, published by Hartknock, 1773.

not pleasure but a sort of delightful horror, a sort of tranquillity tinged with terror.' The beautiful, which he grounds on love (from which, still, he would have desire kept separate), he reduces to ' the relaxing, slackening, and enervating of the
5 fibres of the body, and consequently a softening, a dissolving, a languor, and a fainting, dying, and melting away for pleasure '. And this explanation he supports, not alone by instances in which the feeling of the beautiful as well as of the sublime is capable of being excited in us by the imagination in conjunction
10 with the understanding, but even by instances when it is in conjunction with sensations.—As psychological observations these analyses of our mental phenomena are extremely fine, and supply a wealth of material for the favourite investigations of empirical anthropology. But, besides that, there is no
15 denying the fact that all representations within us, no matter whether they are objectively merely sensible or wholly in tellectual, are still subjectively associable with gratification or pain, however imperceptible either of these may be. (For these representations one and all have an influence on the
20 feeling of life, and none of them, so far as it is a modification of the Subject, can be indifferent). We must even admit that, as Epicurus maintained, *gratification* and *pain* though proceeding from the imagination or even from representations of the understanding, are always in the last resort corporeal,
25 since apart from any feeling of the bodily organ life would be 278 merely a consciousness of one's existence, and could not include any feeling of well-being or the reverse, i.e. of the furtherance or hindrance of the vital forces. For, of itself alone, the mind is all life (the life-principle itself), and hindrance or
30 furtherance has to be sought outside it, and yet in the man himself, consequently in the connexion with his body.

But if we attribute the delight in the object wholly and entirely to the gratification which it affords through charm or emotion, then we must not exact from *any one else* agreement with the aesthetic judgement passed by *us*. For in such matters each person rightly consults his own personal feeling alone.   But in that case there is an end of all censorship of taste—unless the example afforded by others as the result of a contingent coincidence of their judgements is to be held over us as *commanding* our assent.   But this principle we would presumably resent, and appeal to our natural right of submitting a judgement to our own sense, where it rests upon the immediate feeling of personal well-being, instead of submitting it to that of others.   10

Hence if the import of the judgement of taste, where we appraise it as a judgement entitled to require the concurrence of every one, cannot be *egoistic*, but must necessarily, from its inner nature, be allowed a *pluralistic* validity, i.e. on account of what taste itself is, and not on account of the examples which others give of their taste, then it must found upon some *a priori* principle, (be it subjective or objective,) and no amount of prying into the empirical laws of the changes that go on within the mind can succeed in establishing such a principle.   For these laws only yield a knowledge of how we do judge, but they do not give us a command as to how we ought to judge, and, what is more, such a command as is *unconditioned*—and commands of this kind are presupposed by judgements of taste, inasmuch as they require delight to be taken as *immediately* connected with a representation.   Accordingly, though the empirical exposition of aesthetic judgements may be a first step towards accumulating the material for a higher investigation, yet a transcendental examination of this faculty is possible, and forms an essential part of the Critique of Taste.   For, were not taste in possession of *a priori* principles, it could not possibly sit in judgement upon the judgements of others, and pass sentence of commendation or condemnation upon them, with even the least semblance of authority.

The remaining part of the Analytic of the aesthetic judgement contains first of all the :—

DEDUCTION OF PURE AESTHETIC JUDGEMENTS 279

§ 30

The Deduction of aesthetic judgements upon objects of nature must not be directed to what we call sublime in nature, but only to the beautiful.

THE claim of an aesthetic judgement to universal validity for every Subject, being a judgement which must rely on some *a priori* principle, stands in need of a Deduction (i. e. a derivation of its title). Further, where the delight or aversion turns on the *form of the object* this has to be something over and above the Exposition of the judgement. Such is the case with judgements of taste upon the beautiful in nature. For there the finality has its foundation in the Object and its outward form—although it does not signify the reference of this to other objects according to concepts (for the purpose of cognitive judgements), but is merely concerned in general with the apprehension of this form so far as it proves accordant in the mind with the *faculty* of concepts as well as with that of their presentation (which is identical with that of apprehension). With regard to the beautiful in nature, therefore, we may start a number of questions touching the cause of this finality of their forms : e. g. How we are to explain why nature has scattered beauty abroad with so lavish a hand, even in the depth of the ocean where it can but seldom be reached by the eye of man—for which alone it is final.

But the sublime in nature—if we pass upon it a pure aesthetic judgement unmixed with concepts of perfection, as objective finality, which would make the judgement teleological—may be regarded as completely wanting in form or figure, and none the less be looked upon as an object of pure delight, and indicate a subjective finality of the given representation.   So, now, the question suggests itself, whether in addition to the exposition of what is thought in an aesthetic 5 judgement of this kind, we may be called upon to give a Deduction of its claim to some (subjective) *a priori* principle.

280   This we may meet with the reply that the sublime in nature is improperly so called, and that sublimity should, in strictness, be attributed merely to the attitude of thought, or, 10 rather, to that which serves as basis for this in human nature. The apprehension of an object otherwise formless and in conflict with ends supplies the mere occasion for our coming to a consciousness of this basis ; and the object is in this way put to a subjectively-final *use*, but it is not estimated as subjec- 15 tively-final *on its own account* and because of its form. (It is, as it were, a *species finalis accepta*, *non data*.)   Consequently the Exposition we gave of judgements upon the sublime in nature was at the same time their Deduction.   For in our analysis of the reflection on the part of judgement in this case we found 20 that in such judgements there is a final relation of the cognitive faculties, which has to be laid *a priori* at the basis of the faculty of ends (the will), and which is therefore itself *a priori* final.   This, then, at once involves the Deduction, i. e. the justification of the claim of such a judgement to universally- 25 necessary validity.

Hence we may confine our search to one for the Deduction of judgements of taste, i. e. of judgements upon the beauty of things of nature, and this will satisfactorily dispose of the problem for the entire aesthetic faculty of judgement.   30

§ 31

Of the method of the deduction of judgements of taste.

THE obligation to furnish a Deduction, i. e. a guarantee of the legitimacy of judgements of a particular kind, only arises where
5 the judgement lays claim to necessity. This is the case even where it requires subjective universality, i.e. the concurrence of every one, albeit the judgement is not a cognitive judgement, but only one of pleasure or displeasure in a given object, i. e. an assumption of a subjective finality that has a thorough-going
10 validity for every one, and which, since the judgement is one of Taste, is not to be grounded upon any concept of the thing.

Now, in the latter case, we are not dealing with a judgement of cognition—neither with a theoretical one based on the concept of a *nature* in general, supplied by understanding, nor
15 with a (pure) practical one based on the Idea of *freedom*, as given *a priori* by reason—and so we are not called upon to justify *a priori* the validity of a judgement which represents either what a thing is, or that there is something which I ought to do in order to produce it. Consequently, if for judge-
20 ment generally we demonstrate the *universal validity* of a *singular* judgement expressing the subjective finality of an 281 empirical representation of the form of an object, we shall do all that is needed to explain how it is possible that something can please in the mere formation of an estimate of it (without
25 sensation or concept), and how, just as the estimate of an object for the sake of a *cognition* generally has universal rules, the delight of any one person may be pronounced as a rule for every other.

Now if this universal validity is not to be based on a
30 collection of votes and interrogation of others as to what sort of sensations they experience, but is to rest, as it were, upon an autonomy of the Subject passing judgement on the feeling

of pleasure (in the given representation), i.e. upon his own taste, and yet is also not to be derived from concepts ; then it follows that such a judgement—and such the judgement of taste in fact is—has a double and also logical peculiarity. For, *first*, it has universal validity *a priori*, yet without having a logical universality according to concepts, but only the universality of a singular judgement. *Secondly*, it has a necessity, (which must invariably rest upon *a priori* grounds,) but one which depends upon no *a priori* proofs by the representation of which it would be competent to enforce the assent which the judgement of taste demands of every one.

The solution of these logical peculiarities, which distinguish a judgement of taste from all cognitive judgements, will of itself suffice for a Deduction of this strange faculty, provided we abstract at the outset from all content of the judgement, viz. from the feeling of pleasure, and merely compare the aesthetic form with the form of objective judgements as prescribed by logic. We shall first try, with the help of examples, to illustrate and bring out these characteristic properties of taste.

§ 32

First peculiarity of the judgement of taste.

THE judgement of taste determines its object in respect of delight (as a thing of beauty) with a claim to the agreement of *every one*, just as if it were objective.

To say : This flower is beautiful, is tantamount to repeating its own proper claim to the delight of every one.   The agreeableness of its smell gives it no claim at all.   One man revels in it, but it gives another a headache.   Now what else are we to suppose from this than that its beauty is to be taken for a property of the flower itself which does not adapt itself to the diversity of heads and the individual senses of the multitude, but to which they must adapt themselves, if they are going to pass judgement upon it. And yet this is not the way the matter stands. For the judgement of taste consists precisely in a thing being called beautiful solely in respect of that quality in which it adapts itself to our mode of taking it in.

5 Besides, every judgement which is to show the taste of the individual, is required to be an independent judgement of the individual himself. There must be no need of groping about among other people's judgements and getting previous instruction from their delight in or aversion to the same object.
10 Consequently his judgement should be given out *a priori*, and not as an imitation relying on the general pleasure a thing gives as a matter of fact. One would think, however, that a judgement *a priori* must involve a concept of the object for the cognition of which it contains the principle. But the judge-
15 ment of taste is not founded on concepts, and is in no way a cognition, but only an aesthetic judgement.

Hence it is that a youthful poet refuses to allow himself to be dissuaded from the conviction that his poem is beautiful, either by the judgement of the public or of his friends. And
20 even if he lends them an ear, he does so, not because he has now come to a different judgement, but because, though the whole public, at least so far as his work is concerned, should have false taste, he still, in his desire for recognition, finds good reason to accommodate himself to the popular error (even against
25 his own judgement). It is only in aftertime, when his judgement has been sharpened by exercise, that of his own free will and accord he deserts his former judgements—behaving in just the same way as with those of his judgements which depend wholly upon reason. Taste lays claim simply to autonomy. To
30 make the judgements of others the determining ground of one's own would be heteronomy.

The fact that we recommend the works of the ancients as models, and rightly too, and call their authors classical, as constituting a sort of nobility among writers that leads

the way and thereby gives laws to the people, seems to indicate
a posteriori sources of taste, and to contradict the autonomy
of taste in each individual.   But we might just as well say that
283 the ancient mathematicians, who, to this day, are looked upon
as the almost indispensable models of perfect thoroughness and 5
elegance in synthetic methods, prove that reason also is on our
part only imitative, and that it is incompetent with the deepest
intuition to produce of itself rigorous proofs by means of the
construction of concepts.   There is no employment of our
powers, no matter how free, not even of reason itself, (which 10
must create all its judgements from the common *a priori*
source,) which, if each individual had always to start afresh
with the crude equipment of his natural state, would not get
itself involved in blundering attempts, did not those of others
lie before it as a warning.   Not that predecessors make those 15
who follow in their steps mere imitators, but by their methods
they set others upon the track of seeking in themselves for
the principles, and so of adopting their own, often better,
course.   Even in religion—where undoubtedly every one has
to derive his rule of conduct from himself, seeing that he him 20
self remains responsible for it, and, when he goes wrong, cannot
shift the blame upon others as teachers or leaders—general
precepts learned at the feet either of priests or philosophers, or
even drawn from one's own resources, are never so efficacious
as an example of virtue or holiness, which, historically por- 25
trayed, does not dispense with the autonomy of virtue drawn
from the spontaneous and original idea of morality (*a priori*),
or convert this into a mechanical process of imitation.   *Following* which has reference to a precedent, and not imitation, is
the proper expression for all influence which the products of 30
an exemplary *author* may exert upon others—and this means
no more than going to the same sources for a creative work
as those to which he went for his creations, and learning from
one's predecessor no more than the mode of availing oneself

of such sources. Taste, just because its judgement cannot be determined by concepts or precepts, is among all faculties and talents the very one that stands most in need of examples of what has in the course of culture maintained itself longest in
5 esteem. Thus it avoids an early lapse into crudity, and a return to the rudeness of its earliest efforts.

§ 33   284

Second peculiarity of the judgement of taste.

PROOFS are of no avail whatever for determining the judge-
10 ment of taste, and in this connexion matters stand just as they would were that judgement simply *subjective.*

If any one does not think a building, view, or poem beautiful, then, *in the first place* he refuses, so far as his inmost conviction goes, to allow approval to be wrung from him by a
15 hundred voices all lauding it to the skies. Of course he may affect to be pleased with it, so as not to be considered as wanting in taste. He may even begin to harbour doubts as to whether he has formed his taste upon an acquaintance with a sufficient number of objects of a particular kind (just as one
20 who in the distance recognizes, as he believes, something as a wood, which every one else regards as a town, becomes doubtful of the judgement of his own eyesight). But, for all that, he clearly perceives that the approval of others affords no valid proof, available for the estimate of beauty. He recog-
25 nizes that others, perchance, may see and observe for him, and that, what many have seen in one and the same way may, for the purpose of a theoretical, and therefore logical judgement, serve as an adequate ground of proof for him, albeit he believes he saw otherwise, but that what has pleased others can never serve him
30 as the ground of an aesthetic judgement. The judgement of others, where unfavourable to ours, may, no doubt, rightly make

us suspicious in respect of our own, but convince us that it is
wrong it never can.   Hence there is no empirical *ground of
proof* that can coerce any one's judgement of taste.

In the second place, a proof *a priori* according to definite rules
is still less capable of determining the judgement as to beauty. 5
If any one reads me his poem, or brings me to a play, which, all
said and done, fails to commend itself to my taste, then let him
adduce *Batteux* or *Lessing*, or still older and more famous
critics of taste, with all the host of rules laid down by them, as
a proof of the beauty of his poem ; let certain passages particu- 10
larly displeasing to me accord completely with the rules of
beauty, (as set out by these critics and universally recognized) :
I stop my ears : I do not want to hear any reasons or any argu-
ing about the matter.   I would prefer to suppose that those
rules of the critics were at fault, or at least have no application, 15
than to allow my judgement to be determined by *a priori*
285 proofs.   I take my stand on the ground that my judgement is
to be one of taste, and not one of understanding or reason.

This would appear to be one of the chief reasons why this
faculty of aesthetic judgement has been given the name of 20
taste.   For a man may recount to me all the ingredients of a
dish, and observe of each and every one of them that it is just
what I like, and, in addition, rightly commend the wholesome-
ness of the food ; yet I am deaf to all these arguments.   I try
the dish with *my own* tongue and palate, and I pass judgement 25
according to their verdict (not according to universal principles).

As a matter of fact the judgement of taste is invariably laid
down as a singular judgement upon the Object.   The understanding can, from the comparison of the Object, in point of
delight, with the judgements of others, form a universal judge- 30
ment, e. g. ' All tulips are beautiful '.   But that judgement is
then not one of taste, but is a logical judgement which converts
the reference of an Object to our taste into a predicate belonging to things of a certain kind.   But it is only the judgement

whereby I regard an individual given tulip as beautiful, i.e. regard my delight in it as of universal validity, that is a judgement of taste. Its peculiarity, however, consists in the fact that, although it has merely subjective validity, still it extends its
5 claims to *all* Subjects, as unreservedly as it would if it were an objective judgement, resting on grounds of cognition and capable of being proved to demonstration.

§ 34

An objective principle of taste is not possible.

10 A PRINCIPLE of taste would mean a fundamental premiss under the condition of which one might subsume the concept of an object, and then, by a syllogism, draw the inference that it is beautiful. That, however, is absolutely impossible. For I must feel the pleasure immediately in the representation
15 of the object, and I cannot be talked into it by any grounds of proof. Thus although critics, as Hume says, are able to reason more plausibly than cooks, they must still share the same fate. For the determining ground of their judgement they are not able to look to the force of demonstrations, but
20 only to the reflection of the Subject upon his own state (of 286 pleasure or displeasure), to the exclusion of precepts and rules.

There is, however, a matter upon which it is competent for critics to exercise their subtlety, and upon which they ought to do so, so long as it tends to the rectification and extension
25 of our judgements of taste. But that matter is not one of exhibiting the determining ground of aesthetic judgements of this kind in a universally applicable formula—which is impossible. Rather is it the investigation of the faculties of cognition and their function in these judgements, and the illustration, by the
30 analysis of examples, of their mutual subjective finality, the form of which in a given representation has been shown above to constitute the beauty of their object. Hence with regard to

the representation whereby an Object is given, the Critique of
Taste itself is only subjective ; viz. it is the art or science of
reducing the mutual relation of the understanding and the
imagination in the given representation (without reference to
antecedent sensation or concept), consequently their accordance 5
or discordance, to rules, and of determining them with regard
to their conditions.   It is *art* if it only illustrates this by
examples ; it is *science* if it deduces the possibility of such an
estimate from the nature of these faculties as faculties of knowledge in general.   It is only with the latter, as Transcendental 10
Critique, that we have here any concern.   Its proper scope
is the development and justification of the subjective principle
of taste, as an *a priori* principle of judgement.   As an art,
Critique merely looks to the physiological (here psychological),
and, consequently, empirical rules, according to which in actual 15
fact taste proceeds, (passing by the question of their possibility,)
and seeks to apply them in estimating its objects.   The latter
Critique criticizes the products of fine art, just as the former
does the faculty of estimating them.

§ 35   20

The principle of taste is the subjective principle of the general power of judgement.

THE judgement of taste is differentiated from logical judgement by the fact that, whereas the latter subsumes a representation under a concept of the Object, the judgement of 25
taste does not subsume under a concept at all—for, if it did,
necessary and universal approval would be capable of being
enforced by proofs.   And yet it does bear this resemblance
to the logical judgement, that it asserts a universality and
287 necessity, not, however, according to concepts of the Object, 30
but a universality and necessity that are, consequently, merely
subjective.   Now the concepts in a judgement constitute its

content (what belongs to the cognition of the Object). But the judgement of taste is not determinable by means of concepts. Hence it can only have its ground in the subjective formal condition of a judgement in general. The subjective
5 condition of all judgements is the judging faculty itself, or judgement. Employed in respect of a representation whereby an object is given, this requires the harmonious accordance of two powers of representation. These are, the imagination (for the intuition and the arrangement of the manifold of
10 intuition), and the understanding (for the concept as a representation of the unity of this arrangement). Now, since no concept of the Object underlies the judgement here, it can consist only in the subsumption of the imagination itself (in the case of a representation whereby an object is given) under
15 the conditions enabling the understanding in general to advance from the intuition to concepts. That is to say, since the freedom of the imagination consists precisely in the fact that it schematizes without a concept, the judgement of taste must found upon a mere sensation of the mutually
20 quickening activity of the imagination in its *freedom*, and of the understanding with its *conformity to law*. It must therefore rest upon a feeling that allows the object to be estimated by the finality of the representation (by which an object is given) for the furtherance of the cognitive faculties in their
25 free play. Taste, then, as a subjective power of judgement, contains a principle of subsumption, not of intuitions under *concepts*, but of the *faculty* of intuitions or presentations, i.e. of the imagination, under the *faculty* of concepts, i.e. the understanding, so far as the former *in its freedom* accords with the
30 latter *in its conformity to law*.

For the discovery of this title by means of a Deduction of judgements of taste, we can only avail ourselves of the guidance of the formal peculiarities of judgements of this kind, and consequently the mere consideration of their logical form.

§ 36

The problem of a Deduction of judgements of taste.

To form a cognitive judgement we may immediately connect
with the perception of an object the concept of an object in
288 general, the empirical predicates of which are contained in 5
that perception.   In this way a judgement of experience is
produced.   Now this judgement rests on the foundation of
a priori concepts of the synthetical unity of the manifold of
intuition enabling it to be thought as the determination of an
Object.   These concepts (the categories) call for a Deduction, 10
and such was supplied in the Critique of Pure Reason.   That
Deduction enabled us to solve the problem, How are synthetical *a priori* cognitive judgements possible?   This problem had,
accordingly, to do with the *a priori* principles of pure understanding and its theoretical judgements.   15

But we may also immediately connect with a perception a
feeling of pleasure (or displeasure) and a delight attending the
representation of the Object and serving it instead of a predicate.   In this way there arises a judgement which is aesthetic
and not cognitive.   Now, if such a judgement is not merely one 20
of sensation, but a formal judgement of reflection that exacts
this delight from every one as necessary, something must lie at
its basis as its *a priori* principle.   This principle may, indeed,
be a mere subjective one, (supposing an objective one should be
impossible for judgements of this kind,) but, even as such, it 25
requires a Deduction to make it intelligible how an aesthetic
judgement can lay claim to necessity.   That, now, is what lies
at the bottom of the problem upon which we are at present
engaged, i.e. How are judgements of taste possible?   This
problem, therefore, is concerned with the *a priori* principles 30
of pure judgement in *aesthetic* judgements, i.e. not those in
which (as in theoretical judgements) it has merely to subsume
under objective concepts of understanding, and in which it

comes under a law, but rather those in which it is itself, subjectively, object as well as law.

We may also put the problem in this way : How is a judgement possible which, going merely upon the individual's *own* feeling of pleasure in an object independent of the concept of it, estimates this as a pleasure attached to the representation of the same Object *in every other individual,* and does so *a priori,* i. e. without being allowed to wait and see if other people will be of the same mind ?

It is easy to see that judgements of taste are synthetic, for they go beyond the concept and even the intuition of the Object, and join as predicate to that intuition something which is not even a cognition at all, namely, the feeling of pleasure (or displeasure).   But, although the predicate (the *personal* pleasure that is connected with the representation) is empirical, still we need not go further than what is involved in the expressions of their claim to see that, so far as concerns the agreement required of *every one,* they are *a priori* judge- 289 ments, or mean to pass for such.   This problem of the Critique of Judgement, therefore, is part of the general problem of transcendental philosophy : How are synthetic *a priori* judgements possible ?

§ 37

What exactly it is, that is asserted a priori *of an object in a judgement of taste.*

THE immediate synthesis of the representation of an object with pleasure can only be a matter of internal perception, and, were nothing more than this sought to be indicated, would only yield a mere empirical judgement.   For with no representation can I *a priori* connect a determinate feeling (of pleasure or displeasure) except where I rely upon the basis of an *a priori* principle in reason determining the will. The truth is that the pleasure (in the moral feeling) is the consequence of the determination of the will by the principle. It cannot, therefore, be compared with the pleasure in taste. For it requires a determinate concept of a law: whereas the pleasure in taste has to be connected 5 immediately with the simple estimate prior to any concept. For the same reason, also, all judgements of taste are singular judgements, for they unite their predicatè of delight, not to a concept, but to a given singular empirical representation.

Hence, in a judgement of taste, what is represented *a priori* 10 as a universal rule for the judgement and as valid for every one, is not the pleasure but the *universal validity* of this pleasure perceived, as it is, to be combined in the mind with the mere estimate of an object. A judgement to the effect that it is with pleasure that I perceive and estimate some object is an 15 empirical judgement. But if it asserts that I think the object beautiful, i. e. that I may attribute that delight to every one as necessary, it is then an *a priori* judgement.

§ 38

Deduction of judgements of taste. 20

ADMITTING that in a pure judgement of taste the delight in the object is connected with the mere estimate of its form, then what we feel to be associated in the mind with the representation 290 of the object is nothing else `than its subjective finality for judgement. Since, now, in respect of the formal rules of 25 estimating, apart from all matter (whether sensation or concept), judgement can only be directed to the subjective conditions of its employment in general, (which is not restricted to the particular mode of sense nor to a particular concept of the understanding,) and so can only be directed to that subjective 30 factor which we may presuppose in all men (as requisite for a possible experience generally), it follows that the accordance of a representation with these conditions of the judgement must

admit of being assumed valid *a priori* for every one. In other words, we are warranted in exacting from every one the pleasure or subjective finality of the representation in respect of the relation of the cognitive faculties engaged in the estimate of a
5 sensible object in general.[1]

Remark.

What makes this Deduction so easy is that it is spared the necessity of having to justify the objective reality of a concept. For beauty is not a concept of the Object, and the judgement
10 of taste is not a cognitive judgement. All that it holds out for is that we are justified in presupposing that the same subjective conditions of judgement which we find in ourselves are universally present in every man, and further that we have rightly subsumed the given Object under these conditions.
15 The latter, no doubt, has to face unavoidable difficulties which do not affect the logical judgement. (For there the subsumption is under concepts ; whereas in the aesthetic judgement it is under a mere sensible relation of the imagination and under- 291 standing mutually harmonizing with one another in the re-
20 presented form of the Object, in which case the subsumption may easily prove fallacious.) But this in no way detracts from

---

[1] In order to be justified in claiming universal agreement for an aesthetic judgement merely resting on subjective grounds it is sufficient to assume : (1) that the subjective conditions of this faculty of aesthetic
25 judgement are identical with all men in what concerns the relation of the cognitive faculties, there brought into action, with a view to a cognition in general. This must be true, as otherwise men would be incapable of communicating their representations or even their knowledge ; (2) that the judgement has paid regard merely to this relation (consequently
30 merely to the *formal condition* of the faculty of judgement), and is pure, i. e. is free from confusion either with concepts of the Object or sensations as determining grounds. If any mistake is made in this latter point this only touches the incorrect application to a particular case of the right which a law gives us, and does not do away with the right
35 generally.

the legitimacy of the claim of the judgement to count upon universal agreement—a claim which amounts to no more than this : the correctness of the principle of judging validly for every one upon subjective grounds. For as to the difficulty and uncertainty concerning the correctness of the subsumption 5 under that principle, it no more casts a doubt upon the legitimacy of the claim to this validity on the part of an aesthetic judgement generally, or, therefore, upon the principle itself, than the mistakes (though not so often or easily incurred), to which the subsumption of the logical judgement under its 10 principle is similarly liable, can render the latter principle, which is objective, open to doubt.   But if the question were : How is it possible to assume *a priori* that nature is a complex of objects of taste ? the problem would then have reference to teleology, because it would have to be regarded as an end of 15 nature belonging essentially to its concept that it should exhibit forms that are final for our judgement.   But the correctness of this assumption may still be seriously questioned, while the actual existence of beauties of nature is patent to experience.   20

§ 39

The communicability of a sensation.

SENSATION, as the real in perception, where referred to knowledge, is called organic sensation and its specific Quality may be represented as completely communicable to others in 25 a like mode, provided we assume that every one has a like sense to our own.   This, however, is an absolutely inadmissible presupposition in the case of an organic sensation.   Thus a person who is without a sense of smell cannot have a sensation of this kind communicated to him, and, even if he does not 30 suffer from this deficiency, we still cannot be certain that he gets precisely the same sensation from a flower that we get from it. But still more divergent must we consider men to be in respect of the *agreeableness* or *disagreeableness* derived from the sensation of one and the same object of sense, and it is absolutely out of the question to require that pleasure in such objects should be acknowledged by every one. Pleasure of this kind, since it enters into the mind through sense—our rôle, 292 therefore, being a passive one—may be called the pleasure of *enjovment*.

On the other hand delight in an action on the score of its moral character is not a pleasure of enjoyment, but one of self-asserting activity and in this coming up to the idea of what it is meant to be. But this feeling, which is called the moral feeling, requires concepts, and is the presentation of a finality, not free, but according to law. It, therefore, admits of communication only through the instrumentality of reason and, if the pleasure is to be of the same kind for every one, by means of very determinate practical concepts of reason.

The pleasure in the sublime in nature, as one of rationalizing contemplation, lays claim also to universal participation, but still it presupposes another feeling, that, namely, of our super-sensible sphere, which feeling, however obscure it may be, has a moral foundation. But there is absolutely no authority for my presupposing that others will pay attention to this, and take a delight in beholding the uncouth dimensions of nature, (one that in truth cannot be ascribed to its aspect, which is terrifying rather than otherwise). Nevertheless, having regard to the fact that attention ought to be paid upon every appropriate occasion to this moral birthright, we may still demand that delight from every one ; but we can do so only through the moral law, which, in its turn, rests upon concepts of reason.

The pleasure in the beautiful is, on the other hand, neither a pleasure of enjoyment nor of an activity according to law, nor yet one of a rationalizing contemplation according to ideas, but rather of mere reflection. Without any guiding-line of end or

principle this pleasure attends the ordinary apprehension of an
object by means of the imagination, as the faculty of intuition,
but with a reference to the understanding as faculty of concepts,
and through the operation of a process of judgement which has
also to be invoked in order to obtain the commonest experience. 5
In the latter case, however, its functions are directed to perceiving an empirical objective concept, whereas in the former
(in the aesthetic mode of estimating) merely to perceiving the
adequacy of the representation for engaging both faculties of
knowledge in their freedom in an harmonious (subjectively- 10
final) employment, i.e. to feeling with pleasure the subjective
bearings of the representation.   This pleasure must of necessity
depend for every one upon the same conditions, seeing that
they are the subjective conditions of the possibility of a cognition in general, and the proportion of these cognitive faculties 15
293 which is requisite for taste is requisite also for ordinary sound
understanding, the presence of which we are entitled to presuppose in every one.   And, for this reason also, one who judges
with taste, (provided he does not make a mistake as to this
consciousness, and does not take the matter for the form, or 20
charm for beauty,) can impute the subjective finality, i.e. his
delight in the Object, to every one else, and suppose his feeling
universally communicable, and that, too, without the mediation
of concepts.

§ 40   25

Taste as a kind of sensus communis.

THE name of sense is often given to judgement where what
attracts attention is not so much its reflective act as merely its
result.   So we speak of a sense of truth, of a sense of propriety,
or of justice, &c.   And yet, of course, we know, or at least 30
ought well enough to know, that a sense cannot be the true abode
of these concepts, not to speak of its being competent, even in

the slightest degree, to pronounce universal rules. On the
contrary, we recognize that a representation of this kind,
be it of truth, propriety, beauty, or justice, could never enter
our thoughts were we not able to raise ourselves above the
5 level of the senses to that of higher faculties of cognition.
Common human understanding which, as mere sound (not yet
cultivated) understanding, is looked upon as the least we can
expect from any one claiming the name of man, has therefore the doubtful honour of having the name of common sense
10 (*sensus communis*) bestowed upon it ; and bestowed, too, in an
acceptation of the word *common* (not merely in our own language,
where it actually has a double meaning, but also in many
others) which makes it amount to what is *vulgar*—what is every-
where to be met with—a quality which by no means confers
15 credit or distinction upon its possessor.

However, by the name *sensus communis* is to be understood
the idea of a *public* sense, i. e. a critical faculty which in its
reflective act takes account (*a priori*) of the mode of representation of every one else, in order, *as it were*, to weigh its judge-
20 ment with the collective reason of mankind, and thereby avoid
the illusion arising from subjective and personal conditions
which could readily be taken for objective, an illusion that
would exert a prejudicial influence upon its judgement.   This 294
is accomplished by weighing the judgement, not so much with
25 actual, as rather with the merely possible, judgements of others,
and by putting ourselves in the position of every one else, as
the result of a mere abstraction from the limitations which
contingently affect our own estimate.   This, in turn, is effected
by so far as possible letting go the element of matter, i. e.
30 sensation, in our general state of representative activity, and
confining attention to the formal peculiarities of our representation or general state of representative activity.   Now it
may seem that this operation of reflection is too artificial to be
attributed to the faculty which we call *common* sense.   But this

is an appearance due only to its expression in abstract formulae. In itself nothing is more natural than to abstract from charm and emotion where one is looking for a judgement intended to serve as a universal rule.

While the following maxims of common human understand- 5 ing do not properly come in here as constituent parts of the Critique of Taste, they may still serve to elucidate its fundamental propositions. They are these : (1) to think for oneself; (2) to think from the standpoint of every one else ; (3) always to think consistently. The first is the maxim of *unprejudiced* 10 thought, the second that of *enlarged* thought, the third that of *consistent* thought. The first is the maxim of a never-*passive* reason. To be given to such passivity, consequently to heteronomy of reason, is called *prejudice* ; and the greatest of all prejudices is that of fancying nature not to be subject to rules 15 which the understanding by virtue of its own essential law lays at its basis, i. e. *superstition*. Emancipation from superstition is called *enlightenment* ;[1] for although this term applies also to emancipation from prejudices generally, still superstition deserves pre-eminently (*in sensu eminenti*) to be called a prejudice. For 20 the condition of blindness into which superstition puts one, which 295 it as much as demands from one as an obligation, makes the need of being led by others, and consequently the passive state of the reason, pre-eminently conspicuous. As to the second maxim belonging to our habits of thought, we have quite got into the way 25

[1] We readily see that enlightenment, while easy, no doubt, *in thesi, in hypothesi* is difficult and slow of realization. For not to be passive with one's reason, but always to be self legislative is doubtless quite an easy matter for a man who only desires to be adapted to his essential end, and does not seek to know what is beyond his understanding. But as the tendency 30 in the latter direction is hardly avoidable, and others are always coming and promising with full assurance that they are able to satisfy one's curiosity, it must be very difficult to preserve or restore in the mind (and particularly in the public mind) that merely negative attitude (which constitutes enlightenment proper). 35

of calling a man narrow (*narrow*, as opposed to being *of enlarged
mind*) whose talents fall short of what is required for employment
upon work of any magnitude (especially that involving intensity).
But the question here is not one of the faculty of cognition, but
5 of the *mental habit* of making a final use of it.   This, however
small the range and degree to which a man's natural endowments
extend, still indicates a man of *enlarged mind* : if he detaches
himself from the subjective personal conditions of his judgement, which cramp the minds of so many others, and reflects
10 upon his own judgement from a *universal standpoint* (which
he can only determine by shifting his ground to the standpoint
of others).   The third maxim—that, namely, of *consistent*
thought—is the hardest of attainment, and is only attainable by
the union of both the former, and after constant attention to
15 them has made one at home in their observance.   We may
say : the first of these is the maxim of understanding, the second
that of judgement, the third that of reason.

I resume the thread of the discussion interrupted by the
above digression, and I say that taste can with more justice
20 be called a *sensus communis* than can sound understanding ;
and that the aesthetic, rather than the intellectual, judgement
can bear the name of a public sense,[1] i. e. taking it that we are
prepared to use the word 'sense' of an effect that mere reflection has upon the mind ; for then by sense we mean the
25 feeling of pleasure.   We might even define taste as the faculty
of estimating what makes our feeling in a given representation
universally communicable without the mediation of a concept.

The aptitude of men for communicating their thoughts
requires, also, a relation between the imagination and the
30 understanding, in order to connect intuitions with concepts,
and concepts, in turn, with intuitions, which both unite in
cognition.   But there the agreement of both mental powers is

---

[1] Taste may be designated a *sensus communis aestheticus*, common
human understanding a *sensus communis logicus.*

296 *according to law*, and under the constraint of definite concepts. Only when the imagination in its freedom stirs the understanding, and the understanding apart from concepts puts the imagination into regular play, does the representation communicate itself not as thought, but as an internal feeling of a final state of the mind. 5

Taste is, therefore, the faculty of forming an *a priori* estimate of the communicability of the feelings that, without the mediation of a concept, are connected with a given representation.

Supposing, now, that we could assume that the mere universal communicability of our feeling must of itself carry with it 10 an interest for us (an assumption, however, which we are not entitled to draw as a conclusion from the character of a merely reflective judgement), we should then be in a position to explain how the feeling in the judgement of taste comes to be exacted from every one as a sort of duty. 15

§ 41

The empirical interest in the beautiful.

ABUNDANT proof has been given above to show that the judgement of taste by which something is declared beautiful must have no interest *as its determining ground*. But it does 20 not follow from this that after it has once been posited as a pure aesthetic judgement, an interest cannot then enter into combination with it. This combination, however, can never be anything but indirect. Taste must, that is to say, first of all be represented in conjunction with something else, if the delight 25 attending the mere reflection upon an object is to admit of having further conjoined with it *a pleasure in the real existence* of the object (as that wherein all interest consists). For the saying, *a posse ad esse non valet consequentia*, which is applied to cognitive judgements, holds good here in the case of aesthetic 30 judgements. Now this 'something else' may be something

empirical, such as an inclination proper to the nature of human beings, or it may be something intellectual, as a property of the will whereby it admits of rational determination *a priori*. Both of these involve a delight in the existence of the Object, and so
5 can lay the foundation for an interest in what has already pleased of itself and without regard to any interest whatsoever.

The empirical interest in the beautiful exists only in *society*. And if we admit that the impulse to society is natural to mankind, and that the suitability for and the propensity towards it, i. e.
10 *sociability*, is a property essential to the requirements of man as 297 a creature intended for society, and one, therefore, that belongs to *humanity*, it is inevitable that we should also look upon taste in the light of a faculty for estimating whatever enables us to communicate even our *feeling* to every one else, and hence as
15 a means of promoting that upon which the natural inclination of every one is set.

With no one to take into account but himself a man abandoned on a desert island would not adorn either himself or his hut, nor would he look for flowers, and still less plant them, with
20 the object of providing himself with personal adornments. Only in society does it occur to him to be not merely a man, but a man refined after the manner of his kind (the beginning of civilization)—for that is the estimate formed of one who has the bent and turn for communicating his pleasure to others, and who
25 is not quite satisfied with an Object unless his feeling of delight in it can be shared in communion with others. Further, a regard to universal communicability is a thing which every one expects and requires from every one else, just as if it were part of an original compact dictated by humanity itself. And thus, no
30 doubt, at first only charms, e.g. colours for painting oneself (roucou among the Caribs and cinnabar among the Iroquois), or flowers, sea-shells, beautifully coloured feathers, then, in the course of time, also beautiful forms (as in canoes, wearing-apparel, &c.) which convey no gratification, i.e. delight of enjoyment,

become of moment in society and attract a considerable interest. Eventually, when civilization has reached its height it makes this work of communication almost the main business of refined inclination, and the entire value of sensations is placed in the degree to which they permit of universal communication. At this stage, then, even where the pleasure which each one has in an object is but insignificant and possesses of itself no conspicuous interest, still the idea of its universal communicability almost indefinitely augments its value.

This interest, indirectly attached to the beautiful by the inclination towards society, and, consequently, empirical, is, however, of no importance for us here. For that to which we have alone to look is what can have a bearing *a priori*, even though indirect, upon the judgement of taste. For, if even in this form an associated interest should betray itself, taste would then reveal a transition on the part of our critical faculty from the enjoyment of sense to the moral feeling. This would not merely mean that we should be supplied with a more effectual guide for the final employment of taste, but taste would further be presented as a link in the chain of the human faculties *a priori* upon which all legislation must depend. This much may certainly be said of the empirical interest in objects of taste, and in taste itself, that as taste thus pays homage to inclination, however refined, such interest will nevertheless readily fuse also with all inclinations and passions, which in society attain to their greatest variety and highest degree, and the interest in the beautiful, if this is made its ground, can but afford a very ambiguous transition from the agreeable to the good. We have reason, however, to inquire whether this transition may not still in some way be furthered by means of taste when taken in its purity.

§ 42

The intellectual interest in the beautiful.

IT has been with the best intentions that those who love to see in the ultimate end of humanity, namely the morally good, 5 the goal of all activities to which men are impelled by the inner bent of their nature, have regarded it as a mark of a good moral character to take an interest in the beautiful generally. But they have, not without reason, been contradicted by others who appeal to the fact of experience, that *virtuosi* in matters of 10 taste, being not alone often, but one might say as a general rule, vain, capricious, and addicted to injurious passions, could perhaps more rarely than others lay claim to any pre-eminent attachment to moral principles.   And so it would seem, not only that the feeling for the beautiful is specifically different 15 from the moral feeling (which as a matter of fact is the case), but also that the interest which we may combine with it, will hardly consort with the moral, and certainly not on grounds of inner affinity.

Now I willingly admit that the interest in the *beautiful of art* 20 (including under this heading the artificial use of natural beauties for personal adornment, and so from vanity) gives no evidence at all of a habit of mind attached to the morally good, or even inclined that way.   But, on the other hand, I do maintain that to take an *immediate interest* in the beauty of *nature* (not 25 merely to have taste in estimating it) is always a mark of a good soul ; and that, where this interest is habitual, it is at least 299 indicative of a temper of mind favourable to the moral feeling that it should readily associate itself with the *contemplation of nature*.   It must, however, be borne in mind that I mean 30 to refer strictly to the beautiful *forms* of nature, and to put to one side the *charms* which she is wont so lavishly to combine with them ; because, though the interest in these is no doubt immediate, it is nevertheless empirical.

One who alone (and without any intention of communicating his observations to others) regards the beautiful form of a wild flower, a bird, an insect, or the like, out of admiration and love of them, and being loath to let them escape him in nature, even at the risk of some misadventure to himself—so far from 5 there being any prospect of advantage to him—such a one takes an immediate, and in fact intellectual, interest in the beauty of nature. This means that he is not alone pleased with nature's product in respect of its form, but is also pleased at its existence, and is so without any charm of sense 10 having a share in the matter, or without his associating with it any end whatsoever.

In this connexion, however, it is of note that were we to play a trick on our lover of the beautiful, and plant in the ground artificial flowers (which can be made so as to look just like 15 natural ones), and perch artfully carved birds on the branches of trees, and he were to find out how he had been taken in, the immediate interest which these things previously had for him would at once vanish—though, perhaps, a different interest might intervene in its stead, that, namely, of vanity in decorat- 20 ing his room with them for the eyes of others. The fact is that our intuition and reflection must have as their concomitant the thought that the beauty in question is nature's handiwork ; and this is the sole basis of the immediate interest that is taken in it. Failing this we are either left with a bare judgement of 25 taste void of all interest whatever, or else only with one that is combined with an interest that is mediate, involving, namely, a reference to society ; which latter affords no reliable indication of morally good habits of thought.

The superiority which natural beauty has over that of art, 30 even where it is excelled by the latter in point of form, in yet being alone able to awaken an immediate interest, accords with the refined and well-grounded habits of thought of all men who have cultivated their moral feeling. If a man with taste enough

to judge of works of fine art with the greatest correctness and refinement readily quits the room in which he meets with those 300 beauties that minister to vanity or, at least, social joys, and betakes himself to the beautiful in nature, so that he may there
5 find as it were a feast for his soul in a train of thought which he can never completely evolve, we will then regard this his choice even with veneration, and give him credit for a beautiful soul, to which no connoisseur or art collector can lay claim on the score of the interest which his objects have for him.—Here,
10 now, are two kinds of Objects which in the judgement of mere taste could scarcely contend with one another for a superiority. What then, is the distinction that makes us hold them in such different esteem?

We have a faculty of judgement which is merely aesthetic—
15 a faculty of judging of forms without the aid of concepts, and of finding, in the mere estimate of them, a delight that we at the same time make into a rule for every one, without this judgement being founded on an interest, or yet producing one.—
On the other hand we have also a faculty of intellectual
20 judgement for the mere forms of practical maxims, (so far as they are of themselves qualified for universal legislation,)—a faculty of determining an *a priori* delight, which we make into a law for every one, without our judgement being founded on any interest, *though here it produces one.* The pleasure or dis-
25 pleasure in the former judgement is called that of taste; the latter is called that of the moral feeling.

But, now, reason is further interested in ideas (for which in our moral feeling it brings about an immediate interest,) having also objective reality. That is to say, it is of interest to reason
30 that nature should at least show a trace or give a hint that it contains in itself some ground or other for assuming a uniform accordance of its products with our wholly disinterested delight (a delight which we cognize *a priori* as a law for every one without being able to ground it upon proofs). That being so,

reason must take an interest in every manifestation on the part
of nature of some such accordance.   Hence the mind cannot
reflect on the beauty of *nature* without at the same time finding
its interest engaged. But this interest is akin to the moral. One,
then, who takes such an interest in the beautiful in nature can 5
only do so in so far as he has previously set his interest deep
301 in the foundations of the morally good.   On these grounds we
have reason for presuming the presence of at least the germ of
a good moral disposition in the case of a man to whom the
beauty of nature is a matter of immediate interest.   10

It will be said that this interpretation of aesthetic judgements
on the basis of kinship with our moral feeling has far too studied
an appearance to be accepted as the true construction of the
cypher in which nature speaks to us figuratively in its beautiful
forms.   But, first of all, this immediate interest in the beauty 15
of nature is not in fact common.   It is peculiar to those whose
habits of thought are already trained to the good or else are
eminently susceptible of such training ; and under these circumstances the analogy in which the pure judgement of taste that,
without relying upon any interest, gives us a feeling of delight, 20
and at the same time represents it *a priori* as proper to mankind in general, stands to the moral judgement that does just
the same from concepts, is one which, without any clear, subtle,
and deliberate reflection, conduces to a like immediate interest
being taken in the objects of the former judgement as in those 25
of the latter—with this one difference, that the interest in the
first case is free, while in the latter it is one founded on objective laws.   In addition to this there is our admiration of nature
which in her beautiful products displays herself as art, not as
mere matter of chance, but, as it were, designedly, according to 30
a law-directed arrangement, and as finality apart from any
end.   As we never meet with such an end outside ourselves,
we naturally look for it in ourselves, and, in fact, in that which
constitutes the ultimate end of our existence —the moral side

of our being. (The inquiry into the ground of the possibility of such a natural finality will, however, first come under discussion in the Teleology.)

The fact that the delight in beautiful art does not, in the pure judgement of taste, involve an immediate interest, as does that in beautiful nature, may be readily explained. For the former is either such an imitation of the latter as goes the length of deceiving us, in which case it acts upon us in the character of a natural beauty, which we take it to be; or else it is an intentional art obviously directed to our delight. In the latter case, however, the delight in the product would, it is true, be brought about immediately by taste, but there would be nothing but a mediate interest in the cause that lay beneath—an interest, namely, in an art only capable of interesting by its end, and never in itself. It will, perhaps, be said that this is also the case where an Object of nature only interests by its beauty so far as a moral idea is brought into partnership therewith. But it is not the object that is of immediate interest, but rather the inherent character of the beauty qualifying it for such a partnership—a character, therefore, that belongs to the very essence of beauty.

The charms in natural beauty, which are to be found blended, as it were, so frequently with beauty of form, belong either to the modifications of light (in colouring) or of sound (in tones). For these are the only sensations which permit not merely of a feeling of the senses, but also of reflection upon the form of these modifications of sense, and so embody as it were a language in which nature speaks to us and which has the semblance of a higher meaning. Thus the white colour of the lily seems to dispose the mind to ideas of innocence, and the other seven colours, following the series from the red to the violet, similarly to ideas of (1) sublimity, (2) courage, (3) candour, (4) amiability, (5) modesty, (6) constancy, (7) tenderness. The bird's song tells of joyousness

and contentment with its existence.   At least so we interpret
nature—whether such be its purpose or not.   But it is the
indispensable requisite of the interest which we here take in
beauty, that the beauty should be that of nature, and it vanishes
completely as soon as we are conscious of having been deceived, 5
and that it is only the work of art—so completely that even
taste can then no longer find in it anything beautiful nor sight
anything attractive.   What do poets set more store on than the
nightingale's bewitching and beautiful note, in a lonely thicket
on a still summer evening by the soft light of the moon?   And 10
yet we have instances of how, where no such songster was to
be found, a jovial host has played a trick on the guests with him
on a visit to enjoy the country air, and has done so to their
huge satisfaction, by hiding in a thicket a rogue of a youth
who (with a reed or rush in his mouth) knew how to reproduce 15
this note so as to hit off nature to perfection.   But the instant
one realizes that it is all a fraud no one will long endure
listening to this song that before was regarded as so attractive.
And it is just the same with the song of any other bird.   It
must be nature, or be mistaken by us for nature, to enable us 20
to take an immediate *interest* in the beautiful as such ; and
this is all the more so if we may even call upon others to take
a similar interest.   And such a demand we do in fact make,
303 since we regard as coarse and low the habits of thought of
those who have no *feeling* for beautiful nature (for this is the 25
word we use for susceptibility to an interest in the contemplation of beautiful nature), and who devote themselves to the
mere enjoyments of sense found in eating and drinking.

§ 43

Art in general.   30

(1.) *Art* is distinguished from *nature* as making (*facere*) is
from acting or operating in general (*agere*), and the product or the

result of the former is distinguished from that of the latter as *work* (*opus*) from operation (*effectus*).

By right it is only production through freedom, i.e. through an act of will that places reason at the basis of its action, that should be termed art.   For, although we are pleased to call what bees produce (their regularly constructed cells) a work of art, we only do so on the strength of an analogy with art ; that is to say, as soon as we call to mind that no rational deliberation forms the basis of their labour, we say at once that it is a product of their nature (of instinct), and it is only to their Creator that we ascribe it as art.

If, as sometimes happens, in a search through a bog, we light on a piece of hewn wood, we do not say it is a product of nature but of art.   Its producing cause had an end in view to which the object owes its form.   Apart from such cases, we recognize an art in everything formed in such a way that its actuality must have been preceded by a representation of the thing in its cause (as even in the case of the bees), although the effect could not have been *thought* by the cause.   But where anything is called absolutely a work of art, to distinguish it from a natural product, then some work of man is always understood.

(2.) *Art*, as human skill, is distinguished also from *science* (as *ability* from *knowledge*), as a practical from a theoretical faculty, as technic from theory (as the art of surveying from geometry). For this reason, also, what one *can* do the moment one only *knows* what is to be done, hence without anything more than sufficient knowledge of the desired result, is not called art.   To art that alone belongs for which the possession of the most complete knowledge does not involve one's having then and there the skill to do it.   *Camper* describes very exactly how the best shoe must be made, but he, doubtless, was not able to turn one out himself.[1]

---

[1] In my part of the country, if you set a common man a problem like that of Columbus and his egg, he says, ' There is no art in that, it is only

(3.) *Art* is further distinguished from *handicraft*. The first is called *free*, the other may be called *industrial art*. We look on the former as something which could only prove final (be a success) as play, i.e. an occupation which is agreeable on its own account ; but on the second as labour, i.e. a business, 5 which on its own account is disagreeable (drudgery), and is only attractive by means of what it results in (e. g. the pay), and which is consequently capable of being a compulsory imposition.   Whether in the list of arts and crafts we are to rank watchmakers as artists, and smiths on the contrary as craftsmen, 10 requires a standpoint different from that here adopted—one, that is to say, taking account of the proportion of the talents which the business undertaken in either case must necessarily involve.   Whether, also, among the so-called seven free arts some may not have been included which should be reckoned 15 as sciences, and many, too, that resemble handicraft, is a matter I will not discuss here.   It is not amiss, however, to remind the reader of this : that in all free arts something of a compulsory character is still required, or, as it is called, a *mechanism*, without which the *soul*, which in art must be *free*, and which alone 20 gives life to the work, would be bodyless and evanescent (e. g. in the poetic art there must be correctness and wealth of language, likewise prosody and metre).   For not a few leaders of a newer school believe that the best way to promote a free art is to sweep away all restraint, and convert it from 25 labour into mere play.

science ' : i. e. you *can* do it if you know *how* ; and he says just the same of all the would-be arts of jugglers.   To that of the tight-rope dancer, on the other hand, he has not the least compunction in giving the name of art.   30

§ 44

Fine art.

THERE is no science of the beautiful, but only a Critique. Nor, again, is there an elegant (*schöne*) science, but only a fine 5 (*schöne*) art. For a science of the beautiful would have to de-termine scientifically, i.e. by means of proofs, whether a thing 305 was to be considered beautiful or not; and the judgement upon beauty, consequently, would, if belonging to science, fail to be a judgement of taste. As for a beautiful science—a science 10 which, as such, is to be beautiful, is a nonentity. For if, treating it as a science, we were to ask for reasons and proofs, we would be put off with elegant phrases (*bons mots*). What has given rise to the current expression *elegant sciences* is, doubt-less, no more than this, that common observation has, quite 15 accurately, noted the fact that for fine art, in the fulness of its perfection, a large store of science is required, as, for example, knowledge of ancient languages, acquaintance with classical authors, history, antiquarian learning, &c. Hence these his-torical sciences, owing to the fact that they form the necessary 20 preparation and groundwork for fine art, and partly also owing to the fact that they are taken to comprise even the knowledge of the products of fine art (rhetoric and poetry), have by a con-fusion of words, actually got the name of elegant sciences.

Where art, merely seeking to actualize a possible object to 25 the *cognition* of which it is adequate, does whatever acts are required for that purpose, then it is *mechanical*. But should the feeling of pleasure be what it has immediately in view it is then termed *aesthetic* art. As such it may be either *agreeable* or *fine* art. The description 'agreeable art' applies where the end of 30 the art is that the pleasure should accompany the representa-tions considered as mere *sensations*, the description 'fine art' where it is to accompany them considered as *modes of cognition*.

Agreeable arts are those which have mere enjoyment for

their object. Such are all the charms that can gratify a dinner party: entertaining narrative, the art of starting the whole table in unrestrained and sprightly conversation, or with jest and laughter inducing a certain air of gaiety. Here, as the saying goes, there may be much loose talk over the glasses, 5 without a person wishing to be brought to book for all he utters, because it is only given out for the entertainment of the moment, and not as a lasting matter to be made the subject of reflection or repetition. (Of the same sort is also the art of arranging the table for enjoyment, or, at large banquets, the 10 music of the orchestra—a quaint idea intended to act on the mind merely as an agreeable noise fostering a genial spirit, which, without any one paying the smallest attention to the 306 composition, promotes the free flow of conversation between guest and guest.) In addition must be included play of every 15 kind which is attended with no further interest than that of making the time pass by unheeded.

Fine art, on the other hand, is a mode of representation which is intrinsically final, and which, although devoid of an end, has the effect of advancing the culture of the mental 20 powers in the interests of social communication.

The universal communicability of a pleasure involves in its very concept that the pleasure is not one of enjoyment arising out of mere sensation, but must be one of reflection. Hence aesthetic art, as art which is beautiful, is one having for its 25 standard the reflective judgement and not organic sensation.

§ 45

Fine art is an art, so far as it has at the same time the appearance of being nature.

A PRODUCT of fine art must be recognized to be art and not 30 nature. Nevertheless the finality in its form must appear just as free from the constraint of arbitrary rules as if it were

a product of mere nature.   Upon this feeling of freedom in the play of our cognitive faculties — which play has at the same time to be final—rests that pleasure which alone is universally communicable without being based on concepts.   Nature proved
5 beautiful when it wore the appearance of art ; and art can only be termed beautiful, where we are conscious of its being art, while yet it has the appearance of nature.

For, whether we are dealing with beauty of nature or beauty of art, we may make the universal statement : *that is beautiful*
10 *which pleases in the mere estimate of it* (not in sensation or by means of a concept).   Now art has always got a definite intention of producing something.   Were this ' something ', however, to be mere sensation (something merely subjective), intended to be accompanied with pleasure, then such product would, in our
15 estimation of it, only please through the agency of the feeling of the senses.   On the other hand, were the intention one directed to the production of a definite object, then, supposing this were attained by art, the object would only please by means of a concept.   But in both cases the art would please, not
20 in *the mere estimate of it*, i.e. not as fine art, but rather as mechanical art.

Hence the finality in the product of fine art, intentional 307 though it be, must not have the appearance of being intentional ; i.e. fine art must be clothed *with the aspect* of nature,
25 although we recognize it to be art.   But the way in which a product of art seems like nature, is by the presence of perfect *exactness* in the agreement with rules prescribing how alone the product can be what it is intended to be, but with an absence of *laboured effect*, (without academic form betraying itself,)
30 i.e. without a trace appearing of the artist having always had the rule present to him and of its having fettered his mental powers.

§ 46

Fine art is the art of genius.

Genius is the talent (natural endowment) which gives the rule to art.   Since talent, as an innate productive faculty of the artist, belongs itself to nature, we may put it this way : *Genius* is the innate mental aptitude (*ingenium*) *through which* nature gives the rule to art.

Whatever may be the merits of this definition, and whether it is merely arbitrary, or whether it is adequate or not to the concept usually associated with the word *genius* (a point which the following sections have to clear up), it may still be shown at the outset that, according to this acceptation of the word, fine arts must necessarily be regarded as arts of *genius*.

For every art presupposes rules which are laid down as the foundation which first enables a product, if it is to be called one of art, to be represented as possible.   The concept of fine art, however, does not permit of the judgement upon the beauty of its product being derived from any rule that has a *concept* for its determining ground, and that depends, consequently, on a concept of the way in which the product is possible.   Consequently fine art cannot of its own self excogitate the rule according to which it is to effectuate its product.   But since, for all that, a product can never be called art unless there is a preceding rule, it follows that nature in the individual (and by virtue of the harmony of his faculties) must give the rule to art, i.e. fine art is only possible as a product of genius.

From this it may be seen that genius (1) is a *talent* for producing that for which no definite rule can be given : and not an aptitude in the way of cleverness for what can be learned according to some rule ; and that consequently *originality* must be its primary property.   (2) Since there may also be original nonsense, its products must at the same time be models, i.e. be *exemplary* ; and, consequently, though not themselves derived

from imitation, they must serve that purpose for others, i. e. as a standard or rule of estimating. (3) It cannot indicate scientifically how it brings about its product, but rather gives the rule as *nature*. Hence, where an author owes a product to his genius, he
5 does not himself know how the *ideas* for it have entered into his head, nor has he it in his power to invent the like at pleasure, or methodically, and communicate the same to others in such precepts as would put them in a position to produce similar products. (Hence, presumably, our word *Genie* is derived from
10 *genius*, as the peculiar guardian and guiding spirit given to a man at his birth, by the inspiration of which those original ideas were obtained.) (4) Nature prescribes the rule through genius not to science but to art, and this also only in so far as it is to be fine art.

15
§ 47
Elucidation and confirmation of the above explanation of genius.

EVERY one is agreed on the point of the complete opposition between genius and the *spirit of imitation*. Now since learning
20 is nothing but imitation, the greatest ability, or aptness as a pupil (capacity), is still, as such, not equivalent to genius. Even though a man weaves his own thoughts or fancies, instead of merely taking in what others have thought, and even though he go so far as to bring fresh gains to art and science, this does not
25 afford a valid reason for calling such a man of *brains*, and often great brains, a *genius*, in contradistinction to one who goes by the name of *shallow-pate*, because he can never do more than merely learn and follow a lead. For what is accomplished in this way is something that *could* have been learned. Hence it all lies in
30 the natural path of investigation and reflection according to rules, and so is not specifically distinguishable from what may be acquired as the result of industry backed up by imitation. So all

that *Newton* has set forth in his immortal work on the Principles of Natural Philosophy may well be learned, however great a mind it took to find it all out, but we cannot learn to write in 309 a true poetic vein, no matter how complete all the precepts of the poetic art may be, or however excellent its models. The reason is that all the steps that Newton had to take from the first elements of geometry to his greatest and most profound discoveries were such as he could make intuitively evident and plain to follow, not only for himself but for every one else. On the other hand no *Homer* or *Wieland* can show how his ideas, so rich at once in fancy and in thought, enter and assemble themselves in his brain, for the good reason that he does not himself know, and so cannot teach others. In matters of science, therefore, the greatest inventor differs only in degree from the most laborious imitator and apprentice, whereas he differs specifically from one endowed by nature for fine art. No disparagement, however, of those great men, to whom the human race is so deeply indebted, is involved in this comparison of them with those who on the score of their talent for fine art are the elect of nature. The talent for science is formed for the continued advances of greater perfection in knowledge, with all its dependent practical advantages, as also for imparting the same to others. Hence scientists can boast a ground of considerable superiority over those who merit the honour of being called geniuses, since genius reaches a point at which art must make a halt, as there is a limit imposed upon it which it cannot transcend. This limit has in all probability been long since attained. In addition, such skill cannot be communicated, but requires to be bestowed directly from the hand of nature upon each individual, and so with him it dies, awaiting the day when nature once again endows another in the same way—one who needs no more than an example to set the talent of which he is conscious at work on similar lines.

Seeing, then, that the natural endowment of art (as fine art) must furnish the rule, what kind of rule must this be? It cannot be one set down in a formula and serving as a precept—for then the judgement upon the beautiful would be determinable according to concepts. Rather must the rule be gathered from 5 the performance, i.e. from the product, which others may use to put their own talent to the test, so as to let it serve as a model, not for *imitation*, but for *following*. The possibility of this is difficult to explain. The artist's ideas arouse like ideas on the part of his pupil, presuming nature to have visited him with 10 a like proportion of the mental powers. For this reason the models of fine art are the only means of handing down this art 310 to posterity. This is something which cannot be done by mere descriptions (especially not in the line of the arts of speech), and in these arts, furthermore, only those models can become 15 classical of which the ancient, dead languages, preserved as learned, are the medium.

Despite the marked difference that distinguishes mechanical art, as an art merely depending upon industry and learning, from fine art, as that of genius, there is still no fine art in which 20 something mechanical, capable of being at once comprehended and followed in obedience to rules, and consequently something *academic* does not constitute the essential condition of the art. For the thought of something as end must be present, or else its product would not be ascribed to an art at all, but would be 25 a mere product of chance. But the effectuation of an end necessitates determinate rules which we cannot venture to dispense with. Now, seeing that originality of talent is one (though not the sole) essential factor that goes to make up the character of genius, shallow minds fancy that the best evidence they can 30 give of their being full-blown geniuses is by emancipating themselves from all academic constraint of rules, in the belief that one cuts a finer figure on the back of an ill-tempered than of a trained horse. Genius can do no more than furnish rich *material* for products of fine art; its elaboration and its *form* require a

talent academically trained, so that it may be employed in such
a way as to stand the test of judgement.   But, for a person to
hold forth and pass sentence like a genius in matters that fall to
the province of the most patient rational investigation, is ridiculous in the extreme.   One is at a loss to know whether to 5
laugh more at the impostor who envelops himself in such a
cloud—in which we are given fuller scope to our imagination at
the expense of all use of our critical faculty,—or at the simple-
minded public which imagines that its inability clearly to cognize
and comprehend this masterpiece of penetration is due to 10
its being invaded by new truths *en masse*, in comparison with
which, detail, due to carefully weighed exposition and an
academic examination of root-principles, seems to it only the
work of a tyro.

311   § 48   15

The relation of genius to taste.

FOR *estimating* beautiful objects, as such, what is required
is *taste*; but for fine art, i.e. the *production* of such objects,
one needs *genius*.

If we consider genius as the talent for fine art (which the 20
proper signification of the word imports), and if we would analyse
it from this point of view into the faculties which must concur
to constitute such a talent, it is imperative at the outset
accurately to determine the difference between beauty of nature,
which it only requires taste to estimate, and beauty of art, which 25
requires genius for its possibility (a possibility to which regard
must also be paid in estimating such an object).

A beauty of nature is a *beautiful thing*; beauty of art is
a *beautiful representation* of a thing.

To enable me to estimate a beauty of nature, as such, I do 30
not need to be previously possessed of a concept of what sort of
a thing the object is intended to be, i.e. I am not obliged to

know its material finality (the end), but, rather, in forming an estimate of it apart from any knowledge of the end, the mere form pleases on its own account.   If, however, the object is presented as a product of art, and is as such to be declared 5 beautiful, then, seeing that art always presupposes an end in the cause (and its causality), a concept of what the thing is intended to be must first of all be laid at its basis.   And, since the agreement of the manifold in a thing with an inner character belonging to it as its end constitutes the perfection of the thing, 10 it follows that in estimating beauty of art the perfection of the thing must be also taken into account—a matter which in estimating a beauty of nature, as beautiful, is quite irrelevant. —It is true that in forming an estimate, especially of animate objects of nature, e. g. of a man or a horse, objective finality is 15 also commonly taken into account with a view to judgement upon their beauty ; but then the judgement also ceases to be purely aesthetic, i. e. a mere judgement of taste.   Nature is no longer estimated as it appears like art, but rather in so far as it actually *is* art, though superhuman art ; and the teleological 20 judgement serves as basis and condition of the aesthetic, and 312 one which the latter must regard.   In such a case, where one says, for example, 'that is a beautiful woman,' what one in fact thinks is only this, that in her form nature excellently portrays the ends present in the female figure.   For one has to 25 extend one's view beyond the mere form to a concept, to enable the object to be thought in such manner by means of an aesthetic judgement logically conditioned.

Where fine art evidences its superiority is in the beautiful descriptions it gives of things that in nature would be ugly or 30 displeasing.   The Furies, diseases, devastations of war, and the like, can (as evils) be very beautifully described, nay even represented in pictures.   One kind of ugliness alone is incapable of being represented conformably to nature without destroying all aesthetic delight, and consequently artistic beauty, namely, that which excites *disgust*. For, as in this strange sensation, which depends purely on the imagination, the object is represented as insisting, as it were, upon our enjoying it, while we still set our face against it, the artificial representation of the object is no longer distinguishable from the nature of the object 5 itself in our sensation, and so it cannot possibly be regarded as beautiful. The art of sculpture, again, since in its products art is almost confused with nature, has excluded from its creations the direct representation of ugly objects, and, instead, only sanctions, for example, the representation of death (in 10 a beautiful genius), or of the warlike spirit (in Mars), by means of an allegory, or attributes which wear a pleasant guise, and so only indirectly, through an interpretation on the part of reason, and not for the pure aesthetic judgement.

So much for the beautiful representation of an object, which 15 is properly only the form of the presentation of a concept, and the means by which the latter is universally communicated. To give this form, however, to the product of fine art, taste merely is required. By this the artist, having practised and corrected his taste by a variety of examples from nature or art, 20 controls his work and, after many, and often laborious, attempts to satisfy taste, finds the form which commends itself to him. Hence this form is not, as it were, a matter of inspiration, or of a free swing of the mental powers, but rather of a slow and even painful process of improvement, directed to 25 313 making the form adequate to his thought without prejudice to the freedom in the play of those powers.

Taste is, however, merely a critical, not a productive faculty ; and what conforms to it is not, merely on that account, a work of fine art. It may belong to useful and mechanical art, or 30 even to science, as a product following definite rules which are capable of being learned and which must be closely followed. But the pleasing form imparted to the work is only the vehicle of communication and a mode, as it were, of

execution, in respect of which one remains to a certain extent free, notwithstanding being otherwise tied down to a definite end. So we demand that table appointments, or even a moral dissertation, and, indeed, a sermon, must bear this form of fine art, yet
5 without its appearing *studied*. But one would not call them on this account works of fine art. A poem, a musical composition, a picture-gallery, and so forth, would, however, be placed under this head ; and so in a would-be work of fine art we may frequently recognize genius without taste, and in another taste
10 without genius.

§ 49

The faculties of the mind which constitute genius.

OF certain products which are expected, partly at least, to stand on the footing of fine art, we say they are *soul*less ; and this,
15 although we find nothing to censure in them as far as taste goes. A poem may be very pretty and elegant, but is soulless. A narrative has precision and method, but is soulless. A speech on some festive occasion may be good in substance and ornate withal, but may be soulless. Conversation frequently is not
20 devoid of entertainment, but yet soulless. Even of a woman we may well say, she is pretty, affable, and refined, but soulless. Now what do we here mean by 'soul' ?

'*Soul*' (*Geist*) in an aesthetical sense, signifies the animating principle in the mind. But that whereby this principle animates
25 the psychic substance (*Seele*)—the material which it employs for that purpose—is that which sets the mental powers into a swing that is final, i.e. into a play which is self-maintaining and which strengthens those powers for such activity.

Now my proposition is that this principle is nothing else than
30 the faculty of presenting *aesthetic ideas*. But, by an aesthetic 314 idea I mean that representation of the imagination which induces much thought, yet without the possibility of any definite

thought whatever, i.e. *concept*, being adequate to it, and which
language, consequently, can never get quite on level terms with
or render completely intelligible.—It is easily seen, that an
aesthetic idea is the counterpart (pendant) of a *rational idea*,
which, conversely, is a concept, to which no *intuition* (repre- 5
sentation of the imagination) can be adequate.

The imagination (as a productive faculty of cognition) is a
powerful agent for creating, as it were, a second nature out of
the material supplied to it by actual nature. It affords us
entertainment where experience proves too commonplace ; and 10
we even use it to remodel experience, always following, no doubt,
laws that are based on analogy, but still also following principles
which have a higher seat in reason (and which are every whit
as natural to us as those followed by the understanding in laying
hold of empirical nature). By this means we get a sense of 15
our freedom from the law of association (which attaches to the
empirical employment of the imagination), with the result that
the material can be borrowed by us from nature in accordance
with that law, but be worked up by us into something else—
namely, what surpasses nature.   20

Such representations of the imagination may be termed *ideas*.
This is partly because they at least strain after something lying
out beyond the confines of experience, and so seek to approximate to a presentation of rational concepts (i.e. intellectual
ideas), thus giving to these concepts the semblance of an 25
objective reality. But, on the other hand, there is this most
important reason, that no concept can be wholly adequate to
them as internal intuitions. The poet essays the task of
interpreting to sense the rational ideas of invisible beings, the
kingdom of the blessed, hell, eternity, creation, &c. Or, again, 30
as to things of which examples occur in experience, e.g. death,
envy, and all vices, as also love, fame, and the like, transgressing
the limits of experience he attempts with the aid of an imagination which emulates the display of reason in its attainment of

a maximum, to body them forth to sense with a completeness of which nature affords no parallel ; and it is in fact precisely in the poetic art that the faculty of aesthetic ideas can show itself to full advantage.   This faculty, however, regarded solely on
5 its own account, is properly no more than a talent (of the imagination).

If, now, we attach to a concept a representation of the imagination belonging to its presentation, but inducing solely on its 315 own account such a wealth of thought as would never admit of
10 comprehension in a definite concept, and, as a consequence, giving aesthetically an unbounded expansion to the concept itself, then the imagination here displays a creative activity, and it puts the faculty of intellectual ideas (reason) into motion—a motion, at the instance of a representation, towards an extension
15 of thought, that, while germane, no doubt, to the concept of the object, exceeds what can be laid hold of in that representation or clearly expressed.

Those forms which do not constitute the presentation of a given concept itself, but which, as secondary representations of
20 the imagination, express the derivatives connected with it, and its kinship with other concepts, are called (aesthetic) *attributes* of an object, the concept of which, as an idea of reason, cannot be adequately presented.   In this way Jupiter's eagle, with the lightning in its claws, is an attribute of the mighty king of
25 heaven, and the peacock of its stately queen.   They do not, like *logical attributes*, represent what lies in our concepts of the sublimity and majesty of creation, but rather something else— something that gives the imagination an incentive to spread its flight over a whole host of kindred representations that provoke
30 more thought than admits of expression in a concept determined by words.   They furnish an *aesthetic idea*, which serves the above rational idea as a substitute for logical presentation, but with the proper function, however, of animating the mind by opening out for it a prospect into a field of kindred representa-

tions stretching beyond its ken. But it is not alone in the arts of painting or sculpture, where the name of attribute is customarily employed, that fine art acts in this way; poetry and rhetoric also derive the soul that animates their works wholly from the aesthetic attributes of the objects—attributes which go 5 hand in hand with the logical, and give the imagination an impetus to bring more thought into play in the matter, though in an undeveloped manner, than allows of being brought within the embrace of a concept, or, therefore, of being definitely formulated in language.—For the sake of brevity I must confine 10 myself to a few examples only. When the great king expresses himself in one of his poems by saying :

> Oui, finissons sans trouble, et mourons sans regrets,
> En laissant l'Univers comblé de nos bienfaits.
> Ainsi l'Astre du jour, au bout de sa carrière, 15
> Répand sur l'horizon une douce lumière,
> Et les derniers rayons qu'il darde dans les airs
> Sont les derniers soupirs qu'il donne à l'Univers;

316

he kindles in this way his rational idea of a cosmopolitan sentiment even at the close of life, with the help of an attribute 20 which the imagination (in remembering all the pleasures of a fair summer's day that is over and gone—a memory of which pleasures is suggested by a serene evening) annexes to that representation, and which stirs up a crowd of sensations and secondary representations for which no expression can be found. 25 On the other hand, even an intellectual concept may serve, conversely, as attribute for a representation of sense, and so animate the latter with the idea of the supersensible; but only by the aesthetic factor subjectively attaching to the consciousness of the supersensible being employed for the purpose. 30 So, for example, a certain poet says in his description of a beautiful morning : 'The sun arose, as out of virtue rises peace.' The consciousness of virtue, even where we put ourselves only in thought in the position of a virtuous man, diffuses in the mind a multitude of sublime and tranquillizing feelings, and gives a boundless outlook into a happy future, such as no expression within the compass of a definite concept completely attains.[1]

5 In a word, the aesthetic idea is a representation of the imagination, annexed to a given concept, with which, in the free employment of imagination, such a multiplicity of partial representations are bound up, that no expression indicating a definite concept can be found for it—one which on that account 10 allows a concept to be supplemented in thought by much that is indefinable in words, and the feeling of which quickens the cognitive faculties, and with language, as a mere thing of the letter, binds up the spirit (soul) also.

The mental powers whose union in a certain relation 15 constitutes *genius* are imagination and understanding. Now, since the imagination, in its employment on behalf of cognition, is subjected to the constraint of the understanding and the restriction of having to be conformable to the concept belonging thereto, whereas aesthetically it is free to furnish of its own 317 20 accord, over and above that agreement with the concept, a wealth of undeveloped material for the understanding, to which the latter paid no regard in its concept, but which it can make use of, not so much objectively for cognition, as subjectively for quickening the cognitive faculties, and hence also indirectly 25 for cognitions, it may be seen that genius properly consists in the happy relation, which science cannot teach nor industry learn, enabling one to find out ideas for a given concept, and,

---

[1] Perhaps there has never been a more sublime utterance, or a thought more sublimely expressed, than the well-known inscription upon the 30 Temple of *Isis* (Mother *Nature*) : 'I am all that is, and that was, and that shall be, and no mortal hath raised the veil from before my face.' *Segner* made use of this idea in a suggestive vignette on the frontispiece of his Natural Philosophy, in order to inspire his pupil at the threshold of that temple into which he was about to lead him, with such a holy awe as 35 would dispose his mind to serious attention.

besides, to hit upon the *expression* for them—the expression by
means of which the subjective mental condition induced by the
ideas as the concomitant of a concept may be communicated
to others.   This latter talent is properly that which is termed
soul.   For to get an expression for what is indefinable in the 5
mental state accompanying a particular representation and
to make it universally communicable—be the expression in
language or painting or statuary—is a thing requiring a faculty
for laying hold of the rapid and transient play of the imagination, and for unifying it in a concept (which for that very reason 10
is original, and reveals a new rule which could not have been
inferred from any preceding principles or examples) that admits
of communication without any constraint of rules.

If, after this analysis, we cast a glance back upon the above
definition of what is called *genius*, we find : *First,* that it is a 15
talent for art—not one for science, in which clearly known rules
must take the lead and determine the procedure.   *Secondly,*
being a talent in the line of art, it presupposes a definite concept
of the product—as its end.   Hence it presupposes understanding, but, in addition, a representation, indefinite though 20
it be, of the material, i. e. of the intuition, required for the
presentation of that concept, and so a relation of the imagination
to the understanding.   *Thirdly,* it displays itself, not so much
in the working out of the projected end in the presentation of
a definite *concept,* as rather in the portrayal, or expression of 25
aesthetic ideas containing a wealth of material for effecting that
intention.   Consequently the imagination is represented by it
in its freedom from all guidance of rules, but still as final for the
presentation of the given concept.   *Fourthly,* and lastly, the un-
318 sought and undesigned subjective finality in the free harmonizing 30
of the imagination with the understanding's conformity to law
presupposes a proportion and accord between these faculties

such as cannot be brought about by any observance of rules, whether of science or mechanical imitation, but can only be produced by the nature of the individual.

Genius, according to these presuppositions, is the exemplary originality of the natural endowments of an individual in the *free* employment of his cognitive faculties. On this showing, the product of a genius (in respect of so much in this product as is attributable to genius, and not to possible learning or academic instruction,) is an example, not for imitation (for that would mean the loss of the element of genius, and just the very soul of the work), but to be followed by another genius— one whom it arouses to a sense of his own originality in putting freedom from the constraint of rules so into force in his art, that for art itself a new rule is won—which is what shows a talent to be exemplary.   Yet, since the genius is one of nature's elect—a type that must be regarded as but a rare pheno- menon—for other clever minds his example gives rise to a school, that is to say a methodical instruction according to rules, collected, so far as the circumstances admit, from such products of genius and their peculiarities. And, to that extent, fine art is for such persons a matter of imitation, for which nature, through the medium of a genius, gave the rule.

But this imitation becomes *aping* when the pupil *copies* every- thing down to the deformities which the genius only of necessity suffered to remain, because they could hardly be removed without loss of force to the idea. This courage has merit only in the case of a genius. A certain *boldness* of expression, and, in general, many a deviation from the common rule becomes him well, but in no sense is it a thing worthy of imitation. On the contrary it remains all through intrinsically a blemish, which one is bound to try to remove, but for which the genius is, as it were, allowed to plead a privilege, on the ground that a scrupulous carefulness would spoil what is inimitable in the impetuous ardour of his soul. *Mannerism* is another kind of aping—an aping of *peculiarity* (originality) in general, for the sake of removing oneself as far as possible from imitators, while the talent requisite to enable one to be at the same time *exemplary* is absent.—There are, in fact, two modes (*modi*) in general of arranging one's thoughts for utterance. The one is called a *manner* (*modus aestheticus*), the other a *method* (*modus logicus*). The distinction between them is this: the former possesses no standard other than the *feeling* of unity in the presentation, whereas the latter here follows definite *principles*. As a consequence the former is alone admissible for fine art. It is only, however, where the manner of carrying the idea into execution in a product of art is *aimed at* singularity instead of being made appropriate to the idea, that *mannerism* is properly ascribed to such a product. The ostentatious (*précieux*), forced, and affected styles, intended to mark one out from the common herd (though soul is wanting), resemble the behaviour of a man who, as we say, hears himself talk, or who stands and moves about as if he were on a stage to be gaped at—action which invariably betrays a tyro.

§ 50

The combination of taste and genius in products of fine art.

To ask whether more stress should be laid in matters of fine art upon the presence of genius or upon that of taste, is equivalent to asking whether more turns upon imagination or upon judgement. Now, imagination rather entitles an art to be called an *inspired* (*geistreiche*) than a *fine* art. It is only in respect of judgement that the name of fine art is deserved. Hence it follows that judgement, being the indispensable condition (*conditio sine qua non*), is at least what one must look to as of capital importance in forming an estimate of art as fine art. So far as beauty is concerned, to be fertile and original in ideas is not such an imperative requirement as it is that the imagina-

tion in its freedom should be in accordance with the understanding's conformity to law. For in lawless freedom imagination, with all its wealth, produces nothing but nonsense ; the power of judgement, on the other hand, is the faculty that
5 makes it consonant with understanding.

Taste, like judgement in general, is the discipline (or corrective) of genius. It severely clips its wings, and makes it orderly or polished ; but at the same time it gives it guidance, directing and controlling its flight, so that it may preserve its
10 character of finality. It introduces a clearness and order into the plenitude of thought, and in so doing gives stability to the ideas, and qualifies them at once for permanent and universal approval, for being followed by others, and for a continually progressive culture. And so, where the interests of
15 both these qualities clash in a product, and there has to be a sacrifice of something, then it should rather be on the side of 320 genius ; and judgement, which in matters of fine art bases its decision on its own proper principles, will more readily endure an abatement of the freedom and wealth of the imagination,
20 than that the understanding should be compromised.

The requisites for fine art are, therefore, *imagination, understanding, soul*, and *taste*.[1]

§ 51

The division of the fine arts.

25 BEAUTY (whether it be of nature or of art) may in general be termed the *expression* of aesthetic ideas. But the proviso must be added that with beauty of art this idea must be excited

---

[1] The first three faculties are first *brought into union* by means of the fourth. *Hume*, in his history, informs the English that although they
30 are second in their works to no other people in the world in respect of the evidences they afford of the three first qualities *separately* considered, still in what unites them they must yield to their neighbours, the French.

through the medium of a concept of the Object, whereas with beauty of nature the bare reflection upon a given intuition, apart from any concept of what the object is intended to be, is sufficient for awakening and communicating the idea of which that Object is regarded as the *expression*.   5

Accordingly, if we wish to make a division of the fine arts, we can choose for that purpose, tentatively at least, no more convenient principle than the analogy which art bears to the mode of expression of which men avail themselves in speech, with a view to communicating themselves to one another as 10 completely as possible, i. e. not merely in respect of their concepts but in respect of their sensations also.[1]—Such expression consists in *word, gesture,* and *tone* (articulation, gesticulation, and modulation). It is the combination of these three modes of expression which alone constitutes a complete 15 communication of the speaker. For thought, intuition, and sensation are in this way conveyed to others simultaneously and in conjunction.

Hence there are only three kinds of fine art: the art of
321 *speech, formative* art, and the art of the *play of sensations* 20 (as external sense impressions). This division might also be arranged as a dichotomy, so that fine art would be divided into that of the expression of thoughts or intuitions, the latter being subdivided according to the distinction between the form and the matter (sensation). It would, however, in that case 25 appear too abstract, and less in line with popular conceptions.

(1) The arts of SPEECH are *rhetoric* and *poetry*. *Rhetoric* is the art of transacting a serious business of the understanding as if it were a free play of the imagination ; *poetry* that of conducting a free play of the imagination as if it were a serious 30 business of the understanding.

---

[1] The reader is not to consider this scheme for a possible division of the fine arts as a deliberate theory. It is only one of the various attempts that can and ought to be made.

Thus the *orator* announces a serious business, and for the purpose of entertaining his audience conducts it as if it were a mere *play* with ideas.   The *poet* promises merely an entertaining *play* with ideas, and yet for the understanding there enures
5 as much as if the promotion of its business had been his one intention.   The combination and harmony of the two faculties of cognition, sensibility and understanding, which, though, doubtless, indispensable to one another, do not readily permit of being united without compulsion and reciprocal abatement,
10 must have the appearance of being undesigned and a spontaneous occurrence—otherwise it is not *fine* art.   For this reason what is studied and laboured must be here avoided.   For fine art must be free art in a double sense : i.e. not alone in a sense opposed to contract work, as not being a work the magnitude
15 of which may be estimated, exacted, or paid for according to a definite standard, but free also in the sense that, while the mind, no doubt, occupies itself, still it does so without ulterior regard to any other end, and yet with a feeling of satisfaction and stimulation (independent of reward).

20 The orator, therefore, gives something which he does not promise, viz. an entertaining play of the imagination.   On the other hand, there is something in which he fails to come up to his promise, and a thing, too, which is his avowed business, namely, the engagement of the understanding to some end.
25 The poet's promise, on the contrary, is a modest one, and a mere play with ideas is all he holds out to us, but he accomplishes something worthy of being made a serious business, namely, the using of play to provide food for the understanding, and the giving of life to its concepts by means of the
30 imagination.   Hence the orator in reality performs less than he promises, the poet more.

(2) The FORMATIVE arts, or those for the expression of ideas in *sensuous intuition* (not by means of representations of mere imagination that are excited by words) are arts either of 322

sensuous truth or of *sensuous semblance.* The first is called *plastic* art, the second *painting.* Both use figures in space for the expression of ideas : the former makes figures discernible to two senses, sight and touch (though, so far as the latter sense is concerned, without regard to beauty), the latter makes 5 them so to the former sense alone. The aesthetic idea (archetype, original) is the fundamental basis of both in the imagination ; but the figure which constitutes its expression (the ectype, the copy) is given either in its bodily extension (the way the object itself exists) or else in accordance with the 10 picture which it forms of itself in the eye (according to its appearance when projected on a flat surface). Or, whatever the archetype is, either the reference to an actual end or only the semblance of one may be imposed upon reflection as its condition. 15

To *plastic* art, as the first kind of formative fine art, belong *sculpture* and *architecture.* The first is that which presents concepts of things corporeally, as they *might exist in nature* (though as fine art it directs its attention to aesthetic finality). The *second* is the art of presenting concepts of things which are 20 possible *only through art,* and the determining ground of whose form is not nature but an arbitrary end—and of presenting them both with a view to this purpose and yet, at the same time, with aesthetic finality. In architecture the chief point is a certain *use* of the artistic object to which, as the condition, 25 the aesthetic ideas are limited. In sculpture the mere *expression* of aesthetic ideas is the main intention. Thus statues of men, gods, animals, &c., belong to sculpture ; but temples, splendid buildings for public concourse, or even dwelling-houses, triumphal arches, columns, mausoleums, &c., erected 30 as monuments, belong to architecture, and in fact all household furniture (the work of cabinet-makers, and so forth— things meant to be used) may be added to the list, on the ground that adaptation of the product to a particular use

is the essential element in a *work of architecture*. On the other hand, a mere *piece of sculpture*, made simply to be looked at, and intended to please on its own account, is, as a corporeal presentation, a mere imitation of nature, though one
5 in which regard is paid to aesthetic ideas, and in which, therefore, *sensuous truth* should not go the length of losing the appearance of being an art and a product of the elective will.

Painting, as the second kind of formative art, which presents the *sensuous semblance* in artful combination with ideas, I 323
10 would divide into that of the beautiful *portrayal of nature*, and that of the beautiful *arrangement* of its *products*. The first is *painting proper*, the second *landscape gardening*. For the first gives only the semblance of bodily extension ; whereas the second, giving this, no doubt, according to its truth, gives
15 only the semblance of utility and employment for ends other than the play of the imagination in the contemplation of its forms.[1] The latter consists in no more than decking out the ground with the same manifold variety (grasses, flowers, shrubs, and trees, and even water, hills, and dales) as that with which
20 nature presents it to our view, only arranged differently and in obedience to certain ideas. The beautiful arrangement of

[1] It seems strange that landscape gardening may be regarded as a kind of painting, notwithstanding that it presents its forms corporeally. But, as it takes its forms bodily from nature (the trees, shrubs, grasses,
25 and flowers taken, originally at least, from wood and field) it is to that extent not an art such as, let us say, plastic art. Further, the arrangement which it makes is not conditioned by any concept of the object or of its end (as is the case in sculpture), but by the mere free play of the imagination in the act of contemplation. Hence it bears a degree of
30 resemblance to simple aesthetic painting that has no definite theme (but by means of light and shade makes a pleasing composition of atmosphere, land, and water).—Throughout, the reader is to weigh the above only as an effort to connect the fine arts under a principle, which, in the present instance, is intended to be that of the expression of
35 aesthetic ideas (following the analogy of a language), and not as a positive and deliberate derivation of the connexion.

corporeal things, however, is also a thing for the eye only, just like painting—the sense of touch can form no intuitable representation of such a form. In addition I would place under the head of painting, in the wide sense, the decoration of rooms by means of hangings, ornamental accessories, and all beautiful furniture the sole function of which is *to be looked at*; and in the same way the art of tasteful dressing (with rings, snuff-boxes, &c.). For a *parterre* of various flowers, a room with a variety of ornaments (including even the ladies' attire), go to make at a festal gathering a sort of picture which, like pictures in the true sense of the word, (those which are not intended *to teach* history or natural science,) has no business beyond appealing to the eye, in order to entertain the imagination in free play with ideas, and to engage actively the aesthetic judgement independently of any definite end. No matter how heterogeneous, on the mechanical side, may be the craft involved in all this decoration, and no matter what a variety of artists may be required, still the judgement of taste, so far as it is one upon what is beautiful in this art, is determined in one and the same way : namely, as a judgement only upon the forms (without regard to any end) as they present themselves to the eye, singly or in combination, according to their effect upon the imagination.—The justification, however, of bringing formative art (by analogy) under a common head with gesture in a speech, lies in the fact that through these figures the soul of the artist furnishes a bodily expression for the substance and character of his thought, and makes the thing itself speak, as it were, in mimic language—a very common play of our fancy, that attributes to lifeless things a soul suitable to their form, and that uses them as its mouthpiece.

(3) The art of the BEAUTIFUL PLAY OF SENSATIONS, (sensations that arise from external stimulation,) which is a play of sensations that has nevertheless to permit of universal communication, can only be concerned with the proportion of the

different degrees of tension in the sense to which the sensation belongs, i. e. with its tone. In this comprehensive sense of the word it may be divided into the artificial play of sensations of hearing and of sight, consequently into *music* and the *art*
5 *of colour.*—It is of note that these two senses, over and above such susceptibility for impressions as is required to obtain concepts of external objects by means of these impressions, also admit of a peculiar associated sensation of which we cannot well determine whether it is based on sense or reflection ;
10 and that this sensibility may at times be wanting, although the sense, in other respects, and in what concerns its employment for the cognition of objects, is by no means deficient but particularly keen. In other words, we cannot confidently assert whether a colour or a tone (sound) is merely an agree-
15 able sensation, or whether they are in themselves a beautiful play of sensations, and in being estimated aesthetically, convey, as such, a delight in their form. If we consider the velocity of the vibrations of light, or, in the second case, of the air, which in all probability far outstrips any capacity on our part
20 for forming an immediate estimate in perception of the time interval between them, we should be led to believe that it is only the *effect* of those vibrating movements upon the elastic parts of our body, that can be evident to sense, but that the *time-interval* between them is not noticed nor involved in our
25 estimate, and that, consequently, all that enters into combin- 325 ation with colours and tones is agreeableness, and not beauty, of their composition. But, let us consider, on the other hand, *first*, the mathematical character both of the proportion of those vibrations in music, and of our judgement upon it, and,
30 as is reasonable, form an estimate of colour contrasts on the analogy of the latter. *Secondly*, let us consult the instances, albeit rare, of men who, with the best of sight, have failed to distinguish colours, and, with the sharpest hearing, to distinguish tones, while for men who have this ability the perception

of an altered quality (not merely of the degree of the sensation) in the case of the different intensities in the scale of colours or tones is definite, as is also the number of those which may be *intelligibly* distinguished.   Bearing all this in mind we may feel compelled to look upon the sensations afforded by both, not 5 as mere sense-impressions, but as the effect of an estimate of form in the play of a number of sensations.   The difference which the one opinion or the other occasions in the estimate of the basis of music would, however, only give rise to this much change in its definition, that either it is to be interpreted, 10 as we have done, as the *beautiful* play of sensations (through hearing), or else as one of *agreeable* sensations.   According to the former interpretation, alone, would music be represented out and out as a *fine* art, whereas according to the latter it would be represented as (in part at least) an *agreeable* art.   15

§ 52

The combination of the fine arts in one and the same product.

RHETORIC may in a *drama* be combined with a pictorial presentation as well of its Subjects as of objects ; as may poetry with music in a *song* ; and this again with a pictorial 20 (theatrical) presentation in an *opera* ; and so may the play of sensations in a piece of music with the play of figures in a *dance*, and so on.   Even the presentation of the sublime, so far as it belongs to fine art, may be brought into union with beauty in a *tragedy in verse*, a *didactic poem* or an *oratorio*, 25 and in this combination fine art is even more artistic.   Whether it is also more beautiful (having regard to the multiplicity of different kinds of delight which cross one another) may in 326 some of these instances be doubted.   Still in all fine art the essential element consists in the form which is final for 30 observation and for estimating.   Here the pleasure is at the

same time culture, and disposes the soul to ideas, making it thus susceptible of such pleasure and entertainment in greater abundance. The matter of sensation (charm or emotion) is not essential. Here the aim is merely enjoyment, which leaves
5 nothing behind it in the idea, and renders the soul dull, the object in the course of time distasteful, and the mind dissatisfied with itself and ill-humoured, owing to a consciousness that in the judgement of reason its disposition is perverse.
10   Where fine arts are not, either proximately or remotely, brought into combination with moral ideas, which alone are attended with a self-sufficing delight, the above is the fate that ultimately awaits them. They then only serve for a diversion, of which one continually feels an increasing need in proportion
15 as one has availed oneself of it as a means of dispelling the discontent of one's mind, with the result that one makes oneself ever more and more unprofitable and dissatisfied with oneself. With a view to the purpose first named the beauties of nature are in general the most beneficial, if one is
20 early habituated to observe, estimate, and admire them.

§ 53

Comparative estimate of the aesthetic worth of the fine arts.

Poetry (which owes its origin almost entirely to genius and is
25 least willing to be led by precepts or example) holds the first rank among all the arts. It expands the mind by giving freedom to the imagination and by offering, from among the boundless multiplicity of possible forms accordant with a given concept, to whose bounds it is restricted, that one which couples
30 with the presentation of the concept a wealth of thought to which no verbal expression is completely adequate, and by thus rising aesthetically to ideas. It invigorates the mind by letting

it feel its faculty—free, spontaneous, and independent of determination by nature—of regarding and estimating nature as phenomenon in the light of aspects which nature of itself does not afford us in experience, either for sense or understanding, and of employing it accordingly in behalf of, and as a sort 5 of schema for, the supersensible. It plays with semblance, which it produces at will, but not as an instrument of deception; for its avowed pursuit is merely one of play, which, however, understanding may turn to good account and employ for its own purpose.—Rhetoric, so far as this is taken to mean the art of 10 persuasion, i. e. the art of deluding by means of a fair semblance (as *ars oratoria*), and not merely excellence of speech (eloquence and style), is a dialectic, which borrows from poetry only so much as is necessary to win over men's minds to the side of the speaker before they have weighed the matter, and to rob their 15 verdict of its freedom. Hence it can be recommended neither for the bar nor the pulpit. For where civil laws, the right of individual persons, or the permanent instruction and determination of men's minds to a correct knowledge and a conscientious observance of their duty is at stake, then it is below the dignity 20 of an undertaking of such moment to exhibit even a trace of the exuberance of wit and imagination, and, still more, of the art of talking men round and prejudicing them in favour of any one. For although such art is capable of being at times directed to ends intrinsically legitimate and praiseworthy, still 25 it becomes reprehensible on account of the subjective injury done in this way to maxims and sentiments, even where objectively the action may be lawful. For it is not enough to do what is right, but we should practise it solely on the ground of its being right. Further, the simple lucid concept of human 30 concerns of this kind, backed up with lively illustrations of it, exerts of itself, in the absence of any offence against the rules of euphony of speech or of propriety in the expression of ideas of reason (all which together make up excellence of speech), a

327

sufficient influence upon human minds to obviate the necessity of having recourse here to the machinery of persuasion, which, being equally available for the purpose of putting a fine gloss or a cloak upon vice and error, fails to rid one completely of the
5 lurking suspicion that one is being artfully hoodwinked. In poetry everything is straight and above board. It shows its hand: it desires to carry on a mere entertaining play with the imagination, and one consonant, in respect of form, with the laws of understanding; and it does not seek to steal upon and
10 ensnare the understanding with a sensuous presentation.[1]

After poetry, *if we take charm and mental stimulation into* 328 *account*, I would give the next place to that art which comes nearer to it than to any other art of speech, and admits of very natural union with it, namely the art of *tone*. For though it
15 speaks by means of mere sensations without concepts, and so does not, like poetry, leave behind it any food for reflection, still it moves the mind more diversely, and, although with transient,

---

[1] I must confess to the pure delight which I have ever been afforded by a beautiful poem; whereas the reading of the best speech of a Roman
20 forensic orator, a modern parliamentary debater, or a preacher, has invariably been mingled with an unpleasant sense of disapproval of an insidious art that knows how, in matters of moment, to move men like machines to a judgement that must lose all its weight with them upon calm reflection. Force and elegance of speech (which together constitute
25 rhetoric) belong to fine art; but oratory (*ars oratoria*), being the art of playing for one's own purpose upon the weaknesses of men (let this purpose be ever so good in intention or even in fact) merits no *respect* whatever. Besides, both at Athens and at Rome, it only attained its greatest height at a time when the state was hastening to its decay, and
30 genuine patriotic sentiment was a thing of the past. One who sees the issue clearly, and who has a command of language in its wealth and its purity, and who is possessed of an imagination that is fertile and effective in presenting his ideas, and whose heart, withal, turns with lively sympathy to what is truly good—he is the *vir bonus dicendi peritus*, the
35 orator without art, but of great impressiveness, as *Cicero* would have him, though he may not himself always have remained faithful to this ideal.

still with intenser effect. It is certainly, however, more a matter
of enjoyment than of culture—the play of thought incident-
ally excited by it being merely the effect of a more or less
mechanical association—and it possesses less worth in the
eyes of reason than any other of the fine arts.   Hence, like all 5
enjoyment, it calls for constant change, and does not stand
frequent repetition without inducing weariness.   Its charm,
which admits of such universal communication, appears to
rest on the following facts.   Every expression in language has
an associated tone suited to its sense.   This tone indicates, 10
more or less, a mode in which the speaker is affected, and in
turn evokes it in the hearer also, in whom conversely it then
also excites the idea which in language is expressed with such a
tone.   Further, just as modulation is, as it were, a universal
language of sensations intelligible to every man, so the art of 15
tone wields the full force of this language wholly on its own
account, namely, as a language of the affections, and in this
way, according to the law of association, universally communicates the aesthetic ideas that are naturally combined therewith.
But, further, inasmuch as those aesthetic ideas are not concepts 20
or determinate thoughts, the form of the arrangement of these
sensations (harmony and melody), taking the place of the form
of a language, only serves the purpose of giving an expression
to the aesthetic idea of an integral whole of an unutterable
wealth of thought that fills the measure of a certain theme 25
forming the dominant *affection* in the piece.   This purpose is
effectuated by means of a proportion in the accord of the
sensations (an accord which may be brought mathematically
under certain rules, since it rests, in the case of tones, upon the
numerical relation of the vibrations of the air in the same time, 30
so far as there is a combination of the tones simultaneously or
in succession).   Although this mathematical form is not represented by means of determinate concepts, to it alone belongs
the delight which the mere reflection upon such a number of

329

concomitant or consecutive sensations couples with this their play, as the universally valid condition of its beauty, and it is with reference to it alone that taste can lay claim to a right to anticipate the judgement of every man.

5   But mathematics, certainly, does not play the smallest part in the charm and movement of the mind produced by music. Rather is it only the indispensable condition (*conditio sine qua non*) of that proportion of the combining as well as changing impressions which makes it possible to grasp them all in one and prevent them from destroying one another, and to let them, rather, conspire towards the production of a continuous movement and quickening of the mind by affections that are in unison with it, and thus towards a serene self-enjoyment.

If, on the other hand, we estimate the worth of the fine arts by the culture they supply to the mind, and adopt for our standard the expansion of the faculties whose confluence, in judgement, is necessary for cognition, music, then, since it plays merely with sensations, has the lowest place among the fine arts —just as it has perhaps the highest among those valued at the same time for their agreeableness. Looked at in this light it is far excelled by the formative arts. For, in putting the imagination into a play which is at once free and adapted to the understanding, they all the while carry on a serious business, since they execute a product which serves the concepts of understanding as a vehicle, permanent and appealing to us on its own account, for effectuating their union with sensibility, and thus for promoting, as it were, the urbanity of the higher powers of cognition. The two kinds of art pursue completely different 330 courses.   Music advances from sensations to indefinite ideas : formative art from definite ideas to sensations. The latter gives a *lasting* impression, the former one that is only *fleeting*. The former sensations imagination can recall and agreeably entertain itself with, while the latter either vanish entirely, or else, if involuntarily repeated by the imagination, are more annoying

to us than agreeable.   Over and above all this, music has a
certain lack of urbanity about it.   For owing chiefly to the
character of its instruments, it scatters its influence abroad to
an uncalled-for extent (through the neighbourhood), and thus,
as it were, becomes obtrusive and deprives others, outside 5
the musical circle, of their freedom.   This is a thing that
the arts that address themselves to the eye do not do, for if
one is not disposed to give admittance to their impressions,
one has only to look the other way.   The case is almost on
a par with the practice of regaling oneself with a perfume that 10
exhales its odours far and wide.   The man who pulls his per-
fumed handkerchief from his pocket gives a treat to all around
whether they like it or not, and compels them, if they want to
breathe at all, to be parties to the enjoyment, and so the habit
has gone out of fashion.[1]   15

Among the formative arts I would give the palm to *painting* :
partly because it is the art of design and, as such, the groundwork of all the other formative arts ; partly because it can
penetrate much further into the region of ideas, and in conformity with them give a greater extension to the field of 20
intuition than it is open to the others to do.

§ 54

Remark.

As we have often shown, an essential distinction lies between
what *pleases simply in the estimate formed of it* and what *gratifies* 25
(pleases in sensation).   The latter is something which, unlike

[1] Those who have recommended the singing of hymns at family
prayers have forgotten the amount of annoyance which they give to the
general public by such *noisy* (and, as a rule, for that very reason, phari-
saical) worship, for they compel their neighbours either to join in the 30
singing or else abandon their meditations.

the former, we cannot demand from every one. Gratification (no matter whether its cause has its seat even in ideas) appears 331 always to consist in a feeling of the furtherance of the entire life of the man, and, hence, also of his bodily well-being, i. e.
5 his health. And so, perhaps, Epicurus was not wide of the mark when he said that at bottom all gratification is bodily sensation, and only misunderstood himself in ranking intellectual and even practical delight under the head of gratification. Bearing in mind the latter distinction, it is readily
10 explicable how even the gratification a person feels is capable of displeasing him (as the joy of a necessitous but good-natured individual on being made the heir of an affectionate but penurious father), or how deep pain may still give pleasure to the sufferer (as the sorrow of a widow over the death of her de-
15 serving husband), or how there may be pleasure over and above gratification (as in scientific pursuits), or how a pain (as, for example, hatred, envy, and desire for revenge) may in addition be a source of displeasure. Here the delight or aversion depends upon reason, and is one with *approbation* or *disappro-*
20 *bation.* Gratification and pain, on the other hand, can only depend upon feeling, or upon the prospect of a possible *well-being* or the *reverse* (irrespective of source).

The changing free play of sensations (which do not follow any preconceived plan) is always a source of gratification,
25 because it promotes the feeling of health ; and it is immaterial whether or not we experience delight in the object of this play or even in the gratification itself when estimated in the light of reason. Also this gratification may amount to an affection, although we take no interest in the object itself, or none,
30 at least, proportionate to the degree of the affection. We may divide the above play into that of *games of chance* (*Glückspiel*), *harmony* (*Tonspiel*), and *wit* (*Gedankenspiel*). The *first* stands in need of an *interest*, be it of vanity or self-seeking, but one which falls far short of that centered in the adopted mode of

procurement. All that the *second* requires is the change of *sensations*, each of which has its bearing on affection, though without attaining to the degree of an affection, and excites aesthetic ideas. The *third* springs merely from the change of the representations in the judgement, which, while unpro- 5 ductive of any thought conveying an interest, yet enlivens the mind.

What a fund of gratification must be afforded by play, without our having to fall back upon any consideration of interest, is a matter to which all our evening parties bear witness—for with- 10 out play they hardly ever escape falling flat. But the affections 332 of hope, fear, joy, anger, and derision here engage in play, as every moment they change their parts, and are so lively that, as by an internal motion, the whole vital function of the body seems to be furthered by the process—as is proved by a vivacity 15 of the mind produced—although no one comes by anything in the way of profit or instruction. But as the play of chance is not one that is beautiful, we will here lay it aside. Music, on the contrary, and what provokes laughter are two kinds of play with aesthetic ideas, or even with representations of 20 the understanding, by which, all said and done, nothing is thought. By mere force of change they yet are able to afford lively gratification. This furnishes pretty clear evidence that the quickening effect of both is physical, despite its being excited by ideas of the mind, and that the feeling of health, 25 arising from a movement of the intestines answering to that play, makes up that entire gratification of an animated gather-ing upon the spirit and refinement of which we set such store. Not any estimate of harmony in tones or flashes of wit, which, with its beauty, serves only as a necessary vehicle, but rather 30 the stimulated vital functions of the body, the affection stirring the intestines and the diaphragm, and, in a word, the feeling of health (of which we are only sensible upon some such provoca-tion) are what constitute the gratification we experience at being able to reach the body through the soul and use the latter as the physician of the former.

In music the course of this play is from bodily sensation to aesthetic ideas (which are the Objects for the affections), and 5 then from these back again, but with gathered strength, to the body. In jest (which just as much as the former deserves to be ranked rather as an agreeable than a fine art) the play sets out from thoughts which collectively, so far as seeking sensuous expression, engage the activity of the body. In this presenta-10 tion the understanding, missing what it expected, suddenly lets go its hold, with the result that the effect of this slackening is felt in the body by the oscillation of the organs. This favours the restoration of the equilibrium of the latter, and exerts a beneficial influence upon the health.

15 Something absurd (something in which, therefore, the under-standing can of itself find no delight) must be present in whatever is to raise a hearty convulsive laugh. *Laughter is an affection arising from a strained expectation being suddenly re-duced to nothing.* This very reduction, at which certainly under-20 standing cannot rejoice, is still indirectly a source of very lively enjoyment for a moment. Its cause must consequently lie 333 in the influence of the representation upon the body, and the reciprocal effect of this upon the mind. This, moreover, cannot depend upon the representation being objectively an object of 25 gratification, (for how can we derive gratification from a dis-appointment?) but must rest solely upon the fact that the reduction is a mere play of representations, and, as such, pro-duces an equilibrium of the vital forces of the body.

Suppose that some one tells the following story : An Indian 30 at an Englishman's table in Surat saw a bottle of ale opened, and all the beer turned into froth and flowing out. The repeated exclamations of the Indian showed his great astonishment. ' Well, what is so wonderful in that ? ' asked the Englishman. ' Oh, I'm not surprised myself,' said the Indian, ' at its getting out, but at how you ever managed to get it all in.' At this we laugh, and it gives us hearty pleasure. This is not because we think ourselves, maybe, more quick-witted than this ignorant Indian, or because our understanding here brings to our notice any other ground of delight. It is rather that the bubble of our expectation was extended to the full and suddenly went off into nothing. Or, again, take the case of the heir of a wealthy relative being minded to make preparations for having the funeral obsequies on a most imposing scale, but complaining that things would not go right for him, because (as he said) 'the more money I give my mourners to look sad, the more pleased they look'. At this we laugh outright, and the reason lies in the fact that we had an expectation which is suddenly reduced to nothing. We must be careful to observe that the reduction is not one into the positive contrary of an expected object—for that is always something, and may frequently pain us—but must be a reduction to nothing. For where a person arouses great expectation by recounting some tale, and at the close its untruth becomes at once apparent to us, we are displeased at it. So it is, for instance, with the tale of people whose hair from excess of grief is said to have turned white in a single night. On the other hand, if a wag, wishing to cap the story, tells with the utmost circumstantiality of a merchant's grief, who, on his return journey from India to Europe with all his wealth in merchandise, was obliged by stress of storm to throw everything overboard, and grieved to such an extent that in the selfsame night his *wig* turned grey, we laugh and enjoy the tale. This is because we keep for a time playing on our own mistake about an object otherwise indifferent to us, or rather on the idea we ourselves were following out, and, beating it to and fro, just as if it were a ball eluding our grasp, when all we intend to do is just to get it into our hands and hold it tight. Here our gratification is not excited by a knave or a fool getting a rebuff: for, even on its own account, the latter

tale told with an air of seriousness would of itself be enough to
set a whole table into roars of laughter; and the other matter
would ordinarily not be worth a moment's thought.

It is observable that in all such cases the joke must have
5 something in it capable of momentarily deceiving us.   Hence,
when the semblance vanishes into nothing, the mind looks back
in order to try it over again, and thus by a rapidly succeeding
tension and relaxation it is jerked to and fro and put in oscillation.   As the snapping of what was, as it were, tightening up
10 the string takes place suddenly (not by a gradual loosening),
the oscillation must bring about a mental movement and a
sympathetic internal movement of the body. This con-
tinues involuntarily and produces fatigue, but in so doing
it also affords recreation (the effects of a motion conducive
15 to health).

For supposing we assume that some movement in the bodily
organs is associated sympathetically with all our thoughts, it is
readily intelligible how the sudden act above referred to, of
shifting the mind now to one standpoint and now to the other,
20 to enable it to contemplate its object, may involve a corresponding and reciprocal straining and slackening of the elastic parts
of our intestines, which communicates itself to the diaphragm
(and resembles that felt by ticklish people), in the course of
which the lungs expel the air with rapidly succeeding interrup-
25 tions, resulting in a movement conducive to health. This alone,
and not what goes on in the mind, is the proper cause of the
gratification in a thought that at bottom represents nothing.—
Voltaire said that heaven has given us two things to compensate
us for the many miseries of life, *hope* and *sleep*. He might have
30 added *laughter* to the list—if only the means of exciting it in
men of intelligence were as ready to hand, and the wit or
originality of humour which it requires were not just as rare as
the talent is common for inventing stuff *that splits the head*, as
mystic speculators do, or *that breaks your neck*, as the genius

does, or that *harrows the heart* as sentimental novelists do (aye, and moralists of the same type).

We may, therefore, as I conceive, make Epicurus a present of the point that all gratification, even when occasioned by concepts that evoke aesthetic ideas, is *animal*, i.e. bodily 5 sensation. For from this admission the *spiritual* feeling of respect for moral ideas, which is not one of gratification, but a self-esteem, (an esteem for humanity within us,) that raises us above the need of gratification, suffers not a whit—no nor even the less noble feeling of *taste*. 10

In *naïveté* we meet with a joint product of both the above. *Naïveté* is the breaking forth of the ingenuousness originally natural to humanity, in opposition to the art of disguising oneself that has become a second nature. We laugh at the simplicity that is as yet a stranger to dissimulation, but we 15 rejoice the while over the simplicity of nature that thwarts that art. We await the commonplace manner of artificial utterance, thoughtfully addressed to a fair show, and lo! nature stands before us in unsullied innocence—nature that we were quite unprepared to meet, and that he who laid it bare had also no 20 intention of revealing. That the outward appearance, fair but false, that usually assumes such importance in our judgement, is here, at a stroke, turned to a nullity, that, as it were, the rogue in us is nakedly exposed, calls forth the movement of the mind, in two successive and opposite directions, agitating 25 the body at the same time with wholesome motion. But that something infinitely better than any accepted code of manners, namely purity of mind, (or at least a vestige of such purity,) has not become wholly extinct in human nature, infuses seriousness and reverence into this play of judgement. But since it is 30 only a manifestation that obtrudes itself for a moment, and the veil of a dissembling art is soon drawn over it again, there enters into the above feelings a touch of pity. This is an emotion of tenderness, playful in its way, that thus readily admits of com-

bination with this sort of genial laughter. And, in fact, this emotion is as a rule associated with it, and, at the same time, is wont to make amends to the person who provides such food for our merriment for his embarrassment at not being wise
5 after the manner of men.—For that reason an art of being *naïf* is a contradiction. But it is quite possible to give a representation of *naïveté* in a fictitious personage, and, rare as the art is, it is a fine art. With this *naïveté* we must not confuse homely simplicity, which only avoids spoiling nature by artifici-
10 ality, because it has no notion of the conventions of good society.

The *humorous* manner may also be ranked as a thing which in its enlivening influence is clearly allied to the gratification provoked by laughter. It belongs to originality of mind (*des*
15 *Geistes*), though not to the talent for fine art. *Humour*, in a good sense, means the talent for being able to put oneself at will into a certain frame of mind in which everything is estimated on lines that go quite off the beaten track, (a topsy-turvy view of things,) and yet on lines that follow certain principles,
20 rational in the case of such a mental temperament. A person with whom such variations are not a matter of choice is said *to have humours* ; but if a person can assume them voluntarily, and of set purpose (on behalf of a lively presentation drawn from a ludicrous contrast), he and his way of speaking are termed
25 *humorous*. This manner belongs, however, to agreeable rather than to fine art, because the object of the latter must always have an evident intrinsic worth about it, and thus demands a certain seriousness in its presentation, as taste does in estimating it.

337 ## CRITIQUE OF AESTHETIC JUDGEMENT

SECOND SECTION

DIALECTIC OF AESTHETIC JUDGEMENT

§ 55

FOR a power of judgement to be dialectical it must first of all be rationalizing ; that is to say, its judgements must lay claim to universality,[1] and do so *a priori*, for it is in the antithesis of such judgements that dialectic consists. Hence there is nothing dialectical in the irreconcilability of aesthetic judgements of sense (upon the agreeable and disagreeable). And in so far as each person appeals merely to his own private taste, even the conflict of judgements of taste does not form a dialectic of taste —for no one is proposing to make his own judgement into a universal rule. Hence the only concept left to us of a dialectic affecting taste is one of a dialectic of the *Critique* of taste (not of taste itself) in respect of its *principles* : for, on the question of the ground of the possibility of judgements of taste in general, mutually conflicting concepts naturally and unavoidably make their appearance. The transcendental Critique of taste will, therefore, only include a part capable of bearing the name of a dialectic of the aesthetic judgement if we find an antinomy of the principles of this faculty which throws doubt upon its conformity to law, and hence also upon its inner possibility.

[1] Any judgement which sets up to be universal may be termed a rationalizing judgement (*iudicium ratiocinans*) ; for so far as universal it may serve as the major premiss of a syllogism. On the other hand, only a judgement which is thought as the conclusion of a syllogism, and, therefore, as having an *a priori* foundation, can be called rational (*iudicium ratiocinatum*).

§ 56

Representation of the antinomy of taste.

THE first commonplace of taste is contained in the proposition under cover of which every one devoid of taste thinks to
5 shelter himself from reproach : *every one has his own taste.*
This is only another way of saying that the determining ground
of this judgement is merely subjective (gratification or pain),
and that the judgement has no right to the necessary agreement of others.

10 Its second commonplace, to which even those resort who
concede the right of the judgement of taste to pronounce with
validity for every one, is : *there is no disputing about taste.* This
amounts to saying that even though the determining ground
of a judgement of taste be objective, it is not reducible to
15 definite concepts, so that in respect of the judgement itself no
decision can be reached by proofs, although it is quite open to
us to *contend* upon the matter, and to contend with right. For
though *contention* and *dispute* have this point in common,
that they aim at bringing judgements into accordance out of
20 and by means of their mutual opposition ; yet they differ in the
latter hoping to effect this from definite concepts, as grounds of
proof, and, consequently, adopting *objective concepts* as grounds
of the judgement. But where this is considered impracticable,
dispute is regarded as alike out of the question.

25 Between these two commonplaces an intermediate proposition
is readily seen to be missing. It is one which has certainly not
become proverbial, but yet it is at the back of every one's mind.
It is that *there may be contention about taste* (although not a
dispute). This proposition, however, involves the contrary of
30 the first one. For in a matter in which contention is to be
allowed, there must be a hope of coming to terms. Hence one
must be able to reckon on grounds of judgement that possess
more than private validity and are thus not merely subjective.

And yet the above principle, *every one has his own taste*, is directly opposed to this.

The principle of taste, therefore, exhibits the following antinomy :

1. *Thesis.* The judgement of taste is not based upon 5 concepts ; for, if it were, it would be open to dispute (decision by means of proofs).

2. *Antithesis.* The judgement of taste is based on concepts ; for otherwise, despite diversity of judgement, there could be no 339 room even for contention in the matter (a claim to the necessary 10 agreement of others with this judgement).

§ 57

Solution of the antinomy of taste.

THERE is no possibility of removing the conflict of the above principles, which underlie every judgement of taste (and which 15 are only the two peculiarities of the judgement of taste previously set out in the Analytic) except by showing that the concept to which the Object is made to refer in a judgement of this kind is not taken in the same sense in both maxims of the aesthetic judgement ; that this double sense, or point of view, 20 in our estimate, is necessary for our power of transcendental judgement ; and that nevertheless the false appearance arising from the confusion of one with the other is a natural illusion, and so unavoidable.

The judgement of taste must have reference to some concept 25 or other, as otherwise it would be absolutely impossible for it to lay claim to necessary validity for every one.   Yet it need not on that account be provable from a concept.   For a concept may be either determinable, or else at once intrinsically undetermined and indeterminable.   A concept of the under- 30 standing, which is determinable by means of predicates borrowed from sensible intuition and capable of corresponding to it, is of the first kind. But of the second kind is the transcendental rational concept of the supersensible, which lies at the basis of all that sensible intuition and is, therefore, incapable of being 5 further determined theoretically.

Now the judgement of taste applies to objects of sense, but not so as to determine a *concept* of them for the understanding ; for it is not a cognitive judgement. Hence it is a singular representation of intuition referable to the feeling of pleasure, 10 and, as such, only a private judgement. And to that extent it would be limited in its validity to the individual judging : the object is *for me* an object of delight, for others it may be otherwise ;—every one to his taste.

For all that, the judgement of taste contains beyond doubt 15 an enlarged reference on the part of the representation of the Object (and at the same time on the part of the Subject also), which lays the foundation of an extension of judgements of this kind to necessity for every one. This must of necessity be founded upon some concept or other, but such a concept as 340 20 does not admit of being determined by intuition, and affords no knowledge of anything. Hence, too, it is a concept *which does not afford any proof* of the judgement of taste. But the mere pure rational concept of the supersensible lying at the basis of the object (and of the judging Subject for that matter) 25 as Object of sense, and thus as phenomenon, is just such a concept. For unless such a point of view were adopted there would be no means of saving the claim of the judgement of taste to universal validity. And if the concept forming the required basis were a concept of understanding, though a mere 30 confused one, as, let us say, of perfection, answering to which the sensible intuition of the beautiful might be adduced, then it would be at least intrinsically possible to found the judgement of taste upon proofs, which contradicts the thesis.

All contradiction disappears, however, if I say : The judgement 35 of taste does depend upon a concept (of a general ground of the subjective finality of nature for the power of judgement), but one from which nothing can be cognized in respect of the Object, and nothing proved, because it is in itself indeterminable and useless for knowledge. Yet by means of this very concept it acquires at the same time validity for every one (but with each 5 individual, no doubt, as a singular judgement immediately accompanying his intuition): because its determining ground lies, perhaps, in the concept of what may be regarded as the supersensible substrate of humanity.

The solution of an antinomy turns solely on the possibility 10 of two apparently conflicting propositions not being in fact contradictory, but rather being capable of consisting together, although the explanation of the possibility of their concept transcends our faculties of cognition. That this illusion is also natural and for human reason unavoidable, as well as 15 why it is so, and remains so, although upon the solution of the apparent contradiction it no longer misleads us, may be made intelligible from the above considerations.

For the concept, which the universal validity of a judgement must have for its basis, is taken in the same sense in both the 20 conflicting judgements, yet two opposite predicates are asserted of it. The thesis should therefore read: The judgement of taste is not based on *determinate* concepts; but the antithesis: The judgement of taste does rest upon a concept, although an *indeterminate* one, (that, namely, of the supersensible substrate 25 of phenomena); and then there would be no conflict between them.

Beyond removing this conflict between the claims and counter-claims of taste we can do nothing. To supply a determinate objective principle of taste in accordance with which its 30 judgements might be derived, tested, and proved, is an absolute impossibility, for then it would not be a judgement of taste. The subjective principle—that is to say, the indeterminate idea of the supersensible within us—can only be indicated as the unique key to the riddle of this faculty, itself concealed from us in its sources ; and there is no means of making it any more intelligible.

The antinomy here exhibited and resolved rests upon the
5 proper concept of taste as a merely reflective aesthetic judgement, and the two seemingly conflicting principles are reconciled on the ground that *they may both be true*, and this is sufficient. If, on the other hand, owing to the fact that the representation lying at the basis of the judgement of taste is singular,
10 the determining ground of taste is taken, as by some it is, to be *agreeableness*, or, as others, looking to its universal validity, would have it, the principle of *perfection*, and if the definition of taste is framed accordingly, the result is an antinomy which is absolutely irresolvable unless we show *the falsity of both*
15 *propositions* as contraries (not as simple contradictories). This would force the conclusion that the concept upon which each is founded is self-contradictory. Thus it is evident that the removal of the antinomy of the aesthetic judgement pursues a course similar to that followed by the Critique in the solution
20 of the antinomies of pure theoretical reason ; and that the antinomies, both here and in the Critique of Practical Reason, compel us, whether we like it or not, to look beyond the horizon of the sensible, and to seek in the supersensible the point of union of all our faculties *a priori* : for we are left with no other
25 expedient to bring reason into harmony with itself.

Remark 1.

We find such frequent occasion in transcendental philosophy for distinguishing ideas from concepts of the understanding that it may be of use to introduce technical terms answering to 342
30 the distinction between them. I think that no objection will be raised to my proposing some.—Ideas, in the most comprehensive sense of the word, are representations referred to an

object according to a certain principle (subjective or objective), in so far as they can still never become a cognition of it. They are either referred to an intuition, in accordance with a merely subjective principle of the harmony of the cognitive faculties (imagination and understanding), and are then called *aesthetic* ; 5 or else they are referred to a concept according to an objective principle and yet are incapable of ever furnishing a cognition of the object, and are called *rational ideas*. In the latter case the concept is a *transcendent* concept, and, as such, differs from a concept of understanding, for which an adequately answering 10 experience may always be supplied, and which, on that account, is called *immanent*.

An *aesthetic idea* cannot become a cognition, because it is an *intuition* (of the imagination) for which an adequate concept can never be found. A *rational idea* can never become a cognition, 15 because it involves a *concept* (of the supersensible), for which a commensurate intuition can never be given.

Now the aesthetic idea might, I think, be called an *inexponible* representation of the imagination, the rational idea, on the other hand, an *indemonstrable* concept of reason. The pro- 20 duction of both is presupposed to be not altogether groundless, but rather, (following the above explanation of an idea in general,) to take place in obedience to certain principles of the cognitive faculties to which they belong (subjective principles in the case of the former and objective in that of the 25 latter).

Concepts of the understanding must, as such, always be demonstrable (if, as in anatomy, demonstration is understood in the sense merely of *presentation*). In other words, the object answering to such concepts must always be capable of being 30 given in intuition (pure or empirical) ; for only in this way can they become cognitions. The concept of *magnitude* may be given *a priori* in the intuition of space, e.g. of a right line, &c. ; the concept of *cause* in impenetrability, in the impact of

bodies, &c. Consequently both may be verified by means of an empirical intuition, i.e. the thought of them may be indicated (demonstrated, exhibited) in an example ; and this it must be 343 possible to do : for otherwise there would be no certainty of
5 the thought not being empty, i.e. having no object.

In logic the expressions demonstrable or indemonstrable are ordinarily employed only in respect of *propositions*. A better designation would be to call the former, propositions only mediately, and the latter, propositions *immediately, certain*. For
10 pure philosophy, too, has propositions of both these kinds— meaning thereby true propositions which are in the one case capable, and in the other incapable, of proof. But, in its character of philosophy, while it can, no doubt, prove on *a priori* grounds, it cannot demonstrate—unless we wish to give the
15 complete go-by to the meaning of the word which makes demonstrate (*ostendere, exhibere*) equivalent to giving an accompanying presentation of the concept in intuition (be it in a proof or in a definition). Where the intuition is *a priori* this is called its construction, but when even the intuition is
20 empirical, we have still got the illustration of the object, by which means objective reality is assured to the concept. Thus an anatomist is said to demonstrate the human eye when he renders the concept, of which he has previously given a discursive exposition, intuitable by means of the dissection of that
25 organ.

It follows from the above that the rational concept of the supersensible substrate of all phenomena generally, or even of that which must be laid at the basis of our elective will in respect of moral laws, i.e. the rational concept of transcendental
30 freedom, is at once specifically an indemonstrable concept, and a rational idea, whereas virtue is so in a measure. For nothing can be given which in itself qualitatively answers in experience to the rational concept of the former, while in the case of virtue no empirical product of the above causality attains the degree
35 that the rational idea prescribes as the rule.

Just as the *imagination*, in the case of a rational idea, fails with its intuitions to attain to the given concept, so *understanding*, in the case of an aesthetic idea, fails with its concepts ever to attain to the completeness of the internal intuition which imagination conjoins with a given representation. Now since 5 the reduction of a representation of the imagination to concepts is equivalent to giving its *exponents*, the aesthetic idea may be called an *inexponible* representation of the imagination (in its free play). I shall have an opportunity hereafter of dealing more fully with ideas of this kind. At present I confine myself 10 344 to the remark, that both kinds of ideas, aesthetic ideas as well as rational, are bound to have their principles, and that the seat of these principles must in both cases be reason—the latter depending upon the objective, the former upon the subjective, principles of its employment. 15

Consonantly with this, GENIUS may also be defined as the faculty of *aesthetic ideas*. This serves at the same time to point out the reason why it is nature (the nature of the individual) and not a set purpose, that in products of genius gives the rule to art (as the production of the beautiful). For the beautiful 20 must not be estimated according to concepts, but by the final mode in which the imagination is attuned so as to accord with the faculty of concepts generally ; and so rule and precept are incapable of serving as the requisite subjective standard for that aesthetic and unconditioned finality in fine art which has to make 25 a warranted claim to being bound to please every one. Rather must such a standard be sought in the element of mere nature in the Subject, which cannot be comprehended under rules or concepts, that is to say, the supersensible substrate of all the Subject's faculties (unattainable by any concept of understand- 30 ing), and consequently in that which forms the point of reference for the harmonious accord of all our faculties of cognition—the production of which accord is the ultimate end set by the intelligible basis of our nature. Thus alone is it possible for a subjective and yet universally valid principle *a priori* to lie at the basis of that finality for which no objective principle can be prescribed.

Remark 2.

5 The following important observation here naturally presents itself: There are *three kinds of antinomies* of pure reason, which, however, all agree in forcing reason to abandon the otherwise very natural assumption which takes the objects of sense for things-in-themselves, and to regard them, instead, 10 merely as phenomena, and to lay at their basis an intelligible substrate (something supersensible, the concept of which is only an idea and affords no proper knowledge). Apart from some such antinomy reason could never bring itself to take such a step as to adopt a principle so severely restricting the 15 field of its speculation, and to submit to sacrifices involving the complete dissipation of so many otherwise brilliant hopes. For even now that it is recompensed for this loss by the prospect of a proportionately wider scope of action from a practical point of view, it is not without a pang of regret that 345 20 it appears to part company with those hopes, and to break away from the old ties.

The reason for there being three kinds of antinomies is to be found in the fact that there are three faculties of cognition, understanding, judgement, and reason, each of which, being 25 a higher faculty of cognition, must have its *a priori* principles. For, so far as reason passes judgement upon these principles themselves and their employment, it inexorably requires the unconditioned for the given conditioned in respect of them all. This can never be found unless the sensible, instead of being 30 regarded as inherently appurtenant to things-in-themselves, is treated as a mere phenomenon, and, as such, being made to rest upon something supersensible (the intelligible substrate of external and internal nature) as the thing-in-itself. There is then

(1) *for the cognitive faculty* an antinomy of reason in respect of the theoretical employment of understanding carried to the point of the unconditioned ; (2) for *the feeling of pleasure and displeasure* an antinomy of reason in respect of the aesthetic employment of judgement ; (3) *for the faculty of desire* an 5 antinomy in respect of the practical employment of self-legislative reason. For all these faculties have their fundamental *a priori* principles, and, following an imperative demand of reason, must be able to judge and to determine their Object *unconditionally* in accordance with these principles. 10

As to two of the antinomies of these higher cognitive faculties, those, namely, of their theoretical and of their practical employment, we have already shown elsewhere both that they are *inevitable*, if no cognisance is taken in such judgements of a supersensible substrate of the given Objects as 15 phenomena, and, on the other hand, that they *can be solved* the moment this is done. Now, as to the antinomy incident to the employment of judgement in conformity with the demand of reason, and the solution of it here given, we may say that to avoid facing it there are but the following alterna- 20 tives. It is open to us to deny that any *a priori* principle lies at the basis of the aesthetic judgement of taste, with the result that all claim to the necessity of a universal consensus of opinion is an idle and empty delusion, and that a judgement of taste only deserves to be considered to this extent correct, 25 that *it so happens* that a number share the same opinion, and even this, not, in truth, because an *a priori* principle is *presumed* to lie at the back of this agreement, but rather (as with the taste of the palate) because of the contingently resembling organization of the individuals. *Or else*, in the 30 346 alternative, we should have to suppose that the judgement of taste is in fact a disguised judgement of reason on the perfection discovered in a thing and the reference of the manifold in it to an end, and that it is consequently only called aesthetic on account of the confusion that here besets our reflection, although fundamentally it is teleological. In this latter case the solution of the antinomy with the assistance of transcendental ideas might be declared otiose and nugatory, 5 and the above laws of taste thus reconciled with the Objects of sense, not as mere phenomena, but even as things-in-themselves. How unsatisfactory both of those alternatives alike are as a means of escape has been shown in several places in our exposition of judgements of taste.

10 If, however, our deduction is at least credited with having been worked out on correct lines, even though it may not have been sufficiently clear in all its details, three ideas then stand out in evidence. *Firstly*, there is the supersensible in general, without further determination, as substrate of nature ; *secondly*, 15 this same supersensible as principle of the subjective finality of nature for our cognitive faculties ; *thirdly*, the same supersensible again, as principle of the ends of freedom, and principle of the common accord of these ends with freedom in the moral sphere.

20

§ 58

The idealism of the finality alike of nature and of art, as the unique principle of the aesthetic judgement.

THE principle of taste may, to begin with, be placed on either of two footings. For taste may be said invariably to judge on 25 empirical grounds of determination and such, therefore, as are only given *a posteriori* through sense, or else it may be allowed to judge on an *a priori* ground. The former would be the *empiricism* of the Critique of Taste, the latter its *rationalism*. The first would obliterate the distinction that marks off the 30 object of our delight from the *agreeable* ; the *second*, supposing the judgement rested upon determinate concepts, would obliterate its distinction from the *good*. In this way *beauty* would have its *locus standi* in the world completely denied, and nothing but the dignity of a separate name, betokening, maybe, a certain blend of both the above-named kinds of 347 delight, would be left in its stead. But we have shown the existence of grounds of delight which are *a priori*, and which, 5 therefore, can consist with the principle of rationalism, and which are yet incapable of being grasped by *definite concepts*.

As against the above we may say that the rationalism of the principle of taste may take the form either of the *realism* of finality or of its *idealism*. Now, as a judgement of taste is not 10 a cognitive judgement, and as beauty is not a property of the object considered on its own account, the rationalism of the principle of taste can never be placed in the fact that the finality in this judgement is regarded in thought as objective. In other words, the judgement is not directed theoretically, nor, 15 therefore, logically, either, (no matter if only in a confused estimate,) to the perfection of the object, but only *aesthetically* to the harmonizing of its representation in the imagination with the essential principles of judgement generally in the Subject. For this reason the judgement of taste, and the 20 distinction between its realism and its idealism, can only, even on the principle of rationalism, depend upon its subjective finality interpreted in one or other of two ways. Either such subjective finality is, in the first case, a harmony with our judgement pursued as an actual (intentional) *end* of nature 25 (or of art), or else, in the second case, it is only a supervening final harmony with the needs of our faculty of judgement in its relation to nature and the forms which nature produces in accordance with particular laws, and one that is independent of an end, spontaneous and contingent. 30

The beautiful forms displayed in the organic world all plead eloquently on the side of the realism of the aesthetic finality of nature in support of the plausible assumption that beneath the production of the beautiful there must lie a preconceived idea in the producing cause—that is to say an *end* acting in the interest of our imagination. Flowers, blossoms, even the shapes of plants as a whole, the elegance of animal formations of all kinds, unnecessary for the discharge of any function on their part, but chosen as it were with an eye to our taste; and, beyond all else, the variety and harmony in the array of colours (in the pheasant, in crustacea, in insects, down even to the meanest flowers), so pleasing and charming to the eyes, but which, inasmuch as they touch the bare surface, and do not even here in any way affect the structure, of these creatures— a matter which might have a necessary bearing on their internal ends—seem to be planned entirely with a view to outward appearance: all these lend great weight to the mode of ex- 348 planation which assumes actual ends of nature in favour of our aesthetic judgement.

On the other hand, not alone does reason, with its maxims enjoining upon us in all cases to avoid, as far as possible, any unnecessary multiplication of principles, set itself against this assumption, but we have nature in its free formations display- ing on all sides extensive mechanical proclivity to producing forms seemingly made, as it were, for the aesthetic employment of our judgement, without affording the least support to the supposition of a need for anything over and above its mechan- ism, as mere nature, to enable them to be final for our judgement apart from their being grounded upon any idea. The above expression, '*free formations*' of nature, is, however, here used to denote such as are originally set up in a *fluid at rest* where the volatilization or separation of some constituent (sometimes merely of caloric) leaves the residue on solidifica- tion to assume a definite shape or structure (figure or texture) which differs with specific differences of the matter, but for the same matter is invariable. Here, however, it is taken for granted that, as the true meaning of a fluid requires, the matter in the fluid is completely dissolved and not a mere admixture of solid particles simply held there in suspension.

The formation, then, takes place by a *concursion*, i.e. by a sudden solidification—not by a gradual transition from the fluid to the solid state, but, as it were, by a leap. This transition is termed *crystallization*. Freezing water offers the most familiar instance of a formation of this kind. There 5 the process begins by straight threads of ice forming. These unite at angles of 60°, whilst others similarly attach themselves to them at every point until the whole has turned into ice. But while this is going on the water between the threads of ice does not keep getting gradually more viscous, but remains as 10 thoroughly fluid as it would be at a much higher temperature, although it is perfectly ice-cold. The matter that frees itself— that makes its sudden escape at the moment of solidification— is a considerable quantum of caloric. As this was merely required to preserve fluidity, its disappearance leaves the exist- 15 ing ice not a whit colder than the water which but a moment before was there as fluid.

There are many salts and also stones of a crystalline figure which owe their origin in like manner to some earthy substance being dissolved in water under the influence of agencies little 20 349 understood. The drusy configurations of many minerals, of the cubical sulphide of lead, of the red silver ore, &c., are presumably also similarly formed in water, and by the concursion of their particles, on their being forced by some cause or other to relinquish this vehicle and to unite among them- 25 selves in definite external shapes.

But, further, all substances rendered fluid by heat, which have become solid as the result of cooling, give, when broken, internal evidences of a definite texture, thus suggesting the inference that only for the interference of their own weight or 30 the disturbance of the air, the exterior would also have exhibited their proper specific shape. This has been observed in the case of some metals where the exterior of a molten mass has hardened, but the interior remained fluid, and then, owing to the withdrawal of the still fluid portion in the interior, there has been an undisturbed concursion of the remaining parts on the inside. A number of such mineral crystallizations, such as *spars, hematite, aragonite,* frequently present extremely beautiful shapes such as it might take art all its time to devise; and the halo in the grotto of Antiparos is merely the work of water percolating through strata of gypsum.

The fluid state is, to all appearance, on the whole older than the solid, and plants as well as animal bodies are built up out of fluid nutritive substance, so far as this takes form undisturbed—in the case of the latter, admittedly, in obedience, primarily, to a certain original bent of nature directed to ends (which, as will be shown in Part II, must not be judged aesthetically, but teleologically by the principle of realism); but still all the while, perhaps, also following the universal law of the affinity of substances in the way they shoot together and form in freedom. In the same way, again, where an atmosphere, which is a composite of different kinds of gas, is charged with watery fluids, and these separate from it owing to a reduction of the temperature, they produce snow-figures of shapes differing with the actual composition of the atmosphere. These are frequently of very artistic appearance and of extreme beauty. So without at all derogating from the teleological principle by which an organization is judged, it is readily conceivable how with beauty of flowers, of the plumage of birds, of crustacea, both as to their shape and their colour, we have only what may be ascribed to nature and its capacity for originating in free activity aesthetically final forms, independently of any particular guiding ends, according to chemical laws, by means of the chemical integration of the substance requisite for the organization. 350

But what shows plainly that the principle of the *ideality* of the finality in the beauty of nature is the one upon which we ourselves invariably take our stand in our aesthetic judgements, forbidding us to have recourse to any realism of a natural end in favour of our faculty of representation as a principle of explanation, is that in our general estimate of beauty we seek its standard *a priori* in ourselves, and, that the aesthetic faculty is itself legislative in respect of the judgement whether anything 5 is beautiful or not.   This could not be so on the assumption of a realism of the finality of nature ; because in that case we should have to go to nature for instruction as to what we should deem beautiful, and the judgement of taste would be subject to empirical principles.   For in such an estimate the question 10 does not turn on what nature is, or even on what it is for us in the way of an end, but on how we receive it.   For nature to have fashioned its forms for our delight would inevitably imply an objective finality on the part of nature, instead of a subjective finality resting on the play of imagination in its freedom, 15 where it is we who receive nature with favour, and not nature that does us a favour.   That nature affords us an opportunity for perceiving the inner finality in the relation of our mental powers engaged in the estimate of certain of its products, and, indeed, such a finality as arising from a supersensible basis is to be 20 pronounced necessary and of universal validity, is a property of nature which cannot belong to it as its end, or rather, cannot be estimated by us to be such an end.   For otherwise the judgement that would be determined by reference to such an end would found upon heteronomy, instead of founding 25 upon autonomy and being free, as befits a judgement of taste.

The principle of the idealism of finality is still more clearly apparent in fine art.   For the point that sensations do not enable us to adopt an aesthetic realism of finality (which would 30 make art merely agreeable instead of beautiful) is one which it enjoys in common with beautiful nature.   But the further point that the delight arising from aesthetic ideas must not be made dependent upon the successful attainment of determinate ends

(as an art mechanically directed to results), and that, consequently, even in the case of the rationalism of the principle, an
ideality of the ends and not their reality is fundamental,
is brought home to us by the fact that fine art, as such, must
5 not be regarded as a product of understanding and science, 351
but of genius, and must, therefore, derive its rule from *aesthetic*
ideas, which are essentially different from rational ideas of
determinate ends.

Just as the *ideality* of objects of sense as phenomena is the
10 only way of explaining the possibility of their forms admitting
of *a priori* determination, so, also, the *idealism* of the finality
in estimating the beautiful in nature and in art is the only
hypothesis upon which a Critique can explain the possibility of
a judgement of taste that demands *a priori* validity for
15 every one (yet without basing the finality represented in the
Object upon concepts).

§ 59

Beauty as the symbol of morality.

INTUITIONS are always required to verify the reality of our
20 concepts. If the concepts are empirical the intuitions are
called *examples* : if they are pure concepts of the understanding
the intuitions go by the name of *schemata*. But to call for a
verification of the objective reality of rational concepts, i.e. of
ideas, and, what is more, on behalf of the theoretical cognition
25 of such a reality, is to demand an impossibility, because
absolutely no intuition adequate to them can be given.

All *hypotyposis* (presentation, *subjectio sub adspectum*) as a
rendering in terms of sense, is twofold. Either it is *schematic*,
as where the intuition corresponding to a concept comprehended
30 by the understanding is given *a priori*, or else it is *symbolic*, as
where the concept is one which only reason can think, and to
which no sensible intuition can be adequate. In the latter case
the concept is supplied with an intuition such that the pro-

cedure of judgement in dealing with it is merely analogous to that which it observes in schematism. In other words, what agrees with the concept is merely the rule of this procedure, and not the intuition itself. Hence the agreement is merely in the form of reflection, and not in the content. 5

Notwithstanding the adoption of the word *symbolic* by modern logicians in a sense opposed to an *intuitive* mode of represen- tation, it is a wrong use of the word and subversive of its true meaning; for the symbolic is only a *mode* of the intuitive. The intuitive mode of representation is, in fact, divisible into 10 352 the *schematic* and the *symbolic*. Both are hypotyposes, i.e. presentations (*exhibitiones*), not mere *marks*. Marks are merely designations of concepts by the aid of accompanying sensible signs devoid of any intrinsic connexion with the intuition of the Object. Their sole function is to afford a means of reinvoking 15 the concepts according to the imagination's law of association— a purely subjective rôle. Such marks are either words or visible (algebraic or even mimetic) signs, simply as *expressions* for concepts.[1]

All intuitions by which *a priori* concepts are given a foothold 20 are, therefore, either *schemata* or *symbols*. Schemata contain direct, symbols indirect, presentations of the concept. Schemata effect this presentation demonstratively, symbols by the aid of an analogy (for which recourse is had even to empirical intuitions), in which analogy judgement performs a double 25 function: first in applying the concept to the object of a sensible intuition, and then, secondly, in applying the mere rule of its reflection upon that intuition to quite another object, of which the former is but the symbol. In this way a monarchical state is represented as a living body when it is governed by 30

---

[1] The intuitive mode of knowledge must be contrasted with the dis- cursive mode (not with the symbolic). The former is either *schematic*, by means of *demonstration*, or *symbolic*, as a representation following a mere *analogy*.

constitutional laws, but as a mere machine (like a hand-mill) when it is governed by an individual absolute will; but in both cases the representation is merely *symbolic*. For there is certainly no likeness between a despotic state and a hand-mill,
5 whereas there surely is between the rules of reflection upon both and their causality. Hitherto this function has been but little analysed, worthy as it is of a deeper study. Still this is not the place to dwell upon it. In language we have many such indirect presentations modelled upon an analogy enabling the
10 expression in question to contain, not the proper schema for the concept, but merely a symbol for reflection. Thus the words *ground* (support, basis), *to depend* (to be held up from above), to *flow* from (instead of to follow), *substance* (as Locke puts it : the support of accidents), and numberless others, are
15 not schematic, but rather symbolic hypotyposes, and express concepts without employing a direct intuition for the purpose, but only drawing upon an analogy with one, i. e. transferring the reflection upon an object of intuition to quite a new concept, 353 and one with which perhaps no intuition could ever directly
20 correspond. Supposing the name of knowledge may be given to what only amounts to a mere mode of representation (which is quite permissible where this is not a principle of the theoretical determination of the object in respect of what it is in itself, but of the practical determination of what the idea of it ought to
25 be for us and for its final employment), then all our knowledge of God is merely symbolic; and one who takes it, with the properties of understanding, will, and so forth, which only evidence their objective reality in beings of this world, to be schematic, falls into anthropomorphism, just as, if he abandons
30 every intuitive element, he falls into Deism which furnishes no knowledge whatsoever—not even from a practical point of view.

Now, I say, the beautiful is the symbol of the morally good, and only in this light (a point of view natural to every one,
35 and one which every one exacts from others as a duty) does

it give us pleasure with an attendant claim to the agreement of every one else, whereupon the mind becomes conscious of a certain ennoblement and elevation above mere sensibility to pleasure from impressions of sense, and also appraises the worth of others on the score of a like maxim of their judgement. This is that *intelligible* to which taste, as noticed in the preceding paragraph, extends its view. It is, that is to say, what brings even our higher cognitive faculties into common accord, and is that apart from which sheer contradiction would arise between their nature and the claims put forward by taste. In this faculty judgement does not find itself subjected to a heteronomy of laws of experience as it does in the empirical estimate of things—in respect of the objects of such a pure delight it gives the law to itself, just as reason does in respect of the faculty of desire. Here, too, both on account of this inner possibility in the Subject, and on account of the external possibility of a nature harmonizing therewith, it finds a reference in itself to something in the Subject itself and outside it, and which is not nature, nor yet freedom, but still is connected with the ground of the latter, i.e. the supersensible—a something in which the theoretical faculty gets bound up into unity with the practical in an intimate and obscure manner. We shall bring out a few points of this analogy, while taking care, at the same time, not to let the points of difference escape us.

(1) The beautiful pleases *immediately* (but only in reflective intuition, not, like morality, in its concept). (2) It pleases *apart from all interest* (pleasure in the morally good is no doubt necessarily bound up with an interest, but not with one of the kind that are antecedent to the judgement upon the delight, but with one that judgement itself for the first time calls into existence). (3) *The freedom* of the imagination (consequently of our faculty in respect of its sensibility) is, in estimating the beautiful, represented as in accord with the understanding's conformity to law (in moral judgements the freedom of the will is thought as the

harmony of the latter with itself according to universal laws of Reason). (4) The subjective principle of the estimate of the beautiful is represented as *universal,* i. e. valid for every man, but as incognizable by means of any universal concept (the objective principle of morality is set forth as also universal, i. e. for all individuals, and, at the same time, for all actions of the same individual, and, besides, as cognizable by means of a universal concept). For this reason the moral judgement not alone admits of definite constitutive principles, but is *only* possible by adopting these principles and their universality as the ground of its maxims.

Even common understanding is wont to pay regard to this analogy ; and we frequently apply to beautiful objects of nature or of art names that seem to rely upon the basis of a moral estimate. We call buildings or trees majestic and stately, or plains laughing and gay ; even colours are called innocent, modest, soft, because they excite sensations containing something analogous to the consciousness of the state of mind produced by moral judgements. Taste makes, as it were, the transition from the charm of sense to habitual moral interest possible without too violent a leap, for it represents the imagination, even in its freedom, as amenable to a final determination for understanding, and teaches us to find, even in sensuous objects, a free delight apart from any charm of sense.

§ 60

APPENDIX

The methodology of taste.

THE division of a Critique into Elementology and Methodology—a division which is introductory to science—is one inapplicable to the Critique of Taste. For there neither is, nor can be, a science of the beautiful, and the judgement of taste is not determinable by principles. For, as to the element of science in every art—a matter which turns upon *truth* in the presentation of the Object of the art—while this is, no doubt, the indispensable condition (*conditio sine qua non*) of fine art, it is not itself fine art. Fine art, therefore, has only got a *manner* (*modus*), and not a *method* of teaching (*methodus*). 5 The master must illustrate what the pupil is to achieve, and how achievement is to be attained, and the proper function of the universal rules to which he ultimately reduces his treatment is rather that of supplying a convenient text for recalling its chief moments to the pupil's mind, than of prescribing them to him. 10 Yet, in all this, due regard must be paid to a certain ideal which art must keep in view, even though complete success ever eludes its happiest efforts. Only by exciting the pupil's imagination to conformity with a given concept, by pointing out how the expression falls short of the idea to which, as aesthetic, the con- 15 cept itself fails to attain, and by means of severe criticism, is it possible to prevent his promptly looking upon the examples set before him as the prototypes of excellence, and as models for him to imitate, without submission to any higher standard or to his own critical judgement. This would result in genius being 20 stifled, and, with it, also the freedom of the imagination in its very conformity to law—a freedom without which a fine art is not possible, nor even as much as a correct taste of one's own for estimating it.

The propaedeutic to all fine art, so far as the highest degree 25 of its perfection is what is in view, appears to lie, not in precepts, but in the culture of the mental powers produced by a sound preparatory education in what are called the *humaniora* —so called, presumably, because *humanity* signifies, on the one hand, the universal *feeling of sympathy*, and, on the other, the 30 faculty of being able to *communicate* universally one's inmost self—properties constituting in conjunction the befitting *social spirit* of mankind, in contradistinction to the narrow life of the lower animals. There was an age and there were nations

in which the active impulse towards a social life *regulated by laws*—what converts a people into a permanent community—grappled with the huge difficulties presented by the trying problem of bringing freedom (and therefore equality also) into
5 union with constraining force (more that of respect and dutiful submission than of fear). And such must have been the age, and such the nation, that first discovered the art of reciprocal 356 communication of ideas between the more cultured and ruder sections of the community, and how to bridge the difference be-
10 tween the amplitude and refinement of the former and the natural simplicity and originality of the latter—in this way hitting upon that mean between higher culture and the modest worth of nature, that forms for taste also, as a sense common to all mankind, that true standard which no universal rules can supply.
15 Hardly will a later age dispense with those models. For nature will ever recede farther into the background, so that eventually, with no permanent example retained from the past, a future age would scarce be in a position to form a concept of the happy union, in one and the same people, of the law-directed
20 constraint belonging to the highest culture, with the force and truth of a free nature sensible of its proper worth.

However, taste is, in the ultimate analysis, a critical faculty that judges of the rendering of moral ideas in terms of sense (through the intervention of a certain analogy in our reflection
25 on both); and it is this rendering also, and the increased sensibility, founded upon it, for the feeling which these ideas evoke (termed moral sense), that are the origin of that pleasure which taste declares valid for mankind in general and not merely for the private feeling of each individual. This makes
30 it clear that the true propaedeutic for laying the foundations of taste is the development of moral ideas and the culture of the moral feeling. For only when sensibility is brought into harmony with moral feeling can genuine taste assume a definite unchangeable form.

ANALYTICAL INDEX TO
AESTHETIC JUDGEMENT

Abstraction. From content of judgement of taste, 136 ; from concept of object, 72, 74 ; from the agreeable and good, 57.

Admiration. Definition of, 125.

Aesthetic. Aesthetic quality, defined, 29 ; transcendental, of judgement, only deals with pure judgements, 121 ; faculty, legislative, 220, and mathematical estimation of magnitude contrasted, 99 ; all estimation of magnitude in the last resort, 98. *See* Attributes.

Aesthetic ideas. Meaning of, 175 ; justification for name, 175 ; soul, the faculty of presenting, 175 ; counterpart of rational idea, 176 ; contrasted with intellectual ideas, 176 ; faculty of, best displayed in poetry, 177 ; serves rational idea instead of logical presentation, 177 ; beauty, the expression of, 183 ; the mere expression of, the main intention in sculpture, 186 ; fine art must derive its rule from, 221 ; distinguished from rational ideas of determinate ends, 221 ; music and what provokes laughter two kinds of play with, 198.

Aesthetic judgement. *A priori* principle of, difficulty of discovering, 5 ; evidences a bearing of faculty of knowledge on feeling of pleasure, 6 ; defined, 36 ; compared with teleological judgement, 36 ; compared with logical judgement, 42 ; pleasure in, 65 ; division of, 65 ; does not afford even a confused knowledge of objects, 71 ; subjective reference of, 71 ; the *ought* in, 82 ; logical peculiarities of, 136 ; arises by delight being attached as predicate to object, 144 ; contrasted with cognitive judgements, 144, cf. 5, l. 35 ; contrasted with judgements of experience, 144 ; the principle in, both object and law, 145 ; dialectic of, 204 ; unique principle of, 287.

Affection. Physiological concomitants, 16, n. ; freedom from, represented as sublime, 124 ; of strenuous type, sublime, 125 ; of languid type not sublime, 125.

Agreeable. The, defined, 44 ; delight in, interested, 44 ; the, does not merely please but gratifies, 45 ; compared with the good, 46, 48 ; contrasted with delight in the beautiful, 46, 53, 55 ; rests entirely on sensation, 46 ; contrasted with the beautiful and good, 49, 51, 81 ; difference of opinion as to, tolerated, 53 ; abstraction from, 57 ; contrasted with the beautiful, the sublime, and the good, 116, cf. 90 ; as motive of desire, always of one and the same kind, 117 ; difference among men as to the, 149 ; empiricism confuses, with aesthetic delight, 215 ; art, agreeable or beautiful, 165 ; music and jest belong to agreeable rather than to fine art, 198, cf. 193, 194, but see also 190.

Agreement. As to the beautiful, necessity of, 82 ; of different judging Subjects, 85 ; the judgement of taste exacts agreement from every one, 84 ; as a duty, 154, cf. 82, 84, 132, 223, 224 ; of all ages, empirical criterion, 75.

respective worth of different, 191 ; the nature of the individual and not a set purpose gives the rule to, 213 ; no rule or precept can serve as standard for, 211 ; finality of, 215 ; successful attainment of, ends only a determining ground of judgement in mechanical, 221 ; must derive its rule from aesthetic ideas, 221 ; the element of science in, only an indispensable condition, 226 ; has only a manner and not a method of teaching, 226 ; propaedeutic to all fine, 226.

Assent. (*See* Agreement.) Necessity of universal, 84.

Association. Law of, imagination borrows material supplied according to law of, 176 ; laws of, 86, 121.

Astonishment. Defined, 125 ; cf. 120.

Attributes. Aesthetic, defined, 177 ; logical, 177 ; examples of the use of aesthetic, 178.

Autonomy. Of higher faculties, 38 ; does not belong to imagination itself, 86 ; judgement of taste should found on, 220.

Batteux. Referred to as an art critic, 140.

Beautiful. Analytic of the, 41 ; definition of the, 118 ; definitions of the, resulting from moments, 50, 60, 80, 85 ; pleases in the mere reflection, 149, and in the mere estimate of it, 167 ; independent of definite concept, 46, 72, 150 ; the, contrasted with the agreeable, the sublime, and the good, 49, 52, 53, 54, 90, 117 ; points of agreement and difference between the, and the sublime, 90, 93, 104, 107, 115 ; in judging of the, mind in restful contemplation, 94, 107, 110 ; we dwell on the contemplation of the, 64 ; charms compatible with the, 91 ; person captivated by inclination and appetite cannot judge of the, 110 ; delight in the, connected with representation of quality, 91 ; implies a necessary reference to delight, 81 ; the, a presentation of an indeterminate concept of understanding, 90 ; delight in the, is positive, 120 ; the, requires a certain quality of the object, 117 ; ground of the, sought in what is external to ourselves, 93 ; ground of the estimation of, a mere formal finality, 69 ; what required for calling an object, 43 ; difference of opinion not tolerated when anything described as, 84 ; no criterion or objective rule for determining what is, 75 ; no science of the, 225 ; deduction of judgements upon, 133 ; so called by reference to that character to which the thing adapts itself to our mode of taking it in, 137 ; pleasure in the, attends a process of judgement which must be exercised for the commonest experience, 150 ; pleasure in the, must depend for every one on the same conditions, 150 ; proportion of the faculties necessary for the perception of the, 150 ; mistakes in the judgement upon, 150 ; culture, how far necessary for its appreciation, 115 ; cultivates us, 117 ; the immediate pleasure in, cultivates liberality of mind, 120 ; finality of, in connexion with the moral sense, 119 ; conformity to law of action done from duty may be represented as, 118 ; only pleases universally in reference to morality, 224 ; beautiful representation of an object defined, 174 ; beautiful object distinguished from beautiful views of objects, 89 ; objects, examples of, 46.

Beauty. Not a property of the object, 136, 215, cf. 51 ; the expression of aesthetic ideas, 183 ; finality in this case has its ground in the form and figure of the object, 133 ; of object, consists in the form of mutual subjective finality of faculties of imagination and understanding, 141 ; why scattered abroad so lavishly, 133 ; intellectual an inaccurate expression, 123 ; of nature, mind cannot dwell on, without finding its interest engaged,

160 ; of, nature superior to that of art, in that it awakens an immediate interest, 158 ; symbol of morality, 223 ; has only significance for human beings, 49.

Dance. Combination of arts in a, 190.

Decoration, 188.

Deduction. Of principle of finality, 22 et seq.; of pure aesthetic judgements, 133; in what cases obligatory, 133; only necessary in the case of judgements upon the beautiful, 133; what suffices for, in case of aesthetic judgements, 135, 136; method of the, of judgements of taste, 135; of judgements of taste, problem of, 144; of judgements of taste, 146; also in the sublime, 215.

Definition. Transcendental, 16, *n.*

Deism, 223.

Delight. Disinterested, 42, 49; comparison of the different kinds of, 48; as related to inclination, favour, and respect, 49; universal, 50; taste gains by combination of intellectual with aesthetic, 73; in the good but not in the beautiful, when, 86; in the way a figure strikes the eye, 87; purpose in respect of knowledge combined with, 87; serving instead of a predicate of the object, 144; nature of, in a moral action, 149.

Design. The essential element in the formative arts, 67, 68.

Desire. (*See* Reason.) Faculty of, defined, 16, *n.*; faculty of principles of, 4, 6; definition tested by consideration of fantastic wishes, 16, *n.*; causal reference of, 16, *n.*; purpose of propensity to, consciously vain, 16, *n.*; reference of interest to, 42.

Dialectic. Of the aesthetic judgement, 204; not of taste but of the critique of it, 204.

Disgust. What excites, cannot be represented in fine art, 174.

Disputes. As to questions of taste, 74.

Division. Of philosophy, 7; of philosophy, as theoretical or practical, 8; of metaphysic, 75; why Kant's divisions always threefold, 39; of investigation, into that of the beautiful and the sublime, 33; of the sublime into the mathematically and the dynamically sublime, 94.

Doctrine. Principles belonging to, must be determinant, 36.

Dominion. Defined as might which is superior to resistance of that which itself possesses might, 109.

Drama. Rhetoric combined with pictorial presentation in, 190.

Emotion. Spirited and tender emotions, 125.

Empiricism. Of critique of taste, 215.

End. Defined, 19; natural end, 34; analogy of an, 34; natural beauty and natural ends, contrasted, 34; no reason assignable *a priori* why there should be objective ends of nature, 35; of nature, teleological estimation of, 35; final, condition of possibility of, presupposed by judgement, 38.

Enjoyment. Those intent on, would dispense with all judgement, 45, 47; an obligation to, an absurdity, 48; nature of pleasure of, 149: pleasure in the beautiful not a pleasure of enjoyment, 149.

Enlightenment. Defined, 152.

Entertainment. Of the mental faculties, 88; social, taste in, 53.

Enthusiasm. Sublimity of, 124; compared with fanaticism, 128.

Epicurus. Corporal basis of gratification and pain, 131, 197, 202.

Euler. Colour theory of, 66.

Evil. That which we strive to resist, 109.

Examples. Function of illustration by, 141; intuitions verifying reality of empirical concepts are called, 221.

Judgement. Middle term between understanding and reason, 4, 15 ; principles of, annexed as needful to theoretical or practical philosophy, 4 ; as synonymous for sound understanding, 5 ; *a priori* principle of, difficulty in discovering, 5 ; especially great in case of aesthetic judgements, 5 ; *a priori* principle of, necessary in logical judging of nature, when, 6 ; no reference to feeling of pleasure in logical judging of nature, 6; separate division for, why necessary in Critique, 6 ; Critique plays part of theory in case of, 7 ; principle of, territory of, 15 ; presumption of an *a priori* principle of, that has reference to the feeling of pleasure and displeasure, 15 ; presumption that, effects transition from realm of nature to that of freedom, 17 ; as a faculty that prescribes laws *a priori*, defined, 18 ; determinant and reflective, contrasted, 18 ; reflective compelled to ascend from particular to universal, 18 ; transcendental principle of reflective, 19, 20, 21 ; maxims of, 21, 23; law of specification makes us proceed on principle of conformity of nature to our faculty of cognition, 29 ; reflective, what is final for, 30 ; aesthetic, on finality of object, 30; nature of the principle of, 25 ; empirical, singular, claims universal assent, 32 ; function of, when concept given, 34 ; teleologically employed, assigns determinate conditions, 35 ; connects legislations of understanding and reason, 36 ; provides mediating concept, 38 ; provides constitutive *a priori* principle for feeling of pleasure and displeasure, 39 ; grounds of, clear or confused, 71 ; mathematically determinant and reflective, contrasted, 96 ; of experience, 144, cf. 31, 32 ; cognitive, contrasted with aesthetic, 144.

Judgement of taste. A subdivision of aesthetic judgements, 65 ; is aesthetic, 41 ; defined, 41, *n.* ; involves a reference to understanding, 41 ; not a cognitive judgement, 41, 48, 72, 210 ; affords no knowledge of anything, 207 ; the determining ground of, may be objective, 205, but not reducible to definite concepts, 205 ; the extended reference of, requires a concept for basis, 207 ; a special faculty for estimating by rule and not by concepts, 36 ; is reflective, not determinant, 36 ; is contemplative, 48 ; compared with empirical judgements generally, 32 ; rests on *a priori* grounds, 63 ; hence requires a Critique, 32 ; is both synthetic and *a priori* 145 ; position of, in a Critique, 36 ; constitutive principle in respect of the feeling of pleasure and displeasure, 38 ; can only have its ground in the subjective condition of a judgement in general, 143 ; what asserted in a, 145 ; subjective finality of nature for the judgement of the concept upon which it depends, 207 ; unique principle of, finality of nature and of art, 215 ; how we become conscious of accord in, 59 ; relative priority of feeling of pleasure and estimate of the object in, 57 ; should be founded on autonomy and not heteronomy, 220, 224 ; contrasted with logical judgements, 142, 140, 147 ; logical peculiarities of, 136 ; not determinable by grounds of proof, 139, 205, 206 ; logical quantity of, singular, 55, 90, 146 ; how converted into a logical judgement, 65, cf. 119 ; not determined by interest, 42, 154 ; should be disinterested, 43 ; may be combined with interest, 154 ; what represented *a priori* in, not pleasure but its universal validity, 146 ; universality of delight in, only represented as subjective, 53 ; speaks with a universal voice, 56 ; consistent statement of the view denying any claim to its necessity, 214 ; how imputed as a sort of duty, 154 ; as a faculty of communicating even our feelings to others, 155 ; put forward as example of judgement of common sense, 84 ; pure, independent of charm and emotion, 64 ; not pure, if condition is a definite concept, 72 ; purity of, affected by association with the agreeable or the good, 73 ; pure, when, in respect of object with definite internal end, 73; pure, in estimating a free beauty, 72; independent of concept of perfection, 69; pure, interest may be combined with, 154; false, how possible, 57, cf. 54, 147, 150; conflict of, 204, cf. 74; deduction of, 204; riddle of, key to, supplied by indeterminate idea of supersensible, 208; rational concept of supersensible lies at basis of, 207; universal validity of, explained by reference to rational concept of supersensible, 207; determining ground, perhaps the supersensible substrate of humanity, 208.

Knowledge. (*See* Cognitive faculty.) Of things, aesthetic estimates do not contribute, 5; how far dependent on universal communicability, 83; end in respect of, coupled with delight, 87.

Landscapes. *See* Views.

Laughter. Generally, 196–203; physical character of the cause of, 198; account of its production as a phenomenon, 198; something absurd always its basis, 199; defined, 199; art of inducing an air of gaiety by jest and, an agreeable art, 166.

Law. Contrasted with precepts and rules, 10; conformity to, without a, 86.

Legislation. Of reason and understanding, 12; non-interference of, 13.

Lessing. As an art critic, 140.

Link. In the chain of the faculties *a priori*, the intellectual interest in the beautiful discovers a, 156; mediating, between concept of nature and of freedom, 38.

Logic. Contrasted with philosophy, 8.

Logical judgement. Compared with aesthetic judgement, 42; analogy of judgement of beautiful to, 51; judgement of taste, how converted into a, 50, 140; knowledge to be had only from a, 71; judgement of taste, how distinguished from, 142.

Logical presentation, 177.

Logical quantity. Of aesthetic judgements, 55, 90, 119, 136, 146.

Logical universality. Aesthetic universality compared with, 54.

Logical validity. Defined, 29.

Magnitude. Mathematical and aesthetic estimation of, 98; representation of, 101.

Man. An ideal of beauty only possible in case of, 77.

Mannerism. A mode of aping, 182.

Marsden. His description of Sumatra, 88.

Master. Can only teach by illustration, 226; examples of, not to be imitated without a criticism, 226.

Mathematical. Estimation of magnitude, 98.

Maxims. Of judgement, 21, 23, cf. 217; of empirical science, 21, 24; of common human understanding, 152; of unprejudiced thought, 152; of enlarged thought, 153; of consistent thought, 153; of the aesthetic judgement, 206, cf. 20, 23.

Means. Choice of a means to enjoyment, 44.

Mechanism. Conception of nature as, enlarged to that of nature as art, 92; required in art, 171; of nature, 217.

Metaphysic. Projected system of, 5; requires preliminary Critique, 5; divisible into that of nature and morals, 7; metaphysical principle, 20.

Methodology. Of taste, 225.

sensations, 67 ; as agreeable on its own account, 164 ; art as, 164 ; free,
a source of gratification, 197 ; free, of chance, tone and thought, 197.

Pleasure. (*See* Feeling.) Feeling associated with concept of finality,
26 ; the subjective quality incapable of becoming a cognition, 29 ; when
judged to be combined necessarily with representation, 31 ; only connected
with representation by means of reflective judgement, 31 ; in judgement
of taste, dependent on empirical representation, 32 ; relative priority of,
and estimate of object in judgement of taste, 57 ; what denoted by, 61 ;
causal connexion with representation not determinable *a priori*, 63 ;
mental state identical with, where, 63 ; in aesthetic judgements, contemplative, 64 ; consciousness of formal finality is, 64 ; non-practical, 64.

Poem. Didactic, 190.

Poet. Youthful, not dissuaded from his convictions, 137.

Poetry. Imagination enjoys free play in, 86 ; prosody and measure
required in, 164 ; faculty of aesthetic ideas displays itself to best advantage in, 177 ; contrasted with rhetoric, 184, 192 ; combined with music in
song, 190 ; compared with other arts, 191.

Polycletus. Doryphorus of, 79.

Practical. Philosophy, contrasted with theoretical, 8–11 ; misuse of
word, 9, 10 ; precepts, 10, 11 ; morally, compared with technically, 9,
cf. 13 ; sphere, reason can only prescribe laws in, 12 ; function, distinguished from theoretical, 12 ; reality, of ideas, 14 ; finality, 21 ; faculty,
art as, 163 ; point of view, broadening of mind from, 103.

Prayers. For avoiding inevitable evils, superstition at basis of, 16, n.

Predicate. Pleasure united to concept of object as if it were a predicate, 32.

Prejudice, 152.

Presentation. When the function of judgement, 34 ; of ideas, 119,
176, cf. 209-212, 221, 222.

Principle. Constitutive, 3, 38, 39 ; regulative, 3, 39 ; transcendental
or metaphysical, 20 ; independent, of judgement, 4 ; of judgement,
reference to pleasure the riddle of, 6 ; of cognition, distinct, importance
of, 9 ; practical, 8 ; technically or morally practical, 9 ; of finality of
nature, 19, 21.

Progress. Of art, limit to, 170 ; of culture, 183.

Proof. Grounds of, judgement of taste does not admit of determination by, 139 ; fine art does not appeal to, 165.

Propaedeutic. To fine art, culture the, 226 ; to taste, the development of moral ideas, 227 ; to all philosophy, 36.

Prosody. Required in poetry, 164.

Prudence. Rules of, are mere corollaries to theoretical philosophy,
9, 10.

Psychology. Empirical, modality of aesthetic judgements lifts them
out of the sphere of, 117 ; critique of taste as an art deals with psychological rules, 142.

Pyramids. Sublimity of the, 99.

Quality. Of space, 29 ; delight in the beautiful associated with
representation of, 91 ; of delight in our estimate of the sublime, 105 ; of
feeling of the sublime, a displeasure, 108.

Quantity. Delight in the sublime associated with representation
of, 91.

to be pure, 100, cf. 190 ; not based on finality of the form of the object, 101 ; the mathematically, examples of, 104 ; quality of delight in our estimate of, 105, 106 ; applied to object by a subreption, 106 ; a feeling of displeasure and a pleasure, 106 ; mind moved in representation of the 107 ; finality in case of, one for ideas of reason, 109 ; the dynamically, defined, 109 ; the dynamically, examples, 109 ; we must see ourselves safe to estimate the, 112 ; sublimity of war, 113 ; of a religion, 113 ; of humility, 114 ; culture requisite for appreciation of, 115 ; modality of judgement upon, 93, 116 ; defined, 118, 119 ; finality of the, in connexion with moral feeling, 119 ; feeling for the, requires moral disposition, 120 ; cultivates a liberality in our mental attitude, 120 ; delight in the, is negative, 120 ; represented as a might to overcome hindrances, 123 ; abstractions in presentation of, 127 ; simplicity the style adopted by nature in the, 128 ; freedom from affection, represented as, 124 ; isolation from society regarded as, 129 ; deduction of judgements upon, not necessary, 133, as exposition sufficed for deduction, 134 ; nature only supplies the occasion for the judgement upon the, 134 ; brought into union with beauty in a tragedy, 190.

Subsumption. Logical and aesthetic, contrasted, 147 ; mistake in, 148.

Sumatra. Marsden's description of, 88.

Supersensible. Reference of natural thing to unknowable, 6 ; how made cognizable, 11 ; introduction of idea of, 13; field of, no territory in, 13 ; must be occupied with ideas, 13 ; practical reality of concept of freedom brings us no nearer theoretical knowledge of, 14 ; great gulf fixed between, and sensible, 14, 36 ; ground of unity of, at basis of nature, with what freedom contains in a practical way, 14. cf. 37, 38 ; in the Subject, 36, 37 ; substrate of nature, 37, n. ; how affected by understanding, judgement, and reason respectively, 38 ; freedom, supersensible attribute of subject, 63 ; reference of sublime to supersensible faculty within us, 97 ; estate, our, 106 ; rational idea of, 107 ; faculty, ability to think given infinite evidences, 103 ; nature thought as a presentation of the, 119 ; idea of, as substrate of nature, as principle of subjective finality, and as principle of the ends of freedom, 215 ; nature employed as schema for, 192.

Superstition, 152 ; religion distinguished from, 114.

Symbol. Of morality, beauty the, 221 ; contrasted with schema, 222.

Symbolic. All our knowledge of God is, 223.

Symbolism. Nature of, 222.

Symmetry, 87.

Sympathy. Sense of, implied by word humanity, 226.

Taste. (*See* Judgement of taste.) Culture of, 6 ; impossible to determine *a priori* what object will accord with, 32 ; defined, 31, 41, 153, 154; estimates natural beauty, 34 ; shown by meaning I can give to a representation, 43 ; explanation of, from first moment, 50 ; principle that every one has his own, considered, 52, 205 ; demanded as something one ought to have, 52 ; in social entertainments, 53 ; of sense and of reflection, 54 ; gains by combination of intellectual delight with aesthetic, 73 ; union of, with reason, rules prescribed for, 73 ; disputes about, how frequently settled, 74 ; in respect of models, shown by person only as a critic of the

CRITIQUE OF JUDGEMENT

PART II

CRITIQUE OF
TELEOLOGICAL JUDGEMENT

INTRODUCTION [1]

WE do not need to look beyond the critical explanation of the
possibility of knowledge to find ample reason for assuming a
subjective finality on the part of nature in its particular laws.
This is a finality relative to comprehensibility—man's power of
5 judgement being such as it is—and to the possibility of uniting
particular experiences into a connected system of nature. In
this system, then, we may further anticipate the possible existence of some among the many products of nature that, as if put
there with quite a special regard to our judgement, are of a form
10 particularly adapted to that faculty. Forms of this kind are
those which by their combination of unity and heterogeneity
serve as it were to strengthen and entertain the mental powers
that enter into play in the exercise of the faculty of judgement,
and to them the name of *beautiful forms* is accordingly given.

15   But the universal idea of nature, as the complex of objects of
sense, gives us no reason whatever for assuming that things of
nature serve one another as means to ends, or that their very
possibility is only made fully intelligible by a causality of this
sort. For since, in the case of the beautiful forms above men-
20 tioned, the representation of the things is something in ourselves,
it can quite readily be thought even *a priori* as one well-adapted
and convenient for disposing our cognitive faculties to an inward
and final harmony. But where the ends are not ends of our
own, and do not belong even to nature (which we do not take
25 to be an intelligent being), there is no reason at all for presuming

---

[1] [The heading in the text is not 'Introduction' but '§ 61,
Objective finality in nature'. But the objective finality in nature is
simply the general topic of the Second Part of the *Critique of Judgement*, and therefore the heading in question is equivalent to the
heading 'Introduction'.]

a priori that they may or ought nevertheless to constitute a
360 special kind of causality or at least a quite peculiar order of
nature. What is more, the actual existence of these ends cannot
be proved by experience—save on the assumption of an antecedent process of mental jugglery that only reads the conception 5
of an end into the nature of the things, and that, not deriving
this conception from the Objects and what it knows of them from
experience, makes use of it more for the purpose of rendering
nature intelligible to us by an analogy to a subjective ground
upon which our representations are brought into inner connexion, 10
than for that of cognizing nature from objective grounds.

Besides, objective finality, as a principle upon which physical
objects are possible, is so far from attaching *necessarily* to the
conception of nature, that it is the stock example adduced to
show the contingency of nature and its form. So where the 15
structure of a bird, for instance, the hollow formation of its
bones, the position of its wings for producing motion and of its
tail for steering, are cited, we are told that all this is in the
highest degree contingent if we simply look to the *nexus effectivus*
in nature, and do not call in aid a special kind of causality, 20
namely, that of ends (*nexus finalis*). This means that nature,
regarded as mere mechanism, could have fashioned itself in a
thousand other different ways without lighting precisely on the
unity based on a principle like this, and that, accordingly, it is
only outside the conception of nature, and not in it, that we may 25
hope to find some shadow of ground *a priori* for that unity.

We are right, however, in applying the teleological estimate,
at least problematically, to the investigation of nature ; but only
with a view to bringing it under principles of observation and
research by *analogy* to the causality that looks to ends, while 30
not pretending to *explain* it by this means. Thus it is an estimate of the reflective, not of the determinant, judgement. Yet
the conception of combinations and forms in nature that are
determined by ends is at least *one more principle* for reducing its

phenomena to rules in cases where the laws of its purely mechanical causality do not carry us sufficiently far. For we are bringing 361
forward a teleological ground where we endow a conception of an
object—as if that conception were to be found in nature instead
5 of in ourselves—with causality in respect of the object, or rather
where we picture to ourselves the possibility of the object on the
analogy of a causality of this kind—a causality such as we
experience in ourselves—and so regard nature as possessed of
a capacity of its own for acting *technically* ; whereas if we did not
10 ascribe such a mode of operation to nature its causality would
have to be regarded as blind mechanism. But this is a different
thing from crediting nature with causes acting *designedly*, to
which it may be regarded as subjected in following its particular
laws. The latter would mean that teleology is based, not merely
15 on a *regulative* principle, directed to the simple *estimate* of
phenomena, but is actually based on a *constitutive* principle available for *deriving* natural products from their causes : with the
result that the conception of a physical end no longer exists for
the reflective, but for the determinant, judgement. But in that
20 case the conception would not really be specially connected with
the power of judgement, as is the conception of beauty as a
formal subjective finality. It would, on the contrary, be a conception of reason, and would introduce a new causality into
science—one which we are borrowing all the time solely from
25 ourselves and attributing to other beings, although we do not
mean to assume that they and we are similarly constituted.

ANALYTIC OF TELEOLOGICAL JUDGEMENT

§ 1 (62) [1]

Purely formal, as distinguished from material,
objective finality.

ALL geometrical figures drawn on a principle display an
objective finality which takes many directions and has often
been admired. This finality is one of convenience on the part
of the figure for solving a number of problems by a single
5 principle, and even for solving each one of the problems in an
infinite variety of ways. Here the finality is manifestly objective
and intellectual, not simply subjective and aesthetic. For it
expresses the way the figure lends itself to the production of
many proposed figures, and it is cognized through reason. Yet
10 this finality does not make the conception of the object itself
possible, that is to say, we do not regard the object as possible
simply because it may be turned to such use.

In such a simple figure as the circle lies the key to the solution
of a host of problems every one of which would separately
15 require elaborate materials, and this solution follows, we might
say, directly as one of the infinite number of excellent properties
of that figure. For instance, suppose we have to construct a
triangle, being given the base and vertical angle. The problem
is indeterminate, i. e. it admits of solution in an endless variety
20 of ways. But the circle embraces them all in one, as the geometrical locus of all triangles satisfying this condition. Or two
lines have to intersect one another so that the rectangle under
the two parts of the one shall be equal to the rectangle under
the two parts of the other. The solution of the problem is

---

[1] The figures in brackets are those which appear in the text.

apparently full of difficulty. But all lines intersecting within
363 a circle whose circumference passes through their extremities
are divided directly in this ratio. The remaining curves similarly
suggest to us other useful solutions, never contemplated in the
rule upon which they are constructed. All conic sections, taken 5
separately or compared with one another, are, however simple
their definition, fruitful in principles for solving a host of possible
problems.—It is a real joy to see the ardour with which the older
geometricians investigated these properties of such lines, without allowing themselves to be troubled by the question which 10
shallow minds raise, as to the supposed use of such knowledge.
Thus they investigated the properties of the parabola in ignorance
of the law of terrestrial gravitation which would have shown
them its application to the trajectory of heavy bodies (for the
direction of their gravitation when in motion may be regarded 15
as parallel to the curve of a parabola). So again they investigated
the properties of the ellipse without a suspicion that a gravitation was also discoverable in the celestial bodies, and without
knowing the law that governs it as the distance from the point
of attraction varies, and that makes the bodies describe this 20
curve in free motion. While in all these labours they were
working unwittingly for those who were to come after them,
they delighted themselves with a finality which, although
belonging to the nature of the things, they were able to present
completely *a priori* as necessary. Plato, himself a master of 25
this science, was fired with the idea of an original constitution
of things, for the discovery of which we could dispense with all
experience, and of a power of the mind enabling it to derive
the harmony of real things from their supersensible principle
(and with these real things he classed the properties of numbers 30
with which the mind plays in music). Thus inspired he trans-
cended the conceptions of experience and rose to ideas that
seemed only explicable to him on the assumption of a com-

munity of intellect with the original source of all things real. No wonder that he banished from his school the man that was ignorant of geometry, since he thought that from the pure intuition residing in the depths of the human soul he could 5 derive all that Anaxagoras inferred from the objects of experience and their purposive combination. For it is the necessity of that which, while appearing to be an original attribute belonging to the essential nature of things regardless of service to us, is yet final, and formed as if purposely designed for our use, that is 10 the source of our great admiration of nature—a source not so much external to ourselves as seated in our reason. Surely we 364 may pardon this admiration if, as the result of a misapprehension, it is inclined to rise by degrees to fanatical heights.

This intellectual finality is simply formal, not real. In other 15 words it is a finality which does not imply an underlying end, and which, therefore, does not stand in need of teleology. As such, and although it is objective, not subjective like aesthetic finality, its possibility is readily comprehensible, though only in the abstract. The figure of a circle is an intuition which 20 understanding has determined according to a principle. This principle, which is arbitrarily assumed and made a fundamental conception, is applied to space, a form of intuition which, similarly, is only found in ourselves, and found *a priori*, as a representation. It is the unity of this principle that explains 25 the unity of the numerous rules resulting from the construction of that conception. These rules display finality from many possible points of view, but we must not rest this finality on an *end*, or resort to any explanation beyond the above. This is different from finding order and regularity in complexes of 30 external *things* enclosed within definite bounds, as, for instance, order and regularity in the trees, flower-beds, and walks in a garden, which is one that I cannot hope to deduce *a priori* from any delimitation I may make of space according to some rule out of my own head. For these are things having real

existence—things that to be cognized must be given empirically—
and not a mere representation in myself defined *a priori* on a
principle. Hence the latter (empirical) finality is *real*, and,
being real, is dependent on the conception of an end.

But we can also quite easily see the reason for the admiration, 5
and, in fact, regard it as justified, even where the finality
admired is perceived in the essential nature of the things, they
being things whose conceptions are such as we can construct.
The various rules whose unity, derived from a principle, excites
this admiration are one and all synthetic and do not follow from 10
any *conception* of the Object, as, for instance, from the conception of a circle, but require to have this Object given in
intuition. This gives the unity the appearance of having an
external source of its rules distinct from our faculty of representation, just as if it were empirical. Hence the way the Object 15
answers to the understanding's own peculiar need for rules
appears intrinsically contingent and, therefore, only possible
365 by virtue of an end expressly directed to its production. Now
since this harmony, despite all the finality mentioned, is not
cognized empirically, but *a priori*, it is just what should bring 20
home to us the fact that space, by the limitation of which (by
means of the imagination acting in accordance with a conception) the Object was alone possible, is not a quality of the
things outside me, but a mere mode of representation existing
in myself. Hence, where I draw a figure *in accordance with a* 25
conception, or, in other words, when I form my own representation of what is given to me externally, be its own intrinsic nature
what it may, what really happens is that I *introduce the finality*
into that figure or representation. I derive no empirical instruction as to the finality from what is given to me externally, and 30
consequently the figure is not one for which I require any special
end external to myself and residing in the Object. But this
reflection presupposes a critical use of reason, and, therefore,

it cannot be involved then and there in the estimate of the object and its properties. Hence all that this estimate immediately suggests to me is a unification of heterogeneous rules (united even in their intrinsic diversity) in a principle the truth 5 of which I can cognize *a priori*, without requiring for that purpose some special explanation lying beyond my conception, or, to put it more generally, beyond my own *a priori* representation. Now *astonishment* is a shock that the mind receives from a representation and the rule given through it being incompatible 10 with the mind's existing fund of root principles, and that accordingly makes one doubt one's own eyesight or question one's judgement ; but *admiration* is an astonishment that keeps continually recurring despite the disappearance of this doubt. Admiration is consequently quite a natural effect of observing 15 the above-mentioned finality in the essence of things (as phenomena), and so far there is really nothing to be said against it. For the agreement of the above form of sensuous intuition, which is called space, with the faculty of conceptions, namely understanding, not alone leaves it inexplicable why it is this particular 20 form of agreement and not some other, but, in addition, produces an expansion of the mind in which it gets, so to speak, the secret feeling of the existence of something lying beyond the confines of such sensuous representations, in which, perhaps, although unknown to us, the ultimate source of that accordance 25 could be found. It is true that we have also no need to know this source where we are merely concerned with the formal finality of our *a priori* representations ; but even the mere fact that we are compelled to look out in that direction excites an accompanying admiration for the object which obliges us to do so.

30 The name of *beauty* is customarily given to the properties above 366 referred to—both those of geometrical figures and also those of numbers—on account of a certain finality which they possess for employment in all kinds of ways in the field of knowledge, which finality the simplicity of their construction would not

Part II. Critique of Teleological Judgement

lead us to expect. Thus people speak of this or that *beautiful* property of the circle, brought to light in this or that manner. But it is not by means of any aesthetic appreciation that we consider such properties final. There is no estimate apart from a conception, making us take note of a purely *subjective* finality in the free play of our cognitive faculties. On the contrary it is an intellectual estimate according to conceptions, in which we clearly recognize an objective finality, that is to say, adaptability for all sorts of ends, i. e. an infinite manifold of ends. Such properties should rather be termed a *relative perfection*, than a beauty, of the mathematical figure. We cannot even properly allow the expression *intellectual beauty* at all: as, if we do, the word beauty must lose all definite meaning, and the delight of the intellect all superiority over that of the senses. The term beautiful could be better applied to a *demonstration* of the properties in question; since here understanding, as the faculty of conceptions, and imagination, as the faculty of presenting them *a priori*, get a feeling of invigoration (which, with the addition of the precision introduced by reason, is called the elegance of the demonstration): for in this case the delight, although founded on conceptions, is at least subjective, whereas perfection involves an objective delight.

§ 2 (63)

Relative, as distinguished from intrinsic, finality of nature.

THERE is only one case in which experience leads our judgement to the conception of an objective and material finality, that is to say, to the conception of an end of nature. This is where the relation in which some cause stands to its effect is under review,[1] and where we are only able to see uniformity

---

[1] Pure mathematics can never deal with the real existence of things, but only with their possibility, that is to say, with the possi-

in this relation on introducing into the causal principle the idea of the effect and making it the source of the causality and the basal condition on which the effect is possible. Now this can be done in two ways. We may regard the effect as being, as it stands, an art-product, or we may only regard it as what other possible objects in nature may employ for the purposes of their art. We may, in other words, look upon the effect either as an end, or else as a means which other causes use in the pursuit of ends. The latter finality is termed utility, where it concerns human beings, and adaptability where it concerns any other creatures. It is a purely relative finality. The former, on the contrary, is an intrinsic finality belonging to the thing itself as a natural object.

For example, rivers in their course carry down earth of all kinds good for the growth of plants, and this they deposit sometimes inland, sometimes at their mouths. On some coasts the high-tide carries this alluvial mud inland, or deposits it along the sea-shore. Thus the fruitful soil is increased, especially where man helps to hinder the ebb tide carrying the detritus off again, and the vegetable kingdom gains a home in the former abode of fish and crustaceans. Nature has in this way itself effected most accretions to the land, and is still, though slowly, continuing the process.—There now arises the question if this result is to be considered an end on the part of nature, since it is fraught with benefit to man. I say ' to man ', for the benefit to the vegetable kingdom cannot be taken into account, inasmuch as against the gain to the land there is, as a set off, as much loss to sea-life.

Or we may give an example of the adaptability of particular things of nature as means for other forms of life—setting out with the assumption that these latter are ends. Thus there is no healthier soil for pine trees than a sandy soil. Now before

bility of an intuition answering to the conceptions of the things. Hence it cannot touch the question of cause and effect, and, consequently, all the finality there observed must always be regarded simply as formal, and never as a physical end.

the primeval sea withdrew from the land it left numerous sand
tracts behind it in our northern regions. The result was that
upon this soil, generally so unfavourable for cultivation of any
kind, extensive pine forests were able to spring up—forests which
we frequently blame our ancestors for having wantonly destroyed. 5
Now it may be asked if this primordial deposit of sand tracts
was not an end that nature had in view for the benefit of the
possible pine forests that might grow on them. This much is
clear : that if the pine forests are assumed to be a natural end,
then the sand must be admitted to be an end also—though only 10
a relative end—and one for which, in turn, the primeval sea's
beach and its withdrawal were means ; for in the series of the
mutually subordinated members of a final nexus each intermediate member must be regarded as an end, though not a
final end, to which its proximate cause stands as means. Simi- 15
larly, if it is granted that cattle, sheep, horses, and the like,
were to be in the world, then there had to be grass on the earth,
while alkaline plants had to grow in the deserts if camels were
to thrive. Again, these and other herbivora had to abound if
wolves, tigers, and lions were to exist. Consequently objective 20
finality based on adaptability is not an immanent objective
finality of things : as though the sand, as simple sand, could not
be conceived as the effect of its cause, the sea, unless we made
this cause look to an end, and treated the effect, namely the
sand, as an art-product. It is a purely relative finality, and 25
merely contingent to the thing itself to which it is ascribed ;
and although among the examples cited, the various kinds of
herbs or plants, considered in their own right, are to be estimated
as organized products of nature, and, therefore, as things of
art, yet, in relation to the animals that feed on them, they are 30
to be regarded as mere raw material.

Moreover the freedom of man's causality enables him to adapt
physical things to the purposes he has in view. These purposes

are frequently foolish—as when he uses the gay-coloured feathers of birds for adorning his clothes, and coloured earths or juices of plants for painting himself. Sometimes they are reasonable, as when he uses the horse for riding, and the ox or, as in Minorca, even the ass or pig for ploughing. But we cannot
5 here assume even a relative end of nature—relative, that is, to such uses. For man's reason informs him how to adapt things to his own arbitrary whims—whims for which he was not himself at all predestined by nature. All we can say is that *if* we assume that it is intended that men should live on the earth, then at
10 least, those means without which they could not exist as animals, and even, on however low a plane, as rational animals, must also not be absent. But in that case, those natural things that are indispensable for such existence must equally be regarded as ends of nature.

15 From what has been said we can easily see that the only condition on which extrinsic finality, that is, the adaptability of a thing for other things, can be looked on as an extrinsic physical end, is that the existence of the thing for which it is proximately or remotely adapted is itself, and in its own right,
20 an end of nature. But this is a matter that can never be decided by any mere study of nature. Hence it follows that relative 369 finality, although, on a certain supposition, it points to natural finality, does not warrant any absolute teleological judgement.

In cold countries the snow protects the seeds from the frost.
25 It facilitates human intercourse—through the use of sleighs. The Laplander finds animals in these regions, namely reindeer, to bring about this intercourse. The latter find sufficient food to live on in a dry moss which they have to scrape out for themselves from under the snow, yet they submit to being tamed
30 without difficulty, and readily allow themselves to be deprived of the freedom in which they could quite well have supported themselves. For other dwellers in these ice-bound lands the sea is rich in its supply of animals that afford them fuel for

heating their huts ; in addition to which there are the food and
clothing that these animals provide and the wood which the
sea itself, as it were, washes in for them as material for their
homes.   Now here we have a truly marvellous assemblage of
many relations of nature to an end—the end being the Green- 5
landers, Laplanders, Samoyedes, Jakutes, and the like. But we
do not see why men should live in these places at all.   To say,
therefore, that the *facts* that vapour falls from the atmosphere
in the form of snow, that the ocean has its currents that wash
into these regions the wood grown in warmer lands, and that 10
sea-monsters containing quantities of oil are to be found there,
are due to the idea of some benefit to certain poor creatures
underlying the cause that brings together all these natural
products, would be a very hazardous and arbitrary assertion.
For supposing that all this utility on the part of nature were 15
absent, then the capacity of the natural causes to serve this
order of existence would not be missed.   On the contrary it
would seem audacious and inconsiderate on our part even to ask
for such a capacity, or demand such an end from nature—for
nothing but the greatest want of social unity in mankind could 20
have dispersed men into such inhospitable regions.

§ 3 (64)

The distinctive character of things considered as physical ends.

A THING is possible only as an end where the causality to
which it owes its origin must not be sought in the mechanism of
370 nature, but in a cause whose capacity of acting is determined by
conceptions.   What is required in order that we may perceive 25
that a thing is only possible in this way is that its form is not
possible on purely natural laws—that is to say, such laws as we
may cognize by means of unaided understanding applied to

objects of sense—but that, on the contrary, even to know it empirically in respect of its cause and effect presupposes conceptions of reason. Here we have, as far as any empirical laws of nature go, a *contingency* of the form of the thing in relation
5 to reason. Now reason in every case insists on cognizing the necessity of the form of a natural product, even where it only desires to perceive the conditions involved in its production. In the given form above mentioned, however, it cannot get this necessity. Hence the contingency is itself a ground for making
10 us look upon the origin of the thing as if, just because of that contingency, it could only be possible through reason. But the causality, so construed, becomes the faculty of acting according to ends—that is to say, a will; and the Object, which is represented as only deriving its possibility from such a will, will be
15 represented as possible only as an end.

Suppose a person was in a country that seemed to him uninhabited and was to see a geometrical figure, say a regular hexagon, traced on the sand. As he reflected, and tried to get a conception of the figure, his reason would make him conscious,
20 though perhaps obscurely, that in the production of this conception there was unity of principle. His reason would then forbid him to consider the sand, the neighbouring sea, the winds, or even animals with their footprints, as causes familiar to him, or any other irrational cause, as the ground of the possibility of
25 such a form. For the contingency of coincidence with a conception like this, which is only possible in reason, would appear to him so infinitely great that there might just as well be no law of nature at all in the case. Hence it would seem that the cause of the production of such an effect could not be contained
30 in the mere mechanical operation of nature, but that, on the contrary, a conception of such an Object, as a conception that only reason can give and compare the Object with, must likewise be what alone contains that causality. On these grounds it would appear to him that this effect was one that might without

reservation be regarded as an end, though not as a natural end.
In other words he would regard it as a product of *art—vestigium
hominis video.*

But where a thing is recognized to be a product of nature,
then something more is required—unless, perhaps, our very 5
estimate involves a contradiction—if, despite its being such a
product, we are yet to estimate it as an end, and, consequently,
as a *physical end.* As a provisional statement I would say that
a thing exists as a physical end *if it is* (though in a double sense)
37¹ *both cause and effect of itself.* For this involves a kind of causality 10
that we cannot associate with the mere conception of a nature
unless we make that nature rest on an underlying end, but which
can then, though incomprehensible, be thought without contradiction.   Before analysing the component factors of this
idea of a physical end, let us first illustrate its meaning by an 15
example.

A tree produces, in the first place, another tree, according to
a familiar law of nature.   But the tree which it produces is of the
same genus.   Hence, in its *genus,* it produces itself.   In the genus,
now as effect, now as cause, continually generated from itself 20
and likewise generating itself, it preserves itself generically.

Secondly, a tree produces itself even as an *individual.* It is
true that we only call this kind of effect growth ; but growth is
here to be understood in a sense that makes it entirely different
from any increase according to mechanical laws, and renders it 25
equivalent, though under another name, to generation.   The
plant first prepares the matter that it assimilates and bestows
upon it a specifically distinctive quality which the mechanism
of nature outside it cannot supply, and it develops itself by
means of a material which, in its composite character, is its own 30
product.   For, although in respect of the constituents that it
derives from nature outside, it must be regarded as only an
educt, yet in the separation and recombination of this raw

material we find an original capacity of selection and construction on the part of natural beings of this kind such as
infinitely outdistances all the efforts of art, when the latter
attempts to reconstitute those products of the vegetable kingdom
5 out of the elements which it obtains through their analysis, or else
out of the material which nature supplies for their nourishment.

Thirdly, a part of a tree also generates itself in such a way
that the preservation of one part is reciprocally dependent on the
preservation of the other parts. An eye taken from the sprig
10 of one tree and set in the branch of another produces in the
alien stock a growth of its own species, and similarly a scion
grafted on the body of a different tree. Hence even in the case
of the same tree each branch or leaf may be regarded as en-
grafted or inoculated into it, and, consequently, as a tree with
15 a separate existence of its own, and only attaching itself to
another and living parasitically on it. At the same time the 372
leaves are certainly products of the tree, but they also maintain
it in turn ; for repeated defoliation would kill it, and its growth
is dependent upon the action of the leaves on the trunk. The
20 way nature comes, in these forms of life, to her own aid in the
case of injury, where the want of one part necessary for the
maintenance of the neighbouring parts is made good by the rest ;
the abortions or malformations in growth, where, on account
of some chance defect or obstacle, certain parts adopt a com-
25 pletely new formation, so as to preserve the existing growth, and
thus produce an anomalous form : are matters which I only
desire to mention here in passing, although they are among the
most wonderful properties of the forms of organic life.

§ 4 (65)

Things considered as physical ends are organisms.

WHERE a thing is a product of nature and yet, so regarded,
30 has to be cognized as possible only as a physical end, it must,
from its character as set out in the preceding section, stand to

itself reciprocally in the relation of cause and effect. This is, however, a somewhat inexact and indeterminate expression that needs derivation from a definite conception.

In so far as the causal connexion is thought merely by means of understanding it is a nexus constituting a series, namely of causes and effects, that is invariably progressive. The things that as effects presuppose others as their causes cannot themselves in turn be also causes of the latter. This causal connexion is termed that of efficient causes (*nexus effectivus*). On the other hand, however, we are also able to think a causal connexion according to a rational concept, that of ends, which, if regarded as a series, would involve regressive as well as progressive dependency. It would be one in which the thing that for the moment is designated effect deserves none the less, if we take the series regressively, to be called the cause of the thing of which it was said to be the effect. In the domain of practical matters, namely in art, we readily find examples of a nexus of this kind. Thus a house is certainly the cause of the money that is received as rent, but yet, conversely, the representation of this possible income was the cause of the building of the house. A causal nexus of this kind is termed that of final causes (*nexus finalis*). The former might, perhaps, more appropriately be called the nexus of real, and the latter the nexus of ideal causes, because with this use of terms it would be understood at once that there cannot be more than these two kinds of causality.

373   Now the *first* requisite of a thing, considered as a physical end, is that its parts, both as to their existence and form, are only possible by their relation to the whole. For the thing is itself an end, and is, therefore, comprehended under a conception or an idea that must determine *a priori* all that is to be contained in it. But so far as the possibility of a thing is only thought in this way, it is simply a work of art. It is the product, in other words, of an intelligent cause, distinct from the matter, or parts, of the

thing, and of one whose causality, in bringing together and combining the parts, is determined by its idea of a whole made possible through that idea, and consequently, not by external nature.

5 But if a thing is a product of nature, and in this character is notwithstanding to contain intrinsically and in its inner possibility a relation to ends, in other words, is to be possible only as a physical end and independently of the causality of the conceptions of external rational agents, then this *second* requisite is 10 involved, namely, that the parts of the thing combine of themselves into the unity of a whole by being reciprocally cause and effect of their form. For this is the only way in which it is possible that the idea of the whole may conversely, or reciprocally, determine in its turn the form and combination of all the 15 parts, not as cause—for that would make it an art-product—but as the epistemological basis upon which the systematic unity of the form and combination of all the manifold contained in the given matter becomes cognizable for the person estimating it.

What we require, therefore, in the case of a body which in its 20 intrinsic nature and inner possibility has to be estimated as a physical end, is as follows. Its parts must in their collective unity reciprocally produce one another alike as to form and combination, and thus by their own causality produce a whole, the conception of which, conversely,—in a being possessing the 25 causality according to conceptions that is adequate for such a product—could in turn be the cause of the whole according to a principle, so that, consequently, the nexus of *efficient causes* might be no less estimated as an *operation brought about by final causes.*

30 In such a natural product as this every part is thought as *owing* its presence to the *agency* of all the remaining parts, and also as existing *for the sake of the others* and of the whole, that is as an instrument, or organ. But this is not enough—for it 374 might be an instrument of art, and thus have no more than its

Part II.   Critique of Teleological Judgement

general possibility referred to an end. On the contrary the part
must be an organ *producing* the other parts—each, consequently,
reciprocally producing the others. No instrument of art can
answer to this description, but only the instrument of that nature
from whose resources the materials of every instrument are 5
drawn—even the materials for instruments of art. Only under
these conditions and upon these terms can such a product be an
organized and *self-organized being*, and, as such, be called a
physical end.

In a watch one part is the instrument by which the movement 10
of the others is effected, but one wheel is not the efficient cause
of the production of the other. One part is certainly present for
the sake of another, but it does not owe its presence to the agency
of that other. For this reason, also, the producing cause of the
watch and its form is not contained in the nature of this material, 15
but lies outside the watch in a being that can act according to
ideas of a whole which its causality makes possible. Hence one
wheel in the watch does not produce the other, and, still less,
does one watch produce other watches, by utilizing, or organizing, foreign material ; hence it does not of itself replace parts 20
of which it has been deprived, nor, if these are absent in the
original construction, does it make good the deficiency by the
subvention of the rest ; nor does it, so to speak, repair its own
casual disorders. But these are all things which we are justified
in expecting from organized nature.—An organized being is, 25
therefore, not a mere machine. For a machine has solely *motive
power*, whereas an organized being possesses inherent *formative*
power, and such, moreover, as it can impart to material devoid
of it—material which it organizes. This, therefore, is a self-
propagating formative power, which cannot be explained by the 30
capacity of movement alone, that is to say, by mechanism.

We do not say half enough of nature and her capacity in
organized products when we speak of this capacity as being the

analogue of art. For what is here present to our minds is an artist—a rational being—working from without. But nature, on the contrary, organizes itself, and does so in each species of its organized products—following a single pattern, certainly, as to 5 general features, but nevertheless admitting deviations calculated to secure self-preservation under particular circumstances. We might perhaps come nearer to the description of this impenetrable property if we were to call it an *analogue of life.* But then either we should have to endow matter as mere matter with 10 a property (hylozoism) that contradicts its essential nature ; or else we should have to associate with it a foreign principle *standing in community* with it (a soul). But, if such a product 375 is to be a natural product, then we have to adopt one or other of two courses in order to bring in a soul. Either we must pre-15 suppose organized matter as the instrument of such a soul, which makes organized matter no whit more intelligible, or else we must make the soul the artificer of this structure, in which case we must withdraw the product from (corporal) nature. Strictly speaking, therefore, the organization of nature has nothing 20 analogous to any causality known to us.[1] Natural beauty may justly be termed the analogue of art, for it is only ascribed to the objects in respect of reflection upon the *external* intuition of them and, therefore, only on account of their superficial form. But *intrinsic natural perfection,* as possessed by things that are only 25 possible as *physical ends,* and that are therefore called organisms,

[1] We may, on the other hand, make use of an analogy to the above mentioned immediate physical ends to throw light on a certain union, which, however, is to be found more often in idea than in fact. Thus in the case of a complete transformation, recently undertaken, of a great people into a state, the word *organization* has frequently, and with much propriety, been used for the constitution of the legal authorities and even of the entire body politic. For in a whole of this kind certainly no member should be a mere means, but should also be an end, and, seeing that he contributes to the possibility of the entire body, should have his position and function in turn defined by the idea of the whole.

is unthinkable and inexplicable on any analogy to any known physical, or natural, agency, not even excepting—since we ourselves are part of nature in the widest sense—the suggestion of any strictly apt analogy to human art.

The concept of a thing as intrinsically a physical end is, therefore, not a constitutive conception either of understanding or of reason, but yet it may be used by reflective judgement as a regulative conception for guiding our investigation of objects of this kind by a remote analogy with our own causality according to ends generally, and as a basis of reflection upon their supreme source. But in the latter connexion it cannot be used to promote our knowledge either of nature or of such original source of those objects, but must on the contrary be confined to the service of just the same practical faculty of reason in analogy with which we considered the cause of the finality in question.

Organisms are, therefore, the only beings in nature that, considered in their separate existence and apart from any relation to other things, cannot be thought possible except as ends of nature. It is they, then, that first afford objective reality to the conception of an *end* that is an end *of nature* and not a practical end. Thus they supply natural science with the basis for a teleology, or, in other words, a mode of estimating its Objects on a special principle that it would otherwise be absolutely unjustifiable to introduce into that science—seeing that we are quite unable to perceive *a priori* the possibility of such a kind of causality.

§ 5 (66)

The principle on which the intrinsic finality in organisms is estimated.

THIS principle, the statement of which serves to define what is meant by organisms, is as follows : *an organized natural product is one in which every part is reciprocally both end and means.*

In such a product nothing is in vain, without an end, or to be ascribed to a blind mechanism of nature.

It is true that the occasion for adopting this principle must be derived from experience—from such experience, namely, as is
5 methodically arranged and is called observation. But owing to the universality and necessity which that principle predicates of such finality, it cannot rest merely on empirical grounds, but must have some underlying *a priori* principle. This principle, however, may be one that is merely regulative, and it may be
10 that the ends in question only reside in the idea of the person forming the estimate and not in any efficient cause whatever. Hence the above named principle may be called a *maxim* for estimating the intrinsic finality of organisms.

It is common knowledge that scientists who dissect plants and
15 animals, seeking to investigate their structure and to see into the reasons why and the end for which they are provided with such and such parts, why the parts have such and such a position and interconnexion, and why the internal form is precisely what it is, adopt the above maxim as absolutely necessary. So they say
20 that nothing in such forms of life is in *vain*, and they put the maxim on the same footing of validity as the fundamental principle of all natural science, that *nothing* happens *by chance*. They are, in fact, quite as unable to free themselves from this teleological principle as from that of general physical science.
25 For just as the abandonment of the latter would leave them without any experience at all, so the abandonment of the former would leave them with no clue to assist their observation of a type of natural things that have once come to be thought under the conception of physical ends.

30 Indeed this conception leads reason into an order of things 377 entirely different from that of a mere mechanism of nature, which *mere mechanism* no longer proves adequate in this domain. An idea has to underlie the possibility of the natural product. But this idea is an absolute unity of the representation, whereas

the material is a plurality of things that of itself can afford no
definite unity of composition. Hence, if that unity of the idea
is actually to serve as the *a priori* determining ground of a
natural law of the causality of such a form of the composite, the
end of nature must be made to extend to *everything* contained 5
in its product. For if once we lift such an effect out of the sphere
of the blind mechanism of nature and relate it *as a whole* to a
supersensible ground of determination, we must then estimate
it out and out on this principle. We have no reason for assuming
the form of such a thing to be still partly dependent on blind 10
mechanism, for with such confusion of heterogeneous principles
every reliable rule for estimating things would disappear.

It is no doubt the case that in an animal body, for example,
many parts might be explained as accretions on simple mechanical laws (as skin, bone, hair). Yet the cause that accumulates 15
the appropriate material, modifies and fashions it, and deposits
it in its proper place, must always be estimated teleologically.
Hence, everything in the body must be regarded as organized,
and everything, also, in a certain relation to the thing is itself
in turn an organ.   20

§ 6 (67)

*The principle on which nature in general is estimated
teleologically as a system of ends.*

WE have said above that the *extrinsic* finality of natural things
affords no adequate justification for taking them as ends of nature
to explain the reason of their existence, or for treating their contingently final effects as ideally the grounds of their existence on
the principle of final causes. Thus we are not entitled to consider 25
rivers as physical ends then and there, because they facilitate
international intercourse in inland countries, or *mountains*,
because they contain the sources of the rivers and hold stores
of snow for the maintenance of their flow in dry seasons, or,

similarly, the *slope* of the land, that carries down these waters 378
and leaves the country dry. For, although this configuration of
the earth's surface is very necessary for the origination and sustenance of the vegetable and animal kingdoms, yet intrinsically
5 it contains nothing the possibility of which should make us feel
obliged to invoke a causality according to ends. The same
applies to plants utilized or enjoyed by man ; or to animals, as
the camel, the ox, the horse, dog, &c., which are so variously
employed, sometimes as servants of man, sometimes as food for
10 him to live on, and mostly found quite indispensable. The external
relationship of things that we have no reason to regard as ends
in their own right can only be hypothetically estimated as final.

There is an essential distinction between estimating a thing as
a physical end in virtue of its intrinsic form and regarding the
15 real existence of this thing as an end of nature. To maintain the
latter view we require, not merely the conception of a possible
end, but a knowledge of the final end (*scopus*) of nature. This
involves our referring nature to something supersensible, a reference that far transcends any teleological knowledge we have of
20 nature ; for, to find the end of the real existence of nature itself,
we must look beyond nature. That the origin of a simple blade
of grass is only possible on the rule of ends is, to our human
critical faculty, sufficiently proved by its internal form. But
let us lay aside this consideration and look only to the use to
25 which the thing is put by other natural beings—which means
that we abandon the study of the internal organization and look
only to external adaptations to ends. We see, then, that the
grass is required as a means of existence by cattle, and cattle,
similarly, by man. But we do not see why after all it should be
30 necessary that men should in fact exist (a question that might
not be so easy to answer if the specimens of humanity that we
had in mind were, say, the New Hollanders or Fuegians). We
do not then arrive in this way at any categorical end. On the
contrary all this adaptation is made to rest on a condition that

has to be removed to an ever-retreating horizon. This condition
is the unconditional condition—the existence of a thing as a
final end—which, as such, lies entirely outside the study of the
world on physico-teleological lines. But, then, such a thing is
not a physical end either, since it (or its entire genus) is not to be 5
regarded as a product of nature.

Hence it is only in so far as matter is organized that it necessarily involves the conception of it as a physical end, because here
it possesses a form that is at once specific and a product of nature.
379 But, brought so far, this conception necessarily leads us to the 10
idea of aggregate nature as a system following the rule of ends,
to which idea, again, the whole mechanism of nature has to be
subordinated on principles of reason—at least for the purpose of
testing phenomenal nature by this idea. The principle of reason
is one which it is competent for reason to use as a merely sub- 15
jective principle, that is as a maxim : everything in the world
is good for something or other ; nothing in it is in vain ; we are
entitled, nay incited, by the example that nature affords us in
its organic products, to expect nothing from it and its laws but
what is final when things are viewed as a whole.   20

It is evident that this is a principle to be applied not by the
determinant, but only by the reflective, judgement, that it is
regulative and not constitutive, and that all that we obtain from
it is a clue to guide us in the study of natural things. These
things it leads us to consider in relation to a ground of determina- 25
tion already given, and in the light of a new uniformity, and it
helps us to extend physical science according to another principle, that, namely, of final causes, yet without interfering with
the principle of the mechanism of physical causality. Furthermore,
this principle is altogether silent on the point of whether anything 30
estimated according to it is, or is not, an end of nature *by design* :
whether, that is, the grass exists for the sake of the ox or the
sheep, and whether these and the other things of nature exist

foɩ the sake of man.—We do well to consider even things that are
unpleasant to us, and that in particular connexions are contra-
final, from this point of view also. Thus, for example, one might
say that the vermin which plague men in their clothes, hair, or
5 beds, may, by a wise provision of nature, be an incitement towards cleanliness, which is of itself an important means for
preserving health. Or the mosquitoes and other stinging insects
that make the wilds of America so trying for the savages, may
be so many goads to urge these primitive men to drain the
10 marshes and bring light into the dense forests that shut out the
air, and, by so doing, as well as by the tillage of the soil, to render
their abodes more sanitary. Even what appears to man to be
contrary to nature in his internal organization affords, when
treated on these lines, an interesting, and sometimes even in-
15 structive, outlook into a teleological order of things, to which
mere unaided study from a physical point of view apart from
such a principle would not lead us. Some persons say that men
or animals that have a tapeworm receive it as a sort of com-
pensation to make good some deficiency in their vital organs.
20 Now, just in the same way, I would ask if dreams (from which 380
our sleep is never free, although we rarely remember what we
have dreamed), may not be a regulation of nature adapted to
ends. For when all the muscular forces of the body are relaxed
dreams serve the purpose of internally stimulating the vital
25 organs by means of the imagination and the great activity which
it exerts—an activity that in this state generally rises to psycho-
physical agitation. This seems to be why imagination is usually
more actively at work in the sleep of those who have gone to bed
at night with a loaded stomach, just when this stimulation is
30 most needed. Hence, I would suggest that without this internal
stimulating force and fatiguing unrest that makes us complain
of our dreams, which in fact, however, are probably curative,
sleep, even in a sound state of health, would amount to a complete extinction of life.

Once the teleological estimate of nature, supported by the
physical ends actually presented to us in organic beings, has
entitled us to form the idea of a vast system of natural ends we
may regard even natural beauty from this point of view, such
beauty being an accordance of nature with the free play of our 5
cognitive faculties as engaged in grasping and estimating its
appearance. For then we may look upon it as an objective
finality of nature in its entirety as a system of which man is
a member. We may regard it as a favour [1] that nature has
extended to us, that besides giving us what is useful it has dis- 10
pensed beauty and charms in such abundance, and for this we
may love it, just as we view it with respect because of its im-
mensity, and feel ourselves ennobled by such contemplation—
just as if nature had erected and decorated its splendid stage with
this precise purpose in its mind.   15

The general purport of the present section is simply this :
once we have discovered a capacity in nature for bringing forth
products that can only be thought by us according to the conception of final causes, we advance a step farther. Even products
381 which do not (either as to themselves or the relation, however 20
final, in which they stand) make it necessarily incumbent upon
us to go beyond the mechanism of blind efficient causes and seek
out some other principle on which they are possible, may nevertheless be justly estimated as forming part of a system of ends.
For the idea from which we started is one which, when we con- 25
sider its foundation, already leads beyond the world of sense,

[1] In the Part on Aesthetics the statement was made : *we regard
nature with favour*, because we take a delight in its form that is
altogether free (disinterested). For in this judgement of mere
taste no account is taken of any end for which these natural beauties
exist : whether to excite pleasure in us, or irrespective of us as
ends. But in a teleological judgement we pay attention to this
relation ; and so we can *regard it as a favour of nature*, that it has
been disposed to promote our culture by exhibiting so many beautiful
forms.

and then the unity of the supersensible principle must be treated,
not as valid merely for certain species of natural beings, but as
similarly valid for the whole of nature as a system.

§ 7 (68)

*The principle of teleology considered as an inherent
principle of natural science.*

THE principles of a science may be inherent in that science
5 itself, and are then termed domestic (*principia domestica*).   Or
they may rest on conceptions that can only be vouched outside
that science, and are *foreign* principles (*peregrina*).   Sciences
containing the latter principles rest their doctrines on auxiliary
propositions (*lemmata*), that is, they obtain some conception or
10 other, and with this conception some basis for a regular procedure, on credit from another science.

Every science is a system in its own right ; and it is not
sufficient that in it we construct according to principles, and so
proceed technically, but we must also set to work architectoni-
15 cally with it as a separate and independent building.   We must
treat it as a self-subsisting whole, and not as a wing or section
of another building—although we may subsequently make a
passage to or fro from one part to another.

Hence if we supplement natural science by introducing the
20 conception of God into its context for the purpose of rendering
the finality of nature explicable, and if, having done so, we turn
round and use this finality for the purpose of proving that there
is a God, then both natural science and theology are deprived
of all intrinsic substantiality.   This deceptive crossing and re-
25 crossing from one side to the other involves both in uncertainty,
because their boundaries are thus allowed to overlap.

The expression, an end of nature, is of itself sufficient to
obviate this confusion and prevent our confounding natural
science or the occasion it affords for a *teleological* estimate of its
30 objects with the contemplation of God, and hence with a *theological* 382

derivation. It is not to be regarded as a matter of no consequence that the above expression should be confused with that of a divine end in the appointment of nature, or that the latter should even be passed off as the more appropriate and the one more becoming to a pious soul, on the ground that, say what we will, 5 it must eventually come back to our deriving these final forms in nature from a wise Author of the universe. On the contrary we must scrupulously and modestly restrict ourselves to the term that expresses just as much as we know, and no more—namely, an end of nature. For before we arrive at the question of the 10 cause of nature itself, we find in nature and in the course of its generative processes examples of these final products produced in nature according to known empirical laws. It is according to these laws that natural science must estimate its objects, and, consequently, it must seek within itself for this causality accord- 15 ing to the rule of ends. Therefore this science must not overleap its bounds for the purpose of drawing into its own bosom, as a domestic principle, one to whose conception no experience can be adequate, and upon which we are not authorized to venture until after natural science has said its last word. 20

Natural qualities that are demonstrable *a priori*, and so reveal their possibility on universal principles without any aid from experience, may involve a technical finality. Yet, being absolutely necessary, they cannot be credited to natural teleologic at all. Natural teleology forms part of physics, and is a 25 method applicable to the solution of the problems of physics. Arithmetical and geometrical analogies, also universal mechanical laws, however strange and worthy of our admiration the union in a single principle of a variety of rules apparently quite disconnected may seem, have no claim on that account to rank 30 as teleological grounds of explanation in physics. They may deserve to be brought under review in the universal theory of the finality of the things of nature in general, but, if so, this is a theory that would have to be assigned to another science, namely metaphysics. It would not form an inherent principle of natural science : whereas in the case of the empirical laws of the physical ends which organisms present it is not alone permissible, 5 but even unavoidable, to use teleological *criticism* as a principle of natural science in respect of a peculiar class of its objects.

For the purpose of keeping strictly within its own bounds physics entirely ignores the question whether physical ends are ends *designedly* or *undesignedly*. To deal with that question 383 10 would be to meddle in the affairs of others—namely, in what is the business of metaphysics. Suffice it that there are objects whose one and only *explanation* is on natural laws that we are unable to conceive otherwise than by adopting the idea of ends as principle, objects which, in their intrinsic form, and with 15 nothing more in view than their internal relations, are *cognizable* in this way alone. It is true that in teleology we speak of nature as if its finality were a thing of design. But to avoid all suspicion of presuming in the slightest to mix up with our sources of knowledge something that has no place in physics at all, namely a 20 supernatural cause, we refer to design in such a way that, in the same breath, we attribute this design to nature, that is to matter. Here no room is left for misinterpretation, since, obviously, no one would ascribe design, in the proper sense of the term, to a lifeless material. Hence our real intention is to indicate that 25 the word design, as here used, only signifies a principle of the reflective, and not of the determinant, judgement, and consequently is not meant to introduce any special ground of causality, but only to assist the employment of reason by supplementing investigation on mechanical laws by the addition of another 30 method of investigation, so as to make up for the inadequacy of the former even as a method of empirical research that has for its object all particular laws of nature. Therefore, when teleology is applied to physics, we speak with perfect justice of the wisdom, the economy, the forethought, the beneficence of nature. But in so doing we do not convert nature into an intelligent being, for that would be absurd ; but neither do we dare to think of placing another being, one that is intelligent, above nature as its architect, for that would be extravagant.[1] On the contrary our only intention is to designate in this way 5 a kind of natural causality on an analogy with our own causality in the technical employment of reason, for the purpose of keeping in view the rule upon which certain natural products are to be investigated.

But why, then, is it that teleology does not usually form a 10 special part of theoretical natural science, but is relegated to 384 theology by way of a propaedeutic or transition ? This is done in order to keep the study of the mechanical aspect of nature in close adherence to what we are able so to subject to our observation or experiment that we could ourselves produce it like nature, 15 or at least produce it according to similar laws. For we have complete insight only into what we can make and accomplish according to our conceptions. But to effect by means of art a presentation similar to organization, as an intrinsic end of nature, infinitely surpasses all our powers. And as for such extrinsic 20 adjustments of nature as are considered final (e.g. winds, rains, &c.), physics certainly studies their mechanism, but it is quite unable to exhibit their relation to ends so far as this relation purports to be a condition necessarily attaching to a cause. For this necessity in the nexus does not touch the constitution of things, 25 but turns wholly on the combination of our conceptions.

---

[1] The German word *vermessen* (presumptuous) is a good word and full of meaning. A judgement in which we forget to take stock of the extent of our powers of understanding may sometimes sound very modest, while yet it presumes a great deal, and is really very presumptuous. Of this type are the majority of those by which we purport to exalt divine wisdom by underlaying the works of creation and preservation with designs that are really intended to do honour to the individual wisdom of our own subtle intellects.

SECOND DIVISION

DIALECTIC OF TELEOLOGICAL JUDGEMENT

§ 8 (69)

Nature of an antinomy of judgement.

THE *determinant* judgement does not possess as its own separate property any principles upon which *conceptions of objects* are founded. It is not an autonomy ; for it *subsumes* merely under given laws, or concepts, as principles. Just for this reason
5 it is not exposed to any danger from inherent antinomy and does not run the risk of a conflict of its principles. Thus transcendental judgement, which was shown to contain the conditions of subsumption under categories, was not independently *nomothetic*. It only specified the conditions of sensuous intuition upon
10 which reality, that is, application, can be afforded to a given conception as a law of understanding. In the discharge of this office it could never fall into a state of internal disunion, at least in the matter of principles.

But the *reflective* judgement has to subsume under a law that
15 is not yet given. It has, therefore, in fact only a principle of reflection upon objects for which we are objectively at a complete loss for a law, or conception of the Object, sufficient to serve as a principle covering the particular cases as they come before us. Now as there is no permissible employment of the cognitive
20 faculties apart from principles, the reflective judgement must in such cases be a principle to itself. As this principle is not objective and is unable to introduce any basis of cognition of the Object sufficient for the required purpose of subsumption, it must serve as a mere subjective principle for the employment
25 of our cognitive faculties in a final manner, namely, for reflecting upon objects of a particular kind. The reflective judgement has,

therefore, its maxims applicable to such cases—maxims that are
386 in fact necessary for obtaining a knowledge of the natural laws
to be found in experience, and which are directed to assist us
in attaining to conceptions, be these even conceptions of reason,
wherever such conceptions are absolutely required for the mere 5
purpose of getting to know nature in its empirical laws.—Between
these necessary maxims of the reflective judgement a conflict
may arise, and consequently an antinomy. This affords the
basis of a dialectic ; and if each of the mutually conflicting
maxims has its foundation in the nature of our cognitive facul- 10
ties, this dialectic may be called a natural dialectic, and it
constitutes an unavoidable illusion which it is the duty of
critical philosophy to expose and to resolve lest it should
deceive us.

§ 9 (70)

Exposition of this Antinomy.

In dealing with nature as the complex of objects of external 15
sense, reason is able to rely upon laws some of which are prescribed by understanding itself *a priori* to nature, while others
are capable of indefinite extension by means of the empirical
determinations occurring in experience. For the application of
the laws prescribed *a priori* by understanding, that is, of the 20
universal laws of material nature in general, judgement does not
need any special principle of reflection ; for there it is determinant, an objective principle being furnished to it by understanding. But in respect of the particular laws with which we
can become acquainted through experience alone, there is such 25
a wide scope for diversity and heterogeneity that judgement
must be a principle to itself, even for the mere purpose of
searching for a law and tracking one out in the phenomena
of nature. For it needs such a principle as a guiding thread,
if it is even to hope for a consistent body of empirical know- 30

ledge based on a thorough-going uniformity of nature—that is
a unity of nature in its empirical laws.   Now from the fact of
this contingent unity of particular laws it may come to pass
that judgement acts upon two maxims in its reflection, one of
5 which it receives *a priori* from mere understanding, but the
other of which is prompted by particular experiences that bring
reason into play to institute an estimate of corporeal nature and
its laws according to a particular principle.   What happens 387
then is that these two different maxims seem to all appearance
10 unable to run in the same harness, and a dialectic arises
that throws judgement into confusion as to the principle of its
reflection.

The first maxim of such reflection is the *thesis* : All production
of material things and their forms must be estimated as possible
15 on mere mechanical laws.

The second maxim is the *antithesis* : Some products of material
nature cannot be estimated as possible on mere mechanical laws
(that is, for estimating them quite a different law of causality is
required, namely, that of final causes).

20 If now these regulative principles of investigation were converted into constitutive principles of the possibility of the
Objects themselves, they would read thus :

Thesis : All production of material things is possible on mere
mechanical laws.

25 *Antithesis* : Some production of such things is not possible on
mere mechanical laws.

In this latter form, as objective principles for the determinant
judgement, they would contradict one another, so that one of
the pair would necessarily be false.   But that would then be
30 an antinomy certainly, though not one of judgement, but rather
a conflict in the legislation of reason.   But reason is unable to
prove either one or the other of these principles : seeing that we
can have no *a priori* determining principle of the possibility of
things on mere empirical laws of nature.

On the other hand, looking to the maxims of a reflective judgement as first set out, we see that they do not in fact contain any contradiction at all. For if I say : I must *estimate* the possibility of all events in material nature, and, consequently, also all forms considered as its products, on mere mechanical laws, I do not thereby assert that they *are solely possible in this way*, that is, to the exclusion of every other kind of causality. On the contrary this assertion is only intended to indicate that I *ought* at all times to *reflect* upon these things *according to the principle* of the simple mechanism of nature, and, consequently, push my investigation with it as far as I can, because unless I make it the basis of research there can be no knowledge of nature in the true sense of the term at all. Now this does not stand in the way of the second maxim when a proper occasion for its employment presents itself—that is to say, in the case of some natural forms (and, at their instance, in the case of entire nature), we may, in our reflection upon them, follow the trail of a principle which is radically different from explanation by the mechanism of nature, namely the principle of final causes. For reflection according to the first maxim is not in this way superseded. On the contrary we are directed to pursue it as far as we can. Further it is not asserted that those forms were not possible on the mechanism of nature. It is only maintained that *human reason*, adhering to this maxim and proceeding on these lines, could never discover a particle of foundation for what constitutes the specific character of a physical end, whatever additions it might make in this way to its knowledge of natural laws. This leaves it an open question, whether in the unknown inner basis of nature itself the physico-mechanical and the final nexus present in the same things may not cohere in a single principle ; it being only our reason that is not in a position to unite them in such a principle, so that our judgement, consequently, remains *reflective*, not determinant,

that is, acts on a subjective ground, and not according to an objective principle of the possibility of things in their inherent nature, and, accordingly, is compelled to conceive a different principle from that of the mechanism of nature as a ground of
5 the possibility of certain forms in nature.

§ 10 (71)

Introduction to the solution of the above antinomy.

WE are wholly unable to prove the impossibility of the production of organized natural products in accordance with the simple mechanism of nature. For we cannot see into the first and inner ground of the infinite multiplicity of the particular
10 laws of nature, which, being only known empirically, are for us contingent, and so we are absolutely incapable of reaching the intrinsic and all-sufficient principle of the possibility of a nature —a principle which lies in the supersensible. But may not the productive capacity of nature be just as adequate for what we
15 estimate to be formed or connected according to the idea of ends as it is for what we believe merely calls for mechanical functions on the part of nature ? Or may it be that in fact things are genuine physical ends (as we must necessarily estimate them to be), and as such founded upon an original causality of a com-
20 pletely different kind, which cannot be an incident of material nature or of its intelligible substrate, namely, the causality of an 389 architectonic understanding ? What has been said shows that these are questions upon which our reason, very narrowly restricted in respect of the conception of causality if this conception has
25 to be specified *a priori*, can give absolutely no information.— But that, relatively to our cognitive faculties, the mere mechanism of nature is also unable to furnish any explanation of the production of organisms, is a matter just as indubitably certain. *For the reflective judgement*, therefore, this is a perfectly sound
30 principle : that for the clearly manifest nexus of things according

to final causes, we must think a causality distinct from mechanism, namely a world-cause acting according to ends, that is, an intelligent cause—however rash and undemonstrable a principle this might be *for the determinant judgement.* In the first case the principle is a simple maxim of judgement. The conception of causality which it involves is a mere idea to which we in no way undertake to concede reality, but only make use of it to guide a reflection that still leaves the door open for any available mechanical explanation, and that never strays from the world of sense. In the second case the principle would be an objective principle. Reason would prescribe it and judgement would have to be subject to it and determine itself accordingly. But in that case reflection wanders from the world of sense into transcendent regions, and possibly gets led astray.

All semblance of an antinomy between the maxims of the strictly physical, or mechanical, mode of explanation and the teleological, or technical, rests, therefore, on our confusing a principle of the reflective with one of the determinant judgement. The *autonomy* of the former, which is valid merely subjectively for the use of our reason in respect of particular empirical laws, is mistaken for the *heteronomy* of the second, which has to conform to the laws, either universal or particular, given by understanding.

§ 11 (72)

The various kinds of systems dealing with the finality of nature.

No one has ever yet questioned the correctness of the principle that when judging certain things in nature, namely organisms and their possibility, we must look to the conception of final causes. Such a principle is admittedly necessary even where we require no more than a *guiding-thread* for the purpose of becoming acquainted with the character of these things by means of observation, without trenching upon an investigation into their first origin. Hence the question can only be, whether this principle is merely subjectively valid, that is, a mere maxim of judgement, or is an objective principle of nature. On the latter alternative there would belong to nature another type of causality beyond its mechanism and its simple dynamical laws, namely, the causality of final causes, under which natural causes (dynamical forces) would stand only as intermediate causes.

Now this speculative question or problem might well be left without any answer or solution. For, if we content ourselves with speculation within the bounds of the mere knowledge of nature, the above maxims are ample for its study as far as human powers extend, and for probing its deepest secrets. So it must be that reason wakens some suspicion, or that nature, so to speak, gives us a hint. With the help of this conception of final causes, might we not be able to take a step, we are prompted to think, beyond and above nature, and connect it to the supreme point in the series of causes ? Why not relinquish the investigation of nature (although we have not advanced so very far with it) or, at least, lay it temporarily aside, and try first to discover whither that stranger in natural science, the conception of physical ends, would lead us ?

Now at this point, certainly, the undisputed maxim above mentioned would have to merge in a problem that opens up a wide field for controversy. For it may be alleged that the nexus of natural finality *proves* the existence of a special kind of causality for nature. Or it may be contended that this nexus, considered in its true nature and on objective principles, is, on the contrary, identical with the mechanism of nature, or rests on one and the same ground, though in the case of many natural products this ground often lies too deeply buried for our investigation. Hence, as is contended, we have recourse to a subjective principle, namely art, or causality according to ideas, in order to introduce it, on an analogy, as the basis of nature—an expedient that in fact proves successful in many cases, in some certainly seems to fail, but in no case entitles us to introduce into natural science a mode of operation different from causality on mere mechanical laws of nature.—Now, in giving to the procedure, or causal operation of nature, the name of technic, on account of the suggestion of an end which we find in its products, we propose to divide this technic into such as is *designed* (*technica intentionalis*) and such as is *undesigned* (*technica naturalis*). The former is intended to convey that nature's capacity for production by final causes must be considered a special kind of causality ; the latter that this capacity is at bottom identical with natural mechanism, and that the contingent coincidence with our artificial conceptions and their rules is a mere subjective condition of our estimating this capacity, and is thus erroneously interpreted as a special mode of natural production.

To speak now of the systems that offer an explanation of nature on the point of final causes, one cannot fail to perceive that they all, without exception, controvert one another dogmatically. In other words they are at issue upon objective principles of the possibility of things, be this possibility one due to causes acting designedly or merely undesignedly. They do not attack the subjective maxim of mere judgement upon the cause of the final products in question. In the latter case *disparate* principles might very well be reconciled, whereas, in *the former, contradictorily opposed* principles annul one another and are mutually inconsistent.

The systems in respect of the technic of nature, that is, of nature's power of production on the rule of ends, are of two kinds : that of the *idealism* and that of the *realism* of physical ends. The former maintains that all finality on the part of nature is *undesigned* ; the latter, that some, namely finality in organized beings, is *designed*. From the latter the hypothetical consequence may be inferred, that the technic of nature is also

designed in what concerns all its other products relatively to
entire nature, that is, is an end.

1. The *idealism* of finality (I am here all along referring to
objective finality) is either that of the *accidentality* or *fatality* of
5 the determination of nature in the final form of its products.
The former principle fixes on the relation of matter to the
physical basis of its form, namely dynamical laws ; the latter
on its relation to the hyperphysical basis of matter and entire
nature.   The system of *accidentality*, which is attributed to
10 Epicurus or Democritus, is, in its literal interpretation, so
manifestly absurd that it need not detain us. On the other hand,
the system of *fatality*, of which Spinoza is the accredited author,
although it is to all appearances much older, rests upon something supersensible, into which our insight, accordingly, is un-
15 able to penetrate.   It is not so easy to refute : the reason being
that its conception of the original being is quite unintelligible.
But this much is clear, that on this system the final nexus in the
world must be regarded as undesigned.   For, while it is derived 392
from an original being, it is not derived from its intelligence,
20 and consequently not from any design on its part, but from the
necessity of the nature of this being and the world-unity flowing
from that nature.   Hence it is clear, too, that the fatalism of
finality is also an idealism of finality.

2. The *realism* of the finality of nature is also either physical
25 or hyperphysical. The *former* bases natural ends on the analogue
of a faculty acting designedly, that is, on the *life of matter*—this
life being either inherent in it or else bestowed upon it by an
inner animating principle or world-soul. This is called *hylozoism*.
The *latter* derives such ends from the original source of the
30 universe. This source it regards as an intelligent Being producing
with design—or essentially and fundamentally living.   It is
theism.[1]

---

[1] We see from this how, as in most speculative matters of pure
reason, the schools of philosophy have, in the way of dogmatic

§ 12 (73)

None of the above systems does what it professes to do.

WHAT is the aim and object of all the above systems ? It is to explain our teleological judgements about nature. To do so they adopt one or other of two courses. One side denies their truth, and consequently describes them as an idealism of nature (represented as art). The other side recognizes their truth, and 5 promises to demonstrate the possibility of a nature according to the idea of final causes.

1. The systems that contend for the idealism of the final causes in nature fall into two classes. One class does certainly concede to the principle of these causes a causality according to 10 dynamical laws (to which causality the natural things owe their 393 final existence). But it denies to it *intentionality*—that is, it denies that this causality is determined designedly to this its final production, or, in other words, that an end is the cause. This is the explanation adopted by Epicurus. It completely 15 denies and abolishes the distinction between a technic of nature and its mere mechanism. Blind chance is accepted as the explanation, not alone of the agreement of the generated products with our conception, and, consequently, of the technic of nature, but even of the determination of the causes of this 20 development on dynamical laws, and, consequently, of its mechanism. Hence nothing is explained, not even the illusion in

assertions, usually attempted every possible solution of the problem before them. Thus in the case of the finality of nature, at one time a *lifeless matter*, or again a *lifeless God*, at another, a *living matter*, or else a *living God*, have been tried. Nothing is left to us except, if needs be, to break away from all these *objective assertions*, and weigh our judgement *critically* in its mere relation to our cognitive faculties. By so doing we may procure for their principle a validity which, if not dogmatic, is yet that of a maxim, and ample for the reliable employment of our reason.

our teleological judgements, so that the alleged idealism in them is left altogether unsubstantiated.

Spinoza, as the representative of the other class, seeks to release us from any inquiry into the ground of the possibility of ends of nature, and to deprive this idea of all reality, by refusing to allow that such ends are to be regarded as products at all. They are, rather, accidents inhering in an original being. This being, he says, is the substrate of the natural things, and, as such, he does not ascribe to it causality in respect of them, but simply subsistence. Thanks, then, to the unconditional necessity both of this being and of all the things of nature, as its inherent accidents, he assures to the natural forms, it is true, that unity of ground necessary for all finality, but he does so at the expense of their contingency, apart from which no *unity of end* is thinkable. In eliminating this unity he eliminates all *trace of design*, and leaves the original ground of the things of nature divested of all intelligence.

But Spinozism does not effect what it intends. It intends to furnish an explanation of the final nexus of natural things, which it does not deny, and it refers us simply to the unity of the subject in which they all inhere. But suppose we grant it this mode of existence for its beings of the world, such ontological unity is not then and there a *unity of end* and does not make it in any way intelligible. The latter is, in fact, quite a special kind of unity. It does not follow from the nexus of things in one subject, or of the beings of the world in an original being. On the contrary, it implies emphatically relation to a *cause* possessed of intelligence. Even if all the things were to be united in one *simple* subject, yet such unity would never exhibit a final relation unless these things were understood to be, first, inner *effects* of the substance as a *cause*, and, secondly, effects of it as cause by *virtue of its intelligence*. Apart from these formal conditions all unity is mere necessity of nature, and, when it is ascribed nevertheless to things that we represent as outside one 394 another, blind necessity. But if what the scholastics call the transcendental perfection of things, in relation to their own proper essence—a perfection according to which all things have inherent in them all the requisites for being the thing they are and not any other thing—is to be termed a natural finality, we 5 then get a childish playing with words in the place of conceptions. For if all things must be thought as ends, then to be a thing and to be an end are identical, so that, all said and done, there is nothing that specially deserves to be represented as an end. 10

This makes it evident that by resolving our conception of natural finality into the consciousness of our own inherence in an all-embracing, though at the same time simple, being, and by seeking the form of finality in the unity of that being, Spinoza must have intended to maintain the idealism of the finality and 15 not its realism. But even this he was unable to accomplish, for the mere representation of the unity of the substrate can never produce the idea of finality, be it even undesigned.

2. Those who not merely maintain the *realism* of physical ends, but purport even to explain it, think they can detect a special 20 type of causality, namely that of causes operating intentionally. Or, at least, they think they are able to perceive the possibility of such causality—for unless they did they could not set about trying to explain it. For even the most daring hypothesis must rely at least on the *possibility* of its assumed foundation being 25 *certain,* and the conception of this foundation must be capable of being assured its objective reality.

But the possibility of a living matter is quite inconceivable. The very conception of it involves self-contradiction, since lifelessness, *inertia,* constitutes the essential characteristic of 30 matter. Then if the possibility of a matter endowed with life and of aggregate nature conceived as an animal is invoked in support of the hypothesis of a finality of nature in the macro-

cosm, it can only be used with the utmost reserve in so far as it
is manifested empirically in the organization of nature in the
microcosm. Its possibility can in no way be perceived *a priori.*
Hence there must be a vicious circle in the explanation, if the
5 finality of nature in organized beings is sought to be derived from
the life of matter and if this life in turn is only to be known in
organized beings, so that no conception of its possibility can be 395
formed apart from such experience. Hence hylozoism does not
perform what it promises.

10   Finally *theism* is equally incapable of substantiating dogmatically the possibility of physical ends as a key to teleology. Yet
the source of its explanation of them has this advantage over all
others, that by attributing an intelligence to the original Being
it adopts the best mode of rescuing the finality of nature from
15 idealism, and introduces an intentional causality for its production.

    For theism would first have to succeed in proving to the satis-
faction of the determinant judgement that the unity of end in
matter is an impossible result of the mere mechanism of nature.
20 Otherwise it is not entitled definitely to locate its ground beyond
and above nature. But the farthest we can get is this. The first
and inner ground of this very mechanism being beyond our ken,
the constitution and limits of our cognitive faculties are such as
to preclude us from in any way looking to matter with a view
25 to finding in it a principle of determinate final relations. We are
left, on the contrary, with no alternative mode of estimating
nature's products as natural ends other than that which resorts
to a supreme Intelligence as the cause of the world. But this is
not a ground for the determinant judgement, but only for the
30 reflective judgement, and it is absolutely incapable of authoriz-
ing us to make any objective assertion.

§ 13 (74)

The impossibility of treating the concept of a technic of nature
dogmatically springs from the inexplicability of a physical end.

EVEN though a conception is to be placed under an empirical
condition we deal dogmatically with it, if we regard it as contained under another conception of the Object—this conception
forming a principle of reason—and determine it in accordance
with the latter. But we deal merely critically with the con- 5
ception if we only regard it in relation to our cognitive faculties
and, consequently, to the subjective conditions of thinking it,
without undertaking to decide anything as to its Object. Hence
the dogmatic treatment of a conception is treatment which is
authoritative for the determinant judgement : the critical 10
treatment is such as is authoritative merely for the reflective
judgement.

396 Now the conception of a thing as a physical end is one that
subsumes nature under a causality that is only thinkable by
the aid of reason, and so subsumes it for the purpose of letting 15
us judge on this principle of what is given of the Object in
experience. But in order to make use of this conception dogmatically for the determinant judgement we should have first
to be assured of its objective reality, as otherwise we could not
subsume any natural thing under it. The conception of a thing 20
as a physical end is, however, certainly one that is empirically
conditioned, that is, is one only possible under certain conditions
given in experience. Yet it is not one to be abstracted from
these conditions, but, on the contrary, it is only possible on a
rational principle in the estimating of the object. Being such 25
a principle we have no insight into its objective reality, that is
to say, we cannot perceive that an Object answering to it is
possible. We cannot establish it dogmatically ; and we do not

know whether it is a mere logical fiction and an objectively empty conception (*conceptus ratiocinans*), or whether it is a rational conception, supplying a basis of knowledge and substantiated by reason (*conceptus ratiocinatus*). Hence it cannot
5 be treated dogmatically on behalf of the determinant judgement. In other words, not alone is it impossible to decide whether or not things of nature, considered as physical ends, require for their production a causality of a quite peculiar kind, namely an intentional causality, but the very question is quite out of order.
10 For the conception of a physical end is altogether unprovable by reason in respect of its objective reality, which means that it is not constitutive for the determinant judgement, but merely regulative for the reflective judgement.

That it is not provable is clear from the following considera-
15 tions. Being a conception of a *natural product* it involves necessity. Yet it also involves in one and the same thing, considered as an end, an accompanying contingency in the form of the Object in respect of mere laws of nature. Hence, if it is to escape self-contradiction, besides containing a basis of the possibility of the
20 thing in nature it must further contain a basis of the possibility of this nature itself and of its reference to something that is not an empirically cognizable nature, namely to something supersensible, and, therefore, to what is not cognizable by us at all. Otherwise in judging of its possibility, we should not have to
25 estimate it in the light of a kind of causality different from that of natural mechanism. Accordingly the conception of a thing as a natural end is transcendent *for the determinant judgement* if its Object is viewed by reason—albeit for the reflective judgement it may be immanent in respect of objects of experience. 397
30 Objective reality, therefore, cannot be procured for it on behalf of the determinant judgement. Hence we can understand how it is that all systems that are ever devised with a view to the dogmatic treatment of the conception of physical ends or of nature as a whole that owes its consistency and coherence to final

Part II.   *Critique of Teleological Judgement*

causes, fail to decide anything whatever either by their objective
affirmations or by their objective denials.   For, if things are
subsumed under a conception that is merely problematic, the
synthetic predicates attached to this conception—as, for example, in the present case, whether the physical end which we 5
suppose for the production of the thing is designed or undesigned
—must yield judgements about the Object of a like problematic
character, be they affirmative or negative, since one does not
know whether one is judging about what is something or nothing.
The conception of a causality through ends, that is, ends of art, 10
has certainly objective reality, just as that of a causality according to the mechanism of nature has.   But the conception of a
physical causality following the rule of ends, and still more of
such a Being as is utterly incapable of being given to us in
experience—a Being regarded as the original source of nature— 15
while it may no doubt be thought without self-contradiction,
is nevertheless useless for the purpose of dogmatic definitive
assertions.   For, since it is incapable of being extracted from
experience, and besides is unnecessary for its possibility, there
is nothing that can give any guarantee of its objective reality. 20
But even if this could be assured, how can I reckon among
products of nature things that are definitely posited as products
of divine art, when it was the very incapacity of nature to
produce such things according to its own laws that necessitated
the appeal to a cause distinct from nature ?   25

§ 14 (75)

The conception of an objective finality of nature is a critical
principle of reason for the use of the reflective judgement.

BUT then it is one thing to say : The production of certain
things of nature, or even of entire nature, is only possible
through the agency of a cause that pursues designs in deter-

mining itself to action. It is a perfectly different thing to say : *By the peculiar constitution of my cognitive faculties* the only way I can judge of the possibility of those things and of their pro- 398 duction is by conceiving for that purpose a cause working 5 designedly, and, consequently, a being whose productivity is analogous to the causality of an understanding. In the former case I desire to ascertain something about the Object, and I am bound to prove the objective reality of a conception I have assumed. In the latter case it is only the employment of my cognitive 10 faculties that is determined by reason in accordance with their peculiar character and the essential conditions imposed both by their range and their limitations. The first principle is, therefore, an *objective* principle intended for the determinant judgement. The second is a subjective principle for the use merely of the 15 reflective judgement, of which it is, consequently, a maxim that reason prescribes.

In fact, if we desire to pursue the investigation of nature with diligent observation, be it only in its organized products, we cannot get rid of the necessity of adopting the conception of 20 a design as basal. We have in this conception, therefore, a maxim absolutely necessary for the empirical employment of our reason. But once such a guide for the study of nature has been adopted, and its application verified, it is obvious that we must at least try this maxim of judgement also on nature as a 25 whole, because many of its laws might be discoverable in the light of this maxim which otherwise, with the limitations of our insight into its mechanism, would remain hidden from us. But in respect of the latter employment, useful as this maxim of judgement is, it is not indispensable. For nature as a whole is 30 not given to us as organized—in the very strict sense above assigned to the word. On the other hand, in respect of those natural products that can only be estimated as designedly formed in the way they are, and not otherwise, the above maxim of reflective judgement is essentially necessary, if for no other purpose, to obtain an empirical knowledge of their intrinsic character. For the very notion that they are organized things is itself impossible unless we associate with it the notion of a production by design.

Now where the possibility of the real existence or form of a thing is represented to the mind as subject to the condition of an end, there is bound up indissolubly with the conception of the thing the conception of its contingency on natural laws. For this reason those natural things which we consider to be only possible as ends constitute the foremost proof of the contingency of the universe. Alike for the popular understanding and for the philosopher they are, too, the only valid argument for its dependence upon and its origin from an extramundane Being, and from one, moreover, that the above final form shows to be intelligent. Thus they indicate that teleology must look to a theology for a complete answer to its inquiries.

But suppose teleology brought to the highest pitch of perfection, what would it all prove in the end ? Does it prove, for example, that such an intelligent Being really exists ? No ; it proves no more than this, that by the constitution of our cognitive faculties, and, therefore, in bringing experience into touch with the highest principles of reason, we are absolutely incapable of forming any conception of the possibility of such a world unless we imagine a highest cause *operating designedly*. We are unable, therefore, objectively to substantiate the proposition : There is an intelligent original Being. On the contrary, we can only do so subjectively for the employment of our power of judgement in its reflection on the ends in nature, which are incapable of being thought on any other principle than that of the intentional causality of a highest cause.

Should we desire to establish the major premiss dogmatically from teleological grounds we should become entangled in inextricable difficulties. For then these reasonings would have to

be supported by the thesis : The organized beings in the world
are not possible otherwise than by virtue of a cause operating
designedly. But are we to say that because we can only push
forward our investigation into the causal nexus of these things
5 and recognize the conformity to law which it displays by following the idea of ends, we are also entitled to presume that for
every thinking and perceiving being the same holds true as a
necessary condition, and as one, therefore, attaching to the
Object instead of merely to the Subject, that is, to our own
10 selves ? For this is the inevitable position that we should have
to be prepared to take up. But we could not succeed in carrying
such a point. For, strictly speaking, we do not *observe* the ends
in nature as designed. We only *read* this conception *into* the facts
as a guide to judgement in its reflection upon the products of
15 nature. Hence these ends are not given to us by the Object.
It is even impossible for us *a priori* to warrant the eligibility of
such a conception if taken to possess objective reality. We can
get absolutely nothing, therefore, out of the thesis beyond a
proposition resting only on subjective conditions, that is to say
20 the conditions of a reflective judgement adapted to our cognitive
faculties. Were this proposition to be expressed in objective
terms and as valid dogmatically, it would read : There is a God.
But all that is permissible for us men is the narrow formula :
We cannot conceive or render intelligible to ourselves the finality 400
25 that must be introduced as the basis even of our knowledge
of the intrinsic possibility of many natural things, except by
representing it, and, in general, the world, as the product of an
intelligent cause—in short, of a God.

Now supposing that this proposition, founded as it is upon
30 an indispensably necessary maxim of our power of judgement,
is perfectly satisfactory from every *human* point of view and for
any use to which we can put our reason, whether speculative or
practical, I should like to know what loss we suffer from our
inability to prove its validity for higher beings also—that is to

say, to substantiate it on pure objective grounds, which un-
fortunately are beyond our reach. It is, I mean, quite certain
that we can never get a sufficient knowledge of organized beings
and their inner possibility, much less get an explanation of them,
by looking merely to mechanical principles of nature. Indeed, 5
so certain is it, that we may confidently assert that it is absurd
for men even to entertain any thought of so doing or to hope
that maybe another Newton may some day arise, to make
intelligible to us even the genesis of but a blade of grass from
natural laws that no design has ordered. Such insight we must 10
absolutely deny to mankind. But, then, are we to think that
a source of the possibility of organized beings amply sufficient
to explain their origin without having recourse to a design,
could never be found buried among the secrets even of nature,
were we able to penetrate to the principle upon which it specifies 15
its familiar universal laws ? This, in its turn, would be a presumptuous judgement on our part. For how do we expect to
get any knowledge on the point ? Probabilities drop entirely
out of count in a case like this, where the question turns on
judgements of pure reason. On the question, therefore, whether 20
or not any being acting designedly stands behind what we
properly term physical ends, as a world cause, and consequently,
as Author of the world, we can pass no objective judgement
whatever, be it affirmative or negative. This much alone is
certain, that if we ought, for all that, to form our judgement 25
on what our own proper nature permits us to see, that is, subject
to the conditions and restrictions of our reason, we are utterly
unable to ascribe the possibility of such physical ends to any
other source than an intelligent Being. This alone squares with
the maxim of our reflective judgement, and, therefore, with a 30
401 subjective ground that is nevertheless ineradicably fixed in the
human race.

§ 15 (76)

Remark.

THE following survey is one that justly merits detailed elaboration in trascendental philosophy, but it can only be introduced here as an explanatory digression, and not as a step in the main argument.

5   Reason is a faculty of principles, and the unconditioned is the ultimate goal at which it aims. Understanding, on the other hand, is at its disposal, but always only under a certain condition that must be given. But, without conceptions of understanding, to which objective reality must be given, reason
10 can pass no objective (synthetical) judgements whatever. As theoretical reason it is absolutely devoid of any constitutive principles of its own. Its principles, on the contrary, are merely regulative. It will readily be perceived that once reason advances beyond pursuit of understanding it becomes transcendent. It
15 displays itself in ideas—that have certainly a foundation as regulative principles—but not in objectively valid conceptions. Understanding, however, unable to keep pace with it and yet requisite in order to give validity in respect of Objects, restricts the validity of these ideas to the judging Subject, though to
20 the Subject in a comprehensive sense, as inclusive of all who belong to the human race. In other words it limits their validity to the terms of this condition : From the nature of our human faculty of knowledge, or, to speak in the broadest terms, even according to any conception that we are able *to form for ourselves*
25 of the capacity of a finite intelligent being in general, it must be conceived to be so and cannot be conceived otherwise—terms which involve no assertion that the foundation of such a judgement lies in the Object. We shall submit some examples which, while they certainly possess too great importance and are also
30 too full of difficulty to be here forced at once on the reader as

propositions that have been proved, may yet give him some food for reflection, and may elucidate the matters upon which our attention is here specially engaged.

Human understanding cannot avoid the necessity of drawing a distinction between the possibility and the actuality of things. The reason of this lies in our own selves and the nature of our cognitive faculties. For were it not that two entirely hetero-geneous factors, understanding for conceptions and sensuous intuition for the corresponding Objects, are required for the exercise of these faculties, there would be no such distinction between the possible and the actual. This means that if our understanding were intuitive it would have no objects but such as are actual. Conceptions, which are merely directed to the possibility of an object, and sensuous intuitions, which give us something and yet do not thereby let us cognize it as an object, would both cease to exist. Now the whole distinction which we draw between the merely possible and the actual rests upon the fact that possibility signifies the position of the representation of a thing relatively to our conception, and, in general, to our capacity of thinking, whereas actuality signifies the positing of the thing in its immediate self-existence apart from this con-ception. Accordingly the distinction of possible from actual things is one that is merely valid subjectively for human under-standing. It arises from the fact that even if something does not exist, we may yet always give it a place in our thoughts, or if there is something of which we have no conception we may nevertheless imagine it given. To say, therefore, that things may be possible without being actual, that from mere possibility, therefore, no conclusion whatever as to actuality can be drawn, is to state propositions that hold true for human reason, without such validity proving that this distinction lies in the things themselves. That this inference is not to be drawn from the propositions stated, and that, consequently, while these are

certainly valid even of Objects, so far as our cognitive faculties
in their subjection to sensuous conditions are also occupied with
Objects of sense, they are not valid of things generally, is apparent when we look to the demands of reason. For reason
never withdraws its challenge to us to adopt something or other
existing with unconditioned necessity—a root origin—in which
there is no longer to be any difference between possibility and
actuality, and our understanding has absolutely no conception
to answer to this idea—that is, it can discover no way of representing to itself any such thing or of forming any notion of its
mode of existence. For if understanding *thinks* it—let it think
it how it will—then the thing is represented merely as possible.
If it is conscious of it as given in intuition, then it is actual, and
no thought of any possibility enters into the case. Hence the
conception of an absolutely necessary being, while doubtless an
indispensable idea of reason, is for human understanding an
unattainable problematic conception Nevertheless it is valid
for the employment of our cognitive faculties according to their
peculiar structure ; consequently not so for the Object nor, as
that would mean, for every knowing being. For I cannot take
for granted that thought and intuition are two distinct conditions subject to which every being exercises its cognitive
faculties, and, therefore, that things have a possibility and
actuality. An understanding into whose mode of cognition this 403
distinction did not enter would express itself by saying : All
Objects that I know *are*, that is, exist ; and the possibility of
some that did not exist, in other words, their contingency supposing them to exist, and, therefore, the necessity that would be
placed in contradistinction to this contingency, would never
enter into the imagination of such a being. But what makes it
so hard for our understanding with its conceptions to rival reason
is simply this, that the very thing that reason regards as constitutive of the Object and adopts as principle is for understanding, in its human form, transcendent, that is, impossible

under the subjective conditions of its knowledge.—In this state
of affairs, then, this maxim always holds true, that once the
knowledge of Objects exceeds the capacity of understanding we
must always conceive them according to the subjective conditions 5
necessarily attaching to our human nature in the exercise of its
faculties.   And if—as must needs be the case with transcendent
conceptions—judgements passed in this manner cannot be constitutive principles determining the character of the Object, we
shall yet be left with regulative principles whose function is 10
immanent and reliable, and which are adapted to the human
point of view.

We have seen that in the theoretical study of nature reason
must assume the idea of an unconditioned necessity of the
original ground of nature.   Similarly in the practical sphere it 15
must presuppose its own causality as unconditioned in respect of
nature, in other words, its freedom, since it is conscious of its own
moral command.   Now here the objective necessity of action as
duty is, however, regarded as opposed to that which it would
have as an event if its source lay in nature instead of in freedom 20
or rational causality.   So the action, with its absolute necessity
of the moral order, is looked on as physically wholly contingent—
that is, we recognize that what *ought* necessarily to happen,
frequently does not happen.   Hence it is clear that it only springs
from the subjective character of our practical faculty that the 25
moral laws must be represented as commands, and the actions
conformable to them as duties, and that reason expresses this
necessity, not by an '*is*' or 'happens' (being or fact), but by
an ' ought to be ' (obligation).   This would not occur if reason
and its causality were considered as independent of sensibility, 30
that is, as free from the subjective condition of its application
to objects in nature, and as being, consequently, a cause in
404 an intelligible world perfectly harmonizing with the moral law.
For in such a world there would be no difference between obliga-

tion and act, or between a practical law as to what is possible through our agency and a theoretical law as to what we make actual. However, although an intelligible world in which everything is actual by reason of the simple fact that, being something
5 good, it is possible, is for us a transcendent conception—as is also freedom itself, the formal condition of that world—yet it has its proper function. For while, as transcendent, it is useless for the purpose of any constitutive principle determining an Object and its objective reality, it yet serves as a universal
10 *regulative principle*. This is due to the constitution of our partly sensuous nature and capacity, which makes it valid for us and, so far as we can imagine from the constitution of our reason, for all intelligent beings that are in any way bound to this world of sense. But this principle does not objectively determine the
15 nature of freedom as a form of causality : it converts, and converts with no less validity than if it did so determine the nature of that freedom, the rule of actions according to that idea into a command for every one.

Similarly, as to the case before us, we may admit that we
20 should find no distinction between the mechanism and the technic of nature, that is, its final nexus, were it not for the type of our understanding. Our understanding must move from the universal to the particular. In respect of the particular, therefore, judgement can recognize no finality, or, consequently,
25 pass any determinate judgements, unless it is possessed of a universal law under which it can subsume that particular. But the particular by its very nature contains something contingent in respect of the universal. Yet reason demands that there shall also be unity in the synthesis of the particular laws of nature,
30 and, consequently, conformity to law—and a derivation *a priori* of the particular from the universal laws in point of their contingent content is not possible by any defining of the conception of the object. Now the above conformity to law on the part of the contingent is termed finality. Hence it follows that the

conception of a finality of nature in its products, while it does
not touch the determination of Objects, is a necessary conception
for the human power of judgement, in respect of nature. It is,
therefore, a subjective principle of reason for the use of judgement, and one which, taken as regulative and not as con- 5
stitutive, is as necessarily valid for our *human judgement* as if it
were an objective principle.

405   § 16 (77)

The peculiarity of human understanding that makes the conception of a physical end possible for us.

In the foregoing Remark we have noted peculiarities belonging
to our faculty of cognition—even to our higher faculty of cognition—which we are easily misled into treating as objective predicates to be transferred to the things themselves. But these 10
peculiarities relate to ideas to which no commensurate object
can be given in experience, and which thus could only serve as
regulative principles in the pursuit of experience. The conception of a physical end stands, no doubt, on the same footing as
regards the source of the possibility of a predicate like this— 15
a source which can only be ideal. But the result attributable
to this source, namely the product itself, is nevertheless given in
nature, and the conception of a causality of nature, regarded as
a being acting according to ends, seems to convert the idea of
a physical end into a constitutive teleological principle. Herein 20
lies a point of difference between this and all other ideas.

But this difference lies in the fact that the idea in question is
a principle of reason for the use, not of understanding, but of
judgement, and is, consequently, a principle solely for the application of an understanding in the abstract to possible objects of 25
experience. Moreover, this application only affects a field where
the judgement passed cannot be determinant but simply reflec-

tive. Consequently, while the object may certainly be given in experience, it cannot even be *judged definitely*—to say nothing of being judged with complete adequacy—in accordance with the idea, but can only be made an object of reflection.

5 The difference turns, therefore, on a peculiarity of *our* (human) understanding relative to our power of judgement in reflecting on things in nature. But, if that is the case, then we must have here an underlying idea of a possible understanding different from the human. (And there was a similar implication in the 10 *Critique of Pure Reason.* We were bound to have present to our minds the thought of another possible form of intuition, if ours was to be deemed one of a special kind, one, namely, for which objects were only to rank as phenomena.) Were this not so it could not be said that certain natural products *must,* from the 15 particular constitution of our understanding, be *considered by us* —if we are to conceive the possibility of their production—as having been produced designedly and as ends, yet without this statement involving any demand that there should, as a matter 406 of fact, be a particular cause present in which the representation 20 of an end acts as determining ground, or, therefore, without involving any assertion as to the powers of an understanding different from the human. This is to say, the statement does not deny that a superhuman understanding may be able to discover the source of the possibility of such natural products even in the 25 mechanism of nature, that is, in the mechanism of a causal nexus for which an understanding is not positively assumed as cause.

Hence what we are here concerned with is the relation which *our* understanding bears to judgement. We have, in fact, to examine this relation with a view to finding a certain element of 30 contingency in the constitution of our understanding, so as to note it as a peculiarity of our own in contradistinction to other possible understandings.

This contingency turns up quite naturally in the *particular* which judgement has to bring under the *universal* supplied by the conceptions of understanding. For the particular is not determined by the universal of *our* (human) understanding. Though different things may agree in a common characteristic, the variety of forms in which they may be presented to our perception is contingent. Our understanding is a faculty of conceptions. This means that it is a discursive understanding for which the character and variety to be found in the particular given to it in nature and capable of being brought under its conceptions must certainly be contingent. But now intuition is also a factor in knowledge, and a faculty of *complete spontaneity of intuition* would be a cognitive faculty distinct from sensibility and wholly independent of it. Hence it would be an understanding in the widest sense of the term. Thus we are also able to imagine an *intuitive* understanding—negatively, or simply as not discursive—which does not move, as ours does with its conceptions, from the universal to the particular and so to the individual. Such an understanding would not experience the above contingency in the way nature and understanding accord in natural products subject to *particular* laws. But it is just this contingency that makes it so difficult for our understanding to reduce the multiplicity of nature to the unity of knowledge. Our understanding can only accomplish this task through the harmonizing of natural features with our faculty of conceptions —a most contingent accord. But an intuitive understanding has no such work to perform. 25

Accordingly our understanding is peculiarly circumstanced in respect of judgement. For in cognition by means of understanding the particular is not determined by the universal. Therefore 407 the particular cannot be derived from the universal alone. Yet in the multiplicity of nature, and through the medium of conception and laws, this particular has to accord with the universal in order to be capable of being subsumed under it. But under the circumstances mentioned this accord must be very contingent and must exist without any determinate principle to guide our judgement.

Nevertheless we are able at least to conceive the possibility of such an accord of the things in nature with the power of judge-
5 ment—an accord which we represent as contingent, and, consequently, as only possible by means of an end directed to its production. But, to do so, we must at the same time imagine an understanding different from our own, relative to which—and, what is more, without starting to attribute an end to it—we may
10 represent the above accord of natural laws with our power of judgement, which for our understanding is only thinkable when ends are introduced as a middle term effecting the connexion, as *necessary*.

It is, in fact, a distinctive characteristic of our understanding,
15 that in its cognition—as, for instance, of the cause of a product— it moves from the *analytic universal* to the particular, or, in other words, from conceptions to given empirical intuitions. In this process, therefore, it determines nothing in respect of the multiplicity of the particular. On the contrary, understanding must
20 wait for the subsumption of the empirical intuition—supposing that the object is a natural product—under the conception, to furnish this determination for the faculty of judgement. But now we are also able to form a notion of an understanding which, not being discursive like ours, but intuitive, moves from the
25 *synthetic universal*, or intuition of a whole as a whole, to the particular—that is to say, from the whole to the parts. To render possible a definite form of the whole a *contingency* in the synthesis of the parts is not implied by such an understanding or its representation of the whole. But that is what our under-
30 standing requires. It must advance from the parts as the universally conceived principles to different possible forms to be subsumed thereunder as consequences. Its structure is such that we can only regard a real whole in nature as the effect of the concurrent dynamical forces of the parts. How then may

we avoid having to represent the possibility of the whole as dependent upon the parts in a manner conformable to our discursive understanding ? May we follow what the standard of the intuitive or archetypal understanding prescribes, and represent the possibility of the parts as both in their form and synthesis dependent upon the whole ? The very peculiarity of our understanding in question prevents this being done in such a way that the whole contains the source of the possibility of the nexus of the parts. This would be self-contradictory in knowledge of the discursive type. But the *representation* of a whole may contain the source of the possibility of the form of that whole and of the nexus of the parts which that form involves. This is our only road. But, now, the whole would in that case be an effect or product the *representation* of which is looked on as the *cause* of its possibility. But the product of a cause whose determining ground is merely the representation of its effect is termed an end. Hence it follows that it is simply a consequence flowing from the particular character of our understanding that we should figure to our minds products of nature as possible according to a different type of causality from that of the physical laws of matter, that is, as only possible according to ends and final causes. In the same way we explain the fact that this principle does not touch the question of how such things themselves, even considered as phenomena, are possible on this mode of production, but only concerns the estimate of them possible to our understanding. On this view we see at the same time why it is that in natural science we are far from being satisfied with an explanation of natural products by means of a causality according to ends. For in such an explanation all we ask for is an estimate of physical generation adapted to our critical faculty, or reflective judgement, instead of one adapted to the things themselves on behalf of the determinant judgement. Here it is also quite unnecessary to prove that an *intellectus archetypus*

like this is possible. It is sufficient to show that we are led to
this idea of an *intellectus archetypus* by contrasting with it our
discursive understanding that has need of images (*intellectus
ectypus*) and noting the contingent character of a faculty of this
5 form, and that this idea involves nothing self-contradictory.

Now where we consider a material whole and regard it as in
point of form a product resulting from the parts and their powers
and capacities of self-integration (including as parts any foreign
material introduced by the co-operative action of the original
10 parts), what we represent to ourselves in this way is a mechanical
generation of the whole. But from this view of the generation of
a whole we can elicit no conception of a whole as end—a whole
whose intrinsic possibility emphatically presupposes the idea of a
whole as that upon which the very nature and action of the parts
15 depend. Yet this is the representation which we must form of
an organized body. But, as has just been shown, we are not to con-
clude from this that the mechanical generation of an organized
body is impossible. For that would amount to saying that it
is impossible, or, in other words, self-contradictory, *for any*
20 *understanding* to form a representation of such a unity in the
conjunction of the manifold without also making the idea of this
unity its producing cause, that is, without representing the production as designed. At the same time this is the conclusion
that we should in fact have to draw were we entitled to look on 409
25 material beings as things in themselves. For in that case the
unity constituting the basis of the possibility of natural formations would only be the unity of space. But space is not a real
ground of the generation of things. It is only their formal condition—although from the fact that no part in it can be deter-
30 mined except in relation to the whole (the representation of
which, therefore, underlies the possibility of the parts) it has
some resemblance to the real ground of which we are in search.
But then it is at least possible to regard the material world as
a mere phenomenon, and to think something which is not a

phenomenon, namely a thing-in-itself, as its substrate. And
this we may rest upon a corresponding intellectual intuition,
albeit it is not the intuition we possess. In this way a supersensible real ground, although for us unknowable, would be
procured for nature, and for the nature of which we ourselves 5
form part. Everything, therefore, which is necessary in this
nature as an object of sense we should estimate according to
mechanical laws. But the accord and unity of the particular
laws and of their resulting subordinate forms, which we must
deem contingent in respect of mechanical laws—these things 10
which exist in nature as an object of reason, and, indeed, nature
in its entirety as a system, we should also consider in the light
of teleological laws. Thus we should estimate nature on two
kinds of principles. The mechanical mode of explanation would
not be excluded by the teleological as if the two principles con- 15
tradicted one another.

Further, this gives us an insight into what we might doubtless
have easily conjectured independently, but which we should
have found it difficult to assert or prove with certainty. It shows
us that while the principle of a mechanical derivation of natural 20
products displaying finality is consistent with the teleological,
it in no way enables us to dispense with it. We may apply to
a thing which we have to estimate as a physical end, that is, to
an organized being, all the laws of mechanical generation known
or yet to be discovered, we may even hope to make good progress 25
in such researches, but we can never get rid of the appeal to
a completely different source of generation for the possibility of
a product of this kind, namely that of a causality by ends. It is
utterly impossible for human reason, or for any finite reason
qualitatively resembling ours, however much it may surpass it in 30
degree, to hope to understand the generation even of a blade of
410 grass from mere mechanical causes. For if judgement finds the
teleological nexus of causes and effects quite indispensable for the

possibility of an object like this, be it only for the purpose of
studying it under the guidance of experience, and if a ground
involving relation to ends and adequate for external objects as
phenomena altogether eludes us, so that we are compelled, al-
5 though this ground lies in nature, to look for it in the supersensible substrate of nature, all possible insight into which is,
however, cut off from us : it is absolutely impossible for us to
obtain any explanation at the hand of nature itself to account
for any synthesis displaying finality.   So by the constitution of
10 our human faculty of knowledge it becomes necessary to look for
the supreme source of this finality in an original understanding
as the cause of the world.

§ 17 (78)

*The union of the principle of the universal mechanism of matter
with the teleological principle in the technic of nature.*

IT is of endless importance to reason to keep in view the
mechanism which nature employs in its productions, and to take
15 due account of it in explaining them, since no insight into the
nature of things can be attained apart from that principle.   Even
the concession that a supreme Architect has directly created the
forms of nature in the way they have existed from all time, or has
predetermined those which in their course of evolution regularly
20 conform to the same type, does not further our knowledge of
nature one whit.   The reason is that we are wholly ignorant of
the manner in which the supreme Being acts and of His ideas,
in which the principles of the possibility of the natural beings
are supposed to be contained, and so cannot explain nature from
25 Him by moving from above downwards, that is *a priori*.   On the
other hand our explanation would be simply tautological if,
relying on the finality found, as we believe, in the forms of
objects of experience, we should set out from these forms and
move from below upwards, that is *a posteriori*, and with a view

to explaining such finality should appeal to a cause acting in accordance with ends. We should be cheating reason with mere words—not to mention the fact that where, by resorting to explanation of this kind, we get lost in the transcendent, and thus stray beyond the pursuit of natural science, reason is 5 betrayed into poetic extravagance, the very thing which it is its pre-eminent vocation to prevent.

411   On the other hand, it is an equally necessary maxim of reason not to overlook the principle of ends in the products of nature. For although this principle does not make the mode in which 10 such products originate any more comprehensible to us, yet it is a heuristic principle for the investigation of the particular laws of nature. And this remains true even though it be understood that, as we confine ourselves rigorously to the term physical ends, even where such products manifestly exhibit a designed final 15 unity, we do not intend to make any use of the principle for the purpose of explaining nature itself—that is to say, in speaking of physical ends, pass beyond the bounds of nature in quest of the source of the possibility of those products. However, inasmuch as the question of this possibility must be met sooner or later, 20 it is just as necessary to conceive a special type of causality for it—one not to be found in nature—as to allow that the mechanical activity of natural causes has its special type. For the receptivity for different forms over and above those which matter is capable of producing by virtue of such mechanism 25 must be supplemented by a spontaneity of some cause—which cannot, therefore, be matter—as in its absence no reason can be assigned for those forms. Of course before reason takes this step it must exercise due caution and not seek to explain as teleological every technic of nature—meaning by this a 30 formative capacity of nature which displays (as in the case of regularly constructed bodies) finality of structure for our mere apprehension. On the contrary it must continue to regard such

technic as possible on purely mechanical principles. But to go
so far as to exclude the teleological principle, and to want to keep
always to mere mechanism, even where reason, in its investigation into the manner in which natural forms are rendered possible
5 by their causes, finds a finality of a character whose relation to
a different type of causality is apparent beyond all denial, is
equally unscientific. It inevitably sends reason on a roving
expedition among capacities of nature that are only cobwebs of
the brain and quite unthinkable, in just the same way as a merely
10 teleological mode of explanation that pays no heed to the
mechanism of nature makes it visionary.

   These two principles are not capable of being applied in conjunction to one and the same thing in nature as co-ordinate
truths available for the explanation or deduction of one thing by
15 or from another. In other words they are not to be united in
that way as dogmatic and constitutive principles affording insight into nature on behalf of the determinant judgement. If
I suppose, for instance, that a maggot is to be regarded as a
product of the mere mechanism of matter, that is of a new
20 formative process which a substance brings about by its own
unaided resources when its elements are liberated as the result
of decomposition, I cannot then turn round and derive the
same product from the same substance as a causality that acts 412
from ends. Conversely, if I suppose that this product is a
25 physical end, I am precluded from relying on its mechanical
generation, or adopting such generation as a constitutive principle for estimating the product in respect of its possibility, and
thus uniting the two principles. For each mode of explanation
excludes the other—even supposing that objectively both
30 grounds of the possibility of such a product rest on a single
foundation, provided this foundation was not what we were
thinking of. The principle which is to make possible the compatibility of the above pair of principles, as principles to be
followed in estimating nature, must be placed in what lies beyond

both (and consequently beyond the possible empirical representation of nature), but in what nevertheless contains the ground of
the representation of nature. It must, in other words, be placed
in the supersensible, and to this each of the two modes of
explanation must be referred. Now the only conception we can 5
have of the supersensible is the indeterminate conception of a
ground that makes possible the estimate of nature according to
empirical laws. Beyond this we cannot go : by no predicate can
we determine this conception any further. Hence it follows that
the union of the two principles cannot rest on one basis of 10
explanation setting out in so many terms how a product is
possible on given laws so as to satisfy the *determinant* judgement,
but can only rest on a single basis of *exposition* elucidating this
possibility for the *reflective* judgement. For explanation means
derivation from a principle, which must, therefore, be capable 15
of being clearly cognized and specified. Now the principle of
the mechanism of nature and that of its causality according to
ends, when applied to one and the same product of nature, must
cohere in a single higher principle and flow from it as their
common source, for if this were not so they could not both enter 20
consistently into the same survey of nature. But if this principle,
which is objectively common to both, and which, therefore,
justifies the association of its dependent maxims of natural
research, is of such a kind that, while it can be indicated, it can
never be definitely cognized or clearly specified for employment 25
in particular cases as they arise, then no explanation can be
extracted from such a principle. There can be no clear and
definite derivation, in other words, of the possibility of a natural
product, as one possible on those two heterogeneous principles.
Now the principle common to the mechanical derivation, on 30
the one hand, and the teleological, on the other, is the *supersensible*, which we must introduce as the basis of nature as
phenomenon. But of this we are unable from a theoretical point

of view to form the slightest positive determinate conception,
How, therefore, in the light of the supersensible as principle, 413
nature in its particular laws constitutes a system for us, and one
capable of being cognized as possible both on the principle of
5 production from physical causes and on that of final causes, is
a matter which does not admit of any explanation. All we can
say is that if it happens that objects of nature present themselves,
whose possibility is incapable of being conceived by us on the
principle of mechanism—which has always a claim upon a
10 natural being—unless we rely on teleological principles, it is
then to be presumed that we may confidently study natural laws
on lines following both principles—according as the possibility
of the natural product is cognizable to our understandings from
one or other principle—without being disturbed by the apparent
15 conflict that arises between the principles upon which our
estimate of the product is formed. For we are at least assured
of the possibility of both being reconciled, even objectively,
in a single principle, inasmuch as they deal with phenomena, and
these presuppose a supersensible ground.

20   We have seen that the principles both of nature's mechanical
operation and of its teleological or designed technique, as bearing
upon one and the same product and its possibility, may alike be
subordinated to a common higher principle of nature in its
particular laws. Nevertheless, this principle being *transcendent*,
25 the narrow capacity of our understanding is such that the above
subordination does not enable us to unite the two principles
in the explanation of the same natural generation, even where,
as is the case with organized substances, the intrinsic possibility
of the product is only *intelligible* by means of a causality accord-
30 ing to ends. Hence we must keep to the statement of the
principle of teleology above given. So we say that by the
constitution of our human understanding no causes but those
acting by design can be adopted as grounds of the possibility of
organized beings in nature, and the mere mechanism of nature

is quite insufficient to explain these its products ; and we add
that this implies no desire to decide anything by that principle
in respect of the possibility of such things themselves.

This principle, we mean to say, is only a maxim of the reflective, not of the determinant judgement. Hence, it is only valid 5
subjectively for us, not objectively to explain the possibility of
things of this kind themselves—in which things themselves both
modes of generation might easily spring consistently from one
and the same ground. Furthermore, unless the teleologically-
conceived mode of generation were supplemented by a conception 10
of a concomitantly presented mechanism of nature, such genesis
414 could not be estimated as a product of nature at all. Hence, we
see that the above maxim immediately involves the necessity
of a union of both principles in the estimate of things as physical
ends. But this union is not to be directed to substituting one 15
principle, either wholly or in part, in the place of the other. For
in the room of what is regarded, by us at least, as only possible
by design, mechanism cannot be assumed, and in the room of
what is cognized as necessary in accordance with mechanism,
such contingency as would require an end as its determining 20
ground cannot be assumed. On the contrary we can only
subordinate one to the other, namely mechanism to designed
technique. And on the transcendental principle of the finality
of nature this may readily be done.

For where ends are thought as the sources of the possibility 25
of certain things, means have also to be supposed. Now the law
of the efficient causality of a means, considered *in its own right*,
requires nothing that presupposes an end, and, consequently,
may be both mechanical and yet a subordinate cause of designed
effects. Hence, looking only to organic products of nature, but 30
still more if, impressed by the endless multitude of such products,
we go on and adopt, at least on an allowable hypothesis, the
principle of design, in the connexion of natural causes following

particular laws, as a *universal principle* of the reflective judgement
in respect of the whole of nature, namely the world, we may
imagine a vast and even universal interconnexion of mechanical
and teleological laws in the generative processes of nature. Here
we neither confuse nor transpose the principles upon which such
processes are estimated. For in a teleological estimate, even if
the form which the matter assumes is estimated as only possible
by design, yet the matter itself, considered as to its nature, may
also be subordinated, conformably to mechanical laws, as means
to the represented end. At the same time, inasmuch as the basis
of this compatibility lies in what is neither the one nor the other,
neither mechanism nor final nexus, but is the supersensible substrate of nature which is shut out from our view, for our human
reason the two modes of representing the possibility of such
Objects are not to be fused into one. On the contrary we are unable to estimate their possibility otherwise than as one founded
in accordance with the nexus of final causes on a supreme understanding. Thus the teleological mode of explanation is in no way
prejudiced.

But now it is an open question, and for our reason must always
remain an open question, how much the mechanism of nature 415
contributes as means to each final design in nature. Further,
having regard to the above-mentioned intelligible principle of
the possibility of a nature in general, we may even assume that
nature is possible in all respects on both kinds of law, the physical
laws and those of final causes, as universally consonant laws,
although we are quite unable to see how this is so. Hence, we
are ignorant how far the mechanical mode of explanation
possible for us may penetrate. This much only is certain, that
no matter what progress we may succeed in making with it, it
must still always remain inadequate for things that we have once
recognized to be physical ends. Therefore, by the constitution
of our understanding we must subordinate such mechanical
grounds, one and all, to a teleological principle.

Now this is the source of a privilege and, owing to the importance of the study of nature on the lines of the principle of mechanism for the theoretical employment of our reason, the source also of a duty. We may and should explain all products and events of nature, even the most purposive, so far as in our 5 power lies, on mechanical lines—and it is impossible for us to assign the limits of our powers when confined to the pursuit of inquiries of this kind. But in so doing we must never lose sight of the fact that among such products there are those which we cannot even subject to investigation except under the con- 10 ception of an end of reason. These, if we respect the essential nature of our reason, we are obliged, despite those mechanical causes, to subordinate in the last resort to causality according to ends.

APPENDIX

§ 18 (79)

Whether teleology must be treated as a branch of natural science

EVERY science must have its definite position in the complete
encyclopedia of the sciences. If it is a philosophical science its
position must be assigned to it either in the theoretical or the
practical division. Further, if its place is in the theoretical
5 division, then the position assigned to it must either be in
natural science—which is its proper position when it considers
things capable of being objects of experience—consequently in
physics proper, psychology, or cosmology, or else in theology—
as the science of the original source of the world as complex of
10 all objects of experience.

Now the question arises : What position does teleology deserve ? Is it a branch of natural science, properly so called,
or of theology ? A branch of one or the other it must be ; for
no science can belong to the transition from one to the other,
15 because this only signifies the articulation or the organization
of the system and not a position in it.

That it does not form a constituent part of theology, although
the use that may there be made of it is most important, is
evident from the nature of the case. For its objects are physical
20 generations and their cause ; and, although it points to this
cause as a ground residing beyond and above nature, namely
a Divine Author, yet it does not do so for the determinant
judgement. It only points to this cause in the interests of the
reflective judgement engaged in surveying nature, its purpose

being to guide our estimate of the things in the world by means of the idea of such a ground, as a regulative principle, in a manner adapted to our human understanding.

417 But just as little does it appear to form a part of natural science. For this science requires determinant, and not merely reflective, principles for the purpose of assigning objective grounds of physical effects. As a matter of fact, also, the theory of nature, or the mechanical explanation of its phenomena by efficient causes, is in no way helped by considering them in the light of the correlation of ends. The exposition of the ends pursued by nature in its products, so far as such ends form a system according to teleological conceptions, is strictly speaking only incident to a description of nature that follows a particular guiding star. Here reason does fine work, and work that is full of practical finality from various points of view. But it gives no information whatever as to the origin and intrinsic possibility of these forms. Yet this is what specially concerns the theoretical science of nature.

Teleology, therefore, in the form of a science, is not a branch of doctrine at all, but only of critique, and of the critique of a particular cognitive faculty, namely judgement. But it does contain *a priori* principles, and to that extent it may, and in fact must, specify the method by which nature has to be judged according to the principle of final causes. In this way the science of its methodical application exerts at least a negative influence upon the procedure to be adopted in the theoretical science of nature. It also in the same way affects the metaphysical bearing which this science may have on theology, when the former is treated as a propaedeutic to the latter.

§ 19 (80)

The necessary subordination of the principle of mechanism to the teleological principle in the explanation of a thing regarded as a physical end.

OUR *right to aim at* an explanation of all natural products on simply mechanical lines is in itself quite unrestricted. But the constitution of our understanding, as engaged upon things in the shape of physical ends, is such that our *power* of *meeting all* 5 *demands* from the unaided resources of mechanical explanation is not alone very limited, but is also circumscribed within clearly marked bounds. For by a principle of judgement that adopts the above procedure alone nothing whatever can be accomplished in the way of explaining physical ends. For this 10 reason our estimate of such products must at all times be subordinated to a concurrent teleological principle.

Hence there is reason, and indeed merit, in pursuing the 418 mechanism of nature for the purpose of explaining natural products so far as this can be done with probable success, and in 15 fact never abandoning this attempt on the ground that it is *intrinsically* impossible to encounter the finality of nature along this road, but only on the ground that it is impossible *for us* as men. For in order to get home along this line of investigation we should require an intuition different from our sensuous in- 20 tuition and a determinate knowledge of the intelligible substrate of nature—a substrate from which we could show the reason of the very mechanism of phenomena in their particular laws. But this wholly surpasses our capacity.

So where it is established beyond question that the conception 25 of a physical end applies to things, as in the case of organized beings, if the naturalist is not to throw his labour away, he must always in forming an estimate of them accept some original organization or other as fundamental. He must consider that this organization avails itself of the very mechanism above mentioned for the purpose of producing other organic forms, or for evolving new structures from those given—such new structures, however, always issuing from and in accordance with the end in question.   5

It is praiseworthy to employ a comparative anatomy and go through the vast creation of organized beings in order to see if there is not discoverable in it some trace of a system, and indeed of a system following a genetic principle.   For otherwise we should be obliged to content ourselves with the mere critical 10 principle—which tells us nothing that gives any insight into the production of such beings—and to abandon in despair all claim to *insight into nature* in this field.   When we consider the agreement of so many genera of animals in a certain common schema, which apparently underlies not only the structure of 15 their bones, but also the disposition of their remaining parts, and when we find here the wonderful simplicity of the original plan, which has been able to produce such an immense variety of species by the shortening of one member and the lengthening of another, by the involution of this part and the evolution of 20 that, there gleams upon the mind a ray of hope, however faint, that the principle of the mechanism of nature, apart from which there can be no natural science at all, may yet enable us to arrive at some explanation in the case of organic life.   This analogy of forms, which in all their differences seem to be pro- 25 duced in accordance with a common type, strengthens the suspicion that they have an actual kinship due to descent from 419 a common parent.   This we might trace in the gradual approximation of one animal species to another, from that in which the principle of ends seems best authenticated, namely from man, 30 back to the polyp, and from this back even to mosses and lichens, and finally to the lowest perceiveable stage of nature. Here we come to crude matter ; and from this, and the forces

which it exerts in accordance with mechanical laws (laws resembling those by which it acts in the formation of crystals) seems to be developed the whole technic of nature which, in the case of organized beings, is so incomprehensible to us that we
5 feel obliged to imagine a different principle for its explanation.

Here the *archaeologist* of nature is at liberty to go back to the traces that remain of nature's earliest revolutions, and, appealing to all he knows of or can conjecture about its mechanism, to trace the genesis of that great family of living things (for it
10 must be pictured as a family if there is to be any foundation for the consistently coherent affinity mentioned). He can suppose that the womb of mother earth as it first emerged, like a huge animal, from its chaotic state, gave birth to creatures whose form displayed less finality, and that these again bore others
15 which adapted themselves more perfectly to their native surroundings and their relations to each other, until this womb, becoming rigid and ossified, restricted its birth to definite species incapable of further modification, and the multiplicity of forms was fixed as it stood when the operation of that fruitful forma-
20 tive power had ceased.—Yet, for all that, he is obliged eventually to attribute to this universal mother an organization suitably constituted with a view to all these forms of life, for unless he does so, the possibility of the final form of the products of the animal and plant kingdoms is quite unthinkable.[1] But when 420

---

[1] An hypothesis of this kind may be called a daring venture on the part of reason ; and there are probably few even among the most acute scientists to whose minds it has not sometimes occurred. For it cannot be said to be absurd, like the *generatio aequivoca*, which means the generation of an organized being from crude inorganic matter. It never ceases to be *generatio univoca* in the widest acceptation of the word, as it only implies the generation of something organic from something else that is also organic, although, within the class of organic beings, differing specifically from it. It would be as if we supposed that certain water animals transformed themselves by degrees into marsh animals, and from these after some generations into land animals. In the judgement of plain reason there is nothing *a priori* self-contradictory in this. But experience

he does attribute all this to nature he has only pushed the explanation a stage farther back.   He cannot pretend to have made the genesis of those two kingdoms intelligible independently of the condition of final causes.

Even as regards the alteration which certain individuals of the organized genera contingently undergo, where we find that the character thus altered is transmitted and taken up into the generative power, we can form no other plausible estimate of it than that it is an occasional development of a purposive capacity originally present in the species with a view to the preservation of the race.   For in the complete inner finality of an organized being, the generation of its like is intimately associated with the condition that nothing shall be taken up into the generative force which does not also belong, in such a system of ends, to one of its undeveloped native capacities.   Once we depart from this principle we cannot know with certainty whether many constituents of the form at present found in a species may not be of equally contingent and purposeless origin, and the principle of teleology, that nothing in an organized being which is preserved in the propagation of the species should be estimated as devoid of finality, would be made very unreliable and could only hold good for the parent stock, to which our knowledge does not go back.

In reply to those who feel obliged to adopt a teleological principle of critical judgement, that is an architectonic understanding in the case of all such physical ends, Hume raises the objection that one might ask with equal justice how such an understanding is itself possible.   By this he means that one may

offers no example of it.   On the contrary, as far as experience goes, all generation known to us is *generatio homonyma*.   It is not merely *univoca* in contradistinction to generation from an unorganized substance, but it brings forth a product which in its very organization is of like kind with that which produced it, and a *generatio heteronyma* is not met with anywhere within the range of our experience.

also ask how it is possible that there should be such a teleological coincidence in one being of the manifold faculties and properties presupposed in the very conception of an understanding possessing at once intellectual and executive capacity. But there is nothing in this point. For the whole difficulty that besets the question as to the genesis of a thing that involves ends and that is solely comprehensible by their means rests upon the demand for unity in the source of the synthesis of the multiplicity of *externally existing* elements in this product. For, if this source 421 is laid in the understanding of a productive cause regarded as a simple substance, the above question, as a teleological problem, is abundantly answered, whereas if the cause is merely sought in matter, as an aggregate of many externally existing substances, the unity of principle requisite for the intrinsically final form of its complex structures is wholly absent. The *autocracy* of matter in productions that by our understanding are only conceivable as ends, is a word with no meaning.

This is the reason why those who look for a supreme ground of the possibility of the objectively final forms of matter, and yet do not concede an understanding to this ground, choose nevertheless to make the world-whole either an all-embracing substance (Pantheism), or else—what is only the preceding in more defined form—a complex of many determinations inhering in a single *simple substance* (Spinozism). Their object is to derive from this substance that *unity* of source which all finality presupposes. And in fact, thanks to their purely ontological conception of a simple substance, they really do something to satisfy *one* condition of the problem—namely, that of the unity implied in the reference to an end. But they have nothing to say on the subject of the *other* condition, namely the relation of the substance to its consequence regarded as an *end*, this relation being what gives to their ontological ground the more precise determination which the problem demands. The result is that they in no way answer the *entire* problem. Also for our understanding it remains absolutely unanswerable except on the following terms. First, the original source of things must be pictured by us as a simple substance. Then its attribute, as simple substance, in its relation to the specific character of the natural forms whose source it is—the character, namely, of final 5 unity—must be pictured as the attribute of an intelligent substance. Lastly, the relation of this intelligent substance to the natural forms must, owing to the contingency which we find in everything which we imagine to be possible only as an end, be pictured as one of *causality*. 10

§ 20 (81)

The association of mechanism with the teleological principle which we apply to the explanation of a physical end considered as a product of nature.

WE have seen from the preceding section that the mechanism of nature is not sufficient to enable us to conceive the possibility 422 of an organized being, but that in its root origin it must be subordinated to a cause acting by design—or, at least, that the type of our cognitive faculty is such that we must conceive it 15 to be so subordinated. But just as little can the mere teleological source of a being of this kind enable us to consider and to estimate it as at once an end and a product of nature. With that teleological source we must further associate the mechanism of nature as a sort of instrument of a cause acting by design and 20 contemplating an end to which nature is subordinated even in its mechanical laws. The possibility of such a union of two completely different types of causality, namely that of nature in its universal conformity to law and that of an idea which restricts nature to a particular form of which nature, as nature, is in 25 no way the source, is something which our reason does not comprehend. For it resides in the supersensible substrate of nature,

of which we are unable to make any definite affirmation, further than that it is the self-subsistent being of which we know merely the phenomenon. Yet, for all that, this principle remains in full and undiminished force, that everything which we assume to
5 form part of phenomenal nature and to be its product must be thought as linked with nature on mechanical laws. For, apart from this type of causality, organized beings, although they are ends of nature, would not be natural products.

Now supposing we adopt the teleological principle of the pro-
10 duction of organized beings, as indeed we cannot avoid doing, we may base their internally final form either on the *occasionalism* or on the *pre-establishment* of the cause. According to occasionalism the Supreme Cause of the world would directly supply the organic formation, stamped with the impress of His idea, on the occasion of each impregnation, to the commingling
15 substances united in the generative process. On the system of pre-establishment the Supreme Cause would only endow the original products of His wisdom with the inherent capacity by means of which an organized being produces another after its
20 own kind, and the species preserves its continuous existence, whilst the loss of individuals is ever being repaired through the agency of a nature that concurrently labours towards their destruction. If the occasionalism of the production of organized beings is assumed, all co-operation of nature in the process is
25 entirely lost, and no room is left for the exercise of reason in judging of the possibility of products of this kind. So we may take it for granted that no one will embrace this system who cares anything for philosophy.

Again the system of pre-establishment may take either of two 423
30 forms. Thus it treats every organized being produced from one of its own kind either as its *educt* or as its *product*. The system which regards the generations as educts is termed that of *individual preformation*, or, sometimes, the *theory of evolution* ; that which regards them as products is called the system of

epigenesis. The latter may also be called the system of *generic preformation,* inasmuch as it regards the productive capacity of the parents, in respect of the inner final tendency that would be part of their original stock, and, therefore, the specific form, as still having been *virtualiter* preformed. On this statement the opposite theory of individual preformation might also more appropriately be called the *theory of involution* (or *encasement*).

The advocates of the *theory of evolution* exclude all individuals from the formative force of nature, for the purpose of deriving them directly from the hand of the Creator. Yet they would not venture to describe the occurrence on the lines of the hypothesis of occasionalism, so as to make the impregnation an idle formality, which takes place whenever a supreme intelligent Cause of the world has made up His mind to form a foetus directly with His own hand and relegate to the mother the mere task of developing and nourishing it. They would avow adherence to the theory of preformation ; as if it were not a matter of indifference whether a supernatural origin of such forms is allowed to take place at the start or in the course of the world-process. They fail to see that in fact a whole host of supernatural contrivances would be spared by acts of creation as occasion arose, which would be required if an embryo formed at the beginning of the world had to be preserved from the destructive forces of nature, and had to keep safe and sound all through the long ages till the day arrived for its development, and also that an incalculably greater number of such preformed entities would be created than would be destined ever to develop, and that all those would be so many creations thus rendered superfluous and in vain. Yet they would like to leave nature some role in these operations, so as not to lapse into unmitigated hyperphysic that can dispense with all explanation on naturalistic lines. Of course they would still remain unshaken in their hyperphysic ; so much so that they would discover even in abortions—which yet cannot possibly be deemed ends of nature—a marvellous finality, be it even directed to no better purpose than that of being a meaningless finality intended to set some chance anatomist at his wit's end, and make him fall on his knees with admiration. However, they would be absolutely unable to make the generation of hybrids fit in with the system of preformation, but would be compelled to allow to the seed of the male creature, to which in other cases they had denied all but the mechanical property of serving as the first means of nourishment for the embryo, a further and additional formative force directed to ends. And yet they would not concede this force to either of the two parents when dealing with the complete product of two creatures of the same genus.

As against this, even supposing we failed to see the enormous advantage on the side of the advocate of *epigenesis* in the matter of empirical evidences in support of his theory, still reason would antecedently be strongly prepossessed in favour of his line of explanation. For as regards things the possibility of whose origin can only be represented to the mind according to a causality of ends, epigenesis none the less regards nature as at least itself productive in respect of the continuation of the process, and not as merely unravelling something. Thus with the least possible expenditure of the supernatural it entrusts to nature the explanation of all steps subsequent to the original beginning. But it refrains from determining anything as to this original beginning, which is what baffles all the attempts of physics, no matter what chain of causes it adopts.

No one has rendered more valuable services in connexion with this theory of epigenesis than Herr Hofr. Blumenbach. This is as true of what he has done towards establishing the correct principles of its application—partly by setting due bounds to an over liberal employment of it—as it is of his contributions to its proof. He makes organic substance the starting-point for physical explanation of these formations. For to suppose that crude matter, obeying mechanical laws, was originally its own architect, that life could have sprung up from the nature of what is void of life, and matter have spontaneously adopted the form of a self-maintaining finality, he justly declares to be contrary to reason. But at the same time he leaves to the mechanism of 5 nature, in its subordination to this inscrutable *principle* of a primordial *organization*, an indeterminable yet also unmistakable function. The capacity of matter here required he terms—in contradistinction to the simply mechanical *formative force* universally residing in it—in the case of an organized body a 10 *formative impulse*, standing, so to speak, under the higher guidance and direction of the above principle.

425 ## § 21 (82)

The teleological system in the extrinsic relations of organisms.

By extrinsic finality I mean the finality that exists where one thing in nature subserves another as means to an end. Now even things which do not possess any intrinsic finality, and whose 15 possibility does not imply any, such as earth, air, water, and the like, may nevertheless extrinsically, that is in relation to other beings, be very well adapted to ends. But then those other beings must in all cases be organized, that is be physical ends, for unless they are ends the former could not be considered means. 20 Thus water, air, and earth cannot be regarded as means to the upgrowth of mountains. For intrinsically there is nothing in mountains that calls for a source of their possibility according to ends. Hence their cause can never be referred to such a source and represented under the predicate of a means sub- 25 servient thereto.

Extrinsic finality is an entirely different conception from that of intrinsic finality, the latter being connected with the possibility of an object irrespective of whether its actuality is itself

an end or not. In the case of an organism we may further inquire : For what end does it exist ? But we can hardly do so in the case of things in which we recognize the simple effect of the mechanism of nature. The reason is that in the case of
5 organisms we have already pictured to ourselves a causality according to ends—a creative understanding—to account for their intrinsic finality, and have referred this active faculty to its determining ground, the design. One extrinsic finality is the single exception—and it is one intimately bound up with the
10 intrinsic finality of an organization. It does not leave open the question as to the ulterior end for which the nature so organized must have existed, and yet it lies in the extrinsic relation of a means to an end. This is the organization of the two sexes in their mutual relation with a view to the propagation of their
15 species. For here we may always ask, just as in the case of an individual : Why was it necessary for such a pair to exist ? The answer is : In this pair we have what first forms an *organizing* whole, though not an organized whole in a single body.

Now when it is asked to what end a thing exists, the answer
20 may take one or other of two forms. It may be said that its existence and generation have no relation whatever to a cause acting designedly. Its origin is then always understood to be 426 derived from the mechanism of nature. Or it may be said that its existence, being that of a contingent natural entity, has some
25 ground or other involving design. And this is a thought which it is difficult for us to separate from the conception of a thing that is organized. For inasmuch as we are compelled to rest its intrinsic possibility on the causality of final causes and an idea underlying this causality, we cannot but think that the
30 real existence of this product is also an end. For where the representation of an effect is at the same time the ground determining an intelligent efficient cause to its production, the effect so represented is termed an *end*. Here, therefore, we may either say that the end of the real existence of a natural being of this

kind is inherent in itself, that is, that it is not merely an end, but also a *final end*; or we may say that the final end lies outside it in other natural beings, that is, that its real existence, which is adapted to ends, is not itself a final end, but is necessitated by its being at the same time a means. 5

But if we go through the whole of nature we do not find in it, as nature, any being capable of laying claim to the distinction of being the final end of creation. In fact it may even be proved *a priori*, that what might do perhaps as an *ultimate end* for nature, endowing it with any conceivable qualities or properties we 10 choose, could nevertheless in its character of a natural thing never be a final end.

Looking to the vegetable kingdom we might at first be induced by the boundless fertility with which it spreads itself abroad upon almost every soil to think that it should be regarded as 15 a mere product of the mechanism which nature displays in its formations in the mineral kingdom. But a more intimate knowledge of its indescribably wise organization precludes us from entertaining this view, and drives us to ask : For what purpose do these forms of life exist ? Suppose we reply : For the animal 20 kingdom, which is thus provided with the means of sustenance, so that it has been enabled to spread over the face of the earth in such a manifold variety of genera. The question again arises : For what purpose then do these herbivora exist ? The answer would be something like this : For the carnivora, which are only 25 able to live on what itself has animal life. At last we get down to the question : What is the end and purpose of these and all the preceding natural kingdoms ? For man, we say, and the multifarious uses to which his intelligence teaches him to put all these forms of life. He is the ultimate end of creation here upon earth, 30 427 because he is the one and only being upon it that is able to form a conception of ends, and from an aggregate of things purposively fashioned to construct by the aid of his reason a system of ends.

We might also follow the chevalier Linné and take the seemingly opposite course. Thus we might say : The herbivorous animals exist for the purpose of checking the profuse growth of the vegetable kingdom by which many species of that kingdom
5 would be choked ; the carnivora for the purpose of setting bounds to the voracity of the herbivora ; and finally man exists so that by pursuing the latter and reducing their numbers a certain equilibrium between the productive and destructive forces of nature may be established. So, on this view, however
10 much man might in a certain relation be esteemed as end, in a different relation he would in turn only rank as a means.

If we adopt the principle of an objective finality in the manifold variety of the specific forms of terrestrial life and in their extrinsic relations to one another as beings with a structure adapted
15 to ends, it is only rational to go on and imagine that in this extrinsic relation there is also a certain organization and a system of the whole kingdom of nature following final causes. But experience seems here to give the lie to the maxim of reason, more especially as regards an ultimate end of nature—an end
20 which nevertheless is necessary to the possibility of such a system, and which we can only place in man. For, so far from making man, regarded as one of the many animal species, an ultimate end, nature has no more exempted him from its destructive than from its productive forces, nor has it made the smallest exception
25 to its subjection of everything to a mechanism of forces devoid of an end.

The first thing that would have to be expressly appointed in a system ordered with a view to a final whole of natural beings upon the earth would be their habitat—the soil or the element
30 upon or in which they are intended to thrive. But a more intimate knowledge of the nature of this basal condition of all organic production shows no trace of any causes but those acting altogether without design, and in fact tending towards destruction rather than calculated to promote genesis of forms, order, and

ends. Land and sea not alone contain memorials of mighty
primeval disasters that have overtaken both them and all their
brood of living forms, but their entire structure—the strata of
the land and the coast lines of the sea—has all the appearance
of being the outcome of the wild and all-subduing forces of a 5
428 nature working in a state of chaos. However wisely the configuration, elevation and slope of the land may now seem to be
adapted for the reception of water from the air, for the sub-
terranean channels of the springs that well up between the
diverse layers of earth (suitable for various products) and for the 10
course of the rivers, yet a closer investigation of them shows
that they have resulted simply as the effect partly of volcanic
eruptions, partly of floods, or even of invasions of the ocean. And
this is not alone true as regards the genesis of this configuration,
but more particularly of its subsequent transformation, attended 15
with the disappearance of its primitive organic productions.[1]
If now the abode for all these forms of life—the lap of the land
and the bosom of the deep—points to none but a wholly undesigned mechanical generation, how can we, or what right have
we to ask for or to maintain a different origin for these latter 20
products? And even if man, as the most minute examination
of the remains of those devastations of nature seems, in Camper's
judgement, to prove, was not comprehended in such revolutions,

[1] If the name of *natural history*, now that it has once been adopted,
is to continue to be used for the description of nature, we may give
the name of *archaeology* of *nature*, as contrasted with art, to that
which the former literally indicates, namely an account of the
bygone or *ancient* state of the earth—a matter on which, though we
dare not hope for any certainty, we have good ground for conjecture.
Fossil remains would be objects for the archaeology of nature, just
as rudely cut stones, and things of that kind, would be for the
archaeology of art. For, as work is actually being done in this
department, under the name of a theory of the earth, steadily
though, as we might expect, slowly, this name would not be given
to a purely imaginary study of nature, but to one to which nature
itself invites and summons us.

yet his dependence upon the remaining forms of terrestrial life is such that, if a mechanism of nature whose power overrides these others is admitted, he must be regarded as included within its scope, although his intelligence, to a large extent at least, has 5 been able to save him from its work of destruction.

But this argument seems to go beyond what it was directed to prove. For it would seem to show not merely that man could not be an ultimate end of nature or, for the same reason, the aggregate of the organized things of terrestrial nature be a system 10 of ends, but that even the products of nature previously deemed to be physical ends could have no other origin than the mechanism of nature.

But, then, we must bear in mind the results of the solution 429 above given of the antinomy of the principles of the mechanical 15 and teleological generation of organic natural beings. These principles, as we there saw, are merely principles of reflective judgement in respect of formative nature and its particular laws, the key to whose systematic correlation is not in our possession. They tell us nothing definite as to the origin of the things in their 20 own intrinsic nature. They only assert that by the constitution of our understanding and our reason we are unable to conceive the origin in the case of beings of this kind otherwise than in the light of final causes. The utmost persistence possible, nay even a boldness, is allowed us in our endeavours to explain them on 25 mechanical lines. More than that, we are even summoned by reason to do so, albeit we know we can never get home with such an explanation—not because there is an inherent inconsistency between the mechanical generation and an origin according to ends, but for subjective reasons involved in the particular 30 type and limitations of our understanding. Lastly, we saw that the reconciliation of the two modes of picturing the possibility of nature might easily lie in the supersensible principle of nature, both external and internal. For the mode of representation based on final causes is only a subjective condition of the exercise of our reason in cases where it is not seeking to know the proper estimate to form of objects arranged merely as phenomena, but is bent rather on referring these phenomena, principles and all, to their supersensible substrate, for the purpose of recognizing the possibility of certain laws of their unity, which are incapable 5 of being figured by the mind otherwise than by means of ends (of which reason also possesses examples of the supersensuous type).

§ 22 (83)

The ultimate end of nature as a teleological system.

WE have shown in the preceding section that, looking to principles of reason, there is ample ground—for the reflective, 10 though not of course for the determinant, judgement—to make us estimate man as not merely a physical end, such as all organized beings are, but as the being upon this earth who is the *ultimate end* of nature, and the one in relation to whom all other natural things constitute a system of ends. What now is the 15 end in man, and the end which, as such, is intended to be promoted by means of his connexion with nature ? If this end is 430 something which must be found in man himself, it must either be of such a kind that man himself may be satisfied by means of nature and its beneficence, or else it is the aptitude and skill for 20 all manner of ends for which he may employ nature both external and internal. The former end of nature would be the *happiness* of man, the latter his *culture.*

The conception of happiness is not one which man abstracts more or less from his instincts and so derives from his animal 25 nature. It is, on the contrary, a mere *idea* of a state, and one to which he seeks to make his actual state of being adequate under purely empirical conditions—an impossible task. He projects this idea himself, and, thanks to his understanding and its complicated relations with imagination and sense, projects it in 30

such different ways, and even alters his conception so often, that were nature a complete slave to his elective will, it would nevertheless be utterly unable to adopt any definite, universal and fixed law by which to accommodate itself to this fluctuating
5 conception and so bring itself into accord with the end that each individual arbitrarily sets before himself. But even if we sought to reduce this conception to the level of the true wants of nature in which our species is in complete and fundamental accord, or, trying the other alternative, sought to increase to the highest
10 level man's skill in compassing his imagined ends, nevertheless what man means by happiness, and what in fact constitutes his peculiar ultimate physical end, as opposed to the end of freedom, would never be attained by him. For his own nature is not so constituted as to rest or be satisfied in any possession
15 or enjoyment whatever. Then external nature is far from having made a particular favourite of man or from having preferred him to all other animals as the object of its beneficence. For we see that in its destructive operations—plague, famine, flood, cold, attacks from animals great and small, and all such
20 things—it has as little spared him as any other animal. But, besides all this, the discord of inner *natural tendencies* betrays him into further misfortunes of his own invention, and reduces other members of his species, through the oppression of lordly power, the barbarism of wars, and the like, to such misery,
25 while he himself does all he can to work ruin to his race, that, even with the utmost goodwill on the part of external nature, its end, supposing it were directed to the happiness of our species, would never be attained in a system of terrestrial nature, because our own nature is not capable of it. Man, therefore, is ever but
30 a link in the chain of physical ends. True, he is a principle in respect of many ends to which nature seems to have predeter- 431 mined him, seeing that he makes himself so ; but, nevertheless, he is also a means towards the preservation of the finality in the mechanism of the remaining members. As the single being upon

earth that possesses understanding, and, consequently, a
capacity for setting before himself ends of his deliberate choice,
he is certainly titular lord of nature, and, supposing we regard
nature as a teleological system, he is born to be its ultimate end.
But this is always on the terms that he has the intelligence and 5
the will to give to it and to himself such a reference to ends as
can be self-sufficing independently of nature, and, consequently,
a final end. Such an end, however, must not be sought in nature.

But, where in man, at any rate, are we to place this *ultimate end*
of nature ? To discover this we must seek out what nature can 10
supply for the purpose of preparing him for what he himself
must do in order to be a final end, and we must segregate it
from all ends whose possibility rests upon conditions that man
can only await at the hand of nature. Earthly happiness is an
end of the latter kind. It is understood to mean the complex of 15
all possible human ends attainable through nature whether in
man or external to him. In other words it is the material substance of all his earthly ends and what, if he converts it into his
entire end, renders him incapable of positing a final end for his
own real existence and of harmonizing therewith. Therefore of 20
all his ends in nature, we are left only with a formal, subjective
condition, that, namely, of the aptitude for setting ends before
himself at all, and, independent of nature in his power of determining ends, of employing nature as a means in accordance
with the maxims of his free ends generally. This alone remains 25
as what nature can effect relative to the final end that lies outside it, and as what may therefore be regarded as its ultimate
end. The production in a rational being of an aptitude for any
ends whatever of his own choosing, consequently of the aptitude
of a being in his freedom, is *culture*. Hence it is only culture 30
than can be the ultimate end which we have cause to attribute
to nature in respect of the human race. His individual happiness
on earth, and, we may say, the mere fact that he is the chief

instrument for instituting order and harmony in irrational external nature, are ruled out.

But not every form of culture can fill the office of this ultimate end of nature. *Skill* is a culture that is certainly the principal
5 subjective condition of the aptitude for the furthering of ends of all kinds, yet it is incompetent for giving assistance to the *will* in its determination and choice of its ends.   But this is an essential factor, if an aptitude for ends is to have its full 432 meaning.   This latter condition of aptitude, involving what
10 might be called culture by way of discipline, is negative.   It consists in the liberation of the will from the despotism of desires whereby, in our attachment to certain natural things, we are rendered incapable of exercising a choice of our own.   This happens when we allow ourselves to be enchained by impulses
15 with which nature only provided us that they might serve as leading strings to prevent our neglecting, or even impairing, the animal element in our nature, while yet we are left free enough to tighten or slacken them, to lengthen or shorten them, as the ends of our reason dictate.

20   Skill can hardly be developed in the human race otherwise than by means of inequality among men.   For the majority, in a mechanical kind of way that calls for no special art, provide the necessaries of life for the ease and convenience of others who apply themselves to the less necessary branches of culture
25 in science and art.   These keep the masses in a state of oppression, with hard work and little enjoyment, though in the course of time much of the culture of the higher classes spreads to them also.   But with the advance of this culture—the culminating point of which, where devotion to what is superfluous begins
30 to be prejudicial to what is indispensable, is called luxury— misfortunes increase equally on both sides.   With the lower classes they arise by force of domination from without, with the upper from seeds of discontent within.   Yet this splendid misery is connected with the development of natural tendencies in the

human race, and the end pursued by nature itself, though it be
not our end, is thereby attained. The formal condition under
which nature can alone attain this its real end is the existence
of a constitution so regulating the mutual relations of men that
the abuse of freedom by individuals striving one against another 5
is opposed by a lawful authority centred in a whole, called a
civil community. For it is only in such a constitution that the
greatest development of natural tendencies can take place. In
addition to this we should also need a *cosmopolitan* whole—had
men but the ingenuity to discover such a constitution and the 10
wisdom voluntarily to submit themselves to its constraint. It
would be a system of all states that are in danger of acting
433 injuriously to one another. In its absence, and with the obstacles
that ambition, love of power, and avarice, especially on the
part of those who hold the reins of authority, put in the way 15
even of the possibility of such a scheme, *war* is inevitable. Sometimes this results in states splitting up and resolving themselves
into lesser states, sometimes one state absorbs other smaller
states and endeavours to build up a larger unit. But if on the
part of men war is a thoughtless undertaking, being stirred up 20
by unbridled passions, it is nevertheless a deep-seated, maybe
far-seeing, attempt on the part of supreme wisdom, if not to
found, yet to prepare the way for a rule of law governing the
freedom of states, and thus bring about their unity in a system
established on a moral basis. And, in spite of the terrible 25
calamities which it inflicts on the human race, and the hardships,
perhaps even greater, imposed by the constant preparation for
it in time of peace, yet—as the prospect of the dawn of an
abiding reign of national happiness keeps ever retreating farther
into the distance—it is one further spur for developing to the 30
highest pitch all talents that minister to culture.

We turn now to the discipline of inclinations. In respect of
these our natural equipment is very purposively adapted to

to the performance of our essential functions as an animal species, but they are a great impediment to the development of our humanity. Yet here again, in respect of this second requisite for culture, we see nature striving on purposive lines to give us that education that opens the door to higher ends than it can itself afford. The preponderance of evil which a taste refined to the extreme of idealization, and which even luxury in the sciences, considered as food for vanity, diffuses among us as the result of the crowd of insatiable inclinations which they beget, is indisputable. But, while that is so, we cannot fail to recognize the end of nature—ever more and more to prevail over the rudeness and violence of inclinations that belong more to the animal part of our nature and are most inimical to education that would fit us for our higher vocation (inclinations towards enjoyment), and to make way for the development of our humanity. Fine art and the sciences, if they do not make man morally better, yet, by conveying a pleasure that admits of universal communication and by introducing polish and refinement into society, make him civilized. Thus they do much to overcome the tyrannical propensities of sense, and so prepare man for a sovereignty in which reason alone shall have sway. Meanwhile the evils visited upon us, now by nature, now by the truculent egoism of man, evoke the energies of the soul, and give 434 it strength and courage to submit to no such force, and at the same time quicken in us a sense that in the depths of our nature there is an aptitude for higher ends.[1]

[1] The value of life for us, measured simply by *what we enjoy* (by the natural end of the sum of all our inclinations, that is by happiness), is easy to decide. It is less than nothing. For who would enter life afresh under the same conditions ? Who would even do so according to a new, self-devised plan (which should, however, follow the course of nature), if it also were merely directed to enjoyment ? We have shown above what value life receives from what it involves when lived according to the end with which nature is occupied in us, and which consists in *what we do*, not merely what we enjoy, we being, however, in that case always but a means

§ 23 (84)

The final end of the existence of a world, that is, of creation itself.

A *final end* is an end that does not require any other end as condition of its possibility.

If the simple mechanism of nature is accepted as the explanation of its finality, it is not open to us to ask : For what end do the things in the world exist ? For on such an idealistic system we have only to reckon with the physical possibility of things,— and things that it would be mere empty sophistry to imagine as ends. Whether we refer this form of things to chance, or whether we refer it to blind necessity, such a question would in either case be meaningless. But if we suppose the final nexus in the world to be real, and assume a special type of causality for it, namely the activity of a cause *acting designedly*, we cannot then stop short at the question : What is the end for which things in the world, namely organized beings, possess this or that form, or are placed by nature in this or that relation to other things ? On the contrary, once we have conceived an understanding that must be regarded as the cause of the possibility of such forms as they are actually found in things, we must go on and seek in this understanding for an objective ground capable of determining such productive understanding to the production of an effect of this kind. That ground is then the final end for which such things exist.

I have said above that the final end is not an end which nature would be competent to realize or produce in terms of its idea, because it is one that is unconditioned. For in nature, as a

to an undetermined final end. There remains then nothing but the worth which we ourselves assign to our life by what we not alone do, but do with a view to an end so independent of nature that the very existence of nature itself can only be an end subject to the condition so imposed.

thing of sense, there is nothing whose determining ground, discoverable in nature itself, is not always in turn conditioned. This is not merely true of external or material nature, but also of internal or thinking nature—it being of course understood
5 that I am only considering what in us is strictly nature. But a thing which by virtue of its objective characterization is to exist necessarily as the final end of an intelligent cause, must be of such a kind that in the order of ends it is dependent upon no further or other condition than simply its idea.

10 Now we have in the world beings of but one kind whose causality is teleological, or directed to ends, and which at the same time are beings of such a character that the law according to which they have to determine ends for themselves is represented by them themselves as unconditioned and not dependent
15 on anything in nature, but as necessary in itself. The being of this kind is man, but man regarded as noumenon. He is the only natural creature whose peculiar objective characterization is nevertheless such as to enable us to recognize in him a supersensible faculty—his *freedom*—and to perceive both the law of
20 the causality and the object of freedom which that faculty is able to set before itself as the highest end—the supreme good in the world.

Now it is not open to us in the case of man, considered as a moral agent, or similarly in the case of any rational being in
25 the world, to ask the further question : For what end (*quem in finem*) does he exist ? His existence inherently involves the highest end—the end to which, as far as in him lies, he may subject the whole of nature, or contrary to which at least he must not deem himself subjected to any influence on its part.—Now
30 assuming that things in the world are beings that are dependent in point of their real existence, and, as such, stand in need of a supreme cause acting according to ends, then man is the final end of creation. For without man the chain of mutually subordinated ends would have no ultimate point of attachment.

Only in man, and only in him as the individual being to whom the moral law applies, do we find unconditional legislation in respect of ends. This legislation, therefore, is what alone qualifies him to be a final end to which entire nature is teleologically subordinated.[1]

§ 24 (85)

Physico-Theology.

Physico-Theology is the attempt on the part of reason to infer the supreme cause of nature and its attributes from the *ends* of

---

[1] It would be possible for the happiness of the rational beings in the world to be an end of nature, and, were it so, it would also be the *ultimate* end of nature.   At least it is not obvious *a priori* why nature should not be so ordered, for, so far as we can see, happiness is an effect which it would be quite possible for nature to produce by means of its mechanism.   But morality, or a causality according to ends that is subordinate to morality, is an absolutely impossible result of natural causes.   For the principle that determines such causality to action is supersensible.   In the order of ends, therefore, it is the sole principle possible which is absolutely unconditioned in respect of nature, and it is what alone qualifies the subject of such causality to be the *final end* of creation, and the one to which entire nature is subordinated.   *Happiness*, on the other hand, as an appeal to the testimony of experience showed in the preceding section, so far from being a *final end of creation*, is not even an *end of nature* as regards man in preference to other creatures.   It may ever be that individual men will make it their ultimate subjective end.   But if, seeking for the final end of creation, I ask : For what end was it necessary that men should exist ? my question then refers to an objective supreme end, such as the highest reason would demand for their creation.   If, then, to this question we reply : So that beings may exist upon whom that supreme Cause may exercise this beneficence, we then belie the condition to which the reason of man subjects even his own inmost wish for happiness, namely, harmony with his own inner moral legislation.   This proves that happiness can only be a conditional end, and, therefore, that it is only as a moral being that man can be the final end of creation ; while, as regards his state of being, happiness is only incident thereto as a consequence proportionate to the measure of his harmony with that end, as the end of his existence.

nature—ends which can only be known empirically. A *moral theology*, or ethico-theology, would be the attempt to infer that cause and its attributes from the moral end of rational beings in nature—an end which can be known *a priori*.

5 The former naturally precedes the latter. For if we seek to infer a world-cause from the things in the world by *teleological* arguments, we must first of all be given ends of nature. Then for these ends so given we must afterwards look for a final end, 437 and this final end obliges us to seek the principle of the causality 10 of the supreme cause in question.

Much natural research can, and indeed must, be conducted in the light of the teleological principle without our having occasion to inquire into the source of the possibility of the final action which we meet with in various products of nature. But 15 should we now desire to have also a conception of this source, we are then in the position of having absolutely no available insight that can penetrate beyond our mere maxim of reflective judgement. According to this maxim, given but a single organized product of nature, then the structure of our cognitive 20 faculty is such that the only source which we can conceive it to have is one that is a cause of nature itself—be it of entire nature or even only of this particular portion of it—and that derives from an understanding the requisite causality for such a product. This is a critical principle which doubtless brings us no whit 25 farther in the explanation of natural things or their origin. Yet it discloses to our view a prospect that extends beyond the horizon of nature and points to our being able perhaps to determine more closely the conception of an original being otherwise so unfruitful.

30 Now I say that no matter how far physico-teleology may be pushed, it can never disclose to us anything about a *final end* of creation; for it never even begins to look for a final end. Thus it can justify, no doubt, the conception of an intelligent world-cause as a conception which subjectively—that is in relation

to the nature of our cognitive faculty alone—is effective to explain the possibility of things that we can render intelligible to ourselves in the light of ends. But neither from a theoretical nor a practical point of view can it determine this conception any farther. Its attempt falls short of its proposed aim of afford- 5 ing a basis of theology. To the last it remains nothing but a physical teleology : for the final nexus which it recognizes is only, and must only, be regarded as subject to natural conditions. Consequently it can never institute an inquiry into the end for which nature itself exists—this being an end whose 10 source must be sought outside nature. Yet it is upon the definite idea of this end that the definite conception of such a supreme intelligent World-Cause, and, consequently, the possibility of a theology, depend.

Of what use are the things in the world to one another ? 15 What good is the manifold in a thing to this thing ? How are we entitled to assume that nothing in the world is in vain, but that, provided we grant that certain things, regarded as ends, ought to exist, everything serves some purpose or other *in nature*? All these questions imply that in respect of our judgement reason 20 438 has at its command no other principle of the possibility of the Object which it is obliged to estimate teleologically than that of subordinating the mechanism of nature to the architectonic of an intelligent Author of the world ; and directed to all these issues the teleological survey of the world plays its part nobly 25 and fills us with intense admiration. But inasmuch as the data, and, consequently, the principles, for determining such a conception of an intelligent World-Cause, regarded as the supreme Artist, are merely empirical, they do not allow us to infer any other attributes belonging to it than those which experience 30 reveals to us as manifested in its operations. But as experience is unable to embrace aggregate nature as a system, it must frequently find support for arguments which, to all appearances,

conflict with that conception and with one another. Yet it can
never lift us above nature to the end of its real existence or thus
raise us to a definite conception of such a higher Intelligence—
not though it were in our power empirically to review the entire
5 system in its purely physical aspect.

If the problem which physico-theology has to solve is set to
a lower key, then its solution seems an easy matter. Thus we
may think of an intelligent being possessing a number of super-
lative attributes, without the full complement of those necessary
10 for establishing a nature harmonizing with the greatest possible
end, and to all beings of this description—of whom there may be
one or more—we might be extravagant enough to apply the
conception of a *Deity*. Or, if we let it pass as of no importance
to supplement by arbitrary additions the proofs of a theory
15 where the grounds of proof are deficient ; and if, therefore,
where we have only reason to assume *much* perfection (and what,
pray, is much for us ?) we deem ourselves entitled to take *all
possible* perfection for granted :—then physical teleology has
important claims to the distinction of affording the basis of a
20 theology. But what is there to lead, and, more than that,
authorize us to supplement the facts of the case in this way ?
If we are called on to point out what it is, we shall seek in vain
for any ground of justification in the principles of the theoretical
employment of reason. For such employment emphatically de-
25 mands that for the purpose of explaining an object of experience
we are not to ascribe to it more attributes than we find in the
empirical data for the possibility of the object. On closer investigation we should see that underlying our procedure is an
idea of a Supreme Being, which rests on an entirely different
30 employment of reason, namely its practical employment, and
that it is this idea, which exists in us *a priori*, that impels us to
supplement the defective representation of an original ground
of the ends in nature afforded by physical teleology, and enlarge 439
it to the conception of a Deity. When we saw this, we should

not erroneously imagine that we had evolved this idea, and, with it, a theology by means of the theoretical employment of reason in the physical cognition of the world—much less that we had proved its reality.

One cannot blame the ancients so very much for imagining that, while there was great diversity among their gods, both in respect of their power and of their purposes and dispositions, they were all, not excepting the sovereign head of the gods himself, invariably limited in human fashion.   For on surveying the order and course of the things in nature they certainly found ample reason for assuming something more than mere mechanism as its cause and for conjecturing the existence of purposes on the part of certain higher causes, which they could only conceive to be superhuman, behind the machinery of this world. But, since they encountered both the good and evil, the final and the contra-final, very much interspersed, at least to human eyes, and could not take the liberty of assuming, for the sake of the arbitrary idea of an all-perfect author, that there were nevertheless mysteriously wise and beneficent ends, of which they did not see the evidence, underlying all this apparent antagonism, their judgement on the supreme world-cause could hardly be other than it was, so long, that is, as they followed maxims of the mere theoretical employment of reason with strict consistency.   Others who were physicists and in that character desired to be theologians also, thought that they would give full satisfaction to reason by providing for the absolute unity of the principle of natural things, which reason demands, by means of the idea of a being in which, as sole substance, the whole assemblage of those natural things would be contained only as inhering modes.   While this substance would not be the cause of the world by virtue of its intelligence, it would nevertheless be a subject in which all the intelligence on the part of the beings in the world would reside.   Hence, although it would

not be a being that produced anything according to ends, it would be one in which all things—owing to the unity of the subject of which they are mere determinations—must necessarily be interconnected in a final manner, though apart from end or
5 design. Thus they introduced the idealism of final Causes, by converting the unity, so difficult to deduce, of a number of sub-stances standing in a final connexion, from a causal dependence *on one* substance into the unity of inherence *in one*. Looked at from the side of the beings that inhere, this system became
10 *pantheism*, and from the side of the sole subsisting subject, as original being, it became, by a later development, *Spinozism*. 440 Thus in the end, instead of solving the problem of the primary source of the finality of nature, it represented the whole question as idle, for the conception of such finality, being shorn of all
15 reality, was reduced to a simple misinterpretation of the universal ontological conception of a thing in the abstract.

So we see that the conception of a Deity, such as would meet the demands of our teleological estimate of nature, can never be evolved according to mere theoretical principles of the em-
20 ployment of reason—and these are the only principles upon which physico-theology relies. For, suppose we assert that all teleology is a delusion on the part of judgement in its estimate of the causal nexus of things and take refuge in the sole principle of a mere mechanism of nature. Then nature only appears to us
25 to involve a universal relation to ends, owing to the unity of the substance that contains it as no more than the multiplicity of its modes. Or, suppose that instead of adopting this idealism of final causes, we wish to adhere to the principle of the realism of this particular type of causality. Then—no matter whether
30 we base natural ends on a number of intelligent original beings or on a single one—the moment we find ourselves with nothing upon which to found the conception of realism but empirical principles drawn from the actual nexus of ends in the world, on the one hand we cannot help accepting the fact of the

discordance with final unity of which nature presents many examples, and on the other hand, we can never obtain a sufficiently
definite conception of a single intelligent Cause—so long as we
keep to what mere experience entitles us to extract—to satisfy
any sort of theology whatever which will be of use theoretically 5
or practically.

It is true that physical teleology urges us to go in quest of
a theology.   But it cannot produce one—however far we carry
our investigations of nature, or help out the nexus of ends discovered in it with ideas of reason (which for physical problems 10
must be theoretical).   We may pose the reasonable question :
What is the use of our basing all these arrangements on a great,
and for us unfathomable, intelligence, and supposing it to order
this world according to purposes, if nature does not and cannot
ever tell us anything as to the final purpose in view? For apart 15
from a final purpose we are unable to relate all these natural
ends to a common point, or form an adequate teleological
principle, be it for combining all the ends in a known system, or
be it for framing such a conception of the supreme Intelligence,
441 as cause of a nature like this, as could act as a standard for our 20
judgement in its teleological reflection upon nature.   I should
have, it is true, in that case an *art intelligence* for miscellaneous
ends, but no *wisdom* for a final end, which nevertheless is what
must, properly speaking, contain the ground by which such intelligence is determined. I require a final end, and it is only pure 25
reason that *a priori* can supply this—for all ends in the world
are empirically conditioned and can contain nothing that is
absolutely good, but only what is good for this or that purpose
regarded as contingent.   Such a final end alone would instruct
me how I am to conceive the supreme cause of nature—what 30
attributes I am to assign to it, and in what degree, and how I am
to conceive its relation to nature—if I am to estimate nature as
a teleological system.   In the absence, then, of a final end, what

liberty or what authority have I to extend at will such a very
limited conception of that original intelligence as I can base on
my own poor knowledge of the world, or my conception of the
power of this original being to realize its ideas, or of its will to
5 do so, &c., and expand it to the idea of an all-wise and infinite
Being ? Were I able to do this theoretically it would presuppose
omniscience in myself to enable me to see into the ends of nature
in their entire context, and in addition to conceive all other
possible schemes, as compared with which the present would have
10 to be estimated on reasonable grounds to be the best. For without this perfected knowledge of the effect, my reasoning can
arrive at no definite conception of the supreme cause—which is
only to be found in that of an intelligence in every respect
infinite, that is, in the conception of a Deity—or establish a
15 basis for theology.

Hence, allowing for all possible extension of physical teleology,
we may keep to the principle set out above and say that the
constitution and principles of our cognitive faculty are such
that we can only conceive nature, in respect of those of its ad-
20 justments that are familiar to us and display finality, as the
product of an intelligence to which it is subjected. But whether
this intelligence may also have had a final purpose in view in
the production of nature and in its constitution as a whole,
which final purpose in that case would not reside in nature as
25 the world of sense, is a matter that the theoretical study of
nature can never disclose. On the contrary, however great our
knowledge of nature, it remains an open question whether that
supreme cause is the original source of nature as a cause acting
throughout according to a final end, or whether it is not rather
30 such a source by virtue of an intelligence that is determined by
the simple necessity of its nature to the production of certain
forms (by analogy to what we call the artistic instinct in the 442
lower animals). The latter version does not involve our ascribing
even wisdom to such intelligence, much less wisdom that is

supreme and conjoined with all other properties requisite for ensuring the perfection of its product.

Hence physico-theology is a physical teleology misunderstood. It is of no use to theology except as a preparation or propaedentic, and is only sufficient for this purpose when supplemented by a 5 further principle on which it can rely. But it is not, as its name would suggest, sufficient, even as a propaedentic, if taken by itself.

§ 25 (86)

Ethico-Theology.

THERE is a judgement which even the commonest understanding finds irresistible when it reflects upon the existence of the 10 things in the world and the real existence of the world itself. It is the verdict that all the manifold forms of life, co-ordinated though they may be with the greatest art and concatenated with the utmost variety of final adaptations, and even the entire complex that embraces their numerous systems, incorrectly 15 called worlds, would all exist for nothing, if man, or rational beings of some sort, were not to be found in their midst. Without man, in other words, the whole of creation would be a mere wilderness, a thing in vain, and have no final end. Yet it is not man's cognitive faculty, that is, theoretical reason, that forms 20 the point of reference which alone gives its worth to the existence of all else in the world—as if the meaning of his presence in the world was that there might be some one in it that could make it an object of *contemplation*. For if this contemplation of the world brought to light nothing but things without a final end, 25 the existence of the world could not acquire a worth from the fact of its being known. A final end of the world must be presupposed as that in relation to which the contemplation of the world may itself possess a worth. Neither is it in relation to the feeling of pleasure or the sum of such feelings that we can think 30

that there is a given final end of creation, that is to say, it is
not by well-being, not by enjoyment, whether bodily or mental,
not, in a word, by happiness, that we value that absolute worth.
For the fact that man, when he does exist, makes happiness his
5 own final purpose, affords us no conception of any reason why
he should exist at all, or of any worth he himself possesses, for
which his real existence should be made agreeable to him. Hence 443
man must already be presupposed to be the final end of creation,
in order that we may have a rational ground to explain why
10 nature, when regarded as an absolute whole according to
principles of ends, must be in accord with the conditions of his
happiness.—Accordingly it is only the faculty of desire that can
give the required point of reference—yet not that faculty which
makes man dependent upon nature (through impulses of sense),
15 that is, not that in respect of which the worth of his existence is
dependent upon what he receives and enjoys. On the contrary
it is the worth which he alone can give to himself, and which
consists in what he does—in the manner in which and the
principles upon which he acts in the *freedom* of his faculty of
20 desire, and not as a link in the chain of nature. In other words
a good will is that whereby man's existence can alone possess an
absolute worth, and in relation to which the existence of the
world can have a *final end*.

Even the popular verdict of sound human reason, once its
25 reflection is directed to this question and pressed to its consideration, is in complete accord with the judgement that it is
only as a moral being that man can be a final end of creation.
What, it will be said, does it all avail, that this man has so much
talent, that he is even so active in its employment and thus
30 exerts a useful influence upon social and public life, and that he
possesses, therefore, considerable worth alike in relation to his
own state of happiness and in relation to what is good for others,
if he has not a good will ? Looked at from the point of view of
his inner self, he is a contemptible object ; and, if creation is not

to be altogether devoid of a final end, such a man, though as man he is part of creation, must nevertheless, as a bad man dwelling in a world subject to moral laws, forfeit, in accordance with those laws, his own subjective end, that is happiness, as the sole condition under which his real existence can consist with the final end. 5

Now if we find instances in the world of an order adapted to ends, and if, as reason inevitably requires, we subordinate the ends which are only conditionally ends, to one that is unconditioned and supreme, that is to a final end, we readily see, to begin with, that we are then not dealing with an end of nature, 10 included in nature taken as existent, but with the end of the real existence of nature, with all its orderly adaptations included. Consequently we see that the question is one of the ultimate *end of creation*, and, more precisely, of the supreme condition under which alone there can be a final end, or, in other words, of 15 the ground that determines a highest intelligence to the production of the beings in the world.

444   It is, then, only as a moral being that we acknowledge man to be the end of creation.   Hence we have, first of all, a reason, or at least the primary condition, for regarding the world as a 20 consistent whole of interconnected ends, and as a *system* of final causes.   Now the structure of our reason is such that we necessarily refer natural ends to an intelligent world-cause.   Above all, then, we have *one principle* applicable to this relation, enabling us to think the nature and attributes of this first cause 25 considered as supreme ground in the kingdom of ends, and to form a definite conception of it.   This is what could not be done by physical teleology, which was only able to suggest vague conceptions of such a ground—conceptions which this vagueness made as useless for practical as for theoretical employment.   30

With such a definite principle as this, of the causality of the original being, we shall not have to regard it merely as an intelligence and as legislating for nature, but as the Sovereign Head

legislating in a moral Kingdom of Ends. In relation to the
summum bonum, which is alone possible under His sovereignty,
namely the real existence of rational beings under moral laws,
we shall conceive this Original Being to be *omniscient*, so that
5 even our inmost sentiments—wherein lies the distinctive moral
worth in the actions of rational beings in the world—may not be
hid from Him. We shall conceive Him as *omnipotent*, so that He
may be able to adapt entire nature to this highest end ; as both
all-good and *just*, since these two attributes, which unite to form
10 *wisdom*, constitute the conditions under which a supreme cause
of the world can be the source of the greatest good under moral
laws. Similarly the other remaining transcendental attributes,
such as *eternity*, *omnipresence*, and so forth (for goodness and
justice are moral attributes), all attributes that are presupposed
15 in relation to such a final end, will have to be regarded as belonging to this Original Being.—In this way *moral* teleology supplements the deficiency of *physical* teleology, and for the first time
establishes a *theology*. For physical teleology, if it is not to borrow
secretly from moral teleology, but is to proceed with strict
20 logical rigour, can from its own unaided resources establish
nothing but a demonology, which does not admit of any definite
conception.

But the principle which, because of the moral and teleological
significance of certain beings in the world, refers the world to
25 a Supreme Cause as Deity, does not establish this relation by
being simply a completion of the physico-teleological argument,
and therefore by adopting this necessarily as its foundation. On
the contrary it can rely on *its own* resources, and urges attention 445
to the ends of nature and inquiry after the incomprehensibly
30 great art that lies hidden behind its forms, so as to give to the
ideas produced by pure practical reason an incidental confirmation in physical ends. For the conception of beings of the world
subject to moral laws is an *a priori* principle upon which man
must necessarily estimate himself. Furthermore, if there is a

world-cause acting designedly and directed to an end, the moral relation above mentioned must just as necessarily be the condition of the possibility of a creation as is the relation determined by physical laws—that is, supposing that such an intelligent cause has also a final end. This is a principle which reason regards 5 even *a priori* as one that is necessary for its teleological estimate of the real existence of things. The whole question, then, is reduced to this : Have we any ground capable of satisfying reason, speculative or practical, to justify our attributing a *final end* to the supreme cause that acts according to ends ? For that, 10 judging by the subjective frame of our reason, or even by aught we can at all imagine of the reason of other beings, such final end could be nothing but *man as subject to moral laws*, may be taken *a priori* as a matter of certainty ; whereas we are wholly unable to cognize *a priori* what are the ends of nature in the physical 15 order, and above all it is impossible to see that a nature could not exist apart from such ends.

Remark.

Imagine a man at the moment when his mind is disposed to moral feeling ! If, amid beautiful natural surroundings, he is in calm and serene enjoyment of his existence, he feels within him 20 a need—a need of being grateful for it to some one. Or, at another time, in the same frame of mind, he may find himself in the stress of duties which he can only perform and will perform by submitting to a voluntary sacrifice ; then he feels within him a need—a need of having, in so doing, carried out some command 25 and obeyed a Supreme Lord. Or he may in some thoughtless manner have diverged from the path of duty, though not so as to have made himself answerable to man ; yet words of stern self-reproach will then fall upon an inward ear, and he will seem 446 to hear the voice of a judge to whom he has to render account. 30 In a word, he needs a moral Intelligence ; because he exists for an end, and this end demands a Being that has formed both him and the world with that end in view. It is waste of labour to go burrowing behind these feelings for motives ; for they are immediately connected with the purest moral sentiment : *gratitude,* 5 *obedience,* and *humiliation*—that is, submission before a deserved chastisement—being special modes of a mental disposition towards duty. It is merely that the mind inclined to give expansion to its moral sentiment here voluntarily imagines an object that is not in the world, in order, if possible, to prove its dutiful- 10 ness in the eyes of such an object also. Hence it is at least possible—and, besides, there is in our moral habits of thought a foundation for so doing—to form a representation depicting a pure moral need for the real existence of a Being, whereby our morality gains in strength or even obtains—at least on the side 15 of our representation—an extension of area, that is to say, is given a new object for its exercise. In other words, it is possible to admit a moral Legislator existing apart from the world, and to do so without regard to theoretical proof, and still less to self-interest, but on a purely moral ground, which, while of course 20 only subjective, is free from all foreign influence, on the mere recommendation of a pure practical reason that legislates for itself alone. It may be that such a disposition of the mind is but a rare occurrence, or, again, does not last long, but rather is fleeting and of no permanent effect, or, it may be, passes away 25 without the mind bestowing a single thought upon the object so shadowed forth, and without troubling to reduce it to clear conceptions. Yet the source of this disposition is unmistakable. It is the original moral bent of our nature, as a subjective principle, that will not let us be satisfied, in our review of the world, 30 with the finality which it derives through natural causes, but leads us to introduce into it an underlying supreme Cause governing nature according to moral laws.—In addition to the above there is the fact that we feel ourselves urged by the moral law to strive after a universal highest end, while yet we feel ourselves, and all nature too, incapable of its attainment. Further, it it is only so far as we strive after this end that we can judge ourselves to be in harmony with the final end of an intelligent world-cause—if such there be. Thus we have a pure moral ground derived from practical reason for admitting this Cause (since we may do so without self-contradiction), if for no better reason, in order that we may not run the risk of regarding such striving as quite idle in its effects, and of allowing it to flag in consequence.

447 Let us restate what we intended to convey here by all these remarks. While *fear* doubtless in the first instance may have been able to produce *gods*, that is demons, it is only *reason* by its moral principles that has been able to produce the conception of *God*—and it has been able to do so despite the great ignorance that has usually prevailed in what concerns the teleology of nature, or the considerable doubt that arises from the difficulty of reconciling by a sufficiently established principle the mutually conflicting phenomena that nature presents. Further, the inner *moral* destination of man's existence supplements the short-comings of natural knowledge, by directing us to join to the thought of the final end of the existence of all things—an end the principle of which only satisfies reason from an *ethical* point of view—the thought of the supreme cause as endowed with attributes whereby it is empowered to subject entire nature to that single purpose, and make it merely instrumental thereto. In other words it directs us to think the supreme cause as a *Deity*.

§ 26 (87)

The moral proof of the existence of God.

WE have a *physical teleology* that affords evidence sufficient for our theoretical reflective judgement to enable us to admit the existence of an intelligent world-cause. But in ourselves, and

still more in the general conception of a rational being endowed
with freedom of its causality, we find a *moral teleology*. But as
our own relation to an end, together with the law governing it,
may be determined *a priori*, and consequently cognized as
5 necessary, moral teleology does not stand in need of any intelligent cause outside ourselves to explain this intrinsic conformity
to law any more than what we consider final in the geometrical
properties of figures (their adaptation for all possible kinds of
employment by art) lets us look beyond to a supreme under-
10 standing that imparts this finality to them. But this moral
teleology deals with us for all that as beings of the world and,
therefore, as beings associated with other things in the world ;
and the same moral laws enjoin us to turn our consideration to
these other things in the world, regarded either as ends, or as
15 objects in respect of which we ourselves are the final end. This
moral teleology, then, which deals with the relation of our own
causality to ends, or even to a final end that must be proposed
by us in the world, as well as with the reciprocal relation subsisting between the world and that moral end and the possibility 448
20 of realizing it under external conditions—a matter upon which
no physical teleology can give us any guidance—raises a necessary question. For we must ask : Does this moral teleology
oblige our rational critical judgement to go beyond the world
and seek for an intelligent supreme principle in respect of the
25 relation of nature to the moral side of our being, so that we may
form a representation of nature as displaying finality in relation
also to our inner moral legislation and its possible realization ?
Hence there is certainly a moral teleology. It is as necessarily
implicated with the *nomothetic* of freedom on the one hand, and
30 that of nature on the other, as with civil legislation is implicated
the question of where the executive authority is to be sought.
In fact there is here the same implication as is to be found
in everything in which reason has to assign a principle of the
actuality of a certain uniform order of things that is only possible

A a

according to ideas.—We shall begin by exhibiting how from the above moral teleology and its relation to physical teleology reason advances to *theology.* Having done so, we shall make some observations on the possibility and conclusiveness of this mode of reasoning.   5

If we assume the existence of certain things, or even only of certain forms of things, to be contingent, and consequently to be only possible by means of something else as their cause, we may then look for the supreme source of this causality, and, therefore, for the unconditioned ground of the conditioned, either in the 10 physical or the teleological order—that is, we may look either to the *nexus effectivus* or to the *nexus finalis.* In other words, we may ask which is the supreme efficient cause, or we may ask what is the supreme or absolutely unconditioned end of such cause, that is, what in general is the final end for which it pro- 15 duces these or all its products. In the latter question it is obviously taken for granted that this cause can form a representation of the end, and is consequently an intelligent being, or at least that it must be conceived by us as acting according to the laws of such a being.   20

Now, supposing we follow the teleological order, there is a *fundamental principle* to which even the most ordinary human intelligence is obliged to give immediate assent. It is the principle that if there is to be a *final end* at all, which reason must assign *a priori,* then it can only be *man*—or any rational 25 being in the world—*subject to moral laws.*[1] For—and this is the

[1] I say deliberately : *under* moral laws. It is not man *in accordance* with moral laws, that is to say, human beings living in conformity with such laws, that is the final end of creation. For to use the latter expression would be to assert more than we know, namely, that it is in the power of an author of the world to ensure that man should always conform to the moral laws. But this presupposes a conception of freedom and of nature—of which latter alone we can think an external author—that implies an insight into the supersensible substrate of nature and its identity with what is rendered

verdict of everyone—if the world only consisted of lifeless beings, 449
or even consisted partly of living, but yet irrational beings, the
existence of such a world would have no worth whatever, because
there would exist in it no being with the least conception of what
5 worth is. On the other hand, if there were even rational beings,
and if nevertheless their reason were only able to set the worth
of the existence of things in the bearing which nature has upon
them, that is, in their well-being, instead of being able to procure
such a worth for themselves from original sources, that is, in their
10 freedom, then there would be, it is true, relative ends in the
world, but no absolute end; since the existence of rational beings
of this kind would still always remain devoid of an end. It is,
however, a distinctive feature of the moral laws that they
prescribe something for reason in the form of an end apart from
15 any condition, and consequently in the very form that the conception of a final end requires. Therefore the real existence of a

possible in the world by causality through freedom. Such insight
far exceeds that of our reason. It is only of *man under moral laws*
that we are able to affirm, without transcending the limits of our
insight, that his existence forms the final end of the world. This
statement also accords perfectly with the verdict of human reason in
its reflection upon the course of the world from a moral standpoint.
We believe that even in the case of the wicked we perceive the traces
of a wise design in things if we see that the wanton criminal does not
die before he has suffered the just punishment of his misdeeds.
According to our conceptions of free causality, good or bad conduct
depends upon ourselves. But where we think that the supreme
wisdom in the government of the world lies, is in the fact that the
occasion for the former, and the result following from both, is
ordained according to moral laws. In the latter consists, properly
speaking, the glory of God, which is therefore not inappropriately
termed by theologians the ultimate end of creation.—We should add
that when we make use of the word creation, we only take it to mean
what is spoken of here, namely, the cause of the *existence* of a *world*,
or of the things in it, that is, substances. This is also what the strict
meaning of the word conveys—*actuatio substantiae est creatio*. Consequently it implies no assumption of a cause that acts freely and
that is therefore intelligent. The existence of such an intelligent
cause is what we are set upon proving.

reason like this, that in the order of ends can be the supreme law to itself, in other words the real existence of rational beings 450 subject to moral laws, can alone be regarded as the final end of the existence of a world. But if this is not so, then either no end whatever in the cause underlies the existence of the world, 5 or else only ends without a final end.

The moral law is the formal rational condition of the employment of our freedom, and, as such, of itself alone lays its obligation upon us, independently of any end as its material condition. But it also defines for us a final end, and does so *a priori*, and 10 makes it obligatory upon us to strive towards its attainment. This end is the *summum bonum*, as the highest good *in the world* possible through freedom.

The subjective condition under which man, and, as far as we can at all conceive, every rational finite being also, is able under 15 the above law to set before himself a final end, is happiness. Consequently the highest possible physical good in the world, and the one to be furthered so far as in us lies as the final end, is *happiness*—subject to the objective condition that the individual harmonizes with the law of *morality*, regarded as worthiness to 20 be happy.

But by no faculty of our reason can we represent to ourselves these two requisites for the final end proposed to us by the moral law to be *conjoined* by means of mere natural causes and also conformed to the idea of the final end in contemplation. Accord- 25 ingly, if we do not bring the causality of any other means besides nature into alliance with our freedom, the conception of the *practical necessity* of such an end through the application of our powers does not accord with the theoretical conception of *physical possibility* of its effectuation. 30

Consequently we must assume a moral world-cause, that is, an Author of the world, if we are to set before ourselves a final end in conformity with the requirements of the moral law. And as far as it is necessary to set such an end before us, so far, that is in the same degree and upon the same ground, it is necessary to assume an Author of the world, or, in other words, that there is a God.[1]

5   This proof, to which we may easily give the form of logical precision, does not imply that it is as necessary to assume the existence of God as it is to recognize the validity of the moral 451 law, and that, consequently, one who is unable to convince himself of the former may deem himself absolved from the 10 obligations imposed by the latter.   No ! all that must be abandoned in that case is the *premeditation* of the final end in the world to be effectuated by the pursuit of the moral law, that is the premeditation of a happiness of rational beings harmoniously associated with such pursuit, as the highest good 15 in the world.   Every rational being would have to continue to recognize himself as firmly bound by the precept of morals, for their laws are formal and command unconditionally, paying no regard to ends (as the subject-matter of volition).   But the one requirement of the final end, as prescribed by practical 20 reason to the beings of the world, is an irresistible end planted in them by their nature as finite beings.   Reason refuses to countenance this end except as subject to the moral law *as* inviolable *condition,* and would only have it made universal in accordance with this condition.   Thus it makes the furtherance of happiness 25 in agreement with morality the final end.   To promote this end—

---

[1] This moral argument is not intended to supply an *objectively* valid proof of the existence of God. It is not meant to demonstrate to the sceptic that there is a God, but that he *must adopt* the assumption of this proposition as a maxim of his practical reason, if he wishes to think in a manner consistent with morality.—Further, the argument is not intended to affirm that it is necessary *for the purpose of morality* to assume that the happiness of all rational beings in the world is proportioned to their morality. On the contrary it is *by virtue of morality* that the assumption is necessitated. Consequently it is an argument that is sufficient *subjectively* and for moral persons.

so far, in respect of happiness, as lies in our power—is commanded us by the moral law, whatever the outcome of this endeavour may be. The fulfilment of duty consists in the form of the earnest will, not in the intervening causes that contribute to success.   5

Suppose, then, that a man, influenced partly by the weakness of all the speculative arguments that are thought so much of, and partly by the number of irregularities he finds in nature and the moral world, becomes persuaded of the proposition : There is no God ; nevertheless in his own eyes he would be a worthless 10 creature if he chose on that account to regard the laws of duty as simply fanciful, invalid, and inobligatory, and resolved boldly to transgress them.   Again, let us suppose that such a man were able subsequently to convince himself of the truth of what he had at first doubted ; he would still remain worthless if he held 15 to the above way of thinking.   This is so, were he even to fulfil his duty as punctiliously as could be desired, so far as actual 452 actions are concerned, but were to do so from fear or with a view to reward, and without an inward reverence for duty.   Conversely, if, as a believer in God, he observes his duty according 20 to his conscience, uprightly and disinterestedly, yet if whenever, to try himself, he puts before himself the case of his haply being able to convince himself that there is no God, he straightway believes himself free from all moral obligation, the state of his inner moral disposition could then only be bad.   25

Let us then, as we may, take the case of a righteous man, such, say, as Spinoza, who considers himself firmly persuaded that there is no God and—since in respect of the Object of morality a similar result ensues—no future life either.   How will he estimate his individual intrinsic finality that is derived from the 30 moral law which he reveres in practice ?   He does not require that its pursuit should bring him any personal benefit either in this or any other world.   On the contrary his will is disinterestedly

to establish only that good to which the holy law directs all his energies. But he is circumscribed in his endeavour. He may, it is true, expect to find a chance concurrence now and again, but he can never expect to find in nature a uniform agree-
5 ment—a consistent agreement according to fixed rules, answering to what his maxims are and must be subjectively, with that end which yet he feels himself obliged and urged to realize. Deceit, violence, and envy will always be rife around him, although he himself is honest, peaceable, and benevolent ; and the other
10 righteous men that he meets in the world, no matter how deserving they may be of happiness, will be subjected by nature, which takes no heed of such deserts, to all the evils of want, disease, and untimely death, just as are the other animals on the earth. And so it will continue to be until one wide grave engulfs them all—
15 just and unjust, there is no distinction in the grave—and hurls them back into the abyss of the aimless chaos of matter from which they were taken—they that were able to believe themselves the final end of creation.—Thus the end which this right-minded man would have, and ought to have, in view in his
20 pursuit of the moral law, would certainly have to be abandoned by him as impossible. But perhaps he resolves to remain faithful to the call of his inner moral vocation and would fain not let the respect with which he is immediately inspired to obedience by the moral law be weakened owing to the nullity of the one
25 ideal final end that answers to its high demand—which could not happen without doing injury to moral sentiment. If so he must 453 assume the existence of a *moral* author of the world, that is, of a God. As this assumption at least involves nothing intrinsically self-contradictory he may quite readily make it from a practical
30 point of view, that is to say, at least for the purpose of framing a conception of the possibility of the final end morally prescribed to him.

§ 27 (88)

Limitation of the validity of the moral proof.

PURE reason, regarded as a practical faculty, a capacity, that
is to say, for determining the pure employment of our causality
by means of ideas, or pure rational conceptions, not alone
possesses in its moral law a principle which is regulative of our
actions, but by virtue of that law it furnishes at the same time 5
an additional principle which, from a subjective point of view,
is constitutive. This principle is contained in the conception of
an Object which reason alone is able to think, and which is meant
to be realized in the world through our actions in conformity to
that law. The idea of a final end in the employment of freedom 10
in obedience to moral laws has, therefore, a reality that is subjectively *practical*. We are determined *a priori* by reason to
further the *summum bonum* as far as in us lies. This *summum
bonum* is formed by the union of the greatest welfare of the
rational beings in the world with the supreme condition of their 15
good, or, in other words, by the union of universal happiness
with the strictest morality. Now the possibility of one of the
factors of this final end, namely that of happiness, is empirically
conditioned. It depends upon how nature is constituted—on
whether nature harmonizes or not with this end. It is, therefore, 20
from a theoretical point of view problematic ; whereas the other
factor, namely morality, in respect of which we are independent
of the co-operation of nature, is *a priori* assured of its possibility
and is dogmatically certain. Accordingly, the fact that we have
a final end set before us *a priori* does not meet all the require- 25
ments of the objective and theoretical reality of the conception
of the final end of rational beings in the world. It is further
requisite that creation, that is, the world itself, should, in respect
of its real existence, have a final end. Were we able to prove

a priori that it has such an end, this would supplement the subjective reality of the final end by a reality that is objective. For if creation has a final end at all we cannot conceive it otherwise than as harmonizing necessarily with our moral faculty,
5 which is what alone makes the conception of an end possible. But, now, we do find in the world what are certainly ends. In 454 fact physical teleology exhibits ends in such abundance that if we let reason guide our judgement we have after all justification for assuming, as a principle upon which to investigate nature,
10 that there is nothing whatever in nature that has not got its end. Yet in nature itself we search in vain for its own final end. Hence, just as the idea of this final end resides only in reason, so it is only in rational beings that such an end itself can and must be sought as an objective possibility. But the practical
15 reason of these beings does not merely assign this final end : it also determines this conception in respect of the conditions under which a final end of creation can alone be thought by us.

Now the question arises : Is it not possible to substantiate the objective reality of the conception of a final end in a manner
20 that will meet the theoretical requirements of pure reason ? This cannot indeed be done apodictically for the determinant judgement. Yet may it not be done sufficiently for the maxims of theoretical judgement so far as reflective ? This is the least that could be demanded of speculative philosophy, which undertakes
25 to connect the ethical end with physical ends by means of the idea of a single end.. Yet even this little is still far more than it can ever accomplish.

Let us look at the matter from the standpoint of the principle of the theoretical reflective judgement. To account for the final
30 products of nature are we not justified in assuming a supreme cause of nature, whose causality in respect of the actuality of nature, or whose act of creation, must be regarded as specifically different from that which is required for the mechanism of nature, or, in other words, as the causality of an understanding ?

If we are, then, on the above principle, we should say that we were also sufficiently justified in attributing to this original being, not merely ends prevalent throughout nature, but also a final end. This does not serve the purpose of proving the existence of such a being, yet, at least, as was the case in the physical teleology, it is a justification sufficient to convince us that to make the possibility of such a world intelligible to ourselves we must not merely look to ends, but must also ascribe its real existence to an underlying final end.

But a final end is simply a conception of our practical reason and cannot be inferred from any data of experience for the purpose of forming a theoretical estimate of nature, nor can it be applied to the cognition of nature. The only possible use of this conception is for practical reason according to moral laws ; and the final end of creation is such a constitution of the world as harmonizes with what we can only definitely specify according to laws, namely with the final end of our pure practical reason and of this, moreover, so far as intended to be practical.—Now, by virtue of the moral law which enjoins this final end upon us, we have reason for assuming from a practical point of view, that is for the direction of our energies towards the realization of that end, that it is possible, or, in other words, practicable. Consequently we are also justified in assuming a nature of things harmonizing with such a possibility—for this possibility is subject to a condition which does not lie in our power, and unless nature played into our hands the realization of the final end would be impossible. Hence, we have a moral justification for supposing that where we have a world we have also a final end of creation.

This does not yet bring us to the inference from moral teleology to a theology, that is, to the existence of a moral Author of the world, but only to a final end of creation, which is defined in the above manner. Now must we, to account for this creation,

that is, for the real existence of things conformable to a *final end*, in the first place admit an intelligent being, and, in the second place, not merely an intelligent being—as had to be admitted to account for the possibility of such things in nature as we are
5 compelled to estimate as *ends*—but one that is also *moral*, as Author of the world, and consequently a *God*? This admission involves a further inference, and one of such a nature that we see that it is intended for the power of judging by conceptions of practical reason, and, being so, is drawn for the reflective, not
10 for the determinant judgement. It is true that with us morally practical reason is essentially different in its principles from technically practical reason. But, while this is so, we cannot pretend to see that the same distinction must also hold in the case of the supreme world-cause, if it is assumed to be an intelli-
15 gence, and that a peculiar type of causality is required on its part for the final end, different from that which is requisite simply for natural ends, or, that we have, consequently, in our final end, not merely a *moral ground* for admitting a final end of creation, as an effect, but also a *moral being*, as the original source of
20 creation. But it is quite competent for us to assert that *the nature of our faculty of reason is such* that without an Author and Governor of the world, who is also a moral Lawgiver, we are wholly unable to render intelligible to ourselves the possibility of a finality, related *to the moral law* and its Object, such as exists
25 in this final end.

The actuality of a supreme morally legislative Author is, there- 456 fore, sufficiently proved simply *for the praçtical employment* of our reason, without determining anything theoretically in respect of its existence. For reason has an end which is prescribed inde-
30 pendently by its own peculiar legislation. To make this end possible it requires an idea which removes, sufficiently for the reflective judgement, the obstacle which arises from our inability to carry such legislation into effect when we have a mere physical conception of the world. In that way this idea acquires practical

reality, although for speculative knowledge it fails of every means
that would procure it reality from a theoretical point of view
for explaining nature or determining its supreme cause.   For
theoretical reflective judgement an intelligent world-cause was
sufficiently proved by physical teleology from the ends of nature. 5
For the practical reflective judgement moral teleology effects
the same by means of the conception of a final end, which it is
obliged to ascribe to creation from a practical point of view.
The objective reality of the idea of God, regarded as a moral
Author of the world, cannot, it is true, be substantiated by means 10
of physical ends *alone*. Nevertheless, when the knowledge of
those ends is associated with that of the moral end, the maxim of
pure reason which directs us to pursue unity of principles so far
as we are able to do so lends considerable importance to these
ends for the purpose of reinforcing the practical reality of that 15
idea by the reality which it already possesses from a theoretical
point of view for judgement.

In this connexion there are two points which it is most
necessary to note for the purpose of preventing a misunderstand-
ing which might easily arise. In the first place these attributes of 20
the Supreme Being can only be *conceived* by us on an analogy.
For how are we to investigate its nature when experience can
show us nothing similar ? In the second place, such attributes
also only enable us to conceive a Supreme Being, not to *cognize*
it or to predicate them of it in a more or less theoretical manner. 25
For this could only be done on behalf of the determinant judgement, as a faculty of our reason in its speculative aspect, and
for the purpose of discerning the *intrinsic nature* of the supreme
world-cause. But the only question that concerns us here is as
to what conception we have, by the structure of our cognitive 30
faculties, to form of this Being, and whether we have to admit
its existence on account of an end, which pure practical reason,
apart from any such assumption, enjoins upon us to realize as far

as in us lies, and for which we seek likewise to procure simply practical reality, that is to say, merely to be able to regard a contemplated effect as possible. It may well be that the above conception is transcendent for speculative reason. The attributes 457 also which by means of it we ascribe to the Being in question may, objectively used, involve a latent anthropomorphism. Yet the object which we have in view in employing them is not that we wish to determine the nature of that Being by reference to them—a nature which is inaccessible to us—but rather that we seek to use them for determining our own selves and our will. We may name a cause after the conception which we have of its effect—though only in respect of the relation in which it stands to this effect. And we may do this without on that account seeking to define intrinsically the inherent nature of that cause by the only properties known to us of causes of that kind, which properties must be given to us by experience. We may, for instance, ascribe to the soul, among other properties, a *vis loco-motiva*, because physical movements are actually started, the cause of which lies in the mental representation of them. But this we do without on that account meaning to attribute to the soul the only kind of dynamical force of which we have any knowledge—that is, force exerted by attraction, pressure, impact, and, consequently, by means of a movement, which forces always presuppose a being extended in space. Now in just the same way we have to assume *something* that contains the ground of the possibility and practical reality, or practicability, of a necessary moral final end. But, looking to the character of the effect expected therefrom, we may conceive this ' something ' as a wise Being ruling the world according to moral laws. And, con-formably to the frame of our cognitive faculties, we are obliged to conceive it as a cause of things that is distinct from nature, for the sole purpose of expressing the *relation* in which this being that transcends all our cognitive faculties stands to the Object of *our* practical reason. Yet in so doing we do not mean on that

account to ascribe to this being theoretically the only causality
of this kind familiar to us, namely an understanding and a will.
Nay more, even as to the causality which we think exists in this
Being in respect of what is *for us* a final end, we do not mean to
differentiate it objectively, as it exists in this being itself, from 5
the causality in respect of nature and all its final modes.   On the
contrary we only presume to be able to admit this distinction as
one subjectively necessary for our cognitive faculty, constituted
as it is, and as valid for the reflective, and not for the objectively
determinant judgement.   But, once the question touches practi- 10
cal matters, a *regulative* principle of this kind—one for prudence
or wisdom to follow—which directs us to act in conformity with
something, as an end, the possibility of which, by the frame of
our cognitive faculties, can only be conceived by us in a certain
manner, then becomes also *constitutive*.   In other words it is 15
practically determinant, whereas the very same principle regarded as one upon which to estimate the objective possibility
of things is in no way theoretically determinant, or, in other
words, does not imply that the only type of possibility which our
458 thinking faculty recognizes may also be predicated of the Object 20
of our thought.   On the contrary it is a mere *regulative* principle
for the use of reflective judgement.

Remark.

This moral proof is not in any sense a newly discovered argument, but at the most only an old one in a new form.   For its germ
was lying in the mind of man when his reason first quickened 25
into life, and it only grew and ever developed with the progressive culture of that faculty.   The moment mankind began
to reflect upon right and wrong—at a time when men's eyes
as yet cast but a heedless regard at the finality of nature,
and when they took advantage of it without imagining the 30
presence of anything but nature's accustomed course—one

inevitable judgement must have forced itself upon them. It
could never be that the issue is all alike, whether a man has
acted fairly or falsely, with equity or with violence, albeit to his
life's end, as far at least as human eye can see, his virtues have
5 brought him no reward, his transgressions no punishment. It
seems as though they perceived a voice within them say that
it must make a difference. So there must also have been a
lurking notion, however obscure, of something after which they
felt themselves bound to strive, and with which such a result
10 would be wholly discordant, or with which, once they regarded
the course of the natural world as the sole order of things, they
would then be unable to reconcile that significant bent of their
minds. Now crude as are the various notions they might form
of the way in which such an irregularity could be put straight—
15 and it is one that must be far more revolting to the human mind
than the blind chance which some have sought to make the
underlying principle of their estimate of nature—there is only
one principle upon which they could even conceive it possible for
nature to harmonize with the moral law dwelling within them.
20 It is that of a Supreme Cause ruling the world according to moral
laws. For a final end within, that is set before them as a duty,
and a nature without, that has no final end, though in it the
former end is to be actualized, are in open contradiction. I
admit they might hatch many absurdities anent the inner nature
25 of that world-cause. But that relation to the moral order in the
government of the world always remained the same as is universally comprehensible to the most untutored reason, so far as
it treats itself as practical, though speculative reason is far from 459
being able to keep pace with it.—Further, in all probability, it
30 was this moral interest that first aroused attentiveness to beauty
and the ends of nature. This would be admirably calculated to
strengthen the above idea, though it could not supply its foundation. Still less could it dispense with the moral interest ; for it
is only in relation to the final end that the very study of the ends

of nature acquires that immediate interest displayed to so great an extent in the admiration bestowed upon nature without regard to any accruing advantage.

§ 28 (89)

The use of the moral argument.

THE fact that, in respect of all our ideas of the supersensible, reason is restricted to the conditions of its practical employment, is of obvious use in connexion with the idea of God. It prevents *theology* from losing itself in the clouds of THEOSOPHY, i.e. in transcendent conceptions that confuse reason, or from sinking into the depths of DEMONOLOGY, i.e. an anthropomorphic mode of representing the Supreme Being. Also it keeps *religion* from falling into *theurgy*, which is a fanatical delusion that a feeling can be communicated to us from other supersensible beings and that we in turn can exert an influence on them, or into *idolatry*, which is a superstitious delusion that one can make oneself acceptable to the Supreme Being by other means than that of having the moral law at heart.[1]

For if the vanity or presumption of those who would argue about what lies beyond the world of sense is allowed to determine even the smallest point theoretically, and so as to extend our knowledge ; if any boast is permitted of light upon the existence and constitution of the divine nature, its intelligence and will, and the laws of both these and the attributes which issue there-

[1] A religion is never free from the imputation of idolatry, in a practical sense, so long as the attributes with which it endows the Supreme Being are such that anything that man may do can be taken as in accordance with God's will on any other all-sufficing condition than that of morality. For however pure and free from sensuous images the form of that conception may be from a theoretical point of view, yet, with such attributes, it is from a practical point of view depicted as an idol—the nature of God's will, that is to say, is represented anthropomorphically.

from and influence the world : I should like to know at what
precise point the line is going to be drawn for these pretensions 460
of reason. From whatever source such light is derived still more
may be expected—if, as the idea is, we only rack our brains.
5 Yet it is only on some principle that bounds can be set to such
claims—it is not enough simply to appeal to our experience of
the fact that all attempts of the sort have so far miscarried ;
for that is no disproof of the possibility of a better result. But
the only principle possible in this case is either that of admitting
10 that in respect of the supersensible absolutely nothing can be
determined theoretically (unless solely by way of bare negation),
or that of supposing the existence in our reason of an as yet un-
opened mine of who knows how vast and enlightening information reserved for us and our posterity.—But the result, so far as
15 concerns religion—that is, morality in relation to God as Lawgiver—would be that morality, supposing that the theoretical
knowledge of God has to take the lead, must then conform to
theology. Thus not alone will an extrinsic and arbitrary legislation on the part of a Supreme Being have to be introduced in
20 place of an immanent and necessary legislation of reason, but,
even in such legislation, all the defects of our insight into the
divine nature must spread to the ethical code, and religion in
this way be divorced from morality and perverted.

What now of the hope of a future life ? It is open to us to look
25 to the final end which, in obedience to the injunction of the
moral law, we have ourselves to fulfil, and to adopt it as a guide
to the verdict of reason on our destination—a verdict which is
therefore only regarded as necessary or worthy of acceptance
from a practical point of view. But if, instead of so doing, we
30 consult our faculty of theoretical knowledge, then the same lot
befalls psychology in this connexion as befell theology in the
case above. It supplies no more than a negative conception
of our thinking being. It tells us that not one of the operations of the mind or manifestations of the internal sense can be

B b

explained on materialistic lines ; that, accordingly, no enlightening or determinant judgement as to the separate nature of what
thinks, or of the continuance or discontinuance of its personality
after death, can possibly be passed on speculative grounds by any
exercise of our faculty of theoretical knowledge.   Thus everything is here left to the teleological estimate of our existence from
a point of view that is necessary in the practical sphere, and to
the assumption of the continuance of our existence, as a condition required by the final end that is absolutely imposed upon
us by reason.   Hence in our negative result we see at once a gain
—a gain that at first sight no doubt appears a loss.   For just as
461 theology can never become theosophy, so rational *psychology*
can never become *pneumatology*, as a science that extends our
knowledge, nor yet, on the other hand, be in danger of lapsing
into any sort of *materialism*.   On the contrary we see that it is
really a mere anthropology of the internal sense, a knowledge,
that is to say, of our thinking self *as alive*, and that, in the form
of a theoretical cognition, it also remains merely empirical.   But,
as concerned with the problem of our eternal existence, rational
psychology is not a theoretical science at all.   It rests upon a
single inference of moral teleology, just as the entire necessity
of its employment arises out of moral teleology and our practical
vocation.

§ 29 (90)

The type of assurance in a teleological proof of the existence of God.

WHETHER a proof is derived from immediate empirical
presentation of what is to be proved, as in the case of proof by
observation of the object or by experiment, or whether it is
derived *a priori* by reason from principles, what is primarily
required of it is that it should not *persuade*, but *convince*, or at
least tend to convince.   The argument or inference, in other

words, should not be simply a subjective, or aesthetic, ground of
assent—a mere semblance—but should be objectively valid and
a logical source of knowledge. If it is not this, intelligence is
taken in, not won over. An illusory proof of the type in question
5 is brought forward in natural theology—maybe with the best
of intentions, but nevertheless with a deliberate concealment
of its weakness. The whole host of evidences of an origin of
the things of nature according to the principle of ends is mar-
shalled before us, and capital is made out of the purely subjective
10 foundation of human reason. The latter is inclined of its own
proper motion, wherever it can do so without contradiction, to
think one single principle in place of several. Also, where this
principle only provides one, or, it may be, a large proportion, of
the terms necessary for defining a conception, it supplements
15 this or these by adding the others, so as to complete the conception of the thing by an arbitrary integration. For naturally,
when we find such a number of products of nature pointing us to
an intelligent cause, should we not suppose one single such cause
in preference to supposing a plurality of them ? And why, then,
20 stop at great intelligence, might, and so forth, in this cause, and 462
not rather endow it with omniscience and omnipotence, and, in
a word, regard it as one that contains an ample source of such
attributes for all possible things ? And why not go on and
ascribe to this single all-powerful primordial being, not merely
25 the intelligence necessary for the laws and products of nature,
but also the supreme ethical and practical reason that belongs
to a moral world-cause ? For by this completion of the concept
we are supplied with a principle that meets the joint requirements alike of insight into nature and moral wisdom—and no
30 objection of the least substance can be brought against the
possibility of such an idea. If now, in the course of this argument, the moral springs that stir the mind are touched, and a
lively interest imparted to them with all the force of rhetoric—
of which they are quite worthy—a persuasion arises of the

objective sufficiency of the proof, and, in most cases where it is used, an even beneficent illusion that disdains any examination of its logical accuracy, and in fact abhors and sets its face against logical criticism, as if it sprang from some impious misgiving.— Now there is really nothing to say against all this, so long as we only take popular expediency into consideration. But we cannot and should not be deterred from the analysis of the proof into the two heterogeneous elements which this argument involves, namely into so much as pertains to physical, and so much as pertains to moral teleology. For the fusing of both elements prevents our recognizing where the real nerve of the proof lies, or in what part or in what way it must be reshaped, so that its validity may be able to be upheld under the most searching examination—even though on some points we should be compelled to confess that reason sees but a short way. Hence, the philosopher finds it his duty—supposing that he were even to pay no regard to what he owes to sincerity—to expose the illusion, however wholesome, which such a confusion can produce. He must segregate what is mere matter of persuasion from what leads to conviction—two modes of assent that differ not merely in degree but in kind—so as to be able to present openly in all its clearness the attitude which the mind adopts in this proof, and to subject it frankly to the most rigorous test.

Now a proof which is directed towards conviction may be of one or other of two kinds. It may be intended to decide what the object is *in itself*, or else what it is *for us*, that is, for man in the abstract, according to the rational principles on which it is necessarily estimated by us. It may, in other words, be a proof κατ' ἀλήθειαν or one κατ' ἄνθρωπον—taking the latter word in the broad sense of man in the abstract. In the first case it is founded on principles adequate for the determinant judgement, in the second on such as are adequate merely for the reflective judgement. Where, in the latter case, a proof rests simply on theoretical principles, it can never tend towards conviction. But if it is founded on a practical principle of reason, one which, consequently, is universal and necessary, it may well lay claim to a conviction that is sufficient from a practical point of view, 5 that is to a moral conviction. But a proof *tends towards conviction*, though without producing conviction, if it merely puts us on the road to conviction. This it does where it only involves objective sources of conviction which, while as yet insufficient to produce certitude, are nevertheless of such a kind that they 10 are not subjective grounds of judgement, which, as such, serve merely for persuasion.

Now all arguments that establish a theoretical proof are sufficient either : (1) for proof by logically rigorous *syllogistic inferences* ; or, where this is not the case, (2) for inference by 15 *analogy* ; or, should even such inference be absent, still (3) for *probable opinion* ; or, finally, for what is least of all, (4) the assumption of a merely possible source of explanation as an *hypothesis.*—Now I assert that all arguments without exception that tend towards theoretical conviction, are powerless to pro- 20 duce any assurance of the above type, from its highest degree to its lowest, *where* the proposition that is to be proved is the real existence of an original being, regarded as a God in the sense appropriate to the complete content of this conception, that is to say, regarded as a *moral* Author of the world, and, conse- 25 quently, in such a way that the final end of creation is at once derived from Him.

1. The Critique has abundantly shown how the matter stands as regards proof in *strict logical form*—advancing, that is, from universal to particular. No intuition corresponding to the con- 30 ception of a being which has to be sought beyond nature is possible for us. So far, therefore, as that conception has to be determined theoretically by synthetic predicates, it always remains for us a problematical conception. Hence, there exists absolutely no cognition of such a being that would in the smallest

degree enlarge the compass of our theoretical knowledge.   The
particular conception of a supersensible being cannot possibly be
subsumed in any way under the universal principles of the nature
of things, so as to allow of its being determined by inference
464 from those principles, for they are solely valid for nature as an 5
object of sense.

2.   In the case of two dissimilar things we may admittedly
form some *conception* of one of them by an *analogy* [1] which it

---

[1]   *Analogy*, in a qualitative sense, is the identity of the relation
subsisting between grounds and consequences—causes and effects—
so far as such identity subsists despite the specific difference of the
things, or of those properties, considered in themselves (i. e. apart
from this relation), which are the source of similar consequences.
Thus when we compare the formative operations of the lower animals
with those of man, we regard the unknown source of such effects in
the former case, as compared with the known source of similar effects
produced by man, that is by reason, as the analogon of reason.   By
this we mean to imply that while the source of the formative capacity
of the lower animals, to which we give the name of instinct, is in fact
specifically different from reason, yet, comparing, say, the construc-
tive work of beavers and men, it stands in a like relation to its
effect.—But this does not justify me in inferring that, because man
employs *reason* for what he constructs, beavers must possess reason
also, and in calling this an *inference* from analogy.   But from the
similar mode of operation on the part of the lower animals, the source
of which we are unable directly to perceive, compared with that of
man, of which we are immediately conscious, we may quite correctly
infer, *on the strength of the analogy*, that the lower animals, like man,
act according to *representations*, and are not machines, as Descartes
contends, and that, despite their specific difference, they are living
beings and as such generally kindred to man.   The principle that
authorizes us to draw this inference lies in the fact that we have
exactly the same reason for putting the lower animals in this respect
in the same genus with men as in man for putting men, so far as we
look at them from the outside and compare their acts, in the same
genus with one another.   There is *par ratio*.   In the same way the
causality of the supreme world-cause may be conceived on the
analogy of an understanding, if we compare its final products in
the world with the formative works of man, but we cannot, on the
strength of the analogy, infer such human attributes in the world-
cause.   For the principle that would make such a mode of reasoning

bears to the other, and do so even on the point on which they
are dissimilar ; but from that in which they are dissimilar we
cannot draw any *inference* from one to the other on the strength
of the analogy—that is, we cannot transfer the mark of the
5 specific difference to the second. Thus on the analogy of the law
of the equality of action and reaction in the mutual attraction 465
and repulsion of bodies I am able to picture to my mind the
social relations of the members of a commonwealth regulated
by civil laws ; but I cannot transfer to these relations the former
10 specific modes, that is, physical attraction and repulsion, and
ascribe them to the citizens, so as to constitute a system called
a state.—In the same way the causality of the original being
may, in its relation to the things of the world, regarded as
physical ends, quite properly be conceived on the analogy of an
15 intelligence, regarded as the source of the forms of certain products that we call works of art. For this is only done in the
interests of the theoretical or practical use which our cognitive
faculty has to make of this conception when dealing with the
things in the world. But from the fact that with the beings of
20 the world intelligence must be ascribed to the cause of an effect
that is considered artificial, we are wholly unable to infer by
analogy that, in relation to nature, the very same causality that
we perceive in man belongs also to the being which is entirely
distinct from nature. The reason is that this touches the precise
25 point of dissimilarity between a cause that is sensuously conditioned in respect of its effects and a supersensible original
being. This dissimilarity is implied in the very conception of
such a supersensible being, and the distinguishing feature cannot

possible is absent in this case, namely the *paritas rationis* for including the supreme being and man, in relation to their respective
causalities, in one and the same genus. The causality of the beings
in the world which, like causality by means of understanding, is
always sensuously conditioned, cannot be transferred to a being
which has no generic conception in common with man beyond that
of a thing in the abstract.

therefore be transferred to it.—In this very fact, that I am required to conceive the causality of the Deity only on the analogy of an understanding—a faculty which is not known to us in any other being besides man, subject, as he is, to the conditions of sense—lies the prohibition that forbids me to ascribe to God an understanding in the proper sense of the word.[1]

3. There is no room for *opinion* in *a priori* judgements. Such judgements, on the contrary, enable us to cognize something as quite certain, or else give us no cognition at all. But even where the given premisses from which we start are empirical, as are the natural ends in the present case, yet they cannot help us to form any opinion that extends beyond the world of sense, and to such rash judgements we cannot accord the least claim to probability. For probability is a fraction of a possible certainty distributed over a particular series of grounds—the grounds of the possibility within the series being compared with the sufficient ground of certainty, as a part is compared with a whole. Here the insufficient ground must be capable of being increased to the point of sufficiency. But these grounds, being the determining grounds of the certainty of one and the same judgement, must be of the same order. For unless they are, they would not, when taken together, form a quantum—such as certainty is. Thus one component part cannot lie within the bounds of possible experience, and another lie beyond all possible experience. Consequently, since premisses that are simply empirical do not lead to anything supersensible, nothing can supplement the imperfection of such an empirical series. Not the smallest approximation, therefore, occurs in the attempt to reach the supersensible, or a knowledge of it, from such premisses ; and

[1] This does not involve the smallest loss to our representation of the relation in which this Being stands to the world, so far as concerns the consequences, theoretical or practical, of this conception. To seek to inquire into the intrinsic nature of this Being is a curiosity as senseless as idle.

consequently no probability enters into a judgement about the supersensible, when it rests on arguments drawn from experience.

4. If anything is intended to serve as an *hypothesis* for explaining the possibility of a given phenomenon, then at least the possibility of that thing must be perfectly certain. We give away enough when, in the case of an hypothesis, we waive the knowledge of actual existence—which is affirmed in an opinion put forward as probable—and more than this we cannot surrender. At least the possibility of what we make the basis of an explanation must be open to no doubt, otherwise there would be no end to empty fictions of the brain. But it would be taking things for granted without anything whatever to go upon, if we were to assume the possibility of a supersensible Being defined according to positive conceptions, for no one of the conditions requisite for cognition, so far as concerns the element dependent on intuition, is given. Hence, all that is left as the criterion of this possibility is the principle of contradiction—which can only prove the possibility of the thought and not of the thought object itself.

The net result is that for the existence of the original being, regarded as a Deity, or of the psychic substance, regarded as an immortal soul, it is absolutely impossible for human reason to obtain any proof from a theoretical point of view, so as to produce the smallest degree of assurance. And there is a perfectly intelligible reason for this, since we have no available material for defining the idea of the supersensible, seeing that we should have to draw that material from things in the world of sense, and then its character would make it utterly inappropriate to the supersensible. In the absence, therefore, of all definition, we are left merely with the conception of a not-sensible something containing the ultimate ground of the world of sense. This constitutes no cognition of its intrinsic nature, such as would amplify the conception.

467   § 30 (91)

The type of assurance produced by a practical faith.

If we look merely to the manner in which something can be
an Object of knowledge (*res cognoscibilis*) *for us*, that is, having
regard to the subjective nature of our powers of representation,
we do not in that case compare our conceptions with the objects,
but merely with our faculties of cognition and the use that they 5
are able to make of the given representation from a theoretical
or practical point of view.   So the question whether something
is a cognizable entity or not, is a question which touches, not
the possibility of the things themselves, but the possibility of
our knowledge of them.   10

Things *cognizable* are of three kinds :   *matters of opinion*
(*opinabile*), *matters of fact* (*scibile*), *and matters of faith* (*mere
credibile*).

1. The objects of mere ideas of reason, being wholly incapable
of presentation, on behalf of theoretical knowledge, in any 15
possible experience whatever, are to that extent also things
altogether *unknowable*, and, consequently, we cannot even *form
an opinion* about them.   For to form an opinion *a priori* is
absurd on the face of it and the straight road to pure figments of
the brain.   Either our *a priori* proposition is certain, therefore, 20
or it involves no element of assurance at all.   Hence, *matters
of opinion* are always Objects of an empirical knowledge that
is at least intrinsically possible.   They are, in other words,
objects belonging to the world of sense, but objects of which
an empirical knowledge is impossible *for us* because the degree 25
of empirical knowledge we possess is as it is.   Thus the ether
of our modern physicists—an elastic fluid interpenetrating all
other substances and completely permeating them—is a mere
matter of opinion, yet it is in all respects of such a kind that it

could be perceived if our external senses were sharpened to the highest degree, but its presentation can never be the subject of any observation or experiment. To assume rational inhabitants of other planets is a matter of opinion ; for if we could get
5 nearer the planets, which is intrinsically possible, experience would decide whether such inhabitants are there or not ; but as we never shall get so near to them, the matter remains one of opinion. But to entertain an opinion that there exist in the material universe pure unembodied thinking spirits is mere
10 romancing—supposing, I mean, that we dismiss from our notice, as well we may, certain phenomena that have been passed off for such. Such a notion is not a matter of opinion at all, but an 468 idea pure and simple. It is what remains over when we take away from a thinking being all that is material and yet let it
15 keep its thought. But whether, when we have taken away everything else, the thought—which we only know in man, that is in connexion with a body—would still remain, is a matter we are unable to decide. A thing like this is a *fictitious logical entity* (*ens rationis ratiocinantis*), not a *rational entity* (*ens rationis*
20 *ratiocinatae*). With the latter it is anyway possible to substantiate the objective reality of its conception, at least in a manner sufficient for the practical employment of reason, for this employment, which has its peculiar and apodictically certain *a priori* principles, in fact demands and postulates that conception.
25 2. The objects that answer to conceptions whose objective reality can be proved are *matters of fact* [1] (*res facti*). Such proof may be afforded by pure reason or by experience, and in the former case may be from theoretical or practical data of reason,

---

[1] I here extend the conception of a matter of fact beyond the usual meaning of the term, and, I think, rightly. For it is not necessary, and indeed not practicable, to restrict this expression to actual experience where we are speaking of the relation of things to our cognitive faculties, as we do not need more than a merely possible experience to enable us to speak of things as objects of a definite kind of knowledge.

but in all cases it must be effected by means of an intuition corresponding to the conceptions. Examples of matters of fact are the mathematical properties of geometrical magnitudes, for they admit of *a priori presentation* for the theoretical employment of reason. Further, things or qualities of things that are 5 capable of being verified by experience, be it one's own personal experience or that of others (supported by evidence), are in the same way matters of fact.—But there is this notable point, that one idea of reason, strange to say, is to be found among the matters of fact—an idea which does not of itself admit of any 10 presentation in intuition, or, consequently, of any theoretical proof of its possibility. The idea in question is that of *freedom.* Its reality is the reality of a particular kind of causality (the conception of which would be transcendent if considered theoretically), and as a causality of that kind it admits of 15 verification by means of practical laws of pure reason and in the actual actions that take place in obedience to them, and, consequently, in experience.—It is the only one of all the ideas of pure reason whose object is a matter of fact and must be included among the *scibilia.* 20

469 3. Objects that must be thought *a priori,* either as consequences or as grounds, if pure practical reason is to be used as duty commands, but which are transcendent for the theoretical use of reason, are mere *matters of faith.* Such is the *summum bonum* which has to be realized in the world through freedom— 25 a conception whose objective reality cannot be proved in any experience possible for us, or, consequently, so as to satisfy the requirements of the theoretical employment of reason, while at the same time we are enjoined to use it for the purpose of realizing that end through pure practical reason in the best way possible, 30 and, accordingly, its possibility must be assumed. This effect which is commanded, *together with the only conditions on which its possibility is conceivable by us,* namely the existence of God and

the immortality of the soul, are *matters of faith (res fidei)* and,
moreover, are of all objects the only ones that can be so called.[1]
For although we have to believe what we can only learn by
testimony from the experience of others, yet that does not make
5 what is so believed in itself a matter of faith, for with *one* of
those witnesses it was personal experience and matter of fact, or
is assumed to have been so. In addition it must be possible to
arrive at knowledge by this path—the path of historical faith ;
and the Objects of history and geography, as, in general, every-
10 thing that the nature of our cognitive faculties makes at least
a possible subject of knowledge, are to be classed among matters
of fact, not matters of faith. It is only objects of pure reason
that can be matters of faith at all, and even they must then not
be regarded as objects simply of pure speculative reason ; for
15 this does not enable them to be reckoned with any certainty
whatever among matters, or Objects, of that knowledge which
is possible for us. They are ideas, that is conceptions, whose
objective reality cannot be guaranteed theoretically. On the
other hand, the supreme final end to be realized by us, which is
20 all that can make us worthy of being ourselves the final end of
a creation, is an idea that has objective reality for us in practical
matters, and is a matter. But since we cannot procure objective
reality for this conception from a theoretical point of view, it is 470
a mere matter of faith on the part of pure reason, as are also God
25 and immortality, they being the sole conditions under which,
owing to the frame of our human reason, we are able to conceive
the possibility of that effect of the use of our freedom according
to law. But assurance in matters of faith is an assurance from

[1] Being a matter of faith does not make a thing an *article of faith*,
if by articles of faith we mean such matters of faith as one can be
bound to *acknowledge*, inwardly or outwardly—a kind therefore that
does not enter into natural theology. For, being matters of faith,
they cannot, like matters of fact, depend on theoretical proofs, and,
therefore, the assurance is a free assurance, and it is only as such that
it is compatible with the morality of the subject.

a purely practical point of view. It is a moral faith that proves nothing for pure rational knowledge as theoretical, but only for it as practical and directed to the fulfilment of its obligations. It in no way extends either speculation or the practical rules of prudence actuated by the principle of self-love. If the supreme principle of all moral laws is a postulate, this involves the possibility of its supreme Object, and, consequently, the condition under which we are able to conceive such possibility, being also postulated. This does not make the cognition of the latter any knowledge or any opinion of the existence or nature of these conditions, as a mode of theoretical knowledge, but a mere assumption, confined to matters practical and commanded in practical interests, on behalf of the moral use of our reason.

Were we able with any plausibility to make the ends of nature which physical teleology sets before us in such abundance the basis of a *determinate* conception of an intelligent world-cause, the existence of this being would not even then be a matter of faith. For as it would not be assumed on behalf of the performance of our duty, but only for the purpose of explaining nature, it would simply be the opinion and hypothesis best suited to our reason. Now the teleology in question does not lead in any way to a determinate conception of God. On the contrary such a conception can only be found in that of a moral author of the world, because this alone assigns the final end to which we can attach ourselves only so far as we live in accordance with what the moral law prescribes to us as the final end, and, consequently, imposes upon us as a duty. Hence, it is only by relation to the Object of our duty, as the condition which makes its final end possible, that the conception of God acquires the privilege of figuring in our assurance as a matter of faith. On the other hand, this very same conception cannot make its Object valid as a matter of fact, for although the necessity of duty is quite plain for practical reason, yet the attainment of its final end, so far as it does not lie entirely in our own hands, is merely assumed in the interests of the practical employment of reason, and, there- 471 fore, is not practically necessary in the way duty itself is.[1]

Faith as *habitus*, not as *actus*, is the moral attitude of reason in its assurance of the truth of what is beyond the reach of theoretical knowledge. It is the stedfast principle of the mind, therefore, according to which the truth of what must necessarily be presupposed as the condition of the supreme final end being possible is assumed as true in consideration of the fact that we

---

[1] The final end which we are enjoined by the moral law to pursue is not the foundation of duty. For duty lies in the moral law which, being a formal practical principle, directs categorically, irrespective of the Objects of the faculty of desire—the subject-matter of volition—and, consequently, of any end whatever. This formal character of our actions—their subordination to the principle of universal validity—which alone constitutes their intrinsic moral worth, lies entirely in our own power ; and we can quite easily make abstraction from the possibility or the impracticability of the ends that we are obliged to promote in accordance with that law—for they only form the extrinsic worth of our actions. Thus we put them out of consideration, as what does not lie altogether in our own power, in order to concentrate our attention on what rests in our own hands. But the object in view—the furthering of the final end of all rational beings, namely, happiness so far as consistent with duty—is nevertheless imposed upon us by the law of duty. But speculative reason does not in any way perceive the practicability of that object— whether we look at it from the standpoint of our own physical power or from that of the co-operation of nature. On the contrary, so far as we are able to form a rational judgement on the point, speculative reason must, apart from the assumption of the existence of God and immortality, regard it as a baseless and idle, though well-intentioned, expectation, to hope that mere nature, internal or external, will from such causes bring about such a result of our good conduct, and could it have perfect certainty as to the truth of this judgement, it would have to look on the moral law itself as a mere delusion of our reason in respect of practical matters. But speculative reason is fully convinced that the latter can never happen, whereas those ideas whose object lies beyond nature may be thought without contradiction. Hence for the sake of its own practical law and the task which it imposes, and, therefore, in respect of moral concerns, it must recognize those ideas to be real, in order not to fall into self-contradiction.

are under an obligation to pursue that end [1]—and assumed notwithstanding that we have no insight into its possibility, though
likewise none into its impossibility. Faith, in the plain acceptation of the term, is a confidence of attaining a purpose the furthering of which is a duty, but whose achievement is a thing of which
we are unable to *perceive* the possibility—or, consequently, the
possibility of what we can alone conceive to be its conditions.
Thus the faith that has reference to particular objects is entirely
a matter of morality, provided such objects are not objects of
possible knowledge or opinion, in which latter case, and above all
in matters of history, it must be called credulity and not faith. It
is a free assurance, not of any matter for which dogmatic proofs
can be found for the theoretical determinant judgement, nor of
what we consider a matter of obligation, but of that which we
assume in the interests of a purpose which we set before ourselves in accordance with laws of freedom. But this does not
mean that it is adopted like an opinion formed on inadequate
grounds. On the contrary it is something that has a foundation
in reason (though only in relation to its practical employment),

---

[1] It is a confidence in the promise of the moral law. But this
promise is not regarded as one involved in the moral law itself, but
rather as one which we import into it, and so import on morally
adequate grounds. For a final end cannot be commanded by any
law of reason, unless reason, though it be with uncertain voice, also
promises its attainability, and at the same time authorizes assurance
as to the sole conditions under which our reason can imagine such
attainability. The very word *fides* expresses this ; and it must seem
suspicious how this expression and this particular idea get a place in
moral philosophy, since it was first introduced with Christianity, and
its acceptance might perhaps seem only a flattering imitation of the
language of the latter. But this is not the only case in which this
wonderful religion has in the great simplicity of its statement en-
riched philosophy with far more definite and purer conceptions of
morality than morality itself could have previously supplied. But
once these conceptions are found, they are *freely* approved by reason,
which adopts them as conceptions at which it could quite well have
arrived itself and which it might and ought to have introduced.

and *a foundation that satisfies the purpose of reason*. For without it, when the moral attitude comes into collision with theoretical reason and fails to satisfy its demand for a proof of the possibility of the Object of morality, it loses all its stability, and wavers
5 between practical commands and theoretical doubts. To be *incredulous* is to adhere to the maxim of placing no reliance on testimony ; but a person is *unbelieving* who denies all validity to the above ideas of reason because their reality has no theoretical foundation. Hence, such a person judges dogmatically. But a
10 dogmatic *unbelief* cannot stand side by side with a moral maxim governing the attitude of the mind—for reason cannot command one to pursue an end that is recognized to be nothing but a fiction of the brain. But the case is different with a *doubtful faith*. For with such a faith the want of conviction from grounds
15 of speculative reason is only an obstacle—one which a critical insight into the limits of this faculty can deprive of any influence upon conduct and for which it can make amends by a paramount 473 practical assurance.

.   .   .   .

If we desire to replace certain mistaken efforts in philosophy,
20 and to introduce a different principle, and gain influence for it, it gives great satisfaction to see just how and why such attempts were bound to miscarry.

God, freedom, and the *immortality of the soul* are the problems to whose solution, as their ultimate and unique goal, all the
25 laborious preparations of metaphysics are directed. Now it was believed that the doctrine of freedom was only necessary as a negative condition for practical philosophy, whereas that of God and the nature of the soul, being part of theoretical philosophy, had to be proved independently and separately. Then each
30 of those two conceptions was subsequently to be united with what is commanded by the moral law (which is only possible on terms of freedom) and a religion was to be arrived at in this way. But we perceive at once that such attempts were bound to mis-

C C

carry. For from simple ontological conceptions of things in the
abstract, or of the existence of a necessary being, we can form
absolutely no conception of an original being determined by
predicates which admit of being given in experience and which
are therefore available for cognition. But should the conception 5
be founded on experience of the physical finality of nature, it
could then in turn supply no proof adequate for morality or,
consequently, the cognition of a God. Just as little could knowledge of the soul drawn from experience—which we can only
obtain in this life—furnish a conception of its spiritual and im- 10
mortal nature, or, consequently, one that would satisfy morality.
Theology and *pneumatology*, regarded as problems framed in the
interests of sciences pursued by a speculative reason, are in their
very implication transcendent for all our faculties of knowledge,
and cannot, therefore, be established by means of any empirical 15
data or predicates.—These two conceptions, both that of God
and that of the soul (in respect of its immortality), can only be
defined by means of predicates which, although they themselves
derive their possibility entirely from a supersensible source,
must, for all that, prove their reality in experience, for this is 20
the only way in which they can make possible a cognition of a
wholly supersensible being.—Now the only conception of this
474 kind to be found in human reason is that of the freedom of man
subject to moral laws and, in conjunction therewith, to the final
end which freedom prescribes by means of these laws. These 25
laws and this final end enable us to ascribe, the former to the
author of nature, the latter to man, the properties which contain
the necessary conditions of the possibility of both. Thus it is
from this idea that an inference can be drawn to the real existence
and the nature of both God and the soul—beings that otherwise 30
would be entirely hidden from us.

Hence, the source of the failure of the attempt to attain to
a proof of God and immortality by the merely theoretical route

lies in the fact that no knowledge of the supersensible is possible
if the path of natural conceptions is followed. The reason why
the proof succeeds, on the other hand, when the path of morals,
that is, of the conception of freedom, is followed, is because from
5 the supersensible, which in morals is fundamental (i.e. as freedom), there issues a definite law of causality. By means of this
law the supersensible here not alone provides material for the
knowledge of the other supersensible, that is of the moral final end
and the conditions of its practicability, but it also substantiates
10 its own reality, as a matter of fact, in actions. For that very
reason, however, it is unable to afford any valid argument other
than from a practical point of view—which is also the only one
needful for religion.

There is something very remarkable in the way this whole
15 matter stands. Of the three ideas of pure reason, God, freedom,
and immortality, that of freedom is the one and only conception
of the supersensible which (owing to the causality implied in it)
proves its objective reality in nature by its possible effect there.
By this means it makes possible the connexion of the two other
20 ideas with nature, and the connexion of all three to form a religion.
We are thus ourselves possessed of a principle which is capable
of determining the idea of the supersensible within us, and, in
that way, also of the supersensible without us, so as to constitute
knowledge—a knowledge, however, which is only possible from
25 a practical point of view. This is something of which mere
speculative philosophy—which can only give a simply negative
conception even of freedom—must despair. Consequently the
conception of freedom, as the root-conception of all uncondi-
tionally-practical laws, can extend reason beyond the bounds
30 to which every natural, or theoretical, conception must remain
hopelessly restricted.

IF we ask how the moral argument, which only proves the existence of God as a matter of faith for practical pure reason, ranks with the other arguments in philosophy, the value of the entire stock of the latter may be readily estimated. It turns out that we are left with no choice here, but that philosophy in its theoretical capacity must of its own accord resign all its claims in the face of an impartial critique.

Philosophy must lay the first foundations of all assurance on what is matter of fact, unless such assurance is to be entirely baseless. Hence, the only difference that can arise in the proof is on the point of whether an assurance in the consequence inferred from this matter of fact may be based upon it in the form of *knowledge* for theoretical cognition or in the form of *faith* for practical cognition. All matters of fact come under the head either of the *conception of nature*, which proves its reality in objects of sense that are given, or might be given, antecedently to all conceptions of nature ; or else of the *conception of freedom*, which sufficiently substantiates its reality by the causality of reason in respect of certain effects in the world of sense that are possible by means of that causality—a causality which reason indisputably postulates in the moral law. Now the conception of nature—which pertains merely to theoretical cognition—is either metaphysical and wholly *a priori* ; or physical, that is *a posteriori* and of necessity only conceivable by means of determinate experience. Hence, the metaphysical conception of nature—which does not presuppose any determinate experience —is ontological.

Now *the ontological proof* of the existence of God drawn from the conception of an original being may take one or other of two lines. It may start from the ontological predicates which alone enable that being to be completely defined in thought, and thence infer its absolutely necessary existence. Or it may start from the absolute necessity of the existence of something or other, whatever it may be, and thence infer the predicates of the 5 original being. For an original being implies by its very conception—so that it may not be derived—the unconditional necessity of its existence and—so that this necessity may be formulated to the mind—its determination through and through by its conception. Now these two requirements were both 10 supposed to be found in the conception of the ontological idea of an *ens realissimum* or *superlatively real being*. Thus there arose two metaphysical arguments.

The proof which is based on the purely metaphysical conception of nature—the strictly ontological proof, as it is called— 15 started from the conception of the superlatively real being and 476 thence inferred its absolutely necessary real existence, the argument being that unless it existed it would lack one reality, namely, real existence.—The other, which is also called the metaphysico-*cosmological* proof, started from the necessity of the 20 real existence of something or other—and as much as that I must certainly concede, since an existence is given to me in my own self-consciousness—and thence inferred its complete determination as the superlatively real being. For, as was argued, while all that has real existence is determined in all respects, what is 25 absolutely necessary—that is, what we have to cognize as such, and, consequently, cognize *a priori*—must be completely determined *by its conception*; but such thorough determination can only be found in the conception of a superlatively real thing. The sophistries in both these inferences need not be exposed 30 here, as that has already been done in another place. All I need now say is that, let such proofs be defended with all the forms of dialectical subtlety you please, yet they will never descend from the schools and enter into every-day life or be able to exert the smallest influence on ordinary healthy intelligence.

The proof which is founded on a conception of nature, which, while it can only be empirical, is yet intended to lead beyond the bounds of nature as the complex of objects of sense, can only be the proof derived from the *ends* of nature. Though the conception of these ends, no doubt, cannot be given *a priori*, but only through experience, this proof promises such a conception of the original ground of nature as alone, of all those that we can conceive, is appropriate to the supersensible—the conception, namely, of a supreme intelligence as cause of the world. And in point of fact, so far as principles of the reflective judgement go, that is to say, in respect of our human faculty of cognition, it is as good as its word.—But, now, is this proof in a position to give us that conception of a *supreme* or independent, intelligent being, when further understood as that of a God, that is an Author of a world subject to moral laws, and so as, therefore, to be sufficiently definite for the idea of a final end of the existence of the world ? That is the question on which everything turns, whether we are looking for a theoretically adequate conception of the Original Being on behalf of our knowledge of nature as a whole, or for a practical conception for religion.

This argument, drawn from physical teleology, is deserving of all respect. It appeals to the intelligence of the man in the street with the same convincing force as it does to the most subtle thinker ; and a Reimarus won undying honour for himself by elaborating this line of thought, which he did with his characteristic profundity and clearness in that work of his which has not yet been excelled.—But what is the source of the powerful influence which this proof exerts upon the mind, and exerts especially on a calm and perfectly voluntary assent arising from the cool judgement of reason—for emotion and exaltation of the mind produced by the wonders of nature may be put down to persuasion ? Is it physical ends, which all point to an inscrutable intelligence in the world-cause ? No, they would be an inadequate source, as they do not satisfy the needs of reason or an inquiring mind. For reason asks : For what end do all those things of nature exist which exhibit art-forms ? And for what end does man himself exist—man with whose 5 consideration we are inevitably brought to a halt, he being the ultimate end of nature, so far as we can conceive ? Why does this universal nature exist, and what is the final end of all its wealth and variety of art ? To suggest that it was made for enjoyment, or to be gazed at, surveyed and admired—which 10 if the matter ends there, amounts to no more than enjoy-ment of a particular kind—as though enjoyment was the ultimate and final end of the presence here of the world and of man himself, cannot satisfy reason. For a personal worth, which man can only give to himself, is pre-supposed by reason, as the 15 sole condition upon which he and his existence can be a final end. In the absence of this personal worth—which alone admits of a definite conception—the ends of nature do not dispose of the question. In particular they cannot offer any *definite conception* of the supreme being as an all-sufficient (and for 20 that reason one and, in the strict sense of the term, *Supreme*) Being, or of the laws according to which its intelligence is cause of the world.

That the physico-teleological proof produces conviction just as if it were also a theological proof is, therefore, not due to the 25 use of ends of nature as so many empirical evidences of a *supreme* intelligence. On the contrary it is the moral evidence, which dwells in every man and affects him so deeply, that insinuates itself into the reasoning. One does not stop at the being that manifests itself with such incomprehensible art in the ends of 30 nature, but one goes on to ascribe to it a final end, and, conse-quently, wisdom—although the perception of such physical ends does not entitle one to do this. Thus the above argument is arbitrarily supplemented in respect of its inherent defect. It is, therefore, really the moral proof that alone produces the

conviction, and even this only does so from the point of view of
478 moral considerations to which every one in the depth of his heart
assents. The sole merit of the physico-teleological proof is that
it leads the mind in its survey of the world to take the path of
ends, and guides it in this way to an *intelligent* author of the 5
world. At this point, then, the moral relation to ends and the
idea of a like lawgiver and author of the world, in the form of a
theological conception, though in truth purely an extraneous
addition, seems to grow quite naturally out of the physico-
teleological evidence.   10

Here the matter may be let rest at the popular *statement
of the case*. For where ordinary sound understanding confuses
two distinct principles, and draws its correct conclusion in point
of fact only from one of them, it generally finds it difficult, if
their separation calls for much reflection, to dissociate one from 15
the other as heterogeneous principles. But, besides, the moral
argument for the existence of God does not, strictly speaking,
merely as it were *supplement* the physico-teleological so as to
make it a complete proof. Rather is it a distinct proof which
compensates for the failure of the latter to produce conviction. 20
For the physico-teleological argument cannot in fact do anything more than direct reason in its estimate of the source of
nature and its contingent but admirable order, which is only
known to us through experience, and draw its attention to a
cause that acts according to ends and is as such the source of 25
nature—a cause which by the structure of our cognitive faculty
we must conceive as intelligent—and in this way make it more
susceptible to the influence of the moral proof. For what the
latter conception needs is so essentially different from anything
that is to be found in or taught by physical conceptions that it 30
requires a special premiss and proof entirely independent of the
foregoing if the conception of the original being is to be specified
sufficiently for theology and its existence inferred.—The moral

proof (which of course only proves the existence of God when we take the practical, though also indispensable, side of reason into account) would, therefore, continue to retain its full force were we to meet with no material at all in the world, or only ambiguous
5 material, for physical teleology. We can imagine rational beings finding themselves in the midst of a nature such as to show no clear trace of organization, but only the effects of a mere mechanism of crude matter, so that, looking to them and to the variability of some merely contingently final forms and relations,
10 there would appear to be no reason for inferring an intelligent author. In this nature there would then be nothing to suggest 479 a physical teleology. And yet reason, while receiving no instruction here from physical conceptions, would find in the conception of freedom, and the ethical ideas founded thereon,
15 a ground, sufficient for practice, for postulating the conception of the original being appropriate to those ideas, that is, as a Deity, and nature, including even our own existence, as a final end answering to freedom and its laws, and for doing so in consideration of the indispensable command of practical reason.
20 —However the fact that in the actual world abundant material for physical teleology exists to satisfy the rational beings in it— a fact not antecedently necessary—serves as a desirable confirmation of the moral argument, so far as nature can adduce anything analogous to the ideas of reason (moral ideas in this
25 case). For the conception of a supreme cause that possesses intelligence—a conception that is far from sufficient for a theology—acquires by that means such reality as is sufficient for the reflective judgement. But this conception is not required as a foundation of the moral proof ; nor can the latter proof be
30 used for completing the former, which of itself does not point to morality at all, and making it *one* entire proof by continuing the train of reasoning on the same fundamental lines. Two such heterogeneous principles as nature and freedom cannot but yield two different lines of proof—while the attempt to derive the p oof

.in question from nature will be found inadequate for what is meant to be proved.

If the premises of the physico-teleological argument went the length of the proof sought, the result would be very gratifying to speculative reason. For they would afford hope of producing a theology—that being the name one would have to give to a theoretical knowledge of the divine nature and its existence sufficient for explaining both the constitution of the world and the distinctive scope of the moral laws. Similarly if psychology was sufficient to enable us to attain to a knowledge of the immortality of the soul it would open the door to a pneumatology which would be equally acceptable to reason. But, however much it might flatter the vanity of an idle curiosity, neither of the two fulfil the desire of reason in respect of theory, which would have to be based on a knowledge of the nature of things. But whether they do not better fulfil their final objective purpose, the first in the form of theology, the second in the form of anthropology, when both founded on the moral principle, namely that of freedom, and adapted, therefore, to the practical employment of reason, is a different question, and one which we have here no need to pursue farther.

But the reason why the physico-teleological argument does not go the length that theology requires is that it does not, and cannot, give any conception of the original being that is sufficiently definite for that purpose. Such a conception has to be derived entirely from a different quarter, or (at least) you must look elsewhere to supplement the defects of the conception by what is an arbitrary addition. You infer an intelligent world-cause from the great finality of natural forms and their relations. But what is the degree of this intelligence ? Beyond doubt you cannot assume that it is the highest possible intelligence ; for to do so you would have to see that a greater intelligence than that of which you perceive evidences in the world is inconceivable,

which means attributing omniscience to yourself. In the same
way you infer from the greatness of the world a very great
might on the part of its author. But you will acknowledge that
this has only comparative significance for your power of com-
5 prehension and that, since you do not know all that is possible,
so as to compare it with the magnitude of the world, so far as
known to you, you cannot infer the omnipotence of its author
from so small a standard, and so forth. Now this does not bring
you to any definite conception of an original being suitable for
10 a theology. For that conception can only be found in the
thought of the totality of the perfections associated with an
intelligence, and for this merely *empirical* data can give you no
assistance whatever. But apart from a determinate conception
of this kind you can draw no inference to a *single* intelligent
15 original being ; whatever your purpose, you can only suppose
one.—Now, certainly, one may quite readily give you the liberty
of making an arbitrary addition—since reason raises no valid
objection—and saying that where one meets with so much perfection one may well suppose all perfection to be united in
20 a unique world-cause ; because reason can turn such a definite
principle to better account both theoretically and practically.
But then you cannot cry up this conception of the original being
as one which you have proved, since you have only assumed it
in the interests of a better employment of reason. Hence all
25 lament or impotent rage on account of the supposed enormity
of casting a doubt on the conclusiveness of your chain of reasoning is idle bluster. It would much like us to believe that the
doubt that is freely expressed as to the validity of your argument
is a questioning of sacred truth, so that under this cover its
30 weakness may pass unnoticed.

On the other hand, moral teleology, whose foundations are no
less firm than those of physical teleology, and which in fact 481
should be regarded as in a better position, seeing that it rests
a priori on principles that are inseparable from our reason, leads

to what the possibility of a theology requires, namely to a definite *conception* of the supreme cause as one that is the cause of the world in its accordance with moral laws, and, consequently, of such a cause as satisfies our moral final end. Now that is a cause that requires nothing less than omniscience, omnipotence, 5 omnipresence, and so forth, as the natural attributes character- izing its operation. These attributes must be thought as annexed to the moral final end which is infinite, and accordingly as adequate to that end. Thus moral teleology can alone furnish the conception of a *unique* Author of the world suitable for a 10 theology.

In this way theology also leads directly to *religion*, that is *the recognition of our duties as divine commands*. For it is only the recognition of our duty and of its content—the final end enjoined upon us by reason—that was able to produce a definite 15 conception of God. This conception is, therefore, from its origin indissolubly connected with obligation to that Being. On the other hand, even supposing that by pursuing the theoretical path one could arrive at a definite conception of the original being, namely, as simple cause of nature, one would afterwards 20 encounter considerable difficulty in finding valid proofs for ascribing to this being a causality in accordance with moral laws, and might, perhaps, not be able to do so at all without resorting to arbitrary interpolation. Yet, if the conception of such causality is left out, that would-be theological conception 25 can form no basis for the support of religion. Even if a religion could be established on these theoretical lines, yet in what touches disposition, which is the essential element in religion, it would really be a different religion from one in which the conception of God and the practical conviction of His existence 30 springs from root-ideas of morality. For if omnipotence, omniscience, and so forth on the part of an Author of the world were conceptions given to us from another quarter, and if, regarded in that light, we had to take them for granted for the purpose only of applying our conceptions of duties to our relation to such Author, then these latter conceptions would inevitably betray strong traces of compulsion and forced submission. But what of the alternative ? What if the final end of our true being is delineated to our minds quite freely, and in virtue of the precept of our own reason, by a reverence for the moral law ? Why, then, we accept into our moral perspective a cause harmonizing with that end and with its accomplishment, and accept 482 it with deepest veneration—wholly different from any pathological fear—and we willingly bow down before it.[1]

But why should it be of any consequence to us to have a theology at all ? Well, as to this, it is quite obvious that it is not necessary for the extension or rectification of our knowledge of nature or, in fact, for any theory whatever. We need theology solely on behalf of religion, that is to say, the practical or, in other words, moral employment of our reason, and need it as a subjective requirement. Now if it turns out that the one and only argument which leads to a definite conception of the object of theology is itself a moral argument, the result will not seem strange. But, more than that, we shall not feel that the assurance produced by this line of proof falls in any way short of the final purpose it has in view, provided we are clear on the point that an argument of this kind only proves the existence of God in a way that satisfies the moral side of our nature, that is, from a practical point of view. Speculation does not here display its

---

[1] Both the admiration for beauty and the emotion excited by the profuse variety of ends of nature, which a reflective mind is able to feel prior to any clear representation of an intelligent author of the world, have something about them akin to a *religious* feeling. Hence they seem primarily to act upon the moral feeling (of gratitude and veneration towards the unknown cause) by means of a mode of critical judgement analogous to the moral mode, and therefore to affect the mind by exciting moral ideas. It is then that they inspire that admiration which is fraught with far more interest than mere theoretical observation can produce.

force in any way, nor does it enlarge the borders of its realm. Also the surprise at the fact that we here assert the possibility of a theology, and the alleged contradiction in that assertion with what the *Critique* of speculative reason said of the categories, will disappear on close inspection. What that Critique said was that the categories can only produce knowledge when applied to objects of sense, and that they can in no way do so when applied to the supersensible. But, be it observed, that while the categories are here used on behalf of the knowledge of God, they are so used solely for practical, not for theoretical purposes, that is they are not directed to the intrinsic, and for us inscrutable, nature of God.—Let me take this opportunity of putting an end to the misinterpretation of the above doctrine in the Critique— a doctrine which is very necessary, but which, to the chagrin of blind dogmatists, relegates reason to its proper bounds. With this object I here append the following elucidation.

If I ascribe *motive* force to a body, and conceive it, therefore, by means of the category of *causality*, then at the same time and by the same means I *cognize* it ; that is to say, I determine the conception which I have of it as an Object in general by means of what applies to it in the concrete as an object of sense (this being the condition of the possibility of the relation in question). Thus, suppose the dynamical force that I ascribe to it is that of repulsion, then—even though I do not as yet place beside it another body against which it exerts this force—I may predicate of it a place in space, further an extension or space possessed by the body itself, and, besides, a filling of this space by the repelling forces of its parts, and, finally, the law regulating this filling of space—I mean the law that the force of repulsion in the parts must decrease in the same ratio as the extension of the body increases, and as the space which it fills with the same parts and by means of this force is enlarged.—On the other hand, if I form a notion of a supersensible being as *prime mover*,

and thus employ the category of causality in consideration of
the same mode of action in the world, namely, the movement
of matter, I must not then conceive it to be at any place in space,
or to be extended, nay I am not even to conceive it as existing
5 in time at all or as coexistent with other beings. Accordingly,
I have no forms of thought whatever that could interpret to me
the condition under which movement derived from this being
as its source is possible. Consequently from the predicate of
cause, as prime mover, I do not get the least concrete cognition
10 of it : I have only the representation of a something containing
the source of the movements in the world. And as the relation
in which this something, as cause stands to these movements,
does not give me anything further that belongs to the constitution of the thing which is cause, it leaves the conception of this
15 cause quite empty. The reason is, that with predicates that
only get their Object in the world of sense I may no doubt
advance to the existence of something that must contain the
source of these predicates, but I cannot advance to the determination of the conception of this something as a supersensible
20 being, a conception that excludes all those predicates. If, therefore, I make the category of causality determinate by means of
the conception of a *prime mover*, it does not help me in the
slightest to cognize what God is. But maybe I shall fare better
if I take a line from the order of the world and proceed, not
25 merely to *conceive* the causality of the supersensible being as that
of a supreme *intelligence*, but also to *cognize* it by means of this
determination of the conception in question ; for then the
troublesome terms of space and extension drop out.—Beyond
all doubt the great finality present in the world compels us to 484
30 *conceive* that there is a supreme cause of this finality and one
whose causality has an intelligence behind it. But this in no
way entitles us to *ascribe* such intelligence to that cause. (Thus,
for instance, we are obliged to conceive the eternity of God as an
existence in all time, because we can form no other conception

of mere existence than that of a magnitude, or in other words,
than as duration.   Similarly we have to conceive the divine
omnipotence as an existence in all places, in order to interpret
to ourselves God's immediate presence in respect of things
external to one another.   All this we do without, however, being
at liberty to ascribe any of these thought-forms to God as something cognized in Him.)   If I determine the causality of man in
respect of certain products that are only explicable by reference
to intentional finality by conceiving it as an intelligence on his
part, I need not stop there, but I can ascribe this predicate to
him as a familiar attribute of man and thereby cognize him.   For
I know that intuitions are given to the senses of man, and by
means of understanding are brought under a conception and
thus under a rule ;   that this conception contains only the common mark, letting the particular drop out, and is therefore
discursive ;   that the rules for bringing representations under
the general form of a consciousness are given by understanding
antecedently to those intuitions, and so on.   Accordingly, I
ascribe this attribute to man as one whereby I *cognize* him.   But
supposing, now that I seek to *conceive* a supersensible being
(God) as Intelligence, while this is not alone allowable but unavoidable if I am to exercise certain functions of my reason,
I have no right whatever to flatter myself that I am in a position
to ascribe intelligence to that being and thereby to *cognize* it by
one of its attributes.   For in that case I must omit all the above
conditions under which I know an intelligence.   Consequently,
the predicate that is only available for the determination of
man is quite inapplicable to a supersensible object.   Hence we
are quite unable to cognize what God is by means of any such
definite causality.   And it is so with all categories.   They can
have no significance whatever for knowledge theoretically considered, unless they are applied to objects of possible experience.
—But I am able to form a notion even of a supersensible being

on the analogy of an understanding—nay must do so when I look to certain other considerations—without, however, thereby desiring to cognize it theoretically. I refer to the case of this mode of its causality having to do with an effect in the world that 5 is fraught with an end which is morally necessary but for creatures of sense unrealizable. For in that case a knowledge of God and His existence, that is to say a theology, is possible by 485 means of attributes and determinations of this causality merely conceived in Him according to analogy, and this knowledge has 10 all requisite reality in a practical relation, but also *in respect only of this relation,* that is, in relation to morality.—An ethical theology is therefore quite possible. For while morality without theology may certainly carry on with its own rule, it cannot do so with the final purpose which this very rule enjoins, unless it 15 throws reason to the winds as regards this purpose. But a theological ethics—on the part of pure reason—is impossible, seeing that laws which are not originally given by reason itself, and the observance of which it does not bring about as a practical capacity, cannot be moral. In the same way a theological 20 physics would be a monstrosity, because it would not bring forward any laws of nature but rather ordinances of a supreme will, whereas a physical, or, properly speaking, physico-teleological, theology can at least serve as a propaedeutic to theology proper, since by means of the study of physical ends, of which 25 it presents a rich supply, it awakens us to the idea of a final end which nature cannot exhibit. Consequently it can make us alive to the need of a theology which should define the conception of God sufficiently for the highest practical employment of reason, though it cannot produce a theology or find evidences 30 adequate for its support.

ANALYTICAL INDEX TO
TELEOLOGICAL JUDGEMENT

Beauty. Beautiful forms, existence of, might be anticipated, 3; a formal subjective finality, 5; intellectual, wrong application of term to geometrical properties, 11; natural, the analogue of art, 23; teleological estimate of, 30; of nature, disposing to moral sentiments, 112, 159, *n.*; moral interest, probably first attracted attention to, 129, 130; admiration for, excited by ends of nature, 159, *n.*

Being. Intelligent, producing with design, 43; intelligent original, not objectively substantiated, 52; conception of an absolutely necessary, 57; supreme, conception of affords no explanation, 67; original, determination of conception of, 101; original, attributes of, 110, 111; that has formed man with an end in view, 113; supreme, idea of, resting on practical employment of our reason, 103, 126, cf. 151, 153; supreme, moral need for representation of, 113; supreme, understanding and will not ascribed to, theoretically, 128; supreme, anthropomorphic representation of, 130; supersensible, possibility of a, 139.

Blumenbach. Services of, to theory of epigenesis, 85.

Camper, 90.

Categories. Misapprehension as to what Critique of Pure Reason said in respect of, 160; of causality, 161, 162.

Causality. Final and efficient, the only two kinds of, 20; of ends, possibility of, cannot be perceived *a priori*, 24, l. 25; special ground of, not introduced by teleology, 33, cf. 41, 69, l. 6; of architectonic understanding, 39; of an understanding, 51, 98, 123; of natural causes, subordinated to that of final causes, 41; special kind of, 41, 42, 46, 49, 50, 98, 123, cf. 125; of nature, regarded as a being acting according to ends, 60; union of two types of, 82, cf. 41, l. 30, 125; by means of ideas, 122; freedom a particular kind of. 142; category of, 161, 162.

Cause. Final and efficient, contrasted, 20, 21, 28, 116; intelligent, 40, 110, 116, 125, 126, 144; final, organisms judged on principle of, 40; world cause acting according to ends a mere idea, 40; final, must be a substance, 45; distinct from nature, 50, cf. 75; result corresponding to, 60; final, genesis of organisms not intelligible apart from, 80, cf. 91; supreme, 83, 106, 111, 123, 125; final, representation based on, only a subjective condition of our reason, 92, cf. 110; system of final causes, 110; supreme, governing the world according to moral laws, 113.

Certainty. As a quantum, 138.

Chance. Blind, 44, 129.

Christianity. Idea of faith introduced by, 146, *n.*

Circle. Formal finality of, 7.

Civilization. How fine art and the sciences contribute towards, 97.

Community. Civil, 96.

Conception. Completion of, by arbitrary integration, 133, cf. 103, 107, 156, l. 28, 157.

Conceptus ratiocinans, 49, cf. 141, l. 19.

Contingency. Of nature, 4, 39, 52; apparent, of what displays formal finality, 10; relative finality contingent to thing itself, 14;

of form makes us look to end of reason, 17; of coincidence, 17, cf. 42; unity of end not thinkable apart from, 45; and necessity, physical end implies both, 49; representation of end, association of conception, with, 52, 87; possibility, necessity and, 57; duty implies, 58; particular by its nature contains something contingent in respect of universal, 59, cf. 162, l. 15; conformity to law on part of contingent, termed finality, 59; of the constitution of our understanding, 61, 65; of variety in given particular, 62; makes it difficult to reduce unity to multiplicity, 62; contingent accord, 62, 63; of synthesis, 63; of purpose to which empirical ends refer, 106; points to unconditioned ground, 116.

Contradiction. Principle of, 139; what the moral law postulates can be thought without, 145, *n.*

Conviction. Contrasted with persuasion, 134, cf. 132; proof tending towards, 135.

Cosmopolitan whole. Development of civil communities into a, 96.

Creation. *See* Final end.

Critique. Of Pure Reason, implication in, 61, l. 9; in reference to proof of existence of God, shows what, 135; of Pure Reason, doctrine of categories in, 160; of speculative reason, alleged contradiction with what was said in, 160.

Crystals. Formation of, 79.

Culture. Promotion of, by exhibition of beautiful forms, 30, *n.*; as an end, 92, 94; skill a form of, 95; discipline as a requirement of, 95; how war ministers to, 96; nature's striving in respect of second requisite for culture, 97.

Deduction. Deriving products from their causes, principle for, 5, 70, ll. 15, 25.

Deity. (*See* God, Being, Cause, Attributes.) Physical teleology does not afford adequate conception of, 103, cf. 105, 107, 114; supreme cause as, 111, 114; existence of, no theoretical proof of, 139.

Democritus. Author of system of accidentality, 43.

Demonology, 130.

Descartes. Regarded lower animals as mere machines, 136, *n.*

Descent. Of different species from a common parent, 78; of man, traced back to crude matter, 78, 79.

Design. Nature not to be credited with causes acting designedly, 4; teleological estimate of nature as a whole silent on question of, 28; physics ignores question of, 33; in teleology we speak of nature as if its finality were a thing of, 33; referred to matter, 33; technic divided into designed and undesigned, 42; Idealism denies intentionality, 44, cf. 98; Spinoza eliminates all trace of, 45; question of, problematic character of, 49; cause that pursues, 50, 51, 112; conception of, basal for investigation of organized products, 51, 52, 53, cf. 92; ends not observed as designed, 53; we cannot say that origin of organisms might not be explained without reference to, 54; root origin of organisms must be referred to, 82.

Desire. Faculty of, 109; duty independent of object of, 145.

certainly are ends, found in the world, 123; principle that there is nothing in the world without an, justified, 123; connecting physical and ethical, 123; ends of nature sufficiently prove, for reflective judgement, an intelligent world-cause, 126.

Enjoyment. Value of life measured by, 97 n.; cf. 109, 153.

Ens rationis ratiocinantis, p. 141, cf. 49.

Ens Realissimum. Ontological idea of, 151.

Epicurus. Abolished distinction between technic of nature and mechanism, 44.

Epigenesis. Theory of, 84; theory of, advantages of, 85; services of Blumenbach to theory of, 85.

Ether. An example of a matter of opinion, 141.

Ethics. Theological, impossible, 163.

Evolution. Of new structures, fundamental organization must be assumed, 78; on a genetic principle, 78; or individual preformation, theory of, 83.

Experience. Cannot prove actual existence of ends of nature, 3; occasion for adopting principle on which intrinsic finality is estimated, derived from, 25.

Existence. Can only be conceived as a magnitude, 162.

Explanation. (*See* Deduction, Insight.) Teleology does not afford an, 4, cf. 33, 38, 68, 77; geometrical analogies not a teleological ground of, 32, cf. 48, 54; of organisms, mechanism does not afford an, 39, 71; of finality of nature, systems attempting, 44; finality rendered intelligible by conception of God, 53, cf. 102; of origin of organized beings without reference to design, 54; general explanatory digression, 55; mechanical and teleological modes of, not inconsistent, 66; of nature, none by reference to Supreme Architect, 67; of finality, no, by appeal to final cause, 67; mechanistic excludes teleological, 69; basis of, contrasted with basis of exposition, 70; defined as derivation from a principle, 70; mechanical, ignorant how far it may penetrate, 73; mechanical, not helped by teleology, 76; of physical end, subordination of mechanism to teleology in, 77; of origin, critical principle brings us no nearer, 101.

Fact. Matters of, 140, 141, 143 n. 150; object of freedom, a matter of, 142, 149, cf. 150; matters of, philosophy must lay first foundations of all assurance on, 150; matters of, come under the head either of conceptions of nature or the conception of freedom, 150.

Faculty. Cognitive, peculiar constitution of, 51, 52, 56, 57, 82, 91, 101, 107, 125, 126, 128, 140, 143, 154; peculiar to human race, 54, 55, 58, 59, 60, 61, 64, 67; cognitive, peculiar structure of, the source of teleological representation, 101, cf. 125; cognitive, relativity of theological conception to our, 126, 127; cognitive, representation conformable to, only expresses a relation, 127.

Faith. Practical, type of assurance produced by, 140 et seq.; matters of, 140, 142, cf. 150; *Summum bonum* a matter of, 142; historical, 143; defined, 146; distinguished from credulity, 146; doubtful, 147; contrasted with knowledge, 150.

Fatality. System of, attributed to Spinoza, 43.

good possible in the world through, 118; object of, a matter of fact, 142, 149, cf. 150; formerly regarded as mere negative condition, 147; a basis of knowledge of supersensible from practical point of view, 149; conception of, contrasted with conception of nature, 150; reality of, how substantiated, 150.

Future life. (*See* Immortality, Soul.)   Hope of, 131; view of Spinoza as to, 120.

Geometry. (*See* Figures.)   Plato's conception of importance of, 9.

God. (*See* Being, Deity, Intelligence.)   Introduction of conception of, into natural science, 31; lifeless or living, 44, *n.*; reference to, renders finality intelligible to our understanding, 53, cf. 76; attributes of, 111, cf. 110, 114, 126, 127, 157, 158, 161, 162; existence of, moral proof of, 114 et seq., cf. 122 et seq., 128; existence of, use of moral argument for, 130; effect of belief that there is no, 120; assumption of existence of, involves no contradiction, 121; existence of, steps in advance to inference of, 125; objective reality of idea of, 126; existence of, type of assurance in teleological proof of, 132; real existence of, no theoretical proof of, 135 et seq., 139; understanding in proper sense of word cannot be ascribed to, 138; intrinsic nature of, curiosity as to, senseless, 138, cf. 160, 161; existence of, a matter of faith, 143, cf. 150; conception of, relativity of, to the object of our duty, 144, cf. 147, l. 17; real existence of, only idea from which inference of, possible, 148; Existence of, respective values of moral and other arguments for, 150; existence of, ontological proof of, 150, cf. 148; existence of, metaphysico-cosmological argument for, 151; existence of, teleological argument worthy of respect, 152; existence of, physico-teleological proof of, 153; existence of, relation of moral and physico-teleological arguments for, 154; definite conception of, how obtained, 159.

Grass. Blade of, possibility of generation of, 27, 54, 66, cf. 61, l. 22, 78, l. 22, 39, l. 6.

Ground. Ultimate, purely negative conception of, 139, cf. 161, l. 10.

Guiding-thread. Conception of final causes as, 40, cf. 51, 53, 76.

Habitat. Of organisms, provision for in teleological system, 89.

Happiness. As an end, 92; quite possible as an effect of the mechanism of nature, 100 *n.*; not the final end of creation, or even the ultimate end of nature, 100, *n.*; a consequence of harmony, 100, *n.*, cf. 109; absolute worth not to be valued by, 109; as a subjective condition of final end, 118; empirically conditioned, 122; relation of to final end, 119, 145, *n.*

History. Natural, 90; objects of, matters of fact, 143; credulity in matters of, 146.

Humanity. Development of, 97.

Hume. Criticized, 80.

Hybrid. System of performation cannot explain, 85.

Hylozoism. Contrasted with theism, 43; does not perform what it promises, 47.

Hypothesis. Allowable, in respect of nature as a whole, 72; of evolution, 79; founded on theoretical argument, 135, cf. 144, l. 20; possibility of object must be certain to found an, 139.

Idea. Underlying possibility of natural product, 25, cf. 48, l. 25; world-cause acting according to ends, a mere, 40; of reason, 55, 140; of unconditional necessity of original ground of nature, 58; to which no commensurate object can be given in experience, 60; underlying physical end, difference between, and other ideas, 60; underlying, of possible understanding different from human, 61; of a divine Author as ground, 75, 76; underlying, of final cause, 87; actuality of what is only possible according to, implication, 116; causality by means of, 122; required to make end of reason possible, 125; practical reality of, 125; of supersensible, reason restricted in respect of, 130; of reason, incapable of presentation, 140; of reason, freedom the only, the object of which is a matter of fact, 142, cf. 149, 150.

Idealism. *See* Finality.

Idolatry. Defined, 130.

Illusion. Caused by dialectic of reflective judgement, 36.

Imagination. Function of, in mathematical representations, 10, 12.

Immortality. Of the soul, 143, 147.

Inclinations. Discipline of, 96, 97.

Insight. Complete, only into what we can make according to our conceptions, 34; into nature of things, none apart from mechanistic principle, 67; into supersensible substrate of nature, no, 116, *n.*

Instinct. Of lower animals, 136, cf. 107.

Intelligence. Spinoza divests original ground of all, 45, cf. 104; effect of final cause must be by virtue of, 45; supreme, as cause of the world, 47, cf. 54, 152, 161; Intelligent Original Being, that there is, cannot be substantiated, 52; intelligent world-cause, conception of, subjective, 101, 110, 114, 116, 162; higher, no definite conception of, 103, cf. 106; art-, for miscellaneous ends, controlled with wisdom, 106; determined by simple necessity of its nature, by analogy to art-instinct, 107; intelligent cause, final end of, 112, 113; moral, 112; intelligent world-cause, if such there be, 114, 117, *n.*; highest possible, 156; not *ascribed* to ultimate source, 161.

Intuition. Contrasted with thought, 56, 57; a factor in knowledge, 62; intellectual, 66; an, different from our sensuous, 77.

Involution. Theory of, 84.

Judgement. Determinant and reflective, nature of distinction, 35, 48, 60, 134; teleological estimate is one of reflective not of determinant, 4, 5, 24, 28, 33, 35, 36, 38, 39, 40, 47, 48, 49, 51, 64, 69, 70, 72, 75, 91, 92, 123, 125, 128; teleological, not warranted by relative finality, 15; antinomy of, 35; transcendental, 35; reflective, must be a principle to itself, 35, 36; reflective, principle of, not objective, 35; reflective, maxims of, 36, 37; does not need special principle for applying *a priori* laws, 36; reflective, two antithetical maxims of, 37; maxim of, contrasted with objective principle, 41, 51; indispensible, maxim of, 53; principle of, for application of an understanding in the abstract to possible objects of experience, 60 ; accord of things in nature with our power of, 63 ; teleological, theory of the method of applying, 75 et seq. ; reflective, principles of, tell us nothing as to the origin of things, 91 ; *a priori*, no room for opinion in, 138.

Knowledge. Division of matters in respect of the possibility of, 140 ; contrasted, 150.

Law. Natural laws, physical end must be conceived as not possible on, 16.
Life. Technic of nature the. analogue of, 23 ; value of, measured by enjoyment, 97, *n*. ; future, hope of, 131, 1. 24 ; future, materialism cannot determine question of, 132.
Linné. Theory of, 89.
Luxury. Defined, 95 ; in the sciences, 97.

Machine. Has only motive, not formative power, 22 ; Descartes' view of lower animals as mere machines, 136, *n*.
Macrocosm. Finality of nature in, 46.
Maggot. Mechanistic explanation of, excludes teleological, 64.
Man. As ultimate end of creation, 88, 92 ; titular lord of nature, 94 ; can only be ultimate end of nature by making himself independent of nature, 94 ; as noumenon, the final end of creation, 99 ; only as a moral being the final end of creation, 100, *n*., 109, 110, 112, 116 ; creation in vain without, 108 ; as subject to moral laws, the final end, 112, 116, 117.
Materialism. Cannot determine questions of future life, 131, 132 ; psychology, saved from, 132.
Mathematics. Pure, not concerned with real existence of things, 12, *n*.
Matter. Organic, alone involves conception of physical end, 28 ; design referred to, 33, cf. 73, 1. 9 ; lifelessness the essential characteristic of, 46, cf. 68, l. 27, 81, l. 16 ; formative force of, 86.
Maxim. For estimating intrinsic finality of organisms, 25 ; subjective principle of estimation of nature, 28, 36, 72 ; antinomy between maxims, 36 ; two antithetical maxims of judgement, 37 ; prescribed by reason, 51 ; general, of subjectivity, 58 ; of reflective judgement, in respect of source of final action, 101 ; of pure reason, 126.
Mechanism. Of nature, 25, 123 ; blind, 26 ; of nature, impossibility of production of organisms in accordance with, not provable, 39, 47, cf. 38, 41, 42, 61 ; unable to furnish explanation of production of organisms, 39 ; inner ground of, beyond our ken, 47 ; and technic, distinction between may arise from the type of our understanding, 59 ; conception of whole as end not explicable by reference to, 65 ; principle of, union of teleological principle with, in technic of nature, 67 ; no insight into nature of things apart from, 67 ; subordinated to designed technique, 72 ; subordination of, to teleology, in explanation of physical end, 77 ; mechanical explanation to be pursued as far as possible, 77, 78, 91 ; associated with teleology in explanation of physical end, 82 ; of nature, subordinated to architectonic of an

intelligent Author of the world, 102; possible identity of ground of, and of nexus of final causes, 41, 1. 30, 70, 71, 82, 91.

Metaphysics. Universal theory of finality belongs to, 33; question of design belongs to, 33; all laborious preparations of, directed to problems of God, freedom and immortality, 147.

Method. Of applying the teleological judgement, theory of, 75 et seq.

Misery. Splendid, 95.

Moral feeling. Disposition towards, excited by natural beauty, 112.

Morality. An absolutely impossible result of natural causes, 100; gains by representation of Supreme Being, 113; *a priori* assured of its possibility, 122; one of factors of final end, 122; and religion, 130, *n.*, 131; without theology, position of, 163.

Moral law. Represented as a command, 58; formal condition of freedom, 118; confidence in promise of, 146, *n.*; intelligible world harmonizing with, 58, cf. 109; men as subject to, 112, 116; directs us to strive towards universal highest end, 113; pays no regard to ends, 119.

Nature. (*See* End, Mechanism.) Subjective finality of, in its particular laws, 3; universal idea of, does not lead us to assume that things serve one another as means to ends, 3; contingency of, 4, 39; organizes itself, 23; organization of, has nothing analogous to any causality known to us, 23; as a whole, 26, 28, 31, 44, 1. 2, 46, 49, 50, 51, 66, 73, 89, 102, 109; as a whole, not given as organized, 51, cf. 102; aggregate conceived as an animal, 46; aggregate conceived as a system, 28, 66; as a teleological system, 106, 110, cf. 26, 28, 92; as a whole, referred to design by an allowable hypothesis, 73; ultimate end of, as a teleological system, 92; final end of, 27, cf. 88; for end of real existence of, we must look beyond, 27, cf. 123; mechanism of, 39, 77; hint given by, 41; blind necessity of, according to Spinoza, 45; supersensible substrate of, 67; intelligible substrate of, 77, 116, *n.*; what it can effect relative to final end, 92; strives towards higher ends than it can itself afford, 97; entire, teleologically subordinated ends than it can itself afford, 97; teleologically subordinated to final end, 100; horizon of, prospect beyond, 101; accord of, with conditions of human happiness, 109; harmony of, with final end, 122, 124, 129; nothing in, without an end, 123; final end, not to be found in, 123, cf. 27; conception of, and conception of freedom, 150; metaphysical and physical conception of, 150.

Necessity. Of form of thing, reason insists upon, 17.

Newton, 54.

Noumenon. Man as, the final end of creation, 99.

Occasionalism. Of cause, theory of, 83.

Ontological argument. Criticized, 148, cf. 150, 151; exerts no influence on popular thought, 151.

Opinion. Probable, 135; no room for, in *a priori* judgements, 138; matters of, 140.

PRINTED IN GREAT BRITAIN
AT THE UNIVERSITY PRESS, OXFORD
BY VIVIAN RIDLER
PRINTER TO THE UNIVERSITY